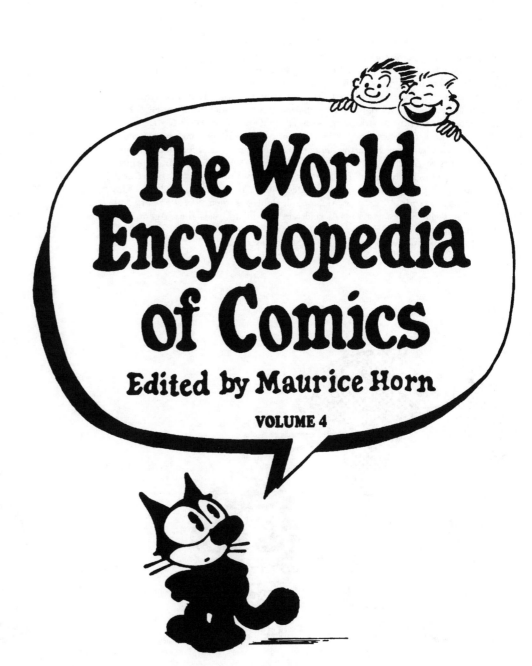

The World
Encyclopedia
of Comics

Edited by Maurice Horn

VOLUME 4

THE CONTRIBUTORS

Manuel Auad (M.A.), *The Philippines*
Bill Blackbeard (B.B.), *U.S.*
Gianni Bono (G.B.), *Italy*
Joe Brancatelli (J.B.), *U.S.*
MaryBeth Calhoun (M.B.C.), *U.S.*
Javier Coma (J.C.), *Spain*
Bill Crouch (B.C.), *U.S.*
Giulio Cesare Cuccolini (G.C.C.), *Italy*
Mark Evanier (M.E.), *U.S.*
Wolfgang Fuchs (W.F.), *Germany*
Luis Gasca (L.G.), *Spain*
Robert Gerson (R.G.), *U.S.*
Denis Gifford (D.G.), *Great Britain*
Paul Gravett (P.G.), *Great Britain*
Peter Harris (P.H.), *Canada*
Hongying Liu-Lengyel (H.Y.L.L.), *China*
Maurice Horn (M.H.), *France/U.S.*
Pierre L. Horn (P.L.H.), *U.S.*
Slobodan Ivkov (S.I.), *Yugoslavia (Serbia)*
Bill Janocha (B.J.), *U.S.*
Orvy Jundis (O.J.), *The Philippines*
Hisao Kato (H.K.), *Japan*
John A. Lent (J.A.L.), *Asia*
Richard Marschall (R.M.), *U.S.*
Alvaro de Moya (A.M.), *Brazil*
Kalmán Rubovszky (K.R.), *Hungary/Poland*
Ervin Rustemagić (E.R.), *Yugoslavia*
John Ryan (J.R.), *Australia*
Matthew A. Thorn (M.A.T.), *Japan*
Dennis Wepman (D.W.), *U.S.*

The World Encyclopedia of Comics

Edited by Maurice Horn

VOLUME 4

Chelsea House Publishers
Philadelphia

Acknowledgments

The editors of *The World Encyclopedia of Comics* wish to extend their sincere thanks to the following persons: Bill Anderson, Jerry Bails, Larry Brill, Mary Beth Calhoun, Frank Clark, Bill Crouch, Leonard Darvin, Tony Dispoto, Jacques Glénat-Guttin, Ron Goulart, George Henderson, Pierre Horn, Pierre Huet, S. M. "Jerry" Iger, Jessie Kahles Straut, Rolf Kauka, Heikki Kaukoranta, Roland Kohlsaat, Maria-M. Lamm, Mort Leav, Vane Lindesay, Ernie McGee, Jacques Marcovitch, Victor Margolin, Doug Murray, Pascal Nadon, Harry Neigher, Walter Neugebauer, Syd Nicholls, Tom Peoples, Rainer Schwarz, Silvano Scotto, Luciano Secchi, David Smith, Manfred Soder, Jim Steranko, Ernesto Traverso, Miguel Urrutía, Jim Vadeboncoeur, Jr., Wendell Washer, Peter Wiechmann, Mrs. John Wheeler and Joe Willicombe.

We would also like to thank the following collectors who donated reproductions of art from their collections: Wendy Gaines Bucci, Mike Burkey, Tony Christopher, Russ Cochran, Robert Gerson, Roger Hill, Bill Leach, Eric Sack, and Jim Steranko.

Special thanks also to Michel Mandry, Bernard Trout, José Maria Conget of Instituto Cervantes in New York, Four-Color Images Gallery, Frederik Schodt, David Astor, Alain Beyrand, Manuel Halffter, Dominique Petitfaux, Annie Baron-Carvais, Janice Silverman.

Our appreciation also to the following organizations: Associated Newspapers Ltd., Bastei Verlag, Bulls Pressedienst, Comics Magazine Association of America, Editions Dupuis, ERB Inc., Field Newspaper Syndicate, Globi Verlag, The Herald and Weekly Times Ltd., Kauka Comic Akademie, King Features Syndicate, Marvel Comics Group, San Francisco Academy of Comic Art, Strip Art Features, Walt Disney Archives and Walt Disney Productions.

Finally, we wish to thank Don Manza for his photographic work.

Chelsea House Publishers
1974 Sproul Road, Suite 400
P.O. Box 914
Broomall PA 19008-0914

Typeset by Alexander Graphics, Indianapolis IN

Library of Congress Cataloging-in-Publication Data

The world encyclopedia of comics / edited by Maurice Horn.
    p.   cm.
    Includes bibliographical references and index.
    ISBN 0-7910-4854-3 (set). — ISBN 0-7910-4857-8 (v. 1). — ISBN
0-7910-4858-6 (v. 2). — ISBN 0-7910-4859-4 (v. 3). — ISBN
0-7910-4860-8 (v. 4). — ISBN 0-7910-4861-6 (v. 5). — ISBN
0-7910-4862-4 (v. 6). — ISBN 0-7910-4863-2 (v. 7)
    1. Comic books, strips, etc.—Dictionaries.   I. Horn, Maurice.
PN6710.W6   1998
741.5'03—dc21   97-50448
                                                              CIP

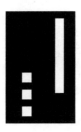

IANIRO, ABEL (1919-) Argentine cartoonist, born in Buenos Aires in 1919. After a career as a caricaturist of political and show business personalities, Abel Ianiro started his collaboration with the magazine *Leoplan* in the early 1940s. There he created his most famous comic strips: *Tóxico y Biberón*, the hilarious saga of a couple of drunks, and *Purapinta*. With this latter creation, the story of a typical bully of the outskirts of Buenos Aires who lives for his depredations but who is at heart a coward, Ianiro reached his major fame. The strip was published for a long time in the humor magazine *Rico Tipo*, run by fellow-cartoonist Guillermo Divito. For *Rico Tipo* Ianiro also contributed a number of caricatures of famous movie actors, a genre in which he was an undisputed master.

L.G.

IBIS THE INVINCIBLE (U.S.) Created by writer/editor Bill Parker in February 1940, *Ibis the Invincible* first appeared in Fawcett's *Whiz* number two. Nattily attired in a black suit and blazing crimson turban, Ibis was one of literally dozens of comic book magicians proliferating during the industry's "golden age." To creator Bill Parker's credit, however, *Ibis the Invincible* was one of very few that did not take their major inspiration from Lee Falk's syndicated *Mandrake* strip. The feature was original in most respects, and that may account for its longevity.

Ibis had two, somewhat related origins, but the one most cited was written by Otto Binder and appeared in *Ibis the Invincible* number one (1942). A captive of the evil Black Pharaoh, Prince Amentep (Ibis) was soon freed by a magic wand called the "Ibistick." Invincible against anything except other magic forces, the stick helped Ibis kill the Pharaoh, but only after the hero's love interest, Taia, had been put to sleep for 4,000 years. Lover that he was, Ibis put himself to sleep for 4,000 years, too. Upon awakening, he freed his beloved, and in the 1940s, they embarked on a war against evil.

Most *Ibis the Invincible* stories were horror tales, and Ibis and Taia were constantly battling vampires, werewolves, winged demons, and all sorts of supernatural creatures. Scenes depicting human sacrifices, rotting corpses, and all types of evil occurrences were not uncommon. But paramount in all the stories, even over and above the skimpy, revealing halter top worn by Taia, was the Ibistick. It could do almost anything—a sort of wooden Superman. Most of the stories were written by Fawcett workhorse Otto Binder, but Bill Woolfolk and Manly Wade Wellman also contributed heavily to the series. Mac Raboy, Carl Pfeufer, Kurt Schaffenberger, and Alex Blum handled the bulk of the artwork, which was always consistent, almost never poor, but not really above ordinary.

Ibis the Invincible appeared in all 155 issues of *Whiz* comics, which was discontinued in June 1953. The feature also had six issues of its own magazine (from 1943 to 1948) and made appearances in many of Fawcett's other magazines.

J.B.

IDÉE FIXE DU SAVANT COSINUS, L' (France) The last part of Christophe's picture-story trilogy, *L'Idée Fixe du Savant Cosinus* ("Learned Cosine's Fixed Idea") is, in many ways, also the funniest. This comic saga started, like Christophe's earlier *La Famille Fenouillard* and *Le Sapeur Camember*, in the pages of *Le Petit Français Illustré*, where it ran from 1893 to 1897.

Zéphyrin Brioche (nicknamed "the learned Cosine") was the prototype of the absentminded professor whose head is always in the clouds. He was leading a sedate life filled with abstruse research and algebraic formulas until the day he learned of his cousin Fenouillard's round-the-world exploits and subsequent fame. Bitten by jealousy, he decided to circle the globe in his turn (his "fixed idea"). Plagued by misfortune, he never made it out of Paris. Cosinus's attempts to start on his journey, on foot and by train, bicycle, horse carriage, and in a variety of outlandish contraptions of his own invention, always ended in abject failure. On this basic theme Christophe wove the most hilarious variations involving the professor's hapless efforts and the implacable quirks of fate that thwarted him at every step.

Le Savant Cosinus has been reprinted in hardbound form by Armand Colin, and in paperback by Hachette.

M.H.

IGAGURI-KUN (Japan) Created by Eiichi Fukui, *Igaguri-kun* ("Mr. Crewcut") made its first appearance in the March 1952 issue of the monthly *Bokeno*, and it grew rapidly in popularity as a judo strip.

Igaguri-kun's real name is Kurisuke Igaya. He is the son of a barber—like Charlie Brown!—but unlike the hapless Charlie he is tall and strong, the captain of his high school's judo team, which he brings to victory over all opponents (again unlike Charlie Brown), finally becoming champion.

The strip's popularity increased by leaps and bounds, and Fukui drew more and more pages as the demand increased. On June 26, 1954, he died suddenly of a heart attack, and the strip passed first into the hands of Ippei Doya, then to Asakazu Arikawa.

Igaguri-kun's success ushered in the boom of sports comic strips (*Daruma-kun* by Yoshiteru Takai, *Inazuma-kun* by Chohei Shimoyama, *Bokutō kun* by Yoshiteru Takano, to name a few). It also inspired a radio program. The strip, however, is no longer being published.

Fukui's work on *Igaguri-kun* was fast-paced, visually striking, and very impressive. If he were alive today Eiichi Fukui could have challenged Osuma Tezuka for the title of "king of the Japanese comic strip" on the strength of his work on *Igagura-kun* alone.

H.K.

IGER, SUMUEL MAXWELL (1903-1990) American comic book and comic strip artist, writer, and editor, born August 22, 1903, in New York City. "Jerry" Iger had no formal art training, but broke directly into the field as a news cartoonist for the *New York American* in 1925. During the late 1920s, he also did advertising artwork for New York Telephone (with Rube Goldberg) and several other companies. In the early 1930s, he began working for Editors Press Service, for which he created features like *Sheena, The Flamingo,* and *Inspector Dayton.* He also formed his own syndicate, Phoenix Features Syndicate, during this time.

Iger became one of the very first people involved in the comic book business. Three of his strips, *Bobby, Peewee,* and *Happy Daze,* appeared in Eastern's *Famous Funnies* in 1935; it is among the first ever produced especially for comic books. In 1936, he was the editor of Herle's *Wow Comics* and published the first work of two later-prominent cartoonists: Bob Kane and Will Eisner. In 1937, he formed the S. M. Iger Studios (in partnership with Eisner, 1937-40) and began packaging material for the slew of new comic book publishers. One of his earliest jobs was Fiction House's *Jumbo,* an oversized comic featuring his Sheena feature (drawn by Mort Meskin). Iger was also Fiction House's feature editor from 1940-55.

Many talented artists passed through the Iger studios over the years (his was the second shop created primarily to package comics); among its best talents were Lou Fine, Reed Crandall, Al Feldstein, Mort Meskin, Will Eisner, Mort Leav, and the under-publicized Mart Baker. His shop contracted and produced work for many of the publishers of the 1940s: Fox, Quality, Harvey, MLJ, Holyoke, Crown, Farrell, EC, and others.

Certainly one of the comic book's earliest pioneers, Iger finally closed his studio in 1955 and became Ajax's art editor until 1957. He then taught art and produced commercial artwork for advertising. He died in a New York City nursing home on September 5, 1990.

J.B.

INDIO, EL (Philippines) *El Indio* ("The Indio" or "The Indian") is not a novel about an Indian of the Old West or an inhabitant of India. The word *Indio* also applies to the non-Spanish inhabitants of the Philippines. The Spaniards who were searching for the Indies mistakenly called the Malayan populace "Indios."

El Indio, written and illustrated by Francisco V. Coching, appeared in *Pilipino Komiks* in 1953 and ran for over 30 chapters. The story is part of a series that featured Barbaro, even though he does not play the main role in this particular tale.

The main character of the novel was Fernando, a constant problem to the Spanish colonists who ruled the Philippines with an iron hand. Using guerrilla tactics, Fernando harassed and attacked his enemies. He was extremely elusive because of his shrewdness and his ability as a horseman. He was equally skilled with a sword as with a dueling pistol.

The other leading characters in this dramatic adventure novel were Victoria, Fernando's girlfriend; Kapitan Castillo, the archenemy; and Blanquita, Fernando's mother and also Castillo's lover.

Fernando's sworn enemy, unknown to him, was his own father. Kapitan Castillo was aware of his son's identity but was powerless to prevent the chain of events that led to the capture and imprisonment of his son and to his eventual facing of the firing squad.

One of the most suspenseful turns of events occurred when Kapitan Castillo faced his son in a duel. The novel was filled with such gripping sequences and emotional scenes. Coching handled each situation with finesse and mastery, qualities that are seldom seen in the comic book medium, where sensationalism and gimmicks have been the tools used by lesser individuals to hide their inability to portray and convey subtle and delicate moments. Coching has the judgment, taste, and control that make him one of the true masters in the comics field. *El Indio* is one of his many contributions to that field.

O.J.

INFANTINO, CARMINE (1925-) American comic book artist, born May 24, 1925, in Brooklyn, New York. After studies at the School of Industrial Arts, the Art Students League, and other institutions, Infantino broke into the comics in 1942 as the illustrator of Timely's *Jack Frost.* After working for a handful of other companies, he landed at National in 1946, illustrating the *Ghost Patrol* adventure feature.

Impressed with his material—mostly done in collaboration with Frank Giacoia—National editor Shelly Mayer assigned work to Infantino on a horde of strips, including *Flash, Johnny Thunder, Green Lantern,* and *Black Canary.* Much of this work was angular and rough, showing heavy influences of the Chester Gould and Harold Gray styles. In the 1950s, however, Infantino refined his style radically, and his work began to show better design and drawing. Strongly influenced by the fine-line illustrations of pulp artists Edd Cartier and Lou Fine, Infantino's work on dozens of science-fiction and Western tales began to show increased maturity and style.

But Infantino's finest career effort was the revived version of *The Flash.* Beginning with its first appearance in *Showcase* number four in October 1956, Infantino guided the strip artistically for 11 years. During that time, although his anatomy drawing was often lacking, his inventive maneuvers to simulate speed became industry standards. During the same time, however, Infantino was also drawing the highly acclaimed *Adam Strange* science-fiction series. There, his tightly knit illustrations and impeccable Hal Foster-inspired layouts were highlighted by some of the most beautiful cityscapes ever to appear in comics. In 1964, Infantino and *Adam Strange* inker Murphy Anderson were called in by Julius Schwartz to revamp the *Batman* strip. The resulting "new look" Infantino brought to the strip reversed the character's 10-year decline, and *Batman, Flash,* and *Adam Strange* all became comic book classics.

Infantino abruptly left the drawing board in 1967 and became National's editorial director. He experimented extensively with the National line and included two Steve Ditko titles; a feature from the 1950s *Bomba* movies, illustrated by comic strip artist Howard Post; *Bat Lash,* a highly acclaimed Western strip by Nick Cardy and Sergio Aragones; and many others. Most of the titles were financially unsuccessful, however. Infantino was appointed publisher in 1971 and continued to experiment. Under his leadership, National revived *Captain Marvel, The Shadow, The Avenger,* and others, introduced the dollar-sized comic, produced the highly acclaimed *Green Lantern-Green Arrow* series, secured the

"DC Special," Carmine Infantino. © DC Comics.

services of Jack Kirby, acquired the comic book rights to *Tarzan,* and issued hardbound and softbound reprints of landmark comic books.

Infantino won several fan awards and was given the National Cartoonist Society award in 1958. He and Stan Lee were instrumental in the founding of The Academy of Comic Book Arts (ACBA), the comic book's equivalent of the NCS.

J.B.

By all accounts Infantino's tenure at DC was a disaster, and he was forced to resign in the late 1970s. Since that time he has had a checkered career, working for Marvel Comics and Warner Publications, then going back to DC in 1982, working principally on *The Flash.* In recent years he has been living in semi-retirement, only occasionally drawing for comic books.

M.H.

INGELS, GRAHAM (1915-1991) American comic book artist, born June 7, 1915, in Cincinnati, Ohio. After several years as a commercial artist, Ingels joined the navy and had his first comic material published in a 1946 issue of Eastern's *Heroic Comics.* After his discharge in 1947, Ingels illustrated for the pulps briefly before joining the Standard group as an editor.

At Standard, which was also known as the Better and Nedor groups, Ingels concerned himself mainly with plotting and scripting, but he did manage to turn out several outstanding cover illustrations for *Startling Comics.* He returned to freelance comic illustrating in 1948 and did some work for the M.E. and Fiction House groups before joining the E.C. group. There he illustrated Western, crime, and love stories in a clean and competent manner.

But it was not until editor and publisher Bill Gaines instituted the E.C. "New Trend" horror line in 1950 that Ingels began to hit his artistic peak. Illustrating horror and crime stories for a wide range of the new titles—including *Crypt of Terror, Vault of Horror,* and *Haunt of Fear*—Ingels made it apparent that he was becoming the definitive Gothic-horror comic illustrator of the day. Adopting the pen name "Ghastly," Ingels began drawing a series of highly regarded covers and stories for the already high quality E.C. line.

Though he was competing with E.C.'s other talents, such as Reed Crandall, Al Williamson, Frank Frazetta, and Jack Davis, it was Ingels's sympathetic handling of gory horror tales that became E.C.'s most popular material. Writer Al Feldstein once commented that "when we did an Ingels script, we did gothic, gooky, horror stories . . . we didn't set limitations . . . we encouraged him to develop his own screw-ball hairy black and white style."

Much of that "screw-ball" style was lost on the color comics. Ingels's horror material was complex and sharp and contained tremendous amounts of fragile linework. But, at the same time they were evoking nerve-shattering horror, his stories would also show brilliant flashes of whimsy, understanding, and even comedy. Some of his best material has been included in the five issues of *E.C. Portfolio,* a large, black-and-white art magazine published by E.C. fan Russ Cochran.

After the E.C. "New Trend" line was scuttled by adverse publicity in late 1954, Ingels spent several years illustrating for *Treasure Chest, Classics Illustrated,* and several of the later E.C. titles. He retired from comic books in 1959 and became a painting instructor in Florida. A born-again Christian, he repudiated his

Graham Ingels, "A Little Stranger." © William M. Gaines, Agent, Inc.

former horror work as "satanic." He died in Florida on April 4, 1991.

J.B.

INSPECTOR DAN, EL (Spain) Created in 1947 by the writer Rafael Gonzalez, *El Inspector Dan de Ia Patrulla Volante* ("Inspector Dan of the Mobile Squad"), as it was first called, enjoyed a long life in the pages of the Spanish weekly *Pulgarcito*, as well as in comic books and newspaper strips produced for the foreign market. The first episodes (there were 38 of them) were drawn by Eugenio Giner, who endowed the character with life and zest and who marked the series with his personal style. Along with the scriptwriter Francisco Gonzalez Ledesma, Giner contributed the best moments of this feature, which cultivated a genre up to then only slightly successful in Spanish comics: the tale of terror.

Dan was a Scotland Yard inspector who was sent on the most dangerous assignments by his superior, Colonel Higgins; he was assisted in his investigations by Inspector Simmons and his beautiful deputy Stella. The locales were the slums of London, filled with fog and teeming with criminals; the British Museum, where mummies sprang back to life; Chinese opium dens; and castles inhabited by mad scientists. Giner's drawings were rendered with care and were very detailed, always effective, with backgrounds lovingly pencilled in. His successors, Macabich, Vivas, Costa, Henares, and Pueyo, did not succeed in re-creating the atmosphere of terror called for by the story line. In the months preceding *El Inspector Dan*'s demise in 1963, Victor Mora wrote the scenarios.

L.G.

INSPECTOR WADE (U.S.) In 1934 King Features Syndicate decided to add yet another entry to its already abundant line of detective strips (*Secret Agent X-9*, *Radio Patrol*, and *Red Barry*). A deal was arranged with the estate of Edgar Wallace to adapt the late British novelist's thrillers into a daily comic strip. The writing was entrusted to Sheldon Stark, Lyman Anderson was hired to do the illustration, and the first release of the *Inspector Wade* feature was scheduled for December 1934. A hitch developed, however; the *London Mirror* was running a strip called *Terror Keep*, based on Edgar Wallace's *Mr. Reeder* stories, and King moved to suppress it. After some legal and business finagling, the *Mirror* dropped the feature, and *Inspector Wade* made its American debut on May 20, 1935. (While King was waiting for the legal dust to settle, its European representatives sold the strip to Mondadori in Italy, where

"Inspector Wade," Lyman Anderson. © King Features Syndicate.

it appeared on May 1, 1935, almost three weeks ahead of its American release.)

The pipe-smoking, tweed-suited Wade of Scotland Yard was a suave gentleman-detective who, with the help of his assistant, the bowler-hatted Donovan, solved the most baffling mysteries. His assignments often took him far afield—for instance, to Arabia, where he put an end to the depredations of a terrorist group—but his usual beat was the teeming streets of London or the peaceful English countryside.

Lyman Anderson drew the strip in a casual way that was not without charm, but failed to grip the reader. He was succeeded on July 4, 1938, by Neil O'Keefe, who changed the mood of the feature to one of suspense and foreboding. The action picked up in pace and violence, and *Inspector Wade* came closer to the hard-boiled school of American gangster movies than to the urbane criminality of Wallace's novels. In spite of O'Keefe's talent, *Inspector Wade* continued on its downward slide, and the daily strip (there never was a Sunday version) finally came to a halt on May 17, 1941, after a six-year run.

M.H.

IN THE LAND OF WONDERFUL DREAMS *see* Little Nemo.

INVISIBLE SCARLET O'NEIL (U.S.) *Invisible Scarlet O'Neil*, distributed by the now-defunct Chicago Times Syndicate, was the creation of former *Dick Tracy* assistant Russell Stamm, and it debuted in June 1940.

Touted in press releases as "America's new superheroine," Scarlet O'Neil was a shapely redhead who had suddenly become endowed with invisibility powers after she was accidentally exposed to "a weird looking ray" in her scientist-father's laboratory. (She was also able to make herself visible again by pressing a nerve in her left wrist, and to revert back to invisibility by the same process.)

Scarlet's early adventures, which were on the mournful side (perhaps in a bid to attract female readership), involved crippled children, kidnapped ingenues, and doe-eyed orphans, but this proved to be a passing phase. By 1944, when Stamm went into military service and left the strip to his assistants, the invisible heroine was fighting foreign agents, subversive organizations, and conspiracies on an international scale. After Stamm's return in 1946, the stories changed once again and became more and more whimsical, even sarcastic, as Stamm appeared to be poking fun at his heroine and her improbable escapades. In 1952 a new character was introduced into the strip (now simply called *Scarlet O'Neil*): Stainless Steel, a Texas swashbuckler with iron fists and a sense of humor. Stainless soon stole the show, and the feature was retitled *Stainless Steel* in 1954, only to disappear two years later.

Russell Stamm drew Scarlet in a loose, broad style with only touches of the tough, *Dick Tracy* treatment. The trouble with the feature was that it was always too cartoony for a straight adventure strip, but not quite funny enough for a parody. What is surprising is that it lasted as long as it did.

M.H.

IRON MAN (U.S.) *Iron Man* was created by Stan Lee and debuted in the March 1963 issue of *Tales of Suspense* (number 39). The origin story, scripted by Lurry Lieber and illustrated by Don Heck, introduced Tony Stark, a wealthy industrialist and munitions builder. While in Vietnam on government work, Stark stumbled across a land mine. He wound up in the clutches of Red Terrorists, having sustained a severe chest injury. The Communists put the American inventor to work on their behalf, working with an elderly physicist, Professor Yinsen. Together, Yinsen and Stark built a suit of invincible armor, equipped with weaponry, flying jets, and devices to keep Stark's injured heart beating. Stark escaped in the suit but Yinsen died. Thereafter, Stark refined the suit and, as Iron Man, devoted himself to fighting tyranny and assorted evils.

Early *Iron Man* adventures, drawn by Heck, Jack Kirby, and Steve Ditko, usually involved Communist villains. Eventually, a Fu Manchu-type named The Mandarin became his major foe. The stories, written by Berns and Lee, centered on Stark's American factory and the various threats to its top-secret work. Stark never completely recovered from his heart injury, and he endured only because of the energy fed into his metal chest plate.

For a time, Heck was the principal artist and Iron Man's outfit was continually being redesigned. In 1966, Gene Colan took over as regular illustrator, and with Stan Lee's scripting, the strip became particularly heavy on "soap opera" aspects, notably in a love triangle involving Stark; his secretary, Pepper Potts; and his sidekick, Happy Hogan. In addition to his health problems, Stark continually faced legal and business problems that his bodyguard, Iron Man (that was the cover

"Iron Man," © Marvel Comics Group.

story for Iron Man's nearness to Stark) couldn't help with. No one suspected that the foppish playboy Tony Stark actually was Iron Man.

In 1968, after a one-shot appearance in a double-feature comic with *Sub-Mariner, Iron Man* began its own magazine. Number one started in May, and by this time, Archie Goodwin had become the regular scripter of the feature. Johnny Craig illustrated a few issues before George Tuska became the regular artist for the strip. A number of temporary artists interrupted Tuska's run on the feature, and after Goodwin left in 1970, several writers handled the chore before Gerry Conway and, finally, Mike Friedrich took over.

Iron Man appeared, as a guest star, in many of Marvel's other magazines, including a regular role as a member of *The Avengers*.

M.E.

Iron Man was put through the wringer in the 1980s: he lost the use of his legs, was elbowed out by an impostor, and turned into an alcoholic, among other vicissitudes. His physical and mental health stabilized somewhat in the 1990s. Among the artists who have worked on the series in this period, mention should be made of John Byrne and Steve Austin.

M.H.

IRVING, JAY (1900-1970) American cartoonist, born in New York City on October 3, 1900. Jay Irving's father, Abraham Rafsky, was a police captain, as his grandfather had been. After studies at Columbia University, Irving shifted from one newspaper job to another, then became police reporter for the *New York Globe*, and later a sports cartoonist. After a stint with the Universal wire service, Irving created a sports strip for King Feature Syndicate, *Bozo Blimp* (1930), which sank with hardly a trace.

Discouraged, Irving went into advertising work for two years before joining (in 1932) *Collier's Weekly*, with which he was to remain for 13 years, doing a weekly panel, *Collier's Cops*, and contributing occasional covers. During World War II, Irving was attached to the Marine Corps as a war artist for *Collier's*.

In 1946 he created a new comic strip, *Willie Doodle*, about a lovable and cuddly police officer, for the Herald-Tribune Syndicate; it did not last long. Then Irving tried to syndicate a TV cartoon show that he had created with Mel Casson, but the project did not succeed either. Finally, in May of 1955, Irving tried his hand at another comic police strip for the Tribune-News Syndicate, *Pottsy*, whose hero was a chubby, cherubic city cop with a penchant for humor and poetry that often put him on a collision course with the police brass.

Irving had been collecting police memorabilia since the 1930s, when his father had given him his own shield and presentation stick, and owned more than 5,000 items related to police work or folklore. He was such an authority on police matters that he was often consulted on the subject by the New York Historical Society and the Museum of the City of New York. Irving was also an honorary member of the New York Police Department, and of more than 200 other departments throughout the country. His stature as a cartoonist, unfortunately, was never as exalted, although with *Pottsy* he made an agreeable, if minor, contribution to American comic art.

Jay Irving.

Jay Irving died of a heart attack in his apartment in New York City on June 5, 1970, and *Pottsy* was discontinued shortly afterward.

M.H.

ISABELLA (Italy) On April 2, 1966, the so-called "fumetti per adulti" ("comics for adults only") underwent an abrupt turnaround with the introduction of their first heroine: Isabella. Considering the tastes prevailing among the comic-book-reading public, it seemed at first a gamble to thrust *Isabella* into this slightly disreputable genre. The new feature clashed violently with the traditional depictions of murder, violence, masked fiends, and assorted evildoers and sadists who were populating the adult comic books. Isabella, on the other hand, was created as a far more complex character, full of courage but also full of apparent contradictions, even flaws.

The new strip, however, made a favorable impression on the public, either because of its very incongruities, or because in the titular heroine it was easy to recognize another very similar feminine firebrand: Anne and Serge Golon's Angélique, who was then enjoying wide popularity in books and movies. No man could dominate Isabella, no woman could outdo her in boldness or passion. Her love was completely free, as was her heart: a passionate heart, or an icy one, according to the situation or the men who came in contact with her. She was an extremely modern heroine, in revolt against the aristocratic caste to which she belonged. Drenched in a splendid, touching, and romantic atmosphere, Isabella stands out from every other female character in the world's comic literature.

Isabella was created by scriptwriter Renzo Barbieri (on the basis of an apocryphal manuscript, "Les Memoires d'Isabella de Frissac") and adapted by Giorgio Cavedon. The artwork was done first by Sandro

Angiolini, who was succeeded by Sergio Rosi (pencils) and Umberto Sammarini (inks), assisted by draftsmen of the Rosi studio in Rome. Released in the beginning through Edizioni RG, *Isabella* moved to Ediperiodici in Milan. It ended in 1976.

G.B.

ISHIMORI, SHŌTARŌ (1938-   ) Japanese comic book artist, born January 25, 1938, in Nakata-machi (Miyagi prefecture). During his years in high school, Shōtarō Ishimori made his debut in *Manga Shōnen* with the work *Nikyu Tenshi* ("Second-Class Angel") in 1954. After his graduation from high school, Ishimori went to Tokyo in the hope of becoming a novelist. Unfortunately, he could not break through, and in order to make a living, he turned again to comic strips. In 1959, he created his first successful strip, *Kaiketsu Harimao*, an adventure story, which was followed by a succession of other creations: *Yureisen* ("The Ghost Ship," 1960), *Mutant Sabu* (1961), *Shōnen Dōmei* ("The Boys' League," 1962), and *Cyborg 009* (1964) All were science-fiction strips. In 1965 Ishimori tried his hand at his first gag strip, *Bon Bon*, but it was not terribly successful and he returned to science fiction with *Genma Taisen*, which traced the epic battles fought by a group of heroes endowed with extrasensory perception against alien creatures who tried to conquer the world (1967).

Shōtarō Ishimori is an extraordinarily versatile artist who has drawn literally hundreds of comic strips of all types for children, young adults, and adults. He has mastered every conceivable genre with dexterity and incredible speed. Under his full name, Ishinomori (of

Shotaro Ishimori.

which Ishimori is a contraction), and in an altogether different register he published in 1985 *Manga Nihon Keizai Nyumon* ("A Comic Strip Survey of the Japanese Economy"), translated with great success in the United States as *Japan Inc.*, and since 1989 he has been working on a monumental history of Japan told in comics form, *Manga Nihon no Rekishi*.

Like most Japanese artists, Ishimori was under the influence of Osamu Tezuka during his formative years, but he has developed a style of his own, which is fluid and airy, even sparse, especially in his gag strips.

H.K.

ISHINOMORI, SHŌTARŌ *see* Ishimori, Shotaro.

JABATO, EL (Spain) *El Jabato* was created by Francisco Darnis in 1958, at a time when adventure comic books were entering their decline, yet it succeeded in gaining an impressive readership in the course of its 381 comic books, published until 1966.

El Jabato was born as a feature designed to emulate the success of *El Capitan Trueno*, which is why the publishers chose Victor Mora, who was already *Capitan Trueno*'s scriptwriter. Ancient Rome provided the background (the so-called peplum films were then in their heyday, with such heroes as Hercules and Maciste), and the hero's companion was named Taurus, like one of those screen hefties. El Jabato was an Iberian warrior enslaved by the Romans, who took him to the capital of the empire and trained him as a gladiator. Not coincidentally this stage of his apprenticeship was similar to that of the historical Spartacus. In Rome El Jabato met his two most loyal admirers, the young Roman girl Claudia, and the stringy poet Fiedo Mileto, who was drawn with such caricatural exaggeration that he clashed with the dominant style of the feature.

The success of *El Jabato* was such that it led to the creation in 1962 of a magazine that bore his name, and his adventures were also being published in other weekly magazines of the same publisher, such as *Ven y Ven, Suplemento de Historietas del DDT, El Campeón,* and *El Capitan Trueno Extra.* In 1965 and 1969 the strip was reprinted, the second time in color.

Francisco Darnis, whose vigorous and personal style did much to establish the series, was helped or succeeded in his weekly labors by Luis Ramos, Martinez Osete, Carregal, and others.

L.G.

JACOBS, EDGAR-PIERRE (1903-1987) Edgar-Pierre Jacobs was probably the most secretive of all European cartoonists. Even his official biographies fail to divulge his exact date and place of birth; however, a close study of his career and several clues provided by the artist himself in his reminiscences lead to the conclusion that he was born in 1903 in Brussels or one of its suburbs.

Jacobs himself stated that "he could not remember a time when he did not draw." In the company of his childhood friend, Jacques van Melkebeke, he haunted Brussels museums and galleries. While preparing for his admission exams for the Royal Academy of Fine Arts, Jacobs did all sorts of small art jobs, from lace design to illustration of mail-order catalogs. Yet Jacobs had another avocation: he was an opera singer. Endowed with a rich baritone voice, he decided to enroll in the Conservatory of Music while pursuing his art studies at the same time! For a while bel canto prevailed as Jacobs graduated with top honors from the Conservatory and promptly found a position with the Lille Opera in France. There he sang all the baritone roles of French, Italian, and German opera. The outbreak of World War I put an end to his promising career, however.

Back in Brussels and penniless, with no further hope of pursuing an opera career, Jacobs decided to go back to drawing. After contributing many cartoons and illustrations to such publications as *Bimbo, Stop, A.B.C.,* and *Lutin,* in 1942 he joined the staff of the comic weekly *Bravo,* which was still publishing a number of American comic strips, including old pages of Raymond's *Flash Gordon.* By the end of 1942 *Bravo* was running out of Raymond pages, and Jacobs was commissioned to bring the current episode to a logical end. His work was of such high quality that the editors asked him to create an original science-fiction feature to replace *Flash.* Thus *Le Rayon U* ("The U-Ray") began to appear in February 1943. In 1944 Jacobs became assistant to Hergé on *Tintin,* which marked the beginning of a long-lasting friendship between the two artists.

In 1946, at the recommendation of Hergé, Jacobs became one of the first artists on the newly created *Tintin* magazine. There he produced his most famous comic strip creation, the universally acclaimed science-fiction adventures of *Blake et Mortimer* (September 1946). In addition to his work on the strip, Jacobs also did many illustrations for *Tintin* (his illustrations for H. G. Wells's *War of the Worlds* are especially worthy of mention).

E. P. Jacobs's reputation as an artist and storyteller stands second only to that of Hergé among European cartoonists. He received a multitude of awards and honors, his works are continuously reprinted, and in 1973 he was the subject of a book-length study titled *Edgar-Pierre Jacobs: 30 Ans de Bandes Dessinées* ("Edgar-Pierre Jacobs: 30 Years of Comic Strips").

In 1977 Jacobs released the first part of the long-awaited Blake and Mortimer album, *Les Trois Formules du Professeur Sato* ("Professor Sato's Three Formulas"). He was laboriously working on the second (and last) part of the story when he died in Brussels on February 21, 1987. (The unfinished project was later completed by Bob de Moor.)

M.H.

JACOBSSON, OSCAR (1889-1945) Oscar Jacobsson, Swedish artist and cartoonist, was born on November 7, 1889, in Göteborg, and died in Solberga on December 25, 1945. Jacobsson's first newspaper illustration was published in 1918 in *Naggen.* It was only two years later that Hasse Zetterström of *Söndags-Nisse* ("Sunday Troll") suggested that Jacobsson create a comic strip for that humor weekly. The resulting comic strip, *Adamson,* premiered in *Söndags-Nisse* number 42/1920 of October 17, 1920. *Adamson* caught on and became immensely popular because of the title character's funny misadventures.

Adamson is a stout little man, bald-headed except for three hairs growing on his head. Rarely is he seen without his cigar dangling from his lips. This offers Adamson the chance to be literally fuming whenever he gets caught in a fix of his own making, like gradually sawing off a chair's legs to keep it from tilting or cutting off loose ends of thread after having sewn a button to a coat and the button's falling off again.

Besides working on *Adamson*, Jacobsson, in the grip of an incurable illness before he turned 60, created *Abu Fakir* for the newspaper *Vi* ("We"). *Abu Fakir* is a strip about a magician, much in the tradition of *Mannen söm gor vad som faller honom in*. The strip was reprinted in album form in 1945. During his career, Jacobsson also worked for newspapers like *Dagens Nyheter, Exlex*, and *Lutfisken*, and exhibited his paintings in Gummeson's art hall in Stockholm in 1930. A memorial exhibition was shown in 1946 in Göteborg, where Jacobsson was a member of the artists' club. Göteborg's museum of art is one of many that exhibits Jacobsson's work.

W.F.

JACOVITTI, BENITO (1923-   ) Italian cartoonist, born March 9, 1923, in Termoli, in the district of Campobasso. At age 15 Franco Benito Jacovitti moved with his family to Florence. He was still a high school student when his first cartoons appeared in the satirical weekly *Il Brivido*. In issue 40 (October 5, 1940) of the weekly *Il Vittorioso*, Jacovitti's most famous character, Pippo, appeared in an episode titled "Pippo e gli Inglesi" ("Pippo and the English"). Later Pippo would be joined by his two inseparable friends, Pertica and Palla, to form the hilarious threesome known as the "three P's."

In addition to *Pippo* (which was published from 1940 to 1967), Jacovitti produced innumerable comic features, such as *Il Barbiere della Prateria* ("The Barber of the Prairie," 1941), *Chicchirichi* (1944), *Raimondo il Vagabondo* ("Raimondo the Tramp," 1946), *Giacinto Corsaro Dipinto* ("Giacinto the Painted Corsair," 1947), *Pasqualino e Pasqualone* (1950), and *Jack Mandolino* (1967). Jacovitti also adapted such enduring works of literature as *Ali Baba* and *Don Quixote* into comic strip form, and drew many parodies of American comic strips, among which *Mandrago il Mago* ("Mandrago the Magician") and *L'Onorevole Tarzan* ("The Honorable Tarzan") are the best known. (A great number of Jacovitti's stories were reprinted in *Albi e Almanacchi del Vittorioso*.)

In 1957 Jacovitti created for the weekly supplement of the Milanese newspaper *Il Giorno* a riotous, nonsensical Western parody, *Cocco Bill*, which appeared on March 28 of that year. For the same publication Jacovitti later produced *Gionni Galassia* ("Johnny Galaxy," a science-fiction parody, 1958) and *Tom Ficcanaso*, about the exploits of a nosy reporter aptly named "nose-sticker" (1957).

After the expiration of his contract with *Il Giorno*, Jacovitti transferred *Cocco Bill* to the *Corriere dei Piccoli* (1968), and in the same year he produced *Zorry Kid*, a clever parody of the famed masked hero Zorro. In 1973 he revived *Jack Mandolino* and *Cip e Zagar* for the *Corriere dei Ragazzi*.

Jacovitti was under exclusive contract to the *Corriere*, while in the past he contributed not only to *Il Vittorioso* and *Il Giorno*, but also to a lesser extent to Taurinia Publications (1940-41); *Intervallo* (1945); *Albi Costellazione*, for which he created the very funny *Ghigno il Maligno* ("Grimace the Evil One") in 1946; *Il Travaso*; *Il Piccolo Missionario*; *L'Automobile*; *L'Europeo*; and *Linus*. In 1980 he transferred most of his creations, including *Cip, Cocco Bill*, and *Zorry Kid*, to the weekly *Il Giornalino*.

Benito Jacovitti (who often signs his work simply "Jac") is probably the best-known Italian satirical cartoonist. His works have been reprinted in hardcover by Milano Libri and Edizione Piero Dami and have appeared in Rizzoli's famous BUR collection. Jacovitti now lives and works in Rome.

G.B.

JAFFEE, ALLAN (1921-   ) American comic book and comic strip artist and writer, born March 13, 1921, in Savannah, Georgia. After studies at New York's High School of Art and Design, Al Jaffee began his comic book career in 1941 as the writer/artist of Quality's *Inferior Man* feature. He moved to Marvel in 1942 and began producing funny animal and humor features, all of them rather standard comic book fare.

In 1955, while packaging two teenage humor books for Marvel, Jaffee produced his first work for Harvey Kurtzman's *Mad*. Intrigued with the possibility of expanding his humorous horizons, Jaffee decided to drop his Marvel titles and concentrate on *Mad*. By that time, however, Kurtzman had left as the magazine's editor, and Jaffee followed him through stints at two highly acclaimed—but short-lived—new humor books, the Playboy-published *Trump* and the artist-owned *Humbug*. Although both books were financial disasters and lasted a total of 13 issues, and although Jaffee had signed on with Kurtzman at about half his old Marvel rate, it was his first real opportunity to develop his humorous abilities. His writing was sharp, snappy, and brilliantly satiric. His artwork was direct, with little emphasis on anatomic perfection, but with considerable time devoted to humorous effect. The two unsuccessful magazines propelled Jaffee into humor's inner circle, and he became recognized as one of the most inventive artists in the field.

Shortly after *Humbug* faded in 1958, Jaffee entered the advertising field, returned to *Mad*, and began the *Tall Tales* syndicated panel. All three were financially and artistically successful. His advertising work is among the most unique and effective in the industry, prompting the NCS to award him its 1973 plaque as the best "Advertising and Illustrations" artist. He soon became one of *Mad*'s most prolific and easily recognizable contributors. In 1964, he invented the "Mad Fold-In," an inside back cover feature that entailed the reader's folding an intricately written and drawn scene into thirds, thus producing an entirely different scene with an always-satiric bite. He has also had many *Mad* paperbacks published, most notably several collections of his "Snappy Answers to Stupid Questions" feature. The *Tall Tales* panel lasted until 1965, and Jaffee went on to write *Debbie Deere* (1966) and *Jason* (1971).

Jaffee continues to produce considerable amounts of advertising work and children's illustrations, has worked on *Little Annie Fanny* (1964-66), and was written about in Nick Meglin's *Art of Humorous Illustration* (Watson-Guptill, 1973). "I did my first job for *Mad* magazine in 1955," Jaffee wrote in 1996, "and have been with it ever since."

J.B.

JAMES, ALFRED see Andriola, Alfred.

JAMES BOND (G.B.) James Bond, the secret agent with the most famous number in the world—007 ("Licensed to Kill"), was created by the late Ian Fleming. Among the most successful popular novels in lit-

Mad *fold-in*, Al Jaffee. © Al Jaffee.

erary history, they were adapted by the *London Daily Express* as a serial strip. The first novel, *Casino Royale*, began picturization in 1957. It was adapted by an *Express* staff writer, was drawn by John McLusky, and ran for 139 days. *Live and Let Die* followed, and then, in order of adaptation, *Diamonds Are Forever, From Russia with Love, Dr. No, Goldfinger, Risico, From a View to Kill, For Your Eyes Only, On Her Majesty's Secret Service,* and *You Only Live Twice*. These were adapted by Henry Gammidge. During the run of the strip, McLusky changed his conception of Bond to fit the likeness of Sean Connery, who had begun playing the role in films, beginning with *Dr. No* in 1962. The strip was

dropped in 1963 when the current supply of novels was exhausted.

The strip resumed in 1964 with an adaptation of *The Man with the Golden Gun*. There was a new artist and a new writer: James Lawrence, an American author of strip stories for *Joe Palooka, Captain Easy,* and *Buck Rogers*. Lawrence proved so successful that, by arrangement with the Fleming Trust, he was permitted to originate Bond stories for the strip. The only non-original in the sequence of stories beginning with *The Living Daylights* (1965) was *Colonel Sun*, the Bond novel written by Kingsley Amis. The new artist was Yaroslav "Larry" Horak. A Russo-Czech born in Manchuria

"James Bond" (promotion piece).

"Jane," Norman Pett. © Daily Mirror Newspapers Ltd.

and naturalized in Australia, he started his art career as a portrait painter, then turned to magazine illustration. In Sydney he began to write comic books, draw them, and finally produced them. He turned to newspaper strips in the *Sydney Morning Herald*, creating an outback adventure feature called *Mike Steel*. McLusky is currently drawing *Laurel and Hardy* in *T.V. Comic*. James Bond's career in British newspapers ended in the 1990s, but the suave secret agent can still be seen in a number of American comic books published as *James Bond 007*.

D.G.

JANE (G.B.) The most famous British newspaper strip, and the first heroine to take the name of her medium literally—strip!—was born out of a true incident that happened to cartoonist Norman Pett's wife. Mrs. Pett received a telegram asking her to look after a dignified visitor from the Continent who spoke no English. "Count Fritz von Pumpernickel" turned out to be a red dachshund! Inspired, Pett drew the incident as a strip and sent it to the *Daily Mirror*. Editor Harry Guy Bartholomew, eager to establish British strips in the American manner, saw the potential immediately, and on December 5, 1932, *Jane's Journal, the Diary of a Bright Young Thing* was opened. For some years it ran as a daily gag, with a hand-lettered text spotted among the pictures to give it the effect of a diary. At the time that panelling was introduced to replace the single landscape box (December 1938), Bartholomew suggested a switch to continuity, and Don Freeman, a writer, came in on the stories.

Always a girl to show a leg, Jane was originally posed by Pett's attractive wife. Other models came in as her clothes were shed more frequently, and during the war Jane toured the music halls with a striptease act. The actress was Christabel Leighton-Porter, and it was she who played the role in a film version, *The Adventures of Jane*, which was made by New World Films in 1949. Her appeal in the war years was tremendous, especially in the armed services. She actually made page-one headlines in *Roundup*, the U.S. Army newspaper in the Far East: *Jane Gives All* commemorated the great day when she finally stripped to the blonde buff!

Jane always topped *Mirror* surveys of readership of their strips: 86 percent in 1937; 85 percent in 1939; 90 percent in 1946; 80 percent in 1947; 79 percent in 1949; 77 percent in 1952. Michael Hubbard, Pett's assistant on backgrounds and male characters, took over the entire strip on May 1, 1948. Pett left to create a similar stripteaser, *Susie*, in the *Sunday Dispatch*, and also drew some rather glamorous strips for the children's comics. Hubbard's version of *Jane* lacked the lightness and fun of Pett's line, and the series became a soap opera. Finally, on Saturday, October 10, 1959, Jane and her beloved Georgie Porgie sailed off into the sunset.

There was an immediate and surprising (to the *Mirror*) outcry, as other national newspapers published articles and obituaries. She was replaced by a teenager, *Patti*, a more "with it" character drawn by Bob Hamilton. *Patti* lasted from October 12, 1959, to April 8, 1961. Then came *Jane Daughter of Jane*, drawn by Albert Mazure, but this, too, failed to last, running from August 28, 1961, to August 30, 1963. *Jane* was irreplaceable.

Norman Pett's *Jane* appeared in several reprints and special paperbacks; *Pett's Journal*, *Jane's Journal*, and *Another Journal* all have special artwork and full color. *Jane's Summer Idle* (1946) reprints a 1945 series; *Jane on the Sawdust Trail* (1947) is a colored reprint of the 1946 series. *Farewell to Jane* (1960) reprints a selection of strips published between 1944 and 1953. There was also a monthly reprint comic book *Jane*, published in Australia.

D.G.

JANE ARDEN (U.S.) *Jane Arden* debuted on November 26, 1928, in the Des Moines *Register and Tribune*, the brainchild of that paper's Henry Martin. The author of the strip was Monte Barrett, and the first artist was Frank Ellis; the strip was among the first sold by the newspaper syndicate operation.

Jane is a newspaper girl, sometime detective, and war correspondent. She is in her early twenties, leggy and predictably attractive. She never marries, but is married to her reporting job on a big-city paper.

The only other permanent character in this early-day *Brenda Starr* is Tubby, the office boy, a comic foil. The bosses change as frequently as do real-life managing editors.

After a few years the syndicate had trouble with artist Ellis; he suddenly disappeared and did not send his drawings in. Russell Ross was recruited from the art department of the newspaper. He had drawn another strip based on a Zane Grey story, *Bullet Benton*, later called *Slim and Tubby*, the latter character switching to become the office boy in *Arden* (the Western feature was continued by Jack McGuire, who was doing the Sunday *Arden*).

Succeeding Ross as artist was Jim Speed, a Toledo cartoonist; a briefly appearing artist from Florida; and finally Bob Schoenke. When Schoenke joined the strip, Walt Graham, who was the writer after Barrett died, retired.

When Schoenke took over the strip, *Jane Arden* underwent a strange transformation. Schoenke had drawn a strip called *Laredo*, and, under his direction, *Arden* became *Jane and Laredo*. It seemed that one day Jane came upon her family history and discovered that her mother was a reporter on a small-town Western paper. Strangely, the strip became one long flashback. Jane became her mother, the time became the 1880s, and Jane Arden and Sheriff Laredo Crockett rode off into the sunset. The strip died in the late 1950s.

The high point of the strip was during the 1940s, when wartime intrigues combined with Ross's attractive blend of the comic and straight styles for a very interesting strip. Ross kept his lines simple and details to the minimum, and he boldly shifted angles and settings. His work had a slick, uncomplicated look that should put many modern artists to shame.

For years *Lena Pry*, a humorous top strip about a hillbilly gal, and Jane Arden fashion cutouts accompanied the Sunday page.

R.M.

JANKOVIĆ, DJORDJE (1908-1974) Serbian artist Djordje Janković was born on April 25, 1908, in the village of Jazak, some 30 miles north of Belgrade. After secondary school, Janković moved to Belgrade and started to work at illustration. He was the staff illustrator for the daily newspaper *Vreme* ("Time"). His first comic strip, *Tajne abisinskih gudura* ("The Secrets of Ethiopian Ravines"), appeared in installments in Serbia's most respected comics magazine of the interwar period, *Mika Miš*, beginning with number 80 (March 16, 1937). The artwork was stiff and somewhat amateurish. Three more strips followed; all, like his initial effort, were realistically rendered adventure strips and were clearly the work of a beginner. But the last of this group, *Džungla Ved* ("Jungle Ved"), shows the influence of Foster's *Tarzan* and Raymond's *Jungle Jim*. With *Put oko sveta* ("Journey Around the World"), based on the popular novel of the Serbian humorist Branislav Nusić, Janković's work begins to assume its mature form, especially in the grotesque drawing that goes with the comic text. Interestingly, with the exception of this text, which was adapted by Branko Vidić, Janković wrote the scenarios for all of his comics.

By early 1938, Janković had become a solid comic artist, adept in the art of the adventure genre. Of his works that year, two were outstanding: *Mysterious Driver No. 13* and a humorous comic titled *Kića*. After discontinuing *Džungla Ved*, Janković devoted himself fully to humorous strips, first *Aga od Rudnika* ("Aga of Rudnik Mountain"), then *Tri bekrije* ("Three Chums"). He reached the apex of his creativity with his last five comics before the German invasion of Yugoslavia on April 6, 1941. The first was an adaptation of another classic Serbian humor novel, *Pop Ćira I pop Spira* ("Reverend Cira and Reverend Spira"), written by Stevan Sremac. The adventures of two Orthodox Christian village priests, it is still popular today. The remaining four were a series of stories about what may be the first Serbian antihero in comics, the loser Maksim. Publication began in *Mika Mis* on December 12, 1939.

During the war, he stopped producing comics, but he did illustrate some fairy-tale books for children. After the war, many Serbs tried to publish their own comics magazines. One such enterprising publisher was Živko V. Rajković, who launched his magazine *Vrabac* ("Sparrow") just before Christmas 1945. All five comics in the premiere issue, four realistic and one grotesque, were written and drawn entirely by Janković. They show continued improvement on his prewar work, and with the grotesque strip, *Nasradin Hodža*, Janković first uses elements of Disney style (smooth soft line, rounded human body and extremities, reduced number of fingers, etc.). Unfortunately, he never got to finish these stories and we will never know how his work would have further developed. After *Vrabac*'s third issue, in January 1946, Communist authorities banned all comics as "capitalist machination." The ban lasted until 1950, when a few comics appeared in youth magazines. In 1951 comics maga-

"Jane Arden," Monte Barrett and Russell Ross. © Register and Tribune.

zines were again legalized; all were strictly state-owned and controlled by the Communist party, but they did present the world's most important comics to their readers. This relaxation, and a general turning toward Western art and culture, was the result of the great ideological schism between Tito's Yugoslavia and Stalin's Soviet Union in 1948.

Unfortunately, Janković did not stay in Yugoslavia long enough to benefit from these changes. In 1950 he slipped illegally across the border and escaped to the West. He remained in Italy, where he changed his name to George Jacoby. From 1951 to 1957 he lived in Rome and only painted, and in 1957 he moved to South Africa. He died in Johannesburg on November 24, 1974, only two days before the opening of a major retrospective of his work.

S.I.

JANSSON, LARS (1928-   ) Finnish artist and writer Lars Jansson was born on October 8, 1926, the younger brother of Tove Jansson. Like her he was endowed by their mother, Signe Hammarsten-Jansson, one of Finland's best-known artists, with a love for literature and art. Having finished his studies, Lars Jansson worked as a freelance writer and artist before joining his sister in producing the extraordinary *Mumin* ("Moomin") comic strip. By 1957 Tove Jansson felt that *Mumin* was too much of a full-time job, keeping her from other art projects, so she assigned her brother the writing duties in 1958. In 1961 he also started drawing the strip and continued to do so until 1974.

Mumin being the highly individual comic strip it is, it was all the more fantastic that Lars could take over the strip without anybody knowing the difference. To be sure, he had had three years in which to get acquainted with the *Mumin* characters by writing their exploits. Nevertheless, this is one of the rare instances in which the artwork continued to have the same fairy-tale quality established by the strip's originator. Free to do what he wanted on the strip, he always ended up doing *Mumin* the way Tove Jansson would have continued it. Although the Mumin trolls were always a bit behind times, Lars Jansson managed to weave into the strip such modern concerns as ecological problems, the youth revolt, and the trials of city life. Throughout the strip's long run, Lars Jansson remained true to its motto. As he put it, "the essential message of the *Mumin* strip is that people should be kind to each other. It sounds terribly naive, but that's the way it is. All members of the Mumin family must be allowed to go their own ways and do what they like, but they still remain interested in each other and follow what the others are doing."

When copyrights went back to Tove and Lars Jansson after the newspaper strip ended, numerous Mumin products were merchandised. The characters appeared in various TV series (in both limited and full animation) over the years. A children's comic and activity magazine—based on the animated series—started being published in the Scandinavian countries in 1991 with stories written and drawn by various Scandinavian artists.

W.F.

JANSSON, TOVE (1914-   ) Tove Jansson, a Finnish painter, artist, and writer, was born on August 9, 1914, in Helsinki. The daughter of artist parents, she readily took to a career in art. She studied art at the academies of Helsinki, Stockholm, and Paris. As it turned out, she was successful both as an artist and as a writer. The first of her novels, *Kometjakten* ("Comet Quest"), was published in 1945, but had been written as early as 1939. Aimed largely at a young readership, the book featured trolls in animal form, the Mumin trolls. Tove Jansson once credited the name of Mumin troll to her uncle, who had used it to warn her not to raid the pantry. The book's success encouraged her to continue in the same vein of illustrated books starring the Mumin family. This resulted in books written in Swedish, such as *Trollkarlens hatt* ("The Wizard's Hat," 1949) and *Muminpappans Bravader* ("Muminpapa's Bravado," 1950). She was awarded the *Svenska Dagbladet's* literary prize in 1952, the Nils Holgersson plaque and the Finnish State's literary prize in 1953.

In 1953 Associated Newspapers of London asked Tove Jansson to do a *Mumin* comic strip to be published in the *Evening News*, the world's largest evening newspaper. Despite warnings from a comic artist friend not to sign a long-running contract, Tove Jansson signed a seven-year deal, and the *Mumin* strip began in 1954. In 1956 Associated Newspapers started an international drive that ultimately resulted in the strip's being published in some 20 languages. All the while Tove Jansson continued writing and illustrating Mumin novels, and raking in awards for her exceptionally fine work. She received the H. C. Andersen diploma in 1956, 1958, 1962, and 1964, and was awarded the Hans Christian Andersen Medal, a kind of Nobel Prize for fairy-tale writers, in 1966, making her the only other female Scandinavian writer besides Astrid Lindgren to win the coveted award.

Tove Jansson continued drawing the *Mumin* strip until 1960, but turned the writing over to Lars Jansson, one of her brothers, in 1958. In 1961, when the contract was renewed, Lars also took over the drawing of the strip. Tove continued working on the books and other art projects.

W.F.

JAPHET AND HAPPY (G.B.) *The Adventures of the Noah Family* began in the *Daily News* in 1919. Originally a serial story in text and illustrated by a single panel, it gradually developed into a four-panel strip, dropping text in favor of balloons. The writer and artist, identified by the single letter "H," eventually appended the flowery signature "Horrabin." He was James Francis Horrabin, illustrator, diagram- and mapmaker, and ultimately artist for another popular daily strip, *Dot and Carrie*.

The Adventures of the Noah Family was based on a traditional children's toy, the wooden Noah's Ark. Mr. and Mrs. Noah, wooden peg dolls, lived at "The Ark" on Ararat Avenue with their sons Ham, Shem, and the bad boy of the family, bespectacled Japhet. Oddly, the animals of "The Ark" were all "real": Polixenes the Parrot, Horatio the Horse (known as "Raish" for short), and Happy the Bear. This chubby little cub, smiling and speechless, arrived somewhere around strip number 2,000 and promptly stole the show. Soon the strip was called *Japhet and Happy*, although for a time it was also known as *The Arkubs*, after the children's club formed by the newspaper; Happy was featured on the badge. When the *Daily News* combined with the *Daily Chronicle* in 1930, the strip continued in the *News-Chronicle*. For a while (1935-39) it expanded to a double

"Japhet and Happy," J. F. Horrabin. © News Chronicle.

"Jean des Flandres," Marcel Moniquet. © Heroic-Albums.

his native Flanders. There our hero becomes one of the leaders of the rebellion against the Spanish crown; with his faithful retainer Claas Platzak and his band of guerrillas, he succeeds in holding back Don Blasco and his henchmen, who were sent from Spain to crush him. Following an abundance of ambushes, fights, massacres, and chases throughout Europe and as far away as North Africa, Jean des Flandres and Doña Flor (whom he had married in the meantime) finally enjoy some peace after 52 action-filled episodes (May 1955).

Jean des Flandres is better enjoyed for its plots, full of twists and turns, than for Moniquet's graphic style. The strip also gives us a fanciful but entertaining re-creation of one of the most eventful periods in European history.

M.H.

JEFF HAWKE (G.B.) Squadron Leader Jeff Hawke, R.A.F. test pilot, took off in the *Daily Express* on February 15, 1954. He flew the experimental X.P.5, the fastest aircraft in the world, which was not quite fast enough for his target, a flying saucer! Rescued from his crashing craft by tentacled aliens, he revived 3,000

bank of strips, but was reduced to three small panels during the war. It ended in the 1950s.

The first reprint in book form, *Some Adventures of the Noah Family*, was published in 1920; it was followed by *The Noahs on Holiday* (1921); *More About the Noahs & Tom Tossett* (1922); *The Japhet Book* (1924); *About Japhet & the Rest of the Noah Family* (1926); *Japhet & Co.* (1927); *Japhet & the Arkubs* (1928); *Japhet & the Arkubs at Sea* (1929); *Japhet & Co. on Arkub Island* (1930); *Japhet & Happy Book* (1931); *Japhet & Happy Annual 1933* (1932). The latter became the regular title until 1951. In addition, there was a paperback comic annual, *The Japhet Holiday Book* (1936-40); a *Japhet & Happy Painting Book* (1949); cutout "shape books," *Mr. Noah* and *Japhet & Fido* (1922); and sheets of colored transfers, postcards, cutouts, and wooden mascots.

D.G.

JEAN DES FLANDRES (Belgium) The series of cheap comic books published in Belgium under the catchall title of "Heroic-Albums" has usually elicited only disdain from comic strip scholars. Yet, amid the generally squalid tenor of the series, a few features stand out: one such is *Jean des Flandres* ("John of Flanders"), created in February 1950 by the prolific Belgian novelist and illustrator Marcel Moniquet.

Jean des Flandres was a young Flemish nobleman raised by the Countess of Hainaut in what was then (1563) the Spanish Low Countries. The action begins in Spain, where Jean delivers the pure and beautiful Doña Flor Della Torres from the clutches of the villainous Don Cesar Blasco de Lopez, and brings her back to

"Jeff Hawke," Sydney Jordan. © Sydney Jordan.

miles beyond the moon, where the Lords of the Universe, responsible for the crash, offered him a choice: safe return to Earth with memory erased, or life as the First Citizen of the Space Age. He opted for the latter, and for 20 years widened the horizons of his readers with his fantastic science-fiction adventures. His partner in many of these adventures was Commander Maclean ("Mac"), from Canada; his worst enemy, Chalcedon, avowed foe of His Excellency the Overlord of the Galactic Federation. Hawke's unexplained disappearance from the *Express* on April 18, 1974, was as fantastic as any of his other adventures, and drew many protests from readers. He was replaced by a sexy instruction strip, *Isometrics*. *Jeff Hawke* wouldn't stay grounded for long, however; the strip was picked up by London Features Syndicate, which distributes it throughout Europe, to Australia, and even in the United States.

Jeff Hawke, Space Rider, to restore its original title, was created by Sydney Jordan of Scotland, who had cut his comic teeth on *Dick Hercules* and other Man's World publications. His original concept was for a comic book hero, Orion, in the space-opera style of *Flash Gordon*, but his hero was renamed by the *Express* editor, who wanted an R.A.F. connection. Assisting, and later taking over the writing, was Willy Patterson, who was responsible for the quirky humor in many of the stories. The early strips were redrawn for *Junior Express* starting on September 4, 1954, changing into a full-color gravure spread in *Express Weekly* from February 18, 1956.

D.G.

JERRY ON THE JOB (U.S.) Walter C. Hoban's best-known comic strip, the daily and Sunday *Jerry on the Job*, began as a rather tentative daily strip in the *New York Journal* on Monday, December 29, 1913. Jerry, a tow-headed, husky kid of about 17 (he is made to appear younger as the strip develops), applies for a job as an office boy in the opening episode with a suave, moustached employer named Frederick Fipp, and immediately tumbles into the sort of office-gag situations used again almost a decade later in *Smitty*. Luckily, Hoban, who had been doing the sports-page cartoons for the *Journal* with Tad Dorgan at the time, had a fey twist to his imagination and a graphically saucy way with his routine figures and backgrounds, which captured the reader's attention virtually on sight.

In a few months, *Jerry* had become one of the *Journal's* standard daily features, going into national distribution with Hearst chain papers. A regular cast of characters had been introduced: Fred Blink, a young rival for Jerry's job; Jerry's younger brother, Herman; a stenographer named Myrtle; and an effeminate bookkeeper (with an odd, rectangular nose) named Pinkie McJunk, who with Jerry and his boss comprised the active figures in the strip. (Within his second month, on February 17, 1914, Hoban introduced 30-panel movie parodies in strip form into the daily continuity of *Jerry*, with such titles as "The Dog Hero," "Jake the Scout," and—written by Jerry himself—"The Country Youth," anticipating the later use of the same idea by Merrill Blosser of NEA and Hearst's Ed Wheelan in his *Midget Movies*.)

Not content with this amusing initial cast and setting, Hoban transferred Jerry after a year or so to a job in a railroad station as a combination ticket-seller, fountain clerk, newsdealer, baggage-smasher, and sweep-out boy, where he worked for a white-haired,

"Jerry on the Job," Walt Hoban. © King Features Syndicate.

middle-aged man named Mr. Givney, and was regularly plagued by passengers and packages all going to a location called New Monia. This final job set the regular format for the strip as it appeared thereafter—except for a vacation in 1917-18, when Hoban was in the armed forces—until its end in 1932. Hoban added a Sunday *Jerry* page in 1921, which ran until 1932, becoming, however, only the page-topper to a new Hoban Sunday strip in 1931 called *Rainbow Duffy* (which featured a young bank clerk and physical culturist). Dropped as a page-topper in 1932, *Jerry* was replaced by an animal gag feature named *Discontinued Stories*, which topped a new strip supplanting *Rainbow Duffy* called *Needlenose Noonan* (narrating the slapstick problems of a comic cop), both running (as Sunday strips only) from 1932 until 1935, when Hoban left King Features to do advertising and other work.

Jerry on the Job is, in its low-keyed way, one of the most graphically innovative and appealing of all humorous comic strips; much of its gag humor is of the "wow-plop" variety, on the level of *Smokey Stover* (another visually inventive strip), but a small part, especially in the earlier years, is sparkling and witty. This latter body of work richly deserves reprinting for contemporary readers.

B.B.

JERRY SPRING (Belgium) Joseph Gillain (who signs his work Jijé) created *Jerry Spring* for the comic weekly *Spirou* in 1954.

Jerry Spring is the Western's equivalent of the knight-errant, the fearless and indomitable figure of lore and legend. With determination and righteousness as his only baggage, and his trusted Colts on his side, he wanders endlessly on the western plains, often sleeping under the stars, always going his own way and being his own man. It is to Jijé's credit that he could take the hackneyed theme of countless horse-operas and make it into a work of significance and even grandeur.

Under Jijé's pen, the magnificent vistas of the West came to life, the action scene took on an added dimension and meaning, and the characters rose from stereotypes to incarnations of myth. The strip, transcending the limitations of plot and situation, became an allegory of life and death centering on the friendship between the dour, inflexible Jerry Spring and his youthful Mexican companion, the cheerful, pragmatic Poncho.

Jerry Spring from the outset caused quite a stir in European comic art circles and was at the center of the revival of the Western strip in Europe. The scenarios for the strip were written by Jijé himself, as well as by his brother Philippe, Lob, Acquaviva, and René Goscinny.

Jerry Spring—which was discontinued in 1967—has been reprinted in book form by Editions Dupuis in Belgium. It was revived in June 1974, again in *Spirou*. It lasted only into 1977, but was resumed again, after Jijé's death, by José-Louis Bocquet (text) and Franz Drappier (drawing) in 1990.

M.H.

JIJÉ *see* Gillain, Joseph.

JIM BOUM (France) One of the first French Western strips, *Jim Boum*, was created in September 1934 in the

"Jerry Spring," Jijé (Joseph Gillain). © Editions Dupuis.

Catholic weekly *Coeurs Vaillants* from the prolific pen of cartoonist Marijac (Jacques Dumas).

Jim Boum was a Galahad of the plains in the tradition of the 1930s. He went through a series of stock situations with the cool aplomb and steely resolve required by the genre. At one time or another, he dutifully rid the range of a gang of cattle rustlers, led a wagon train safely through countless perils and Indian attacks, saved a schoolmarm by stopping her team of runaway horses, and tracked a bunch of desperadoes all the way to Mexico. All these adventures were well plotted and entertaining, in spite of Marijac's inability to draw horses (admittedly a strong handicap for a Western strip).

Marijac may have finally realized his own shortcomings, or he may have tired of the Western scene, for, in 1939, he catapulted his hero all the way to Africa. At the outbreak of World War II, Jim Boum, remembering that he was of French origin, enlisted in the air force and started battling Germans with the same gusto he had previously exhibited fighting outlaws. The French defeat of June 1940 interrupted Jim Boum's war adventures, and he went back to the West, where he remained until 1944 (this was all the more surprising since the German occupation forces were frowning on anything even remotely American).

"Jim Boum," Marijac (Jacques Dumas). © Marijac.

After France's liberation, Jim Boum reappeared in the first issue of *Coq Hardi* (October 1944) as a pilot with the American forces in the Pacific. He later went back to the West, but his best adventure took place on the planet Mars, where Jim had to battle prehistoric monsters and bloodthirsty Martians. *Jim Boum* disappeared from the comic pages in 1950, but some of the earlier episodes were periodically revived in one form or another.

The most striking feature about *Jim Boum* was Marijac's almost total lack of draftsmanship; yet, after a while, the clumsy rendering of characters and the imprecise delineation of action take on an almost endearing quality. On the other hand, the scenarios and situations, trite as they may today appear, were extremely well conceived and brilliantly written. Marijac is a true Western buff (in the 1940s he was made an honorary member of the Blackfeet tribe), and in *Jim Boum* he handled the mythology of the West with integrity and deep affection. These two qualities accounted, more than anything else, for the long-lasting success of the strip: all its episodes were reprinted in softcover albums, and a variety of Jim Boum toys and novelty articles were successfully merchandised over the years.

M.H.

JIM ERIZO (Spain) A humor strip created by Gabriel Arnao (who signs his work "Gabi"), *Jim Erizo y su Papá* ("Porcupine Jim and his Daddy," as it was first called) made its appearance in issue 433 (April 20, 1947) of the comic weekly *Chicos*. Jim Erizo had well-defined characteristics: enormous, with the face of a retired prizefighter, his physical appearance was that of a boy who grew up too fast, and his mental state that of a hapless if lovable moron. His adventures—in which he was accompanied by his father, the Señor Pop, a shrimp of a man who made his first appearance as the father of another protagonist of the magazine, the boxer Rak Tigre—lasted only for the space of four very long episodes, coming to an end in the early 1950s. Jim Erizo, his father, and his father's twin brother, the equally dwarfish Señor Jules Pas, fought witches, criminals, and sadists; most of all, though, they were pitted against the gang called "the intermittently resurrected ones."

In this work, Arnao pursued his experiments in the field of nonsense humor, where language plays an essential role, ahead of the drawing. He also paid great attention to the layout and color, with a cinematic treatment of the panels, which stood out all the more because of the originality and grace of his drawing style, stylized and loose. He later widened these experiments to include the lettering of the onomatopeias and the speech balloons, by which he broke with accepted conventions.

L.G.

JIM HARDY (U.S.) In 1935 Dick Moores, then assistant to Chester Gould on *Dick Tracy*, imagined a toughguy crime strip which he tentatively called "Jim Conley." Mailing samples to various newspaper syndicates, he got a favorable response from United Feature, which eventually bought the strip and rebaptized it *Jim Hardy*. After a series of false starts, the feature, considerably altered and toned down, finally appeared in print in May 1936.

Jim Hardy was at first an ex-convict trying to make it back into straight society. He later underwent several changes of profession, finally settling for that of a newspaper reporter. As such he was a crusader, exposing corrupt politicians, nailing down racketeers, and

"Jimmy das Gummipferd," Roland Kohlsaat. © Kohlsaat.

clearing the names of falsely accused men. *Jim Hardy* was drawn in a graphic style that could only be called a hand-me-down *Dick Tracy,* but it exuded an earthy, rustic charm; and the stories, as neatly done as any in *Tracy,* never displayed the viciousness and self-righteousness of Moores's model. This was probably the strip's undoing, as the readers did not seem to take to medium-boiled detective fiction. At any rate Jim Hardy, as a character, was judged a liability, and he was eased out by a cowboy named Windy and his racehorse, Paddles. *Windy and Paddles* (as the strip was then named) itself disappeared in October 1942.

M.H.

JIMMY DAS GUMMIPFERD (Germany) *Jimmy das Gummipferd* ("Jimmy the Rubber Horse") was created in 1953 by Roland Kohlsaat, who wrote and drew this comic strip published exclusively in the children's supplement *Sternchen* (Starlet) of the renowned German weekly newsmagazine *Stern.* In a readership analysis this popular feature boasted some incredible numbers: 30 percent of all adult readers regularly followed it—besides the youngsters that it was aimed at.

The basic premise of *Jimmy das Gummipferd* is fantastic enough. The gaucho Julio's horse is made of inflatable rubber, yet Jimmy also lives and breathes and carries his master through numerous adventures. It is no small wonder that Julio and Jimmy's adventures more often than not border on science-fantasy and science fiction, despite—or maybe because of—their home on the pampas. It may even be argued, that, wherever Erich von Däniken's high-flying "chariots of the gods" arrived, Julio and Jimmy had already been there, thanks to the inexhaustible fantasy of their creator. Kohlsaat's tongue-in-cheek heroes seem to find lost temples, secret tunnels, vanished civilizations, and flying saucers at every corner of their "pop odyssey" (as Kohlsaat called it), in their never-ending quest to solve all types of intriguing mysteries.

In Kohlsaat's fantasyland everything is believable, even a living horse made of rubber. In fact, his world of dreams would burst like a bubble, were Jimmy not made of rubber. Thus, Kohlsaat managed to spin a fantastic yarn simply by putting a dream on paper. His lit-

erary and artistic styles blended to perfection, and narrative and illustration balanced well. Calm and serenity prevailed, counterbalancing the climactic suspense. The fine-line drawings with their washed-in gray tones—the strip was published in black and white—were graphically satisfying as they blended humoristic and realistic elements. This ruled out graphic spectaculars but seemed to be the ideal way to maintain the special magic of this comic strip.

Jimmy das Gummipferd, which later on was aptly retitled *Julios abenteuerliche Reisen* ("Julio's Adventurous Voyages"), despite continued success for almost a quarter-century, was never reprinted in its entirety in book form. Fan interest generated some book editions, however. The feature ended December 23, 1976, as Roland Kohlsaat was slowly being incapacitated by illness.

W.F.

JIMMY OLSEN (U.S.) "Superman's Pal" Jimmy Olsen was created by producer Bob Maxwell for the *Superman* radio show and did not make his first comic book appearance until the November 1941 issue of National's *Superman* (number 13). For years the red-haired and bow-tied Olsen was a cub reporter for the *Daily Planet.* His freckles set him apart from the other, more serious characters of the *Superman* tableaux, and for a long time, he was the feature's only bit of comic relief.

When gadget-minded Mort Weisinger began directing the "Superman Family," Jimmy Olsen got one of the first gadgets: an emergency signal watch, which sounded whenever Olsen deemed Superman's presence necessary. He was also paired off with Lois's sister, Lucy Lane, and the two carried on a platonic and antiseptic love affair over several years. The character also maintained a Superman trophy room, which supposedly housed much Superman memorabilia.

Jimmy Olsen was finally given his own title in September 1954, and it was here that the character began to develop as an individual. Jimmy Olsen became the Elastic Lad in issue 31, and he would sporadically readopt the guise to foil criminals. He also became a hero in the bottled Kryptonian city of Kandor and was elected an honorary member of the Legion of Super-Heroes.

When Jack Kirby was lured to National in late 1970, *Jimmy Olsen* was his first assignment. He immediately made Olsen the leader of the Newsboy Legion, and he swiftly began severing the Superman/Jimmy Olsen relationship. It was also in this book that Kirby made most of his changes in the Superman mystique, including the introduction of Morgan Edge and the destruction of the *Daily Planet* globe. The *Jimmy Olsen* title was changed to *The Superman Family* in 1974; it ended in 1982.

J.B.

JIMPY (G.B.) On January 5, 1946, Jimpy was thrown out of the Royal College of Magic and into the strip page of the *Daily Mirror*. He had failed to pass his Magiculation Certificate and, despite a fair run of six years, failed to pass the readers' popularity polls. He was thrown out again, this time of the *Mirror*. A low 33 percent liked him from the start; his highest point came in 1949 with 36 percent; and he dropped to 29 percent in 1952. "That was the year Jimpy died," writes Hugh Cudlipp coldly in his biography of a newspaper, *Publish and Be Damned* (1953). He calls Jimpy "the favourite of the intellectuals," and perhaps he was, by *Mirror* standards, but certainly he never reached that sophisticated audience that was delighted by *Flook*. However, he undoubtedly entertained those readers for whom he was intended, the children who had not had a strip of their own in the paper since *Pip Squeak and Wilfred* retired for the war. Indeed, one feels that Jimpy's strip may have been a victim of opinion polls, for the figures Cudlipp quotes are for men and women; he never mentions children.

Hugh McClelland set Jimpy in a medieval world of magic, magic that usually goes wrong or backfires, thanks to his failed sorceror's apprenticeship. He told his story in square panels, with boxed narrative in the present tense; there were no speech balloons. His second adventure, *Jimpy and the Kind Hearted Dragon*, was a great improvement on the first, and introduced the

rival knights Sir Clueless and Sir Binder (names derived from the slang of McClelland's old service, the R.A.F.). Later adventures found Jimpy in an Arabian Nights' setting, crossing Merlin the Magician in the court of King Bonedome, and in 1948 meeting Poco the Llama, who would become his faithful companion and transport. Almost immediately they were transported to Old Spain to meet Christopher Columbus in *Jimpy, Poco and the Admiral of the Ocean Sea*, an adventure that introduced McClelland's wackiest running gag. From here on, at the unlikeliest times, Don Abba de Dab would float by on his umbrella crying, "Beware of the Fiddlygubs!"

Reprints included hardbacks with color, *Jimpy 1952* and *Jimpy Paintbook* (1953); also an Australian monthly comic book.

D.G.

JODELLE (France) The Pop Art movement, which owed so much to the iconography of the comics, in turn inspired a novel in comic strip form, *Jodelle*, illustrated by Guy Pellaert on a script by Pierre Bartier and published by Eric Losfeld in 1966.

Jodelle is a young beauty who gets herself involved in a series of fantastic adventures. The action takes place in an ancient Rome suspiciously resembling New York and Las Vegas (with Cadillacs drawn by horses, neon signs inviting the people to come see Christians tossed to the lions, and toga-clad majorettes). The main characters (aside from Jodelle herself) are the sadistic and scheming Proconsuless, who plots the overthrow of Emperor Augustus, depicted as an effeminate fop; and the lesbian head of the women-spies, always surrounded by a bevy of available young women (among whom Jodelle has infiltrated).

Jodelle was an incredible hit when it came out. The book was translated in many countries (in the United States by Grove Press). Pellaert went on to do a similar opus: *Pravda* (1968), but by then the novelty had worn thin. Pellaert's style, a mixture of Pop Art mannerism, decadent line, and clashing colors, proved a flash in the pan.

M.H.

JODLOMAN, JESS M. (1925-   ) Like many of the comic artists in the Philippines, Jesús Jodloman is self-taught. Born on February 5, 1925, he started to draw at the age of 16. He admired the *Tarzan* and *Prince Valiant* strips done by Hal Foster and the *Flash Gordon* series drawn by Alex Raymond.

Jodloman, who started out as a portrait artist, illustrated a school book for Abive Publishing House. His first break in the comic field was in 1954, when he illustrated a short story for Terry Cinco, publisher of *Luz-vi-minda Klasiks*. It was written by Flor Afable Olazo and was titled *Ang Rosas na Itim* ("The Black Roses").

On January 4, 1955, he wrote and illustrated the heroic epic *Ramir*. It appeared in *Bulaklak*, a weekly comic-oriented magazine written in the Tagalog dialect. The series ran for 83 chapters until August 28, 1957. *Ramir* was so popular that it was made into a movie.

Jodloman has also done cover and interior artwork for such diverse publications as *Hasmin, Paraluman, Maharlika, Top Komiks, Zoom Komiks,* and *Pilipino Komiks*. He has written and drawn other fast-paced visual novels, one of the most popular being *Los Pinta-*

"Jimpy," Hugh McClelland. © *Daily Mirror Newspapers Ltd.*

dos ("The Painted Ones"). He collaborated with the well-known Tagalog novelist Clodualdo del Mundo (who is also the head of the Philippine comics code) to do a science-fiction story about a Filipino astronaut called Brix Virgo.

In addition to his work in the comic medium, Jodloman has done costume and set designs for movie productions, advertising layouts, calendar painting, and biblical illustrations. He did short stories for DC's mystery titles and *Kull* for Marvel comics (both in the United States).

His illustrations are strong and rugged with an earthy feeling about them. His characters, male and female alike, are sensual and endowed with great physical attributes. His heroes are extremely muscular, surging with power and vitality. His heroines are hightly voluptuous, possessing feline grace and independence. He has a loose and detailed rendering style that is very effective for the type of stories he likes to do.

A family man, Jodloman resides in Quezon City with his wife and seven children. His younger brother, Venancio Jr., is also involved in the comic industry.

O.J.

JOE AND ASBESTOS (U.S.) One fine day in the summer of 1925, Ken Kling, then assistant to cartoonist Bud Fisher, accompanied his boss to the Saratoga races. It was Kling's first day at the racetrack, and at the urging of his employer, he bet his whole bankroll on Fisher's horse Cartoonist, which unfortunately finished fourth. There and then Kling decided to create a new comic strip character, Joe Quince, who would perennially bet (and perennially lose) all his money at the racetrack.

Kling's new strip appeared for the first time in the *Baltimore Sun* and used the names of real horses in local races as a gimmick. As the horses started to win (to the cartoonist's amazement) and the circulation of the *Sun* soared, *Joe Quince* was picked up by an increasing number of newspapers (in New York it was carried by the *Mirror* for 25 years, then by the *News* for three more). In 1926 Ken Kling added a new character to the strip, a black stable boy named Asbestos, and changed the name of the feature to *Joe and Asbestos*. When his contract expired later that year, Kling took a year's vacation. Upon his return to New York he started a new strip, *Windy Riley* and revived *Joe and Asbestos* (1928).

Because of the nature of the strip, *Joe and Asbestos* could not be widely syndicated, but Kling's clientele, made up mostly of large metropolitan newspapers, was nonetheless a highly rewarding one (in 1947 his yearly salary was said to be over $100,000). When he decided to discontinue the strip in 1966, Kling retired a millionaire. He died in New York City on May 3, 1970.

Joe and Asbestos was not an outstanding or highly innovative strip. The gags, always revolving around horses and horse races, were slight, the penmanship competent but unremarkable, and the dialogues of the Amos 'n' Andy variety. Yet, as the most successful of American racing strips, it deserves a place all its own: it is a tribute to the appeal and versatility of the medium that Kling was able to sustain so successfully and for so long a feature based on the skimpiest of plots and the most hackneyed of themes.

M.H.

JOE JINKS (U.S.) The ill-starred feature best known as *Joe Jinks* was born *Joe's Car*, the 1918 *New York World* creation of Vic Forsythe.

As the title implied, *Joe's Car* was about automobiles and the passion that they aroused in the hearts of otherwise sedate and meek little men, a theme not unlike that of Frank King's early *Gasoline Alley*. *Joe's Car*, how-

"Joe Jinks," Henry Formhals. © United Feature Syndicate.

ever, never developed the subtle delineation of place and character that King was able to bring to his strip.

From motoring, Joe went on to aviation, and then on to become a cigar-chomping fight manager, the role for which he is best known. In the early 1930s Forsythe left the strip to do *Way Out West* for King Features (he came back a little later). Sports cartoonist Pete Llanuza carried on until 1936. Then came Moe Leff (the best artist on the strip), who drew both the dailies and the Sunday; he was followed by Henry Formhals on the Sunday, while the dailies saw, in quick succession, Harry Homan (creator of the Sunday *Billy Make Believe*) until 1939, then George Storm, Al Kostuk, Morris Weiss, and Al Leiderman. This sorrowful roll call ended in 1944 with Sam Leff (Moe's brother), who soon introduced to the strip its most popular character, a fair-haired young fighter named Curly Kayoe. On the last day of 1945 the daily strip was officially renamed *Curly Kayoe* (the Sunday continued to be called *Joe Jinks* for a while). The feature perked up briefly, then went down without a murmur in the 1950s.

Never a remarkable strip, *Joe Jinks* deserves mention for its long and checkered career.

M.H.

JOE PALOOKA (U.S.) Ham Fisher's famed boxing strip, *Joe Palooka*, began at staggered dates in early 1928 in some 20 newspapers, all of them personally sold on using the strip by Fisher himself. The early episodes, lacking specific release dates, could be started at any time, and were. Most of the first Palooka runs in print were under way by mid-1928, but the strip did not attain any great reader attention until the widely circulated *New York Mirror* took on the feature on January 1, 1931.

Since boxing as a sport had a bad editorial reputation with many papers until the early 1920s (largely because of the Jack Johnson championship and the absence of a "Great White Hope," a strip featuring a prizefighting champion was really only possible at the time when Fisher managed to get his into print. (Some earlier strips, such as *Moon Mullins* and *Smitty*, had touched favorably on boxing, but not as a steady theme.) Fisher's schmaltzy story line and Palooka's naive charm—which subtly controlled the worse excesses of his outwardly tough and cynical manager, Knobby Walsh—caught on big, once readers began to pay prolonged attention to the rather ill-drawn strip, and the ultimately vast popularity of *Palooka* (the *Dondi* of its day) began to take form.

Sharper readers of the strip, rather taken at various times with such amusing Fisher characters as Senator Weidebottom, the French-Canadian Bateese ("by tam, Joe, I keel you!"), Humphrey, and even Jerry Leemy, thought Palooka by far the worst thing in the feature, dreading even glancing exposure to his terrible sweetness and semiliterate platitudes about home, mother, and fair play. The public reaction was, of course, just the reverse: to the general reader, Palooka was the whole strip, and his tepid, unendurable affair with Ann Howe (Joe's totally colorless girlfriend) was endlessly gripping to them, with Joe's ultimate marriage to Ann in 1949 one of the major events of their time.

Fisher's hired art often made up for much of the sentimental and sappy story line: Al Capp and Moe Leff (who had earlier drawn a boy-adventure strip of some merit, *Peter Pat*, for United Feature Syndicate) did the

"Joe Palooka," Ham Fisher. © McNaught Syndicate.

bulk of the work from the early 1930s; they were accomplished draftsmen and graphic storytellers. (Capp even developed a group of hillbilly characters—Big Leviticus and his Mammy and Pappy—while working on *Palooka* who were so amusing that he used them in launching his own strip, *Li'l Abner*, in 1934). But it was Fisher's story and dialogue that held the strip's basic popular appeal, a fact demonstrated by the strip's sharp decline in the hands of its artist for almost two decades, Moe Leff, after Fisher's suicide in 1955. Moe Leff's continuation of *Palooka* did it little good, but it reached an even keel, on a minor level of popularity, with Tony DiPreta's intelligent work on the strip, which extended from October 1959 to the strip's close in November 1984.

Made into a feature film (with Jimmy Durante as Knobby Walsh and Stuart Erwin as Joe) in 1933, and into a series of two-reel comedy shorts in the 1940s, *Joe Palooka* was also a radio program in the 1930s (and later a TV series), and was featured in a long-running comic book series in the 1940s.

B.B.

JOE'S CAR *see* Joe Jinks.

JOHNNY HAZARD (U.S.) At the end of 1943 Frank Robbins, then at the height of his popularity as the artist of *Scorchy Smith*, was asked by King Features Syndicate to create a new strip; Robbins jumped at the chance, and in June 1944 *Johnny Hazard* was born.

In the opening episode, American pilot Johnny Hazard escaped from a German POW camp and rejoined the Allied lines (but not without first inflicting heavy losses on the enemy). With typical comic strip—or military—logic, he was then shifted to the Pacific front (Robbins, like any other armchair strategist, thought that the war in Europe was coming to an end), where he fought an assorted array of Japanese spies and saboteurs, not to mention some of the leading aces of the Imperial Air Force. After the war Johnny became a commercial pilot and the director of a private airline, exercising his talents in the four corners of the world in the rediscovered tradition of *Scorchy Smith*.

This was all changed by the coming of the Cold War (and then the Korean War), which gave Johnny an ill-defined role as a secret agent in a bewildering succession of missions ranging from spy cases to information gathering to rescue operations, from Paris to Rio, and from Greenland to China. Johnny was sometimes accompanied by second bananas like Snap the brassy reporter or Gabby Gillespie the garrulous navigator, but mostly he operated alone. A James Bond before James Bond, Johnny Hazard followed his dangerous calling unfazed by the (countless) beauties who invariably threw themselves at his feet—blondes, brunettes, and redheads with interchangeable faces and evocative feminine names: Brandy, Gloria, Ginny, Maria, and the fittingly named Lady Jaguar.

In the 1970s Johnny shifted gears again, turning into an airline troubleshooter and investigator. In these changing times he looked more and more like an anachronism, and in August 1977 his adventures finally came to their conclusion. *Johnny Hazard*'s passing also marked the end of Robbins's 40-year career in newspaper strips, as he perforce had to return to doing comic books.

"Johnny Hazard," Frank Robbins. © King Features Syndicate.

Robbins's artwork on *Johnny Hazard* had been exemplary. A cartoonist's cartoonist, he never ceased to display his awesome technical skills, even when commercial success (or the lack of it) did not warrant such a superfluity of effort (toward the end of its run, the strip was carried by a mere handful of newspapers). The writing, however, did not keep pace with the times, and that probably was the feature's main weakness. Be that as it may, *Johnny Hazard* remains one of the outstanding adventure strips of the postwar era and one most deserving of study and preservation.

M.H.

JOHNNY-ROUND-THE-WORLD (U.S.) One of King Features' perennial attempts at educating their readers, *Johnny-Round-the-World* came out (as a Sunday page only) in February 1935. The feature was purportedly written by William LaVarre, Fellow of the Royal Geographical Society, and was illustrated (in a straight, unimaginative style) by anonymous artists from the King bullpen.

The titular hero was a teenage boy taken along by his father, Major Jupiter, on a scientific expedition into the jungles of (then) British Guiana and Surinam. The action (or what there was of it) unfolded leisurely as the reader was treated to the sight of native dancers, flash floods, a couple of forest fires, and a number of animal battles, all depicted with actual black-and-white photographs (presumably taken by Johnny's "zoom camera") and with a pontificating, pedestrian text. The strip's comic relief was supplied by Johnny's dog Peppy, who constantly got into trouble, and by the native carriers whose comments often indicated that they did not take the Major's, or his son's, earnest endeavors all too seriously.

This rather wearisome travelogue did not last long: by 1938 it was gone. Its passing was much lamented by the advocates of cultural uplift in the comics. "It seems strange that the public is so exceedingly scared of anything that might add to its knowledge or stretch its mind a notch," bemoaned Coulton Waugh. But the public knew better and recognized *Johnny* not for the genuine attempt at enlightenment that it pretended to be, but for the patronizing bore it actually was.

M.H.

JOHNNY THUNDER (U.S.) Perhaps one of the strangest "superhero" strips ever to appear was National's original *Johnny Thunder* feature. Making its debut in *Flash* number one in January 1940, it was created by writer John Wentworth and artist Stan Asch as a parody of the already-flourishing, deadly dull superhero features of the era.

As described in his initial appearance, the green-suited Johnny Thunder had a "pet thunderbolt working for him." Colored pink with a triangular head perched atop a jagged thunderbolt, it was of Badhnisian origin and Johnny never quite knew what to make of it (him?). "All Johnny knows," the story continued, "is that when the power is on (and it lasts an hour at a time) he can make everything obey his slightest wish. The secret words which Johnny must say to get control of his thunderbolt are 'cei-u'!" To complicate matters, however, Johnny never realized this, and the thunderbolt appeared whenever he accidently uttered the phonetic equivalent "say you."

Given Johnny's admittedly absurd "power" and his own outrageous ignorance, the strip was fairly successful as a parody, but only rarely was it sophisticated or intentionally satiric. Usually the bumbling Johnny fumbled around through an adventure until bailed out by the thunderbolt. Drawbacks aside, however, *Johnny Thunder* was a delightful strip when compared with National's dour *Superman* and its grim and ghastly *Spectre*. Asch and Wentworth plotted the strip's course until 1947, and then gave way to writer Bob Kanigher and artist Carmine Infantino. By that time, however, the Black Canary had already been introduced, and Johnny was soon eased out of his own feature.

Johnny Thunder appeared in all *Flash* issues until January 1948's 91st issue. (It was entitled *Johnny Thunderbolt* in its first 10 strips and *Johnny Thunder and The Black Canary* in its last two.) He was also the Justice Society's comedic relief, appearing in most issues of *All-Star* between 2 (Fall 1940) and 39 (March 1948).

When National exhumed its 1940s characters in the mid-1960s, Johnny and the thunderbolt were revived, too. And while Johnny had gotten a somewhat better grip on himself and his "power," he was still a hopelessly lovable fumbler. His thunderbolt, however, had gained a personality. Writer Gardner Fox—who used the pair in several *Justice League* tales—made him a snappy comic who was infinitely smarter than his master. Their interplay became simultaneously burlesque spoofery and satire.

National premiered a second *Johnny Thunder* strip in *All American* number 100 in August 1948. Created by writer Bob Kanigher and artist Alex Toth, this Western strip was notable only for Toth's rapidly maturing and well-conceived artistic execution. This unrelated feature was short-lived, but three issues of a *Johnny Thunder* reprint title appeared in 1973.

J.B.

JOHNSON, CROCKETT see Leisk, David Johnson.

JOHNSON, FERD (1905-1996) An American cartoonist born on December 18, 1905, to middle-class parents in Spring Creek, Pennsylvania, Ferd Johnson was cartooning before he was in high school. Johnson won a cartoon contest in the *Erie* (Pa.) *Dispatch-Herald* at 12, then earned a gold watch for cartoons he drew for a railroad station agent's magazine at 13. After graduating from the Corry, Pennsylvania, High School in 1923, he attended the Chicago Academy of Fine Arts that fall, only to spend more time hanging around the strip cartoonists' desks at the *Chicago Tribune*. Tired of the eager kid looking over his shoulder, Frank Willard finally handed him a *Moon Mullins* Sunday page to color after it had been statted. Willard liked what he did and had him hired as a Sunday page colorist at $15 a week. Johnson's cartooning talent was so evident, however, that Willard soon engaged him as a full-time assistant, and in late August 1925, Johnson undertook his own Sunday page, called at first *Texas Slim*, concurrent with the *Tribune*'s expansion of its Sunday comic section from four to eight pages. *Texas Slim* was a popular strip where it appeared, but it had to compete for space in the nation's then-small comic sections with other already well-established *Tribune* strips, and Johnson was forced to drop it after two and a half years. Continuing to work with Willard, Johnson married Doris Lee White and began a second Sunday half-page in 1932: *Lovey-Dovey*, with *Texas Slim* as a minor gag appendage at the bottom. After this short-lived strip venture folded, Johnson undertook a sideline

Lynn Johnston, "For Better or For Worse." © *Universal Press Syndicate.*

series of advertising strips for subscribing auto dealers, which ran for years in the 1930s.

Johnson's major break came with the *Tribune*'s second revival of *Texas Slim and Dirty Dalton* in 1940. Read by a mass audience across the country, the cowboy comedy strip had suspenseful continuity and was enthusiastically acclaimed for 18 years until Willard's death in 1958. Johnson then took over *Moon Mullins* as his own. Living in Beverly Hills, California, Johnson, his wife, and son Tom moved down the coast to Corona del Mar in 1969 to escape the smog of Los Angeles. Here Johnson and his son worked on the daily and Sunday *Moon Mullins*. The feature was unhappily retired in 1991, and Johnson went into retirement. He died in Irvine, California, on October 14, 1996.

B.B.

JOHNSTON, LYNN B. (1947-   ) Canadian cartoonist and writer Lynn Johnston was born on May 28, 1947, in Collingwood, Ontario. Her family later moved to Vancouver, British Columbia, where her father was a jeweler and watchmaker and her mother produced calligraphy and illustrations for her grandfather's stamp business.

Early on, Johnston was inspired to draw and create by her mother's artistic ability, her father's humor, and her grandfather's intense interest in newspaper comics. She studied the intricate art of classic comedy by watching the films of Charlie Chaplin, Abbott and Costello, and the Three Stooges and by reading the comic-book work of John Stanley and Carl Barks. Later, the editorial cartoons of the *Vancouver Sun*'s Len Norris and the sarcastic wit of *Mad* magazine appealed to her rowdy, impulsive nature.

As a student at the Vancouver School of Art, she leaned toward commercial illustration and left the school in 1967 to animate Hanna-Barbera's *Abbott and Costello* television series at Canawest Films. At McMaster University Medical Center in Hamilton, Ontario, she spent five years as a medical illustrator, preparing audiovisual graphics for student training. She then obtained a layout position at a packaging firm.

During her first pregnancy she created numerous panel cartoons about her parturient condition for her obstetrician, which led to three books on child rearing, the first of which was published in 1974. The books were *David, We're Pregnant!*; *Hi, Mom! Hi, Dad!*; and *Do They Ever Grow Up?* Universal Press Syndicate's Jim Andrews discovered the series of books and was anx-

ious to add another female creator to the syndicate following the success of Cathy Gusewite's *Cathy*.

Johnston signed a contract in 1978 to originate her masterwork *For Better or For Worse*. Debuting on September 9, 1979, it portrayed the modern family from a woman's viewpoint. With its richly developed characters, artwork, and plot lines, *For Better or For Worse* soon reached the zenith of contemporary humor-story strips. Johnston bases much of the feature on personal experience and emotional retrospect. The strip's fictitious Patterson family loosely mirrors the activities and tribulations of the cartoonist's own kin.

A former president of the National Cartoonists Society, Johnston was given the society's coveted Reuben for 1986 and its Best Newspaper Comic Strip Award in 1991. The International Museum of Cartoon Art inducted her into its Hall of Fame in 1997—making Johnston the first woman to be so honored. Johnston and her family currently live in Corbeil, Ontario, where she continues to produce *For Better or For Worse*.

B.J.

JONAH HEX (U.S.) For some unknown reason a boomlet in Western titles developed among comic-book companies in the late 1960s and early 1970s. Marvel launched *Mighty Marvel Western* in 1968, and in 1970 DC Comics (then called National) resuscitated one of its old titles, *All Star Western*.

At first the *All Star* comic books were, like the rival *Mighty Marvel*, filled chiefly with reprint material; however, because National had a smaller backlist of Western stories than Marvel, original material began to creep in. There was a weak version of *Billy the Kid*, along with *El Diablo*, a good tale of a Zorro-like masked rider by Gray Morrow. But the star of the series was to make its entrance in issue number 10: *Jonah Hex*.

Jonah Hex was an embittered ex-officer of the Confederacy who had had the right side of his face blown away by gunfire in the last days of the Civil War. Since that time, he had been roaming the West, torn between good and evil, each personified by a different side of his face. Hex could sometimes be callous, but he was never intentionally evil. At one point he allowed a woman to be hanged despite the entreaties of his side-kick, Redeye Charlie; but his wrath would habitually turn against the clever crooks, high-placed manipulators, and corrupt lawmen who were forever crossing paths with the disfigured rider. Hex's nemesis was the Yellow Mask Gang, against which he waged an unrelenting and deadly guerrilla war.

The artwork on *Jonah Hex* had been entrusted at the outset to a stable of talented foreign cartoonists: first came the Filipinos Tony de Zuniga and Noly Panaligan, followed by the Latin Americans George (Jorge) Moliterni and José Luis García López. The most notable writer on the series was unquestionably Michael Fleisher, who imparted a dark, despairing tone to the tales.

In 1977 the antihero of the West was given his own comic-book title. While Fleisher remained as the principal writer, other artists came to work on the series, notably Dick Ayers, Gray Morrow, and Joe Kubert. *Jonah Hex* as a title ended in August 1985; the next month the protagonist reappeared in a world that had been devastated by thermonuclear war, with the name of the comic book changed to simply *Hex*. This revamped version didn't take hold, however; it lasted for only 18 issues, to February 1987. DC tried to revive the original character again in two separate miniseries published in the Vertigo line, one in 1993 and the other in 1995.

M.H.

JUDGE, MALCOLM (1918-1989) Cartoonist Malcolm Judge was born in Glasgow, Scotland, in 1918. He began contributing to the newspapers and magazines of D.C. Thomson & Co. while in his twenties, during World War II. When paper shortages were over and the Dundee-based newspaper *Weekly News* expanded, he submitted the idea of a panel gag built around a football-crazy hero named "Saturday Sammy," although the local Scottish edition of the paper preferred to spell his name "Sattorday Sanny." *Saturday Sammy* first appeared on January 5, 1946, and it has yet to miss a week since, despite the artist's death. Judge signed his work with the pen name "Mal."

Mal decided to try his hand at Thomson's comic strips in 1948; he was given the retired *Meddlesome Matty*. This strip, featuring a thoroughly nosy schoolgirl, was first published in *The Dandy* in 1937, when it was drawn by veteran cartoonist Sam Fair. Although *Matty* was fairly popular, it would not be until 1960 that Mal's cartoon career really took off, in the pages of Thomson's new weekly comics tabloid, *The Beezer*. Mal created a gang of three inept crooks called Boss, Fingers, and Knucklehead, collectively Known as *The Badd Lads*. They began their criminal career in *Beezer* number 210 (January 23, 1960). That same year, Mal started in *Beano* (October 15) *Colonel Crackpot's Circus*, which chronicled the Colonel's attempts to keep control over a crazy company of circus performers.

Within the next three years came Mal's two best-loved and most-memorable series, *The Numskulls* in *Beezer* (1962) and *Billy Whizz* in *Beano* (1963). The Numskulls were minute creatures that lived inside a man's head, running such departments as his nose, his eyes, his ears, and his mouth. Billy Whizz was less incredible, despite his phenomenal speed. Some years later Mal added to his comic creations *Ali and His Baba*, a magic strip (*Sparky*, 1970), and *Hop, Skip, and Jack* (*Buzz*, 1973). *Ball Boy* joined *Beano* in 1975, and *Square Eyes* was in *Topper* from 1981. Although his contributions began to taper off, Mal was still drawing *Ball Boy*, *Billy Whizz*, and *Square Eyes* at the time of his death in Bournemouth on January 17, 1989. Many of his characters continue still, penned in the simple style of their

creator by anonymous cartoonists, a tribute to Mal's creativity.

D.G.

JUDGE DREDD (G.B.) The most successful character to emerge from the hard-edged British science-fiction comic *2000 AD*, Judge Dredd was featured every week since he premiered in the second issue, dated March 5, 1977. Modeled after Clint Eastwood in the motion picture *Dirty Harry*, Dredd is essentially one-dimensional in his total dedication to the law. Dressed in black leather and an eyeless helmet that he never removes, he was created by writer John Wagner and artist Carlos Ezquerra and developed by them with contributions from writers Pat Mills and Alan Grant and artists Mike McMahon, Brian Bolland, Ian Gibson, and Ron Smith, among others. The "Lawman of the Future," who hunts down criminals on his LawMaster motorbike, is the toughest in the army of Judges dispensing instant justice through the barrel of a gun. His turf is the gigantic Mega-City One, a 22nd-century conurbation spread across the whole of North America's eastern seaboard.

Dredd was the first British comic character to be exported to and licensed in the United States in his own comic books, at first in reprints from 1983, then in new episodes from 1994 from DC Comics. In 1985 he was awarded his own daily newspaper strip in the *Daily Star*, and from 1990 he also starred in his own title, *Judge Dredd: The Megazine*. In 1991 he had his first encounter with Batman, illustrated by Simon Bisley. In 1995 Dredd was played by Sylvester Stallone in a Hollywood movie, but most of the series' distinctly British irony was lost in the translation, and despite impressive special effects, the film flopped.

Nevertheless, *Judge Dredd* has maintained its popularity in British comics and has grown into a complete, complex future world, adding fresh characters such as the terrifying Judge Death, to whom all life is a crime, and Psi-Judge Anderson, a female psychic. At their best, the stories operate on multiple levels, balancing straight action-adventure and black comedy with satirical commentary on current issues, exaggerated for effect, from food scares and fashion crazes to human rights and world politics. It is no coincidence that Dredd first became popular in Britain during the punk revolution and the rise of Thatcherism. The character has an ambiguous appeal to both ends of the political spectrum. To some readers, he symbolizes the worst excesses of a police state and the erosion of civil liberties; to others, his brand of no-nonsense law enforcement seems to offer the perfect solution to escalating crime and social disorder.

P.G.

JUDGE PARKER (U.S.) *Judge Parker*, which debuted in November 1952, was the product of author Dr. Nicholas Dallis and artist Dan Heilman. It was distributed by Publishers Syndicate of Chicago. It is now distributed by King Features.

Dallis had moved to Toledo, Ohio, where he struck up a friendship with comic strip artist Allen Saunders and created *Rex Morgan, M.D.* four years previously. The title character was based on a progressive juvenile-court judge in Toledo, Dr. Paul Alexander, whom Dallis had come to know during his service as a consulting juvenile psychiatrist. His interest in aspects of the legal

"Judge Dredd," John Howard and Brian Bolland. © IPC Magazines Ltd.

profession in general and Judge Alexander's actions in particular led to the creation of Judge Allan Parker.

Parker, approximately 50 years old, was a widower in the early days of the strip but has since remarried. He has a more youthful look today than when the strip began. Parker has become almost a minor character, with more of the action generated by handsome young attorney Sam Driver. In his mid-thirties, Driver is a moral, aggressive hero who carries the infrequent physical action in the strip. He has a pretty girlfriend, Abbey Spencer, the daughter of wealthy parents.

Other characters come and go with the cases. The strip, though relatively sophisticated, has steered clear of social issues; an exception is a 1975 continuity dealing with ethics in the law profession.

Through the years, *Judge Parker* has come to seem like a continuing series of *Perry Mason* reruns. For the actual and infrequent technical references to the legal profession, author Dallis subscribed to law journals and consulted friends and relatives in the profession. Dan Heilman's art was an easy, straight style that fit well with Dallis's easy, sometimes taut story. Heilman also had a cinematic visual sense.

Upon Heilman's death in July 1965, Harold LeDoux, assistant on the strip since its first year, took it over full-time; his style is less polished and more abrasive—also more stylized—than that of his former boss.

"Judge Parker," Dan Heilman. © Field Newspaper Syndicate.

Woody Wilson has been writing the script since Dallis's death in 1991.

A sturdy item in Publishers' stable of story strips, *Judge Parker* is as predictable as the long-running soap operas on afternoon TV, which it approximates in quality and appeal.

Parker has received awards from the American Bar Association, the Freedom Foundation, and other organizations.

R.M.

JUDGE WRIGHT (U.S.) Try as they might, United Feature Syndicate never succeeded in fielding an even moderately successful mystery strip. In 1945 they tried again with *Judge Wright*, written by Bob Brent and illustrated by Bob Wells.

Wright was a magistrate who spent more time solving crimes than judging cases. In one way or another he got involved with various investigations, and he often had to bring the criminals to justice himself, hampered as he was by the skeptical district attorney on the case (this was probably the same D.A. who, under another name, kept losing to Perry Mason). Judge Wright's adventures, however, were far from the ordinary, as he tracked down desperate wife-killers, murderous nightclub operators, and corrupt politicians, or unraveled complicated conspiracies and bizarre intrigues. A host of characters were always popping in and out of the strip, which was written in a circuitous, almost cryptic, tone and drawn in a hard-edged, black style.

In spite of its good points (entertaining mysteries, varied motivations, and fine suspense), *Judge Wright* did not take hold. In 1947 the syndicate replaced Bob Wells with comic book artist Fred Kida, with no appreciable result. George Roussos was subsequently called in, but he fared no better, and the strip was finally dropped in 1949.

M.H.

JUKES, JOHN L. (1900-1972) John Jukes, a British cartoonist, was born in Birmingham in 1900. After some years in Australia he returned to England and contributed single-joke cartoons to the Amalgamated Press comic papers. His first strips with original characters appeared in 1931: *Merry Mike's Ice Cream Bike* and *Heap Big Beef* in *Comic Cuts*; *Jim Jam* in *Joker*; *Jollity Farm* in *Funny Wonder*. From the start his work was clean and bold, with a firmer line than many of his contemporaries, well in the tradition of Roy Wilson and other mainline masters.

In 1932 came *Ben & Bert the Kid Cops* in *Funny Wonder*, and in 1933 *Dutchy & Dolly* for *Comic Cuts* and *The Wonder Zoo*, a large panel, for *Funny Wonder*. In 1934 he contributed some strips to the comic section of the *Bristol Evening World*, which prompted A.P. to give him more important work; in addition to *Sam Scatterem* and *P. C. Easy*, which he created for *Comic Cuts*, he took over the front page of *Joker*. This popular strip, *Alfie the Air Tramp* (created by Charlie Pease), had been running since 1931, but it is Jukes's image that is recalled today: the rotund Alfie, his "Flying Flea" one-man plane, and his pet pup Wagger, who acted as a rudder.

Especially good were Jukes's full-page designs at Christmas and other special occasions. Oddly, his other best-remembered character was also a "takeover"; Roy Wilson created *George the Jolly Gee Gee* for *Radio Fun*, but Jukes continued it, moving the hayseed horse across to *Funny Wonder*. Another series featuring a horse, *Mike Spike & Greta*, was also given to Jukes, who made it also his own. This Western comic page began on the colored front of *Pilot* (1937) and continued in *Knockout* (1939).

After the war Jukes freelanced for the *Big* series of comic books published by Scion, and then got busier at *Radio Fun*, drawing *Tommy Trinder* (1945), *Archie Andrews* (1949), *Norman Wisdom* (1952), and other radio and film stars. Work dwindled in 1957 as the traditional British style fell from editorial favor, and Jukes took a job with the North Atlantic Treaty Organization drawing instructional material in strip form. He retired to the southern coast of England and was brought back to freelance a weekly page in *Whizzer & Chips* (1971)—*Dinah Mite*, which, curiously, was yet another "takeover." He died in Looe, Cornwall, on October 31, 1972.

D.G.

JULES *see* Radilović, Julio.

JULIOS ABENTEUERLICHE REISE *see* Jimmy das Gummipferd.

JUMPSTART (U.S.) Begun on October 2, 1989, Robb Armstrong's *JumpStart* depicts a young married couple, Joe and Marcy Cobb, in their respective careers of police officer and nurse; at home, where they vainly try to keep up with their baby girl, Sunny; or out and about with friends. The middle-class Cobbs are an average American family. That they are African American is not a central issue but only one detail among many that describes them as they pursue the American dream.

At work, Joe's observations on the human condition resonate: from the one-woman crime wave victim who recognizes everyone in the lineup—plus all the mug shots—as former criminal transgressors but, ironically, can't identify any as her purse snatcher to Joe's own oversensitivity in accusing his curmudgeonly white partner Crusty of a racial remark in referring to four young men as "Hootie and the Blowfish," only to learn that they really are the musical group, the full array of humanity is affectionately represented.

Circumstances in the hospital are no different. Whether it's the patient who grumbles about the food only to discover after Marcy crams a spoonful into his mouth during a tirade that it's actually tasty or the HMO newsletter bigger than the federal budget, there is no respite from human folly. Nor is this environment free from racially based assumptions or blind spots, as when Marcy expresses surprise that an Asian-American colleague has no interest in *The Joy Luck Club*, only to be reminded by a white colleague that she responded identically when he assumed she admired Spike Lee.

The most endearing strips revolve around home and family, with the proud, protective parents either overloading the baby-sitter with cautions or boring the teacher into a trance with their endless commentary on Sunny's talents. With witty glances at sexually explicit films (they ultimately opt for a Barney video) and husband-wife sparring (Joe must scramble when Marcy asks his opinion of another woman's figure, while Marcy has to trick Joe into getting a physical checkup), the Cobbs are a typical couple. As for Sunny, she cries over playtime "wounds" only in sight of her mother,

"JumpStart," Robb Armstrong. © United Feature Syndicate.

exhausts her parents trying to ready her for day care, and at bedtime makes her dad choose between reading *War and Peace* or the Bible or else so befuddles him with questions that she tells her little pals, "My daddy is having difficulty reading."

The strip's panels, with their combination of thick, rounded edges or no borders at all, together with similarly configured balloons (which are sometimes overlaid or with edges whimsically connected or only partially complete), mixed with free-floating dialogue, provide extra appeal. Armstrong's sure handling of his material, gentle character treatment, and generous worldview make his strip the most popular by a black American cartoonist. *JumpStart* is distributed seven days a week by United Feature Syndicate to about 250 newspapers, and selections have been reprinted in *JumpStart: A Love Story* (1996).

M.B.C.

"Jungle Jim," Alex Raymond. © King Features Syndicate.

JUNGLE JIM (U.S.) Alex Raymond created *Jungle Jim* on January 7, 1934, as the companion strip to *Flash Gordon.* Just as *Flash* was King Features Syndicate's answer to *Buck Rogers, Jungle Jim* was designed as competition to Foster's *Tarzan,* which was then dominating the straight adventure field.

"Jungle Jim" Bradley was at first an explorer and animal trapper (in the tradition of Frank Buck's *Bring 'em Back Alive*), but he was soon to take up the role he is best remembered for, that of a professional adventurer. His field of operation is the vast and undefined region known as "east of Suez," where Jim, aided by his faithful companion Kolu, fights brigand chiefs, international agitators, and pirates of every description. In 1935 he meets (and reforms) the shady lady who was later to become his constant companion, Lil' de Vrille, known in her trade as "Shanghai Lil." (The name and the type are obvious borrowings from Josef von Sternberg's 1932 film *Shanghai Express.*)

Alex Raymond's inspired pen endowed Jungle Jim's action-packed adventures with a striking elegance of line, a fine delineation of atmosphere and background, and a visual excitement that gave the strip a highly polished gloss. While it did not succeed in topping *Tarzan's* popularity, Alex Raymond's *Jungle Jim* remains one of the highest-rated adventure strips, and its tone and style were widely imitated all through the 1930s and 1940s.

In the early 1940s, Raymond worked less and less on *Jungle Jim,* leaving the feature in the hands of uninspired "ghosts" (among whom can be found Alex's brother Jim). In May 1944, following Raymond's enlistment in the Marine Corps, *Jungle Jim* (along with *Flash Gordon*) was taken over by Austin Briggs, who did a highly creditable job. After Briggs's departure in May 1948, the strip was given to Paul Norris (who had been doing the comic book version until then) until its final demise in 1954.

Jungle Jim had his own comic book and was the hero of a radio serial. The strip was also made into a movie serial in 1937. In the 1940s and 1950s Johnny Weissmuller had the role in no fewer than 10 *Jungle Jim* pictures for Columbia, and later in a television series.

M.H.

JUNGLE TATEI (Japan) *Jungle Tatei* ("Jungle Emperor"), created by Osamu Tezuka, made its first appearance in the October 1950 issue of the monthly *Manga Shōnen.*

"Jungle Tatei," Osamu Tezuka. © Manga Shōnen.

Leo, the white lion, was the son of Panja, the first Jungle Emperor, but Pancha was killed by white hunters and Leo's mother, Raga, was shipped to the London zoo in a cage, where she gave birth to the white lion. Set free by his mother, Leo escaped on a ship, was adopted by a Japanese boy named Kenichi, and grew up among human beings.

Later returned to Africa, Leo was torn between his animal instincts and his almost-human stirrings. As king of the animals, he tried to fashion a civilized society among the jungle beasts in order to stop the encroaching waves of hunters and other humans trying to despoil the animal kingdom. Within this theme Tezuka wove a variety of subplots involving the animals and parties of explorers who were after the mysterious Moonlight Stone, an extraordinary source of inexhaustible energy.

With *Jungle Tatei*, Tezuka broke sharply with the static, one-dimensional, and slow-paced tradition of old-style Japanese comic strips as he introduced new and exciting cinematic techniques into his strip. *Jungle Tatei* was Osamu Tezuka's first successful magazine feature and ran until April 1954.

Jungle Tatei was adapted into animated form: it was the first color cartoon series produced for Japanese TV. *Jungle Tatei* was awarded the Silver Lion at the International Children's Film Festival held in Venice in 1967.

H.K.

JUST BOY see Elmer.

JUST JAKE (G.B.) It was on Saturday, June 4, 1938, that the British newspaper strip finally came to full fruition and found its first true native hero—not "Jake," the titular hero of the strip, but its villain. "Our Grand New British strip character" heralded the *Daily Mirror*'s introduction to *Just Jake*, by Bernard Graddon, but before long this hayseed hero vanished from the scene, off to fight for king and country at the call of war, leaving the scoundrelly, scurvy squire, all chin and bent cigar, to take over the strip. But he could not win the apple-cheeked, melon-chested Hazel Nutt, the heroine;

she remained true to her tradition as a country maiden, and to her swain, ploughboy Jake.

Captain A.R.P. Reilly-Ffoull, G.G., F.F.I. and bar (a name full of allusions: Air Raid Precautions, Galloping Gertshires, Free From Infection), the Squire of Arntwee Hall, Much Cackling, Gertshire, was present right from the first strip. He was awakened by a large crash. "By carbonate of zodiac!" he cried. Equally aroused were Titus Tallow, his greasy bailiff ("Suffering subpoenas!") and Eric or Buttle by Bottle the scrub-jawed serf ("Lumme! Oozat?"). It was none other than Jake the Hero, returning from Old Australy on his mobile sheep-dipper. In the offing lurked a third member of the Arntwee Hall household, gritty old Maida Grannitt,

"Just Jake," Bernard Graddon. © Daily Mirror Newspapers Ltd.

of the flying hairpins and the broad brogue: "May the awfu' consequences be upon ye'r pesky pates, ye black-hairted bogles!"

Drawing aside, which was brilliant, the dialogue of artist/writer Bernard Graddon has never been equaled this side of *Li'l Abner*: "Stap me sideways, serf, you've snuffled a snozzleful!" Eric could but reply, "Cor!"

Steve Dowling, who worked on the *Mirror* during *Just Jake*'s reign, called Bernard Graddon "a bloody genius but, alas, a drunken one." Dowling had to step in and draw the strip when Graddon was too gone in his cups to ink straight. Often he would disappear in the middle of a serial and another hand had to take over. Ron Gibbs and Tony Royle could work from Graddon's synopsis. But the spark was gone. Graddon died in the night from pneumonia contracted after a particularly sodden office party to celebrate Christmas 1951. The strip ended on April 14, 1952.

A paper-covered reprint of the 1945 saga *Educating Eric* was published by the *Daily Mirror* under the title *The Sly Sinister Scurvy Adventures of Captain Reilly Ffoull*, and the first history of British newspaper strips was named after his classic expletive and dedicated to his memory: *Stap Me! The British Newspaper Strip* (1971).

D.G.

JUST KIDS (U.S.) In 1922 cartoonist Ad Carter, with the encouragement of Clare Briggs, submitted a new child strip to King Features Syndicate. The new feature, named *Just Kids* by KFS, made its appearance on July 23, 1923, as a daily strip, followed by a Sunday page on August 20 of the same year.

Ad Carter filled the strip with characters and reminiscences of his own childhood. Mush Stebbins and his pals, the voracious Fatso Dolan and the far-from-inscrutable Pat Chan, were involved in all the pranks of boyhood and what was essentially high-spirited but harmless mischief. The little band never got involved in anything more dangerous than cutting classes (much to the chagrin of truant officer Bluenose) or wheedling Mr. Trumbull, the soda parlor owner, out of some free chocolate malteds.

The action centered on the suburban town of Barnsville, where the other characters of the strip resided: Mr. Branner, the club-juggling cop; the song-loving street cleaner; the skating oldster; and some other nuts and oddballs. There was never much happening, and the little band of youngsters provided most of the action.

Suddenly, in the mid-1930s, *Just Kids* completely changed character (at least in the daily version). Mush

"Just Kids," Ad Carter. © King Features Syndicate.

and his friends got involved in sinister plots and violent adventures, which were as suspenseful as they were unpredictable. There were secret societies and masked outlaws, and the kids took it all in stride, as if they were playing cops-and-robbers. This probably marked the high point of *Just Kids'* career: from the late 1940s on it was mostly downhill and the strip finally disappeared, without fanfare or notice, following the author's death in 1957.

Just Kids had a crude, even primitive look, and much of its appeal resided in its atmosphere and story line. It enjoyed only middling readership and success, and was never made into a movie; nor did it have its own comic book. Today the strip exhales a nostalgic charm redolent of suburban *Gemütlichkeit* and of quixotic boyhood dreams.

M.H.

JUSTICE LEAGUE OF AMERICA (U.S.) When it became apparent to National that superheroes were again going to be big sellers, editor Julius Schwartz, writer Gardner Fox, and artist Mike Sekowsky combined to create the *Justice League of America* (JLA), a group feature that starred Flash, Green Lantern, Aquaman, Wonder Woman, J'onn J'onzz, Superman, and Batman. Certainly influenced by his earlier experience with the 1940s' *Justice Society of America* (Fox eventually revived this group and wrote an annual two-part super-team-up), Fox's group made their first appearance in February 1960's *Brave and Bold* number 28. They were awarded their own title in October of that year.

Over the years, the membership has changed considerably. Green Arrow, Black Canary, Elongated Man, Sargon, and The Phantom Stranger have all joined; Hawkman joined and then resigned; Wonder Woman resigned and then rejoined; J'onn J'onzz returned to his Martian homeland; and Metamorpho declined entrance altogether. But it was never the "roll call" that made the *JLA* stories among the best produced in the 1960s. Writer Fox had a wide scientific grasp and an empathy for superheroes and used them to create some amazingly poignant stories. "Man, Thy Name Is Brother" is considered by many to be the best antidiscrimination story ever published in comics, and "The Creatures of Nightmare Island" and "The Riddle of the Robot-Justice League" are two of the most subtle stories ever written for a hero feature. When Fox left the feature toward the end of the 1960s, the strip took a sharp downhill slide despite the best efforts of Len Wein and Denny O'Neil, two of the more talented young replacements.

Artistically, the much-maligned Mike Sekowsky handled the first 50 *JLA* tales in a fast-paced and beautifully taut manner. Even panels overcrowded with heroes and villains were well done, and Sekowsky received excellent inking help. His work declined dramatically in the later issues, however, and he was eventually replaced by Dick Dillin and Dick Giordano.

Like the Justice Society before them, the Justice League fought some of the most original villains of their time. Among them were Felix Foust, a wizard of sorts, and the Royal Flush Gang, a group of thugs who dressed like playing-card characters.

J.B.

To revive the fortunes of the group, which had fallen on hard times, National brought in old Fawcett characters it had just acquired—namely, Bulletman,

"Justice League of America." © *National Periodical Publications.*

Spy Smasher, and even Captain Marvel. Initially, it didn't help, and, in quick succession, a bewildering array of writers (Denny O'Neil, Mike Friedrich, Len Wein, Cary Bates, et al.) were ushered in, to no avail. In 1987 the title was changed to simply *Justice League* (it recovered its original appellation a couple of years later). It finally turned around in the late 1980s and became one of the most popular superhero titles of the 1990s, even spawning such spin-offs as *Justice League Europe* and *Justice League International*.

M.H.

JUSTICE SOCIETY OF AMERICA (U.S.) *The Justice Society of America (JSA)* was created by editor Sheldon Mayer and writer Gardner Fox and made its first appearance in National's *All-Star* number three for Winter 1940. The group started a new trend in comic books—the grouping of a company's heroes in a single adventure. Imitators followed in droves, and the group concept is still going strong today. The group began with eight members: Flash, Green Lantern, Hawkman, Hourman, Sandman, Dr. Fate, Spectre, and Atom. Over the years, however, many others have entered and left the convocation. Batman and Superman made their first joint appearance here, and Black Canary, Dr. Mid-Nite, Johnny Thunder, Mr. Terrific, Red Tornado, Starman, Wildcat, and Wonder Woman all became members or made brief cameo appearances.

Gardner Fox wrote 35 of the 57 adventures single-handedly. The format for dealing with so many characters became formularized out of necessity: the heroes gathered for an introductory chapter, were each defeated by their enemies in an individual chapter, and finally reunited to defeat the villains in the last chapter. As patterned as the stories were, however, they were among the finest ever produced, championing democracy, brotherhood, and tolerance. With the 19 tales scripted by John Broome and Bob Kanigher, the series is perhaps the most sensitive and idealistic produced in the 1940s.

The feature boasted a long line of fine illustrators. Among those contributing material to the strip were: Irwin Hasen (1947-49), Alex Toth (1947-48), Carmine Infantino (1947-48), Jack Burnley (1942), and Frank Giacoia (1950-51).

The feature outlasted many of the characters' individual strips, continuing through the 57th issue of *All-Star* (February 1951). The title was then changed to *All-Star Western*.

When the second superhero boom began in the 1960s, it was inevitable that Fox would also reincarnate the *JSA*. The group was revived in the 21st issue of *Justice League of America* (August 1963) and now appears in an annual team-up with the Justice League. The group made a brief return in its own title in 1991-93.

J.B.

KAHLES, CHARLES WILLIAM (1878-1931)

American cartoonist born in Lengfurt, Germany, on January 12, 1878. C. W. Kahles came to the United States at the age of six with his immigrant parents. Settling in Brooklyn, Kahles studied art at the Pratt Institute and the Brooklyn Art School. His career in journalism began at the age of 16 as staff artist for the *New York Recorder* and the *New York Journal*. In 1898 he joined Pulitzer's *New York World* and contributed a great number of comic features. The first of these was *The Little Red Schoolhouse* (1899), followed in rapid succession by *Butch the Butcher's Boy* and *Clarence the Cop* (1900), *The Perils of Submarine Boating* (1901), *Sandy Highflier, the Airship Man* (1902), *Billy Bounce, Pretending Percy,* and *The Merry Nobles Three* (all in 1905), *Clumsy Claude* (1906), *Optimistic Oswald* (1912), and *The Kelly Kids* (1919). In addition, Kahles was a regular contributor to *Life* and *Judge* (where he created *Captain Fibb* in 1905) and did a fair amount of book illustration.

In 1906 Kahles started the feature he is chiefly remembered for, *Hairbreadth Harry,* for the *Philadelphia Press*. In 1923, he began the daily strip of *Hairbreadth Harry* that he drew in addition to the Sunday page, and he discontinued all his other strips. He died of a heart attack on January 21, 1931.

C. W. Kahles was a great innovator, leaving to others the dull task of fully developing his discoveries. As his most constant exegete, his own daughter, Jessie Kahles Straut, wrote: "As a pioneer in American comic art, C. W. Kahles contributed many firsts. Among them were the first suspense serial and the first superhero, *Hairbreadth Harry,* 1906; the first serial story about a policeman, *Clarence the Cop,* 1900; the first comic strip about an aviator, *Sandy Highflier, the Airship Man,* 1902; and the first strip about undersea adventure, *The Perils of Submarine Boating,* 1901."

The sheer number of strips he produced has somewhat obscured Kahles's qualities as a draftsman and a storyteller, but there has been a renewal of interest in his work.

M.H.

KALENBACH, DIETER (1937-   )

Dieter Kalenbach is a German comic artist and graphic artist born August 29, 1937, in Düsseldorf. Having shown a talent for drawing, he decided to develop it further at the Hamburg College of Commercial Arts and Crafts. After concluding his studies there, he worked for various companies and freelanced as a graphic artist, decorator, and scene painter for stage and television. Every

C. W. Kahles, "Clarence the Cop."

now and then Kalenbach interrupted his professional career by extensive traveling. Several times his travels took him to the Balkan countries and to Africa for months. He returned from a voyage to the Arctic regions with an idea for a comic strip about Laplanders, the last nomads of Europe. Their closeness to nature fascinated him. Thus, together with writer Erka, *Turi and Tolk* was created in 1973. The stars of this series are Turi, a young Laplander, and his eagle Tolk. Turi's grandfather, Pavva-Troms, also figures prominently in the stories.

Turi und Tolk appeared in *Zack* magazine when it started including original German material in 1973. The feature ended with the demise of *Zack* in 1981. The magazine did not meet the expectations of the Springer conglomerate managers, who had hoped it would bring in money quickly. Instead, after much criticism at the magazine's inception and a Yellow Kid Award as best foreign comic book at Lucca, Italy, in 1973, sales had leveled off. Despite good licensed and original matter like *Turi und Tolk*, and despite a loyal following of regular buyers, the magazine was axed. With no other publishers wanting original material at the time, Kalenbach more or less left the comic field.

W.F.

KALUTA, MICHAEL WM. (1947-   ) American comic book artist and illustrator born August 25, 1947, in Guatemala to U.S. citizens. As a child of the 1950s, Michael Kaluta was part of a wide-eyed audience of American boys, pencil in hand, watching TV art instructor Jon Gnagy give a weekly drawing lesson. The practice in the fundamentals of drawing gleaned from those TV shows—particularly perspective drawing—poured forth onto the comic pages years later, and to this day Kaluta still mentions Gnagy as his first artistic influence.

Kaluta studied fine arts at the Richmond Professional Institute (now Virginia Commonwealth University). Much to the dismay of his instructors, who were immersed in the Abstract Impressionism trend of the day, Kaluta turned to the comic page for artistic expression. Arriving in New York City in 1969, Kaluta's first published comic book assignment was a three-page story in *Flash Gordon* number 18 (January 1970). His early comic book work, primarily for National Comics (now DC), consisted of filler stories and cover art for many of their horror and fantasy titles. A significant part of his early work illustrated the fantasy stories of Edgar Rice Burroughs, particularly the *Carson of Venus* series. Along with the story work, Kaluta created an impressive number of comic book covers for both DC and Marvel comics. A few of the notable titles that had extended runs with Kaluta covers include *House of Mystery, House of Secrets, Batman, Detective, Conan the King*, and more recently, *Vampirella* and *The Books of Magic*. The original artwork for these covers is highly sought after by art collectors today.

In 1972 DC Comics revived *The Shadow*, a crime-fighting character who originally enjoyed popularity in the 1930s. Kaluta was selected to re-create the character, and his run on the series was brief but brilliant. His artwork manifested a smoky mood and atmosphere. From his art studio on the Upper West Side of Manhattan, Kaluta had every dark alley of Hell's Kitchen, dusty street of Chinatown, and architectural wonder of the city within his reach to cast in The Shadow's

world. His sketchbook-style realism gave *The Shadow* an urban feel that evoked the 1930s but looks fresh and inventive even today. Deadlines conflicted with Kaluta's detailed style, and after five issues and eight covers he left the series. *The Shadow* has become the most notable comic character associated with Kaluta. After the DC series, he brought the character back for several publishers, including Marvel and Dark Horse. In 1994 Kaluta contributed to production of the Universal Pictures film *The Shadow*. Kaluta created illustrations over photos of Alex Baldwin, the film's star, to help develop the makeup design for the Shadow in the movie.

In 1976 Kaluta and two close friends, comic artist and illustrator Bernie Wrightson and painter Jeff Jones, formed an art studio with British comic artist and illustrator Barry Windsor-Smith. Kaluta, Wrightson, and Windsor-Smith all lived in the same apartment building when they first arrived in New York in the late 1960s. A close look at some of Kaluta's and Wrightson's early 1970s comic book work reveals hints of "midnight hour collaborations" as the artists helped each other meet tight deadlines. Each of the studio artists had made contributions to the comic art form in the 1970s but their studio works represented an evolution in illustration and painting for posters, books, and limited-edition prints. Kaluta produced some of his most imaginative work during this period.

The *Starstruck* comic series, which appeared in 1981, was based on an off-Broadway play created by Elaine Lee. The comic book series, which was created by Kaluta and Lee and illustrated by Kaluta, has been published under several imprints, including Marvel's Epic line and most recently at Dark Horse. *Starstruck*, a science fiction satire with feminist overtones, gave Kaluta a fresh vehicle to display his mature drawing and design talents and features some of his most original work in the comic book field. Visually, *Starstruck* is pure Kaluta, with a drawing style that has matured beyond his original comic artist influences. Throughout the 1970s Kaluta's work affectionately reflected his early artistic influences, particularly the virtuoso trio of Frank Frazetta, Al Williamson, and Roy Krenkel. These three brilliant draftsmen created—together and individually—many of the science-fiction comic classics of the 1950s and later reintroduced impeccable draftsmanship and style to the comics at the Warren comic magazines in the 1960s.

Throughout the 1990s, Kaluta has created new works for *The Shadow* and *Starstruck* for various comic publishers. Most recently, he enjoyed a long run of cover designs for DC Comics's Vertigo title *The Books of Magic*. His modern fantasy interpretations of the title, reminiscent of the antiquarian children's illustrators Rackham, Robinson, and Dulac, have been a welcome relief from the ultraviolent and nihilistic subject matter that pervades comic books in the 1990s.

Perhaps Kaluta's most important contribution to the comic field has been his blending of classic visual design and illustration styles within the comic page. Kaluta integrates classical graphic design motifs influenced by the Art Nouveau works of Aubrey Beardsley and the Art Deco patterns of Alfons Mucha—bringing a welcome new look to the comics. Kaluta's comic work represents one of the underappreciated links to the great illustrators and designers of the early part of this century. Perhaps Kaluta can best be described as

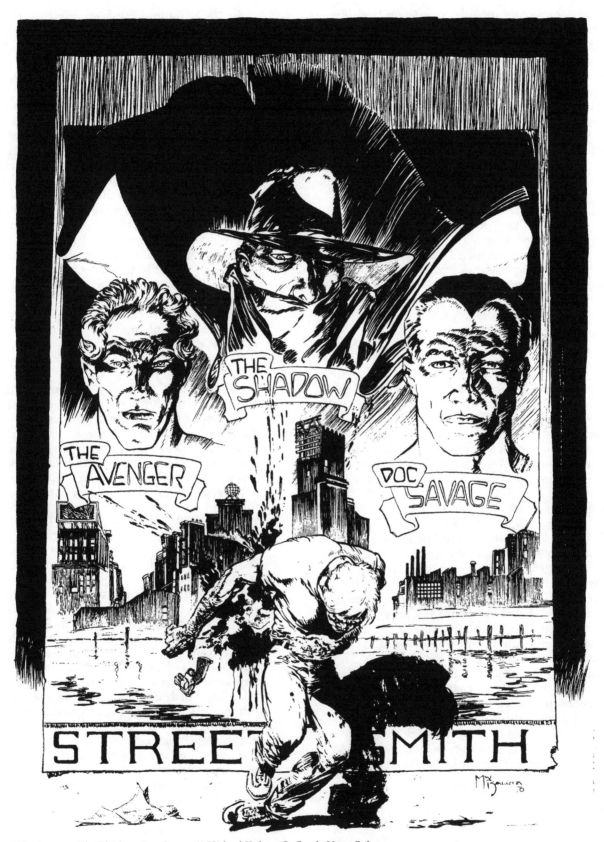

"The Avenger, The Shadow, Doc Savage," Michael Kaluta. © Conde Naste Pub.

an antiquarian-futurist who visually romances the future with the lyrical lines of the past.

Currently working in the digital media, Kaluta is designing characters and environments for several video games, often with famed British designer and illustrator Roger Dean. Hopefully, his love for the art form will continue to draw him back to the pages of comic books in the years ahead.

R.G.

KAMUI DEN (Japan) *Kamui Den*, created by Sanpei Shirato, made its first appearance in the December 1964 issue of the comic monthly *Garo*.

This long-lasting strip depicted the dramatic history of a number of characters during a 20-year period from about 1640 to 1662. The scene was laid mostly in Hioki, and many characters appeared in the strip, from samurais to *hinin* (persons of the lowest class). The main characters were Kamui, son of Yasuke, a hinin who became a ninja spy in order to escape from his class, and his friend, the rebel peasant leader Shousuke, who later became Kamui's brother-in-law. These two were later joined by Ryūnoshin Kusaka, a samurai who wanted to avenge the death of his father and his whole clan at the hands of the wicked lord of Hioki.

Many others appeared in this chronicle of life in the feudal society of the Edo era. Shirato exposed the fundamental conflict besetting this society and he particularly denounced the *Mibun Sida* ("class system") whereby a handful of samurais could oppress the masses of people. The strip also related the wars between the peasants and the samurais, the peasants' uprising (the so-called Ikki) and their defeat under the samurais' superior military power and tactics.

Planned as a trilogy, *Kamui Den* part one ended in July 1971. Part two was published from 1982 to 1987; and in 1988 Shirato started work on the third and final part. A magnificent work of fiction, *Kamui Den* is also the product of painstaking historical research. *Kamu Den* has been reprinted in book form and sold over four million copies.

H.K.

KANE, GIL (1926-   ) American comic book artist and publisher born Eli Katz on April 6, 1926, in Riga, Latvia. Coming to America at the age of three, he broke into the comic book field at age 16. His earliest work began appearing in 1942 while he was with the Binder shop; he also had a short stint in the Baily shop (1944) before turning to freelancing. Throughout the 1940s, Kane worked for all the major comic houses: for MLJ he produced the *Scarlet Avenger* (1941-43); for Street and Smith he backgrounded *Blackstone the Magician* (1942); he drew *Red Hawk, Vision,* and *Young Allies* for Timely (1943-44); produced the *Candy* humor feature for Quality in 1944; produced *Sandman* and *Wildcat* for National (1947-48); and, under pen names like "Scott Edward," "Gil Stack," and "Al Kame," drew material for Fox, Holyoke, Aviation, Hillman, Eastern, Fawcett, Prize, and Avon. As the 1950s brought hard times for superhero strips, Kane spent most of his time producing war, crime, and horror stories for Atlas, and science fiction and mystery comics for National.

It was not until the second superhero boom of the 1960s that Kane was able to cast off the workhorse role. Concentrating on two of National's major features, *Green Lantern* and *The Atom*, Kane refined his style considerably. While most of his work throughout the previous two decades had been rushed and sloppy, these two features were detailed, cleanly illustrated, and sported fast-paced layouts.

Kane's increasing fame and skill also fired his wandering spirit and, by 1967, he was drifting away from the strips. He began a short stint at Marvel illustrating *The Hulk* (1967), drew stories for Warren's black and white horror titles, produced *Flash Gordon* for King in 1967, and contributed stories to Tower's *Thunder Agents* and related strips (1965-67). Kane finally left standard comics in 1968 and published his own black and white adventure comic magazine under the "Adventure House" label. Entitled *His Name Is Savage,* the book lasted only one issue, but presaged the black and white comics boom by several years. Kane returned to Marvel in 1970, producing outstanding material for *Conan, Spider Man,* Marvel covers, and many secondary features.

In 1971, Kane drew a unique feature called *Blackmark*, which was published by Bantam in paperback form. One of the finest sword-and-sorcery strips ever conceived, *Blackmark* was plagued by poor distribution and was financially unsuccessful. But Kane had outpaced the comics establishment once again, and several years later sword-and-sorcery became a saleable product.

Gil Kane came back to newspaper comics with *Star Hawks*, a science fiction strip he drew from 1977 to 1981 on scripts by Ron Goulart. In the mid-1980s, he moved to southern California and went into television animation, working on the *Superman* cartoon and others. After drawing the adaptation of Richard Wagner's *The Ring of Nibelung* (1989-90) for DC Comics, he went on to illustrate *Jurassic Park* for Topps Comics (1993). He has also worked sporadically in recent years on a number of monthly DC titles.

Kane was awarded the NCS's 1971 comic book award and the 1973 Reuben Goldberg Award for Outstanding Achievement in a Story Comic Book. He is considered one of the most articulate and thoughtful comic book artists.

J.B.

KANE, ROBERT (1916-   ) American comic book and comic strip artist born October 24, 1916, in New York City. After attending Cooper Union and the Art Students League, Bob Kane entered the comic book field in 1936 as a staff artist in Jerry Iger's studio. Concentrating primarily on humor features, Kane's first comic book work appeared in *Helne's Wow*, edited and packaged by Iger. This 1936 *Hiram Hick* feature was followed by similar attempts for Fiction House from 1937 to 1939. Titled *Peter Pupp, Jest Laffs,* and *Pluto,* they were all typical "bigfoot" humor types, but studio owner Iger once insisted that Kane "could have been one of the finest humorists of our time if he'd stayed with it."

But by 1938 Kane went out on his own and attempted several adventure strips at National Comics, after creating more humor features like *Gumshoe Gus* and *Jest a Second*. Collaborating with writer Bill Finger, Kane drew two rather pedestrian thrillers, *Rusty and his Pals* and *Clip Carson*. But the times were calling for more *Superman*-types, and, in 1939, National editor Whit Ellsworth assigned the duo the job of finding a suitably costumed companion to cash in on *Superman's* popularity. They developed the quintessential creature of the night: *The Batman*.

Kane drew the original sketches and created the characterizations, but his concept borrowed too heavily from Superman, so Finger suggested the bat-ears and cowl. Thus was born The Batman, a midnight avenger who stalked criminals by preying on their fears, superstitions, and insecurities. Artistically, however, much like Joe Shuster's *Superman* work, Kane's drawing of the strip was amateurish. The backgrounds were nonexistent, characters were stereotypic, usually lifted from the Cagney-Robinson-Bogart genre of crime movies, and the anatomy was still and lifeless. Still, much like the unrealistic and blocky artwork Chester Gould used on the *Dick Tracy* comic strip, Kane's *Batman* work was frighteningly effective. Scenes were eerily quiet, always belying some hideously evil purpose, and shadows were used with unusual success. Finger's stories always utilized the most unsavory of characters, all of whom Kane would render unflatteringly. Batman, on the other hand, although as stiff as the other characters, was drawn to most effectively capitalize on the seedy scenes.

The *Batman* strip began in *Detective* number 27 (May 1939). It quickly spread to several other titles and a comic strip, and Kane immediately began hiring assistants, the first and best of them being Jerry Robinson. Over the years, Kane did less and less of the artwork, but his byline remained on every story until 1964 and Kane claims to have worked actively on the strip until 1968

In recent years, however, Kane has spent most of his time in other fields. He created the *Courageous Cat* animated television show in 1958, the *Cool McCool* animated series in 1969, and has also created several motion picture formats. Kane's serious paintings were first shown at his 1969 one-man show at New York's Gallerie Internationale. He published his autobiography, *Batman and Me*, in 1984, and was involved with the 1989 *Batman* movie.

J.B.

KANIGHER, ROBERT (1915-   ) American comic book writer and editor born 1915. Bob Kanigher began his long comic book career in 1940 at Fox, where he wrote for the *Blue Beetle* and *Samson* adventure strips; *Samson* was a totally forgettable filler, but Kanigher's work on *Blue Beetle* was excellent, even though the character had never been either particularly well-drawn or written throughout its long life. Also during his career, Kanigher wrote for Fawcett (*Captain Marvel*), Marvel (*Iron Man*), MLJ (*Steel Sterling, The Web*), Skywald (*Horror* and *The Heap*) and Pines.

But it was for National that Kanigher did the great majority of his comic writing and editing. He wrote regularly for the company after 1943, and was an editor from 1945 to 1967 and from 1972 until his retirement in the 1980s. He worked in every genre from love to superhero to war to fantasy to adventure.

Strangely enough, there are few specific characters of his that come to mind instantly. Kanigher is known mainly for his outstanding work in two genres: war and Western. Among the many war features he has been acclaimed for are *Sgt. Rock and Easy Co.*, probably the preeminent war strip of all time in the comics; *Enemy Ace*, an affecting series about a good man on the "wrong" side of the war; *Capt. Storm*; *Balloon Buster*, one of the more unique war strips in comics; and *The Haunted Tank*. In the Western group, some of the many strips Kanigher worked on include *El Diablo*, an offbeat and well-received strip; *The Outlaw*; *Johnny Thunder*, where Kanigher did excellent material in collaboration with artist Alex Toth; *Tomahawk*, and later, *Son of Tomahawk*; and many others.

As an editor, he had a reputation as a taskmaster, especially with artists. One of the premier visual storytellers in the medium, Kanigher was once described by a comic-artist-turned-art-director as an editor "who would eat up artists and spit them out for breakfast."

Kanigher has also done extensive amounts of freelance writing, and has published several books, including a 1943 Cambridge House book entitled *How to Make Money Writing for Comic Magazines*. He retired in the 1980s and his contributions to the field since then have been limited to an occasional article or reminiscence.

J.B.

"Kapitein Rob," Pieter-Joseph Kuhn. © Het Parool.

KAPITEIN ROB (Netherlands) *Kapitein Rob* ("Captain Rob"), one of the best-known and cherished Dutch daily adventure strips, started on December 11, 1945, in the newspaper *Het Parool*. Captain Robert van Stoerum lived through some 72 adventures, a total of 5,420 individual strips, before the series came to a sudden end with the untimely death of its creator and artist, Pieter Joseph Kuhn, on January 20, 1966. The first adventure, "De Avonturen van het zeilschip De Vrijheid" ("The Adventures of the Sailing Vessel Freedom"), did not quite live up to Kuhn's own expectations of his abilities as a writer. Therefore, he started a cooperation with Evert Werkman, a Dutch journalist, who wrote most of the exploits of *Kapitein Rob*. Although originally an adventure strip with narrative printed below the pictures, some of the many foreign editions put the narrative and dialogue into captions and speech balloons. The strip worked both ways and Dutch reprints in book form sold by the millions.

Kapitein Rob was written and drawn in the best of adventure traditions. The hero was an adventurer sailing the seven seas, accompanied only by his faithful dog, Skip. His good ship, *De Vrijheid* ("Freedom"), took him to exotic places and faraway lands where the relatively simple and one-dimensionally unalterable character of the Captain was met by unexpected situations and dilemmas. Although the Captain married in 1954 and had a son in 1955, his family, as with Tarzan, rarely figured in the stories. With the addition of Professor Lupardi early in the strip's history, science fiction was added to romanticism. A tunnel under the sea, a trip around the moon, a time machine, or the discovery of a "lost" continent all were made possible and plausible by the very realistic art work of Pieter Joseph Kuhn, himself a sailing enthusiast and the model for his hero. Whenever possible, he traveled to the places Kaptein Rob was to visit. This and extensive research helped to lend the strip an atmosphere and a special flavor that made Kuhn one of the "big three" among Dutch comic strip artists.

W.F.

KAPPIE (Netherlands) Kappie is immediately characterized by his name as a diminutive captain in a humor strip. *Kappie* is one of the many successful strips created by Marten Toonder, possibly the most influential personality in Dutch comics. At one time or another some 80 percent of all Dutch comic artists and writers have worked either as staffers or as freelancers for Toonder's studios. Among those working on the *Kap-*

"Kappie," Marten Toonder. © Marten Toonder.

pie strip were artist Piet Wijn and writer Lo Hartog van Banda, himself as prolific as Toonder and on the Toonder staff for 14 years. "Kappie en het drijvende eiland" ("Cappie and the Floating Island") was the first of the *Kappie* episodes written for Toonder by Hartog van Banda when the latter took over the writing of this strip. *Kappie* was started in 1946, along with Toonder's *Panda*. The strip presented 140 adventures before it ended in 1972. As was usual with most of the earlier Dutch comic strips and with many of the Toonder productions, *Kappie*'s narrative and dialogue was printed below the pictures.

Kappie offered the reader adventures in all kinds of exotic places. In a way this made *Kappie* a cartoon version of Pieter J. Kuhn's adventure strip *Kapitein Rob*. As with Toonder's other strips, money was the driving factor behind the good captain's voyages across the seven seas. Kappie, who, except for a white moustache which lent him added dignity, might have been a relative of *Bugs Bunny's* Elmer Fudd in looks and stature, was aided and abetted by his somewhat stereotyped helmsman and first mate, who followed his every whim to guide the good ship *De Kraak* to wherever the moneymaking mission was to take place.

In outlook and appearance, *Kappie* was more geared for a younger readership than most of Toonder's other work which, like *Tom Poes*, developed an adult appeal over the decades. Like other strips by Toonder, *Kappie*'s comic strip adventures were reprinted in a number of comic books.

W.F.

KAS *See Kasprzak, Zbigniew.*

KASPRZAK, ZBIGNIEW (1955-   ) Cartoonist born May 31, 1955, in Zielona Gora, Poland. During his studies at the Krakow Academy of Fine Arts (1973-80), Zbigniew Kasprzak (who signs "Kas" for obvious reasons) started contributing to the comics magazine *Relax*. After he won a competition sponsored by the magazine, he became a frequent contributor. At the same time, he explored new methods of expression in painting, graphics, and satirical drawing, for which he won a prize at the Lodz Satirical Drawing Triennial in 1980.

In the 1980s, during the difficult period of military emergency in Poland, *Relax* and many other periodicals had to close their doors, so Kas devoted his time to painting because of the lack of opportunity in the comic field. When the situation improved and some houses resumed publishing, he turned out many book and cover illustrations and posters, in addition to the comics he contributed to the magazine *Kaw* and to the Sport y Trystika publishing company. He wrote more than 10 comic stories, mainly on history and science fiction themes.

His big break came in 1988 when he was invited to the International Comics Festival in Sierre, Switzerland. There he met Grzegorz Rosinski, who had already made a name for himself in Western Europe. Rosinski was then drawing both *Thorgal* and *Hans*, and he recommended to his publisher, Brussels-based Editions du Lombard, that Kas take over drawing *Hans*. After being accepted, Kas moved to Brussels with his family. In addition to drawing *Hans*, a postnuclear tale scripted by André-Paul Duchateau, he has also recently started a new series, *Les Voyageurs* ("The Travelers"), of which two volumes have been issued to date.

K.R.

KATO, YOSHIROU (1925-   ) Japanese cartoonist born June 25, 1925, in Tokyo. Under the influence of such childhood readings as *Norakuro*, *Bōken Dankichi*, and other comic strips, Yoshirou Kato decided very early in life to become a cartoonist. In 1938 he started to work at Komagome Hospital while going to night school. At 14 years of age, he sold his first cartoon to *Asahi Graph*; after this he became a frequent contributor to several magazines.

In 1943 he entered Kawabata Academy and took up a new job with the Defense Ministry. Drafted into the army in 1944, Kato departed for the North China front, but was demobilized the next year. Upon his return to civilian life, Kato contributed cartoons, illustrations, and etchings to the cartoon magazine *Manga* while holding an eight-to-five job. In 1947 he became a regular cartoonist for *Manga Shūdan*, and the next year he quit his job, determined to earn his living with cartoon work. Gradually Kato became one of the most prolific cartoonists of the day, contributing to every major publication in Japan. In 1951 he tried his hand at several newspaper strips, but these did not click. Only in 1954 did Kato create a successful comic strip: *Mappirakun*, for the daily *Mainichi*. Many other comic creations then followed: *Onboro Jinsei* (1954); *Ojisama Daimiyō* and *Ore wa Obake dazo* ("I Am a Monster"), both in 1959; *Gejigeji Tarō Gyōjōki* (1961), *Motemote Ojisan* (1963), *Senbiki no Ninja* ("A Thousand Ninjas," 1964); *Benben Monogatari* ("The Story of Benben," 1965); and others.

Yoshirou Kato's comic world is full of fantastic images and far-out concepts. He was the first to break the taboo against showing excrements and filth in comics. While challenging these and other taboos, he created comic strips of interest and high graphic quality, and became famous not only as a comic strip artist, but also as a magazine cartoonist and TV personality. He is still active in the field of comics, although his output has slowed considerably since the 1980s.

H.K.

KATZENJAMMER KIDS, THE (U.S.) Rudolph Dirks created *The Katzenjammer Kids* on December 12, 1897,

"The Katzenjammer Kids," Harold Knerr. © King Features Syndicate.

for the American Humorist, the famed Sunday supplement of the *New York Journal*. Inspired in part by Wilhelm Busch's *Max und Moritz*, *The Katzenjammer Kids* depicts the guerilla war conducted by the twins Hans and Fritz (the Katzenjammer Kids, also called "the Katzies") against any form of authority and indeed against society itself. Their more popular targets include Mama (the mother of the Katzies), the Captain (a former shipwrecked sailor acting as their surrogate father) and the Inspector, (representing school authorities). All these and other assorted characters resort to an Anglo-German pidgin, the effect of which is nothing short of devastating.

In the hands of Rudolph Dirks *The Katzenjammer Kids* became a genuine tale of destruction incarnated in the twin person of Hans and Fritz for whom, in the apt words of the Inspector, "society iss nix."

In 1912 Dirks decided to leave the *Journal* for the *World* and wanted to take *The Katzenjammer Kids* with him, a move fought by William Randolph Hearst in the courts. After much legal maneuvering the case was finally decided in appeal; Dirks retained the rights to the characters while Hearst kept the title.

After an absence of two years *The Katzenjammer Kids* reemerged in 1914, drawn by Harold Knerr. (Dirks started his own strip in the *World*, first titled *Hans and Fritz*, later changed to *The Captain and the Kids*.) During World War I, due to anti-German feelings, Knerr's strip changed its title to *The Shenanigan Kids*, but it reverted back to the original title in 1919.

Knerr not only retained the original flavor of the strip, he also contributed several additions to its cast of characters: the hypocritical little girl Lena, the priggish Miss Twiddle, and the foppish Rollo, whose cunning often proved a match for the Katzies' diabolical inventiveness.

After Knerr's death in 1949, *The Katzenjammer Kids* passed first to Doc Winner, then in 1956 to Joe Musial, while its quality and appeal went steadily downhill. At Musial's death in 1977 it passed into the hands of Joe Senich, who was succeeded in 1981 by Angelo DeCesare. It was then taken over by Hy Eisman, who took the venerable feature to the century mark in December 1997.

The oldest comic strip still in existence, *The Katzenjammer Kids* was adapted to the stage in 1903, and has been the subject of countless animated cartoons. The critic Kenneth Rexroth has hailed it as "one of the two American contributions to modern mythology."

M.H.

KAUKA, ROLF (1917-   ) German writer, editor, and publisher born in Leipzig on April 9, 1917. The Kauka family can be traced through several centuries of Finnish history. Rolf Kauka's great-grandfather had left his village near Vasa, where he had been a kalavala-

singer (a sort of storytelling entertainer in a pretelevision era), in order to move to Germany in 1890.

Rolf Kauka grew up in Leipzig, attending grammar school and high school there. At the age of 17, while still in senior high, he earned some money selling cartoons to the newspapers *Leipziger Neueste Nachrichten* and *Weissenfelser Tageblatt*.

He was three semesters into economic studies when, late in 1937, he was drafted into the German Army. He remained in the service until May 8, 1945, when World War II ended in German capitulation. After the war Kauka found himself in Munich, where he wrote some legal books and a reference work for the police. Finally, in 1950, he started his own publishing house, at first reprinting the romances of Hedwig Courths-Mahler in dime-novel format. Also around this time, with publisher Heinz Ullstein, Kauka got the idea to produce animated cartoons for distribution in the United States, and he planned to keep the cartoon artists busy between films by producing comic books.

Spring of 1952 saw the first issue of *Eulenspiegel*, based on the German folk character. The book was written by Kauka and drawn by Dorul van der Heide. The comic book also featured two characters that became its main attraction with issue number 10, Fix and Foxi, two clever anthropomorphic little foxes. Kauka felt the story potential of the *Eulenspiegel* character would quickly be depleted and had to be replaced. Thus, the perennial *Fix und Foxi* was born. Sales picked up and in time the comic book, now published weekly, was the second most popular comic in Germany, behind *Micky Maus* ("Mickey Mouse").

Fix and Foxi was drawn by various artists, at first almost true to nature, finally in a stylized version. Kauka wrote all the storied and created a great number of additional characters and comic series, but never actually drew them, although it was popular belief that he did because all of the material was published with only his byline and copyright.

Kauka's line of comics expanded over the years, finally including adventure stories which Kauka never really liked. Rolf Kauka sold his publishing company in 1973 but retained control of his characters. In 1975 he founded the Kauka Comic Akademie. This school trains artists and writers to draw and create comics.

In 1972 Kauka turned film producer for the feature-length animated cartoon *Mario d'Oro* and the lead-in cartoon short featuring Fix and Foxi. His earlier efforts in animated cartooning had been *Tom & Biber* and *Baron Münchhausen*.

Kauka's adventure strips ended in 1982 with the demise of *Zack* magazine, which he had taken over. Kauka's funnies continued being produced by the publishing company that had originally just been his distributor, and Kauka left the comic business to retire to a plantation in Georgia. However, in 1994 he was so irked by the noncomic editorial content of the floundering *Fix und Foxi* comic book (especially a photo of pop star Madonna) that—as copyright owner—he filed a court request to suspend publication of the magazine, which was granted. Kauka's characters survived these theatricals, because the quibbling over what was to be in the magazine did not scare off advertisers who wanted to make use of the property. The Kauka comics continue in various types of reprint editions and with more merchandising available than ever before.

W.F.

KAWANABE, GYŌSAI (1831-1889) Gyōsai Kawanabe was a Japanese print artist born in Koga, Shimofusa (now Ibaragi), on April 7, 1831. When he was seven years old, Kawanabe became a pupil of the famous master Kuniyoshi Utagawa. Later he also studied under Douhahu Kanō and Hokusai, and learned Chinese art and Western painting techniques.

Kawanabe used pen names such as Shōjō Kyōsai ("Crazy Orangutan") and Shuransairaisui ("Drunken Bum"), but changed his name to Gyōsai after being thrown in prison because of his cartoons in 1870.

Kawanabe is famous not only for his prints but also for his cartoons. He worked as a staff artist on the cartoon magazine *Eshinbun Nipponchi* from 1874 until his death. He liked to depict the monstrous and the grotesque in such works as *Hyakki Yakō Byōbu* ("The Nightly Walks of the 100 Monsters"), *Gaikotsu no Buyō* ("The Skeleton Dance"), *Namakubi* ("The Freshly Cut-Off Head"), and others. Many of his works were anthologized in book form (*Gyōsai Gadan*, *Gyōsai Donga*, and *Gyōsai Suiga*, among others). In his later years Kawanabe had as his pupil the English architect J. Condre, who later changed his name to Gyōei in admiration of his teacher. After Kawanabe's death on April 26, 1889, Condre collected the artist's works into an anthology titled *Gyōsai Gashū* ("Gyōsai's Art Collection"), released in 1911.

H.K.

KEATON, RUSSELL (1910-1945) American comic strip artist born 1910 in Corinth, Mississippi. Like so many youngsters who loved to draw, Russ Keaton left his hometown after graduation from high school and moved to Chicago, where he enrolled at the Academy of Fine Arts. When Dick Calkins started the daily *Buck Rogers* and *Skyroads* strips in 1929, Keaton, just out of school, was his first assistant. His draftsmanship was so superior to the mediocre Calkins's that he was asked to ghost the *Buck Rogers* Sunday from its inception in 1930. Eventually Keaton got to sign *Skyroads* and continued with the strip into the 1940s, giving it an airy, elegant look.

In 1939 Keaton decided to get his pilot's license and launch his own strip at the same time. In October of that year both ambitions were realized: he graduated from flying school and saw his *Flyin' Jenny* (an aviation feature starring a toothsome, blonde daredevil) get off the ground. For the first few months Keaton both wrote and drew the *Jenny* daily strip and Sunday page, but he later relinquished the scripting chores to Frank Wead, who was succeeded by Glen Chaffin. In 1943 he became a flying instructor and had to turn over the drawing of the Sunday to his assistant, Marc Swayze. Early in 1945 Keaton, feeling ill, entered the hospital for tests; the illness was diagnosed as an acute form of leukemia. On February 13, 1945, Russ Keaton was dead at age 35.

With Russ Keaton's untimely death the comic strip field lost one of its most brilliant craftsmen. Keaton had an instinctive feeling for space, action, and speed, and a sense of drama and style. Both *Skyroads* and *Flyin' Jenny* displayed a genuine air of excitement and expectation. Had his talent been allowed to mature further, Keaton might have gone on to take his place alongside such other greats as Caniff and Sickles.

M.H.

KELLY, WALT (1913-1973) American cartoonist Walter Crawford Kelly Jr. was born August 25, 1913, in Philadelphia. His family moved to Bridgeport, Connecticut, when Walt was two years old. Walt's father was a theatrical scenery painter and taught the boy how to draw. In high school Walt Kelly edited the school paper and after graduation, went to work as a reporter and cartoonist for the *Bridgeport Post*.

In 1935 Kelly went to Hollywood and became an animator for Walt Disney Studios (he worked notably on *Dumbo* and *Fantasia*). Six years later he returned east in the aftermath of the strike at the studios in 1941. He then did comic book work for Western Printing & Lithographing, creating in 1942 *Bumbazine and Albert the Alligator*, about a young boy (Bumbazine) and his pet alligator in the Okefenokee swamp, which was to become the genesis for *Pogo*.

During the war years, Kelly worked as a civilian employee of the Army's language section, illustrating language manuals. In 1948 he became art editor of the short-lived *New York Star*, where *Pogo* first appeared as a daily feature. When the *Star* folded, *Pogo* was taken over by the *New York Post*.

In addition to his work on *Pogo*, Kelly delivered hundreds of lectures, reviewed and illustrated books, drew editorial cartoons, and wrote several thoughtful articles (in one of these, paraphrasing Pogo, he coined the now-famous phrase: "We have met the enemy and he is us.") Kelly also wrote the nonsense verse and some of the music, as well as sang some of the songs on the record "Songs of the Pogo." In 1952 he was named Cartoonist of the Year, and he was elected president of the National Cartoonists Society in 1954.

Walt Kelly, who liked to call himself "the oldest boy cartoonist in the business," was uncompromising in the opinions that he often expressed in his strip. His influence on the so-called "sophisticated cartoonists" has been publicly acknowledged by such artists as Johnny Hart and Mel Lazarus.

Walt Kelly died in Hollywood on October 18, 1973, of complications from diabetes.

M.H.

KENKOY (Philippines) The most popular cartoon character to appear in the Philippines began in Liwayway publications in 1929. It was created by Tony Velasquez, who is considered the father of the Philippine comic industry.

Kenkoy is a typical Filipino male and the series dealt with his life and times as he coped with the prevailing conditions of his environment. The strip underwent several stages as Kenkoy, starting out as a carefree bachelor, went through the agonies of growing up. During this period he got involved with the usual teenage preoccupations—sports, dances, school, and girls (not necessarily in that order).

One of the highlights in the development of the feature was the courtship of Rosing, Kenkoy's eventual wife. Tony Velasquez created many humorous situations and incidents showing the intense rivalry between Kenkoy and the various suitors who vied for Rosing's attention. These episodes kept the readership laughing for many years.

Another interesting and memorable event in the series was the marriage of Rosing to Kenkoy, and their attempts afterwards to solve the numerous problems relating to newlyweds. The strip evolved as the couple produced their first child and eventually became the parents of a large family. The names of some of the children are Junior, Julie, Tsing, Nene, and Etot. One of the really fascinating and unforgettable characters to appear in the feature is Tsikiting Gubat, the non-speaking, wooly-haired, perennial child. As the members of the household grew and matured, Tsikiting remained the same through the years. He is as stubborn as a mule, but cute and lovable.

To this day *Kenkoy* remains the favorite comic creation in the Philippine Islands. Offshoots and imitations often try to duplicate the formula that made the series successful. A movie was made and many *Kenkoy* products emerged, such as comic books and T-shirts.

Despite the tremendous following of the feature, Tony Velasquez had to give up illustrating the escapades of the Kenkoy family due to his heavy commitment to other aspects of the medium. He was chief editor of several publications as well as the writer for other features and strips. The drawing chores were taken over by Celso Trinidad, who later illustrated the

series *Mga Kuwento Ni Kenkoy* ("The Stories of Kenkoy") for *Pinoy Komiks*. After all these years, *Kenkoy* is still going strong in the 1990s.

Tony Velasquez has received the full range of awards in the comic and publication fields. The Citizens Council for Mass Media paid tribute to his many contributions by awarding him the CCMM trophy, the highest honor in Philippine mass communications.

O.J.

KEN PARKER (Italy) Nicknamed "Long Rifle" for his habit of using an outdated muzzle-loading Kentucky rifle, this character is the most peculiar Western hero (better, antihero) made in Italy in a long time. Created by Giancarlo Berardi and drawn by Ivo Milazzo, *Ken Parker* was launched by Bonelli Publishing in 1977 through a series of black and white comics in book form. These enjoyed a sudden success.

In this series, the whole epos of the American frontier is revisited with modern sensibility and critical attitude according to the lesson derived from new and unconventional Western movies such as *Soldier Blue* (1970), *Little Big Man* (1970), and *Jeremiah Johnson* (1972). The genocide of the natives is not the only drama *Ken Parker* dealt with. Many other issues, such as racial prejudice, labor and social conflict, capital punishment, and emancipation of women, have been brought to the attention of the readers through captivating adventures.

Ken Parker has married an Indian woman, Tecumseh; adopted an Indian child, Theba; and roams the West earning a living through different activities: trap-

"Ken Parker," Ivo Milazzo and Giancarlo Berardi. © Edizione Cepim.

per, army scout, detective, actor, lumberjack, and eventually, novelist. For a long time, he was wanted for killing a policeman in self-defense during a strike, but he eventually was imprisoned and paid his debt to society.

The West where Ken wanders is declining and melancholy, and the strip shows how difficult it is to live in the wilderness when an industrial revolution is taking place. Ken lives from day to day, trying to fulfill his ideals with consistency. He is romantic, tenderhearted, and disenchanted, but he never gives up.

Berardi, born in 1949, has written several comic series and has created interesting characters for strips such as *Tiki* (1976), *Welcome to Springville* (1977), *Marvin il detective* (1983), and the graphic novel *L'uomo delle Filippine* ("The Man of the Philippines," 1980). All of these have been drawn by Milazzo, who was also the graphic creator of *Ken Parker*, although the strip has also been drawn by other artists, such as Calegari and Giorgio Trevisan.

The first *Ken Parker* series ended in 1984 with issue 59, but the hero's adventures continued in the comic magazines *Orient Express* and *Comic Art*, and from 1992 to 1996 in the *Ken Parker Magazine*. The old adventures now appear in the bimonthly *Ken Parker Magazine* and the new ones in the semiannual *Ken Parker Special*. Also worth mentioning is a *Ken Parker* graphic novel in four episodes, entitled *Il respiro e il sogno* ("The Breath and the Dream," 1984), with no text and completely based on pantomime. In 1995 Berardi was awarded a Yellow Kid.

G.C.C.

KENT, JACK (1920-1985) American artist and writer born in Burlington, Iowa, on March 10, 1920. John Wellington Kent grew up in various parts of the country, spending his formative years in Chicago and living in different parts of Texas, where he finally settled. He had no formal art training and dropped out of high school to practice commercial art locally. While still in his teens he sold magazine gags to *Collier's* and other publications.

Kent volunteered for service during World War II and saw action with the army in Alaska and the South Pacific; after his discharge he was a partner in a printing plant and worked at nearly every job in the factory. In 1950 his long-cherished dream of producing a comic strip was realized when the McClure Newspaper Syndicate bought *King Aroo*. It first appeared, daily and Sunday, in November 1950.

The strip, like *Krazy Kat*, appealed to a broad but select group of people; it was an "intellectual" strip. Contractual difficulties arose when Bell merged with McClure and the strip was terminated until the newly formed Golden Gate Syndicate of San Francisco took over distribution. In 1965, *King Aroo* died.

Fans of Jack Kent lost touch with him for a while—it was reported that he was driving trucks—but he soon resurfaced drawing greeting cards for Hallmark and others, writing and illustrating children's stories, drawing cartoons for markets from *Humpty Dumpty* magazine to the *Saturday Evening Post* to *Playboy*, and producing children's books.

The children's books brought Kent the acclaim and recognition that was denied him when he was a strip artist. His first, *Just Only John*, won the Chicago Graphics Award and sold over 400,000 copies. Other titles included *Nursery Tales* for Random House, *Mr.*

"Kerry Drake," Alfred Andriola. © Field Newspaper Syndicate.

Elephant's Birthday Party (a reworking of some *King Aroo* gags) for Houghton-Mifflin, and others for Parents Magazine Press, Putnam, McKay, and Golden Press.

Kent's drawing style was incredibly loose—a testament, perhaps, to his lack of formal training—full of broad, wiggly brush lines. In *Aroo*, his panels were freefloating and filled with rolling hills, flowers, and little stars studding the skies. As a writer, Kent produced some of the slickest nonsense in the funnies—literate, absurd, and gay. He died of leukemia on October 18, 1985, in San Antonio, Texas.

R.M.

KERRY DRAKE (U.S.) Fresh from having drawn two police strips in succession, *Charlie Chan* and *Dan Dunn*, Alfred Andriola again picked a detective as the hero of *Kerry Drake*, the new comic strip that he created for Publishers Syndicate on October 1, 1943.

Kerry Drake was a likable, earnest city detective whose adventures were closely related to daily life. Kerry was not a super-cop like Dick Tracy or an accomplished criminologist like Rip Kirby; he did his job with an honest dedication and a dogged determination that ultimately won the day. In the course of his investigations he was helped (and sometimes hampered) by his pretty wife, Mindy, to whom he remained unwaveringly faithful despite all the women (with such evocative names as Pussycat, Ermine, and Cricket) who constantly threw themselves at him. There was a great deal of documentation in *Kerry Drake*, and the atmosphere was suspenseful and violent. While *Kerry Drake*'s gallery of villains was not a match for *Dick Tracy*'s, it did contain some colorful characters like the sadistic Stiches and the warped Mr. Goliath.

Andriola's style on the strip was incisive, somewhat linear, and almost aseptically clean, and Kerry Drake became so popular that a comic book version was printed in the 1940s and '50s. Unfortunately, as time went on Andriola did less and less work on the feature, leaving it almost entirely in the hands of his assistants, and the writing was frequently ghosted by others (most notably Allen Saunders). *Kerry Drake* accordingly (and deservedly) declined in popularity; when the strip was discontinued in March 1983 following Andriola's death it was only being carried by a handful of newspapers.

M.H.

KETCHAM, HENRY KING (1920-   ) American cartoonist born March 14, 1920, in Seattle, Washing-

"Kevin the Bold," Kreigh Collins. © NEA Service.

ton. Hank Ketcham attended the University of Washington in 1938, but soon tired of formal studies and started a career in animation, first with Lantz Productions of Universal Studios (until 1940), then with Walt Disney Productions, where he worked on *Pinocchio*, *Fantasia*, and the Donald Duck shorts.

From 1941 to 1945 Ketcham served as chief photographic specialist with the United States Naval Reserve in Washington, D.C., where he created his first comic strip, *Half Hitch*, about a zany sailor, for a service newspaper. After his return to civilian life, he settled in Westport, Connecticut, and freelanced cartoons and illustrations for magazines and advertising agencies. In 1948 Ketcham moved to Carmel, California, where his most famous creation, *Dennis the Menace*, was conceived. The first daily panel was released by Hall Syndicate on March 12, 1951; its success was so immediate that it earned Ketcham the Billy DeBeck Award the following year. Ketcham devoted most of his professional life to *Dennis*, which he drew with an irreverent yet affectionate pen.

In 1960 the peripatetic Ketcham moved to Geneva, Switzerland. It was there that he decided to revive his old service comic strip *Half Hitch*; written by Ketcham and drawn by Dick Hodgins, the feature was distributed by King Features Syndicate from 1970 to 1975. Hank Ketcham also wrote a book, *I Wanna Go Home* (McGraw-Hill, 1959), based on his experiences during a tour of the Soviet Union.

Hank Ketcham is a facile cartoonist whose drawings and lines flow easily across the comic page. *Dennis the Menace* made him very wealthy, letting him indulge his hobbies: golf and travel. After the 1980s, however, Ketcham left most of the work to his assistants, Ron Ferdinand and Marcus Hamilton. He officially retired in October 1995 and the dailies are now done entirely by Hamilton under Ketcham's signature.

M.H.

KEVIN THE BOLD (U.S.) NEA's *Kevin the Bold* page, which began on October 1, 1950, was created by Kreigh Collins. *Kevin* was a spin-off from another Collins Sunday feature for NEA, *Mitzi McCoy*, which began November 7, 1948, and was used as a Christmas service feature for NEA in December 1949.

Kevin was an Irishman in the days of Henry VIII, a special agent for the king and a troubleshooter whose assignments took him around the globe. His sidekick was a big, strong Spaniard named Pedro who was married to a beauty named Maria. Kevin's young squire,

Brett, provided an outlet for more youthful adventures as Kevin dealt with big-boy troubles and (too infrequently) big-boy romance.

Kevin's adventures took him throughout Europe and into the New World. The strip featured much sailing flavor, a strong dose of history, and passable continuities that nonetheless conveyed a sense of adventure and some sea salt. *Kevin the Bold* was discontinued in 1972.

Collins's art in the 1950s was more exciting than his later work, with broad panoramas and some historical facsimiles. *Kevin* was an obvious answer to King Features's *Prince Valiant*, and, despite other shortcomings, Collins's Irish heroes managed to look Irish. *Kevin the Bold* had a companion piece, *Up Anchor;* this was also a tale of adventure, set on the seven seas.

R.M.

KEWPIES, THE (U.S.) Rose O'Neill's impish, curly-topped cupids, which she nicknamed Kewpies on their first appearance in print in the *Ladies' Home Journal* in 1905, were first corralled into newspaper page form on December 2, 1917. Copyrighted and distributed by the artist herself, the *Kewpies* page—not a comic strip—consisted of a weekly set of verses and drawings with individual titles, without balloons. These early *Kewpies* (unlike Palmer Cox's self-sustaining *Brownies*, on which they were partly based) were generally portrayed dancing and playing pranks around the children and old people to whom their attentions, amused and helpful, seemed to be centered. Some minor identity was given to certain Kewpies (a Wags, a Cook, and a Booky were prominent), but by and large these Kewpies were little more than a wildly tumbling array of small background figures. (O'Neill also distributed a daily *Kewpie* panel at this time; usually only one Kewpie appeared in a panel, along with a cheery slogan or motto.)

This first page and panel lasted barely a year; distress with the American losses in 1918 was said to have caused her to end the feature. Returning to magazine work, O'Neill did not undertake a newspaper feature again until 1935, when she decided once more to copyright and circulate a Sunday page—this time a true comic strip called *The Kewpies*. First appearing in Hearst papers across the country on February 3, 1935, the new strip introduced a jammed roster of characters immediately involved in a complex, continued narrative. Booky, the Information Kewp, survived the years from the first feature; with him were such new figures as Kewpidoodle, Uncle Hob Goblin, Johnny and Katy

Kewp, Frisky Freddie (a frog), Gus the Ghost, Squabby (a duck), and Scoodles Tourist (a human four year old touring Kewpieville). Aside from Scoodles, there were no humans around, and the Kewpies were the whole show.

O'Neill's lovely facility with comic images was the substance of the strip; her stories were often charming and amusing, but rarely more than that (she was not a Kelly or a Johnson), and it was the unfailing delight of her art, her eye into elfland, that sustained attention over weeks of practical jokes, pratfalls, and alarums among the Kewpies. The Hearst papers dropped *The Kewpies* in mid-1937, about the time Rose O'Neill retired from active social life in New York and withdrew to her Ozark Mountain estate to paint and write. No evidence of any continuation of the strip has been found in other papers of the period, and it must be assumed that she ended it at that time.

B.B.

"Keyhole Kate," Allan Morley. © Dandy.

KEYHOLE KATE (G.B.) Keyhole Kate was the first of her kind, an obsessive person whose obsession rebounded to make the reader laugh. She was also that rare species—a comic strip heroine. With her eagle beak, her horn-rimmed spectacles, her twin plaits, her gym-slip, and holes in the knees of her black stockings, Kate arrived complete with keyholes in the first issue of D. C. Thomson's first weekly comic, *Dandy*, on December 4, 1937. She remained in a six-panel strip during her whole career, save once when, perhaps through some editorial crisis, she made the front page in full color, replacing *Korky the Cat*. Every week Kate's snoopy obsession with keyholes proved no problem to her creator, Allan Morley. When forced by Uncle to read a book, she came back from the library with *Keyhole Topics* by O. Howie Peeps! When Cousin Cuthbert took a snap of her yawning, Kate's open mouth came out shaped like a keyhole! Morley's unique neat style never varied, and small oblong panels were his ideal format. He was particularly good with obsessed characters, and drew *Nosey Parker* in *Rover* and *Hungry Horace* in *Dandy* for many years.

Kate's last appearance in *Dandy*, playing a keyhole-shaped triangle, was on September 17, 1955. She returned on January 23, 1965, in number one of *Sparky*, all togged out in a new dress decorated with keyholes. Little else had changed, save the cartoonist. Between her revival and August 1974 when she retired

again, several hands drew the strip, including Drysdale and Brian White, but *Keyhole Kate* was never quite the same.

D.G.

KHALID, MOHAMED NOR (1951-) Mohamed Nor Khalid was born in Kota Baru, a *kampung* ("village") in northern Malaysia. His professional career began at age 13 when his cartoons were published in *Majallah Filem* and *Movie News*; while still in his teens, his first comic book, *Tiga Sekawan*, and regular comic strips saw print. One of these strips, *Si Mamat*, has appeared weekly in *Berita Minggu* for nearly 30 years. However, "Lat" (as he signs himself) was not placed in the art department of the *New Straits Times*, the top English-language daily, when he was hired after graduation; instead, he was made a crime reporter. The *Times* did not take note of his artistic talent until a regional magazine published one of his cartoons in 1974. That same year, Khalid was named editorial cartoonist of the *Times*, and his wildly popular *Scenes of Malaysian Life*, a one-panel depiction of the nation's multicultural society, has appeared on the editorial page since then, even after he left the paper in 1984 to become a freelancer.

Called the Chekhov of the Kampung, Lat often concentrates on the simplistic and humorous aspects of the rural life of his youth, and with more than a touch of nostalgia he laments its loss to the modern day. Because his images and messages are universal, Lat's cartoons have been reprinted widely and translated into other languages. In addition to compiling his strips into books that are issued annually, Lat has written and drawn four stories especially for the book market. His *Kampung Boy* (1979) has sold more than 100,000 copies.

Lat strongly denies any political motives, claiming he makes social commentary, not political cartoons. Yet his satirical works, benefitting from his eagle eye, sharp wit, and societal astuteness, have taken swipes at usually off-limit subjects such as the Malaysian establishment and Singapore's Lee Kuan Yew.

Few cartoonists anywhere have achieved the exposure and status of Lat. A movie, musical play, 13-part animation series, many commercials, all types of merchandise, and even a McDonald's "Kampung-burger" have sprung from his works. Respected by his colleagues, he was elected president of the Malaysian cartoonists association in the 1990s. His many achievements were crowned with the awarding of the Malaysian honorific "datuk" in 1994.

J.A.L.

KIBAŌ (Japan) Kibaō ("King Kiba"), adapted from Yukio Togawa's famous novel *Kibaō Monogatari*, was created by Kyūta Ishikawa for the weekly *Shōnen* magazine in April 1965.

Kiba was born of a male dog called Tetsu and a she-wolf named Devil in the rugged foothills of Daisetsuzan in Hokkaido. While still a cub he fell prey to Gon, the one-eyed bear, but was rescued by a party of hunters. Taken to the Hidaka ranch, the little wolf-dog was raised by Sanae, a young girl who taught him the ways of humans.

When Kiba was grown he was taken on a bear hunt, but his wild instincts returned and he ran away to the mountains. In time he became Kibaō, the King of Daisetsuzan, succeeding his mother, Devil. Hunted

SCENES OF MALAYSIAN LIFE   BY LAT

THE PAHANG GOVERNMENT will consider the idea of using rock music to frighten off wild elephants from plantations....

Mohamed Nor Khalid ("Lat"), "Scenes of Malaysian Life." © Lat.

down by trappers, Kibaō was finally captured and sent to zoos, but he managed to escape and eventually was reunited with Sanae. Happy days ensued but these were brutally interrupted when Sanae was clawed to death by Gon. Enraged by Sanae's death, Kibaō raised a pack of wolves and stray dogs and they hunted down Gon, whom Kibaō himself killed. Then the wolf-king left civilization forever and returned to the wild.

Ishikawa faithfully retained the flavor of the original novel. The top animal artist of Japan, he also adapted many of Ernest Thompson Seton and Yukio Togawa's animal novels, and he created a number of original animal strips. *Kibaō*, his most famous animal strip, ended in February 1966.

H.K.

KIDA, FRED (1920-   ) American comic book and comic strip artist born December 12, 1920, in Manhattan. After attending New York's Textile High School, Fred Kida broke into the comics as an inker and background artist in the Iger Studios in 1941. From there, he moved to Quality (*Phantom Clipper*, 1942-43), MLJ (pencilled *Hangman* strip that was inked by Bob Fuji, 1942), and finally landed at Hillman Publications in 1942. There he produced work on strips like *Iron Ace*, *Boy King*, and *Gunmaster*, but he did not attain much artistic acclaim until he moved over to the Hillman lead

feature, *Airboy*, in 1943. At first he only inked the pencils of Dan Barry—who he later assisted on the *Flash Gordon* newspaper strip in the 1960s—but Kida eventually assumed both the pencilling and inking.

Created by Charles Biro in late 1942, *Airboy* had quickly been relegated to a gimmick strip with most of the emphasis on Davy "Airboy" Nelson's magnificent flying machine, Birdie. But when Kida finally became the strip's artist, he completely reversed the direction of the feature. Whereas Airboy had been subordinate to his plane in earlier adventures, Kida made Davy Nelson a teenaged adventurer and soldier-of-fortune. Birdie was still there, to be sure, but it was for Airboy that people began buying the book. "In Kida's best stories," artist/historian Jim Steranko wrote, "Airboy became a kind of flying Pat Ryan—less a boy aviator in a man's world, more a youthful adventurer with a sophisticated veneer."

To achieve this effect, Kida used simple and tasteful drawings and an amazingly straightforward and direct page composition. His exciting action scenes—both on the ground and in aerial shots—were always busy and utilized an illustrative approach rather than a comic style. Additionally, Kida probably used more blacks in his stories than any other comic artist of the time, and his strips always appeared morose and suspenseful.

After finally leaving the *Airboy* feature in 1948, Kida began to split his time between Charles Biro's crime books and the Atlas line. At the Biro-edited Gleason line, the artist produced several dozen fine crime strips for *Crime Does Not Pay* before leaving in 1953. At Atlas, Kida concentrated on the sometimes-exceptional Western *Ringo Kid*, but also found time to draw some horror and war stories and some fine sword-and-sorcery stories for the Black Knight feature. He left Atlas and comic books in 1959 and his last comic art work was on the *Flash Gordon* daily strip.

J.B.

KIM SONG HWAN (1932-) Kim Song Hwan was born October 8, 1932, in Kaisong City (located in what is now North Korea). His fascination with art was evident from early childhood, when he covered the floors of his home with drawings. During his final year at Kyongbok Middle School in 1949, *Yonhap Shinmun* published his *Mongtongguri* ("Fool") in 15 issues, a long life span for a strip in those days. After graduation, he contributed to *Hwarang* magazine and worked as a reporter for the weekly *Cartoon News* magazine.

The conceptualization of *Old Kobau* ("High, Sturdy Rock"), which made Kim Song Hwan a household name for nearly half a century, occurred in 1950 as he was hiding to avoid conscription in the People's Army. In the beginning, *Kobau* was four to twelve humorous panels dealing with family life, but on December 30, 1950, *Kobau* gained a separate identity in a cartoon meant for soldiers of the Republic of Korea. The character was revived in 1954 in four-panel cartoons for the magazines *Huimang* and *Shinchonji*, and the following year it became a fixture in the daily *Dong-A Ilbo*, where it remained for 26 years before shifting to *Chosun Ilbo*. *Kobau* found its current home in *Munwha Ilbo* in October 1992.

Kim is recognized as a pioneer in Korean newspaper cartooning. He was the first to create an enduring four-panel strip and drew the earliest one-panel political cartoons. More importantly, however, he helped make strips and cartoons, which had previously been for children only, adult fare. Kim can take credit for teaching most major Korean cartoonists the elements of approach and presentation, and can take pride in making *Kobau* (and four-panel strips generally) the most read feature of dailies. (When it was published in *Chosun Ilbo*, the one-inch advertisement directly under *Kobau* was the most expensive space in the entire newspaper.) Through *Kobau*, Kim also fought against a series of authoritarian regimes, for which he suffered censorship, surveillance by the Korean Central Intelligence Agency, torture, and imprisonment.

Kim and *Kobau* have been given many honors. One of the most recent was the issuance of a sheet of postal stamps featuring the bald, bespectacled character.

J.A.L.

KIN-DER-KIDS, THE (U.S.) The famous painter and illustrator Lyonel Feininger created *The Kin-der-Kids* at the request of James Keeley of the *Chicago Tribune*. The title was suggested by Keeley (as an obvious takeoff on *The Katzenjammer Kids*) but the inspiration was all Feininger's. The Sunday page (signed "Your Uncle Feininger") started on April 29, 1906.

The Kin-der-Kids were a motley crew of enterprising youngsters made up of Daniel Webster, the precocious whiz-kid always flanked by his funereal-looking dachshund Sherlock Bones; Pie-Mouth, the ravenous ne'er-do-well; Strenuous Teddy, the group's athlete,

Kim Song Hwan, "Kobau." © Chosun Ilbo.

who could lift the most enormous weights; and Little Japansky, the "clockwork waterbaby" whom the little band had adopted as mascot.

To escape from the clutches of the sinister Aunt Jim-Jam and the hypocritical Cousin Gussie, the Kin-der-Kids embarked on a fantastic round-the-word odyssey aboard the family bathtub. Against a comic-opera background of pointed church steeples, vertiginous staircases, and cobbled meandering streets, the Kids met a host of picturesque characters: Mysterious Pete the outlaw; the sorrowful Mr. Pillsbury, the pill manu-

Frank King, "Gasoline Alley." © Chicago Tribune-New York News Syndicate.

facturer, and his five homely daughters; and Kind-Hearted Pat the Irish chimney sweep.

Aunt Jim-Jam and Cousin Gussie's pursuit, rich in ludicrous events, was not destined to reach a conclusion: following a contractual dispute with his publishers, Feininger abandoned the strip and it was left unfinished. The last page appeared on November 18, 1906.

M.H.

KING, FRANK O. (1883-1969) Frank O. King, whose *Gasoline Alley* family feature was faithfully read by half a nation for 50 years, was born into a middle-class family on June 11, 1883, in Cashton, Wisconsin. The family moved to nearby Tomah in Wisconsin's Kickapoo Hills (source of the name of Al Capp's Kickapoo Joy Juice in *Li'l Abner*) shortly thereafter, and King developed his early cartooning ability through grammar and high school, absorbing local color and family behavior that was reflected later in *Gasoline Alley*. He got his first cartooning job on the old *Minneapolis Times* in 1901 at 19, through the aid of a traveling salesman who saw a comic sign King drew for a Tomah bootblack and mentioned his skill to the *Times* editor. After working four years at the *Times*, King left to study for a year at the Chicago Academy of Fine Arts, then took a new job briefly with Hearst's *Chicago American*, switching later after some advertising agency work to Hearst's other Chicago paper, the *Examiner*. Here he did general cartooning and art work without arousing much attention for three years—except at the *Chicago Tribune*, which was then (1910) developing its own staff of comic strippers and cartoonists and liked the look of King's work. The *Tribune* hired King and put him to work in its Sunday comic supplement (the *Tribune* then had no daily strips) doing such quarter-page and half-page features as *Tough Teddy, The Boy Animal Trainer, Here Comes Motorcycle Mike!*, and *Hi Hopper* (a strip about a frog).

King's first real strip break came on January 31, 1915, when the first episode of his Sunday feature *Bobby Make-Believe* (spelled *Bobbie* in the first episode only) appeared in the *Tribune*. This feature was widely syndicated, and King's income improved considerably. His son, Robert Drew King, on whose behavior his famous Skeezix's childhood antics were largely based, was also born in 1915.

While turning out *Bobby Make-Believe*, King also drew another Sunday feature in black and white for the *Tribune* editorial section's front-page. Nameless as a whole, this page was divided into two half-pages. The upper half was always occupied by a large single panel containing a graphic observation of Chicago life in some form, called *The Rectangle*. The lower half-page was divided into a group of varying-sized panels featuring continued characters (Private Hoozus, etc.), and themes ("Our Movies," "Rubber Stamp," "Is This Your Little Pet Peeve," etc.). As a new addition to this lower group of panels, King introduced *Gasoline Alley* on November 24, 1918, in a panel titled: "Sunday Morning in Gasoline Alley," and subtitled: "Doc's Car Won't Start."

The new panel grew in popularity, and ultimately received more mail than *Bobby Make-Believe*. Accordingly, Joe Patterson of the *Tribune* started King on a daily version of *Gasoline Alley* in August 1919 (starting first in Patterson's *New York Daily News* and beginning in the *Tribune* almost immediately). *Bobby Make-Believe* folded in November 1919, and King's first color Sunday-page *Gasoline Alley* appeared on October 24, 1920.

By his late 30s King was already a wealthy man, and his prosperity increased with the spreading circulation of *Gasoline Alley*. (Essentially an American strip, King's family narrative had little publication outside of the U.S. and Canada.) The owner of two estates, one in Illinois and another in Florida, King spent what spare time the strip left him working at his hobbies: sculpting, collecting old maps, and raising amaryllis bulbs on his Florida property. He retired from the Sunday page in 1951, turning it over to a protege named Bill Perry, then began grooming an artist named Richard Moores to understudy him on the daily strip. Moving at last to the Florida estate near Lake Tohopekaliga at Winter Park, King, the gentlest and most domestic of strip cartoonists, died there of unreported causes at the age of 86 on June 24, 1969. Perry and Moores continued *Gasoline Alley*, which is still appearing today.

B.B.

KING AROO (U.S.) The McClure Newspaper Syndicate introduced *King Aroo* in November 1950 in daily and Sunday versions. The artist was Jack Kent, a high school dropout with no formal art training.

The 1950s was one of the periods in comic history when a new breed seemed to debut almost at once; at that particular time men like Mort Walker, Charles Schulz, Hank Ketcham, Bill Yates, and others entered the scene. Most were college graduates, had drawn for their school papers, and had slick styles. Kent was an exception. Self-taught and wildly individualistic, he quickly carved a niche for himself in comic history.

"King Aroo," Jack Kent. © McClure Syndicate.

King Aroo most certainly belongs in the uncrowded class of such creations as *Little Nemo, Krazy Kat, Barnaby, Pogo, Peanuts,* and *Calvin and Hobbes*: an "intellectual" strip not aimed at any particular age or readership group but cherished by cults in varied categories. Kent quickly created his own world where logic and illogic battled happily to irrelevant ends.

Some of the most literate and sophisticated nonsense in the funnies appeared in *King Aroo*. In one page, as the King learns of the earth's rapid revolution, the wind blows hard against him. A friend informs him that everything is proper, except that the earth revolves in the other direction, whereupon the gales blow from behind. Mixed in with every episode there was a heavy dose of joyful playing with literalism, puns, the consistencies and inconsistencies of the real world, and philosophical satire.

The cast starred King Aroo, a short monarch, the ruler of Myopia. He was an unassuming fellow, almost a child in grownup guise. Yupyop, his companion in a business suit, was the opposite: cynical and authoritative. The King may have had a fatherly image, but Yupyop proclaimed himself the "uncle-type." Professor Yorgle was the expert on everything; Mr. Pennipost was an early satire on the postal service—he was always late and has a coat with pockets like Harpo Marx's; and Wanda Witch, like the King, was the antithesis of everything her job description called for. She was very unwitchlike and none of her spells or tricks quite worked.

Kent freely admitted to inspiration by Herriman, whom he met. If the visual influence was slight, the spiritual bond was there. Kent's art was breezy, with the loosest of brush strokes and the suggestive but heavy indications of sparse backgrounds—hilly horizons, trees, bushes, and flowers—often bordering on surrealism, but the stylistic opposite of the mannered Sterrett.

The strip was carried with moderate success by McClure until it merged with Bell Syndicate. Contractual difficulties arose and Kent decided to surrender his contract. One client paper, however, refused to let the King abdicate; Stanleigh Arnold of the *San Francisco Chronicle* agreed to buy the strip as long as Kent would draw it. Encouraged by soundings from other local fans, Arnold eventually used an inheritance to found a small syndicate operation, Golden Gate Features, principally to distribute *King Aroo*.

Did insufficient promotion do *King Aroo* in? Each syndicate was noted for its very modest sales pushes.

Or was the strip destined to share the fate of most of its select counterparts? The appeal of the intellectual strip is almost always limited to small, albeit loyal, audiences. For whatever reason, *King Aroo* died in 1965. A book of collected strips was published in 1952, and several others were printed in the 1970s and '80s, after the strip's demise.

R.M.

KING OF THE ROYAL MOUNTED (U.S.) King of the Royal Mounted was created in February 1935 as a Sunday page for King Features Syndicate by the noted Western author Zane Grey (from one of his novels) and artist Allen Dean. In March 1936 a daily strip was added with drawings by Dean, who relinquished the Sunday strip to Charles Flanders. In April 1938 Flanders assumed the drawing of the Sunday page as well until April 1939, when Jim Gary took over the feature. *King* was discontinued in March 1954.

A Western with a different touch, *King* took place in Canada. The locale gave it a foreign quality that didn't have to be explained away as in *Red Ryder* or *The Lone Ranger*. At the same time its themes were easily recognizable and never strayed from the tried-and-true conventions of the genre. From the snow fields of the Yukon to the endless plains of Saskatchewan, Sergeant King, true Mountie that he was, always got his man. In his fights against fur thieves, cattle rustlers, smugglers, and assorted miscreants, he was helped by his loyal sidekick Pilot Laroux, his eternal sweetheart Betty Blake, and her brother, Kid.

King of the Royal Mounted does not rank as one of the best adventure strips but its qualities are simple and direct. It was a clean, fast-paced action strip with straightforward dialogue and characterization. The artists who worked on the strip were all good craftsmen (although Dean must be ranked above the other two). *King* was a fairly popular strip in the 1930s and 1940s, and it was made into a movie serial in 1942.

M.H.

KINOWA (Italy) In the jungle of Western comic books crowding the newsstands between the late 1940s and the early 1960s, there are few worthy of mention either for originality of story line or excellence of draftsmanship. Although it did not last long, *Kinowa* is among the features that are worthy. Written by the skilled scriptwriter Andrea Lavezzolo and drawn first by the group Essegesse (Sinchetto, Sartoris, and Guzzon), and later by Pietro Gamba, *Kinowa* appeared in the early months of 1950 as a monthly comic book.

The opening story did not seem to announce anything new; there was the usual Indian ambush of a wagon train, followed by the burning of farms by intoxicated savages, wild chases, and so on. Suddenly, however, a new element was added: an avenger completely different from the others, a being utterly fiendish and evil—or so it appeared to the terror-stricken Indians. Actually the demon was a human being, the long-bearded Sam Boyle, who, in order to wreak vengeance on the Indians who had scalped him when he was a youth, wore a demon mask made all the more terrifying by the light of a campfire or the shining of the moon. The easygoing Sam completely changed his personality once he donned the costume of Kinowa the avenger; he became cruel and ruthless, showing no pity for his fallen enemies.

Called the Spirit of Evil by his Indian foes, Sam was accompanied in his mission of vengeance by his son, even though he was born of an Indian mother. The adventures of Kinowa, which lasted only a few years, were very sophisticated and imaginative. The artwork of the Essegesse group—heavily inspired by Alex Raymond—was characterized by a sharp and firm line and a fine attention to detail.

G.B.

KIRBY, JACK (1917-1994) American comic book and comic strip artist, writer, and editor born in New York City on August 28, 1917. Perhaps the most accomplished of all comic book creators, he is recognized as the comic book king. Jack Kirby began his career in 1935 as an illustrator for Max Fleisher's animation studio, producing material for cartoons like *Betty Boop* and *Popeye*. He moved to Lincoln Newspaper Syndicate in 1936 and produced a horde of short-lived newspaper strips, including *Black Buccaneer*, *Socko the Seadog*, and *Abdul Jones*. Joining the Eisner-Iger comic shop briefly in 1939, he also produced work for Novelty's *Blue Bolt* and Fox's *Blue Beetle*; in 1941, he drew the first issue of *Captain Marvel Adventures*.

Kirby began his famed partnership with Joe Simon in 1941. Together they created *Captain America* for Timely that year. With this comic Kirby developed his artistic style and garnered the most fame. Instantly becoming an American idol, the Captain remains Kirby's most brilliant character. Kirby drew him like a superhuman, complete with a fluid and exaggerated anatomy, and Captain America soon became the country's morale-boosting anti-Nazi. Kirby invented the full-page and double-page comic spread here, and although he handled only 35 stories, his *Captain America* work during 1941 and 1942 is considered among the best ever produced.

Simon and Kirby moved to National in 1942 and produced four strips, including *Boy Commandos* and *Newsboy Legion*. These became the prototypes for all the "kid" comic books to follow. After a stint in the army, Kirby returned to comics and his partnership with Joe Simon in 1945. They immediately created three new titles for Harvey Comics, including *Boy's Ranch*, one of the few Kirby excursions into the Western genre. After originating *My Date*, their first romance comic book for Hillman in 1947, they produced a short-lived line of titles for Crestwood, and then created *Fighting American*, a parody of their own *Captain America*, for Headline in 1954. Simon and Kirby formed Mainline Comics in 1954, but the company folded and their five titles were sold to Charlton.

They dissolved their partnership in 1956, and Kirby began collaborating with Dick, Dave, and Wally Wood on the *Skymasters* newspaper feature in 1957. During this time, Kirby also found the opportunity to create *Challengers of the Unknown* for National (1958) and help ex-partner Simon launch *The Fly* and *Private Strong* for Archie.

Kirby returned permanently to comic books in 1959, joined the Marvel Comics Group, and teamed up with writer-editor Stan Lee. In 1961, they created *Fantastic Four*, a superhero strip Kirby used to further his artistic genius. When he began drawing *Thor* in *Journey Into Mystery* in 1962 and the revived *Captain America* in 1964, Kirby once again captured the comic book market. Kirby, Lee, and Marvel rose to the top of the industry and many claim they completely revamped the comic book world. A festering disagreement with Lee led Kirby to return to National as a writer/editor/ artist in 1970. He created nearly a dozen titles— including several interrelated books and two black- and-white comic magazines—but none were as aesthetically or as financially successful as his Marvel work had been.

Kirby went back to Marvel in the mid-1970s, working on such titles as *The Eternals* and *2001: A Space Odyssey* (both 1976) and turning out a few more Cap-

"King of the Royal Mounted," Allen Dean. © King Features Syndicate.

Jack Kirby, "Fantastic Four." © Marvel Comics.

Jack Kirby, "The Silver Surfer." © Marvel Comics.

tain America stories. In 1981-83 he drew *Captain Victory and the Galactic Rangers* and *Silver Star* for Pacific Comics. He briefly returned to DC in 1985 to work on *Super Powers*. His later years were darkened by his dispute with Marvel over the company's refusal to return his original artwork to him; thanks to fan pressure he finally received partial satisfaction. He died in Los Angeles in February 1994.

In his 50-year career, Jack Kirby produced every conceivable type of comic book work. Many of the field's most successful concepts are his creations and he has been responsible for more comic book sales than any other artist, writer, or editor. "Without him," artist-historian James Steranko said in 1970, "there may not have been comics to write about."

J.B.

KITAZAWA, RAKUTEN (1876-1955) Japanese cartoonist born 1876 in Omiya, Saitama. After learning Western-style painting at the art institute run by Yukihiko Ono, Rakuten Kitazawa joined the magazine *Box of Curios*, where he became influenced by the Australian cartoonist Frank A. Nankivel. Nankivel taught Kitazawa the art of political cartooning, and soon Kitazawa was working as a cartoonist for *Box of Curios*, the only Japanese cartoonist on the staff of the magazine. His talent was recognized by Yukichi Fukuzawa, a famous enlightenment thinker, founder of the Keio Gijuku university, and president of the Jiji Shinpou company. Soon Kitazawa was working for *Jiji Manga*,

the Sunday supplement of the daily *Jiji Shinpou*, where he generalized the term *manga* as meaning both cartoon and comic strip in Japanese.

In addition to his satirical, political, and social cartoons, Kitazawa also drew a number of comic strips, including *Togosaku to Mokubē no Tokyo Kenbutsu* ("The Tokyo Trip of Togosaku and Mokubē," 1901), *Haikara Kidoro no Shippai* ("Fancy Scenes at the Theater," 1901), and *Chame to Dekobo* ("The City Slicker and the Hayseed," 1905). Kitazawa's early comic strips were strongly influenced by the work of American cartoonists such as Outcault, Dirks, and Opper.

In 1905 Kitazawa started the first Japanese cartoon magazine, *Tokyo Puck* (the title was derived from the American *Puck* of which Nankivel was then a cartoonist). *Tokyo Puck*, at first a bimonthly, was soon changed into a weekly due to its enormous success. Kitazawa drew a great many humor and editorial cartoons for *Tokyo Puck* until his departure from the magazine in 1911. The next year he started the bimonthly *Rakuta Puck* (by then the word "Puck" had come to mean any kind of illustrated magazine), and in 1918 he founded the Manga Kourakukai, an association of Japanese cartoonists. In 1929 Kitazawa went on a long journey to America and Europe. In Paris he had a one-man show of his works and was awarded the French Legion of Honor. A complete edition of his works was started in Japan in October 1930, but was never brought to fruition (only seven books were published). After 32 years of working in the Jiji Shinpou Co., Kitazawa left in

1932 (his salary when he left was the highest paid in Japanese newspaper work).

After leaving the company, Kitazawa started his own school, where he taught a new generation of cartoonists and artists. In 1948 he retired to his native Omiya, where he led a peaceful and contented life until he died of a heart attack on August 25, 1955.

Rakuten Kitazawa was the pioneer of Japanese comic art. His greatest merit was the establishment of the modern comic strip in Japan. His influence on the succeeding generation of cartoonists has been tremendous (His disciples included Jihei Ogawa, Outen Shimokawa, Batten Nagasaki, Tetsuo Ogawa, and Tatsumi Nishigawa, to name but a few.) In commemoration of Rakuten Kitazawa's accomplishments, his native city of Omiya inaugurated the City Museum of Cartoon Art in 1966.

H.K.

KIT CARSON (Italy) Rino Albertarelli was the artist who transposed, in a very unconventional and personal fashion, the figure of the legendary frontier hero and guide for John Carles Fremont to the comic strip. *Kit Carson* was the first Italian Western strip, and its titular hero was not some young cowpuncher but a wizened old man, bald and heavily mustached, yet with a determination and an ability that could match those of any man 30 years younger.

Carson, the last representative of a dying era, offered his services and experience to the fight for justice and the redress of wrongs. As a kind of Don Quixote of the West, he had his Sancho Panza in the person of the lazy Uncle Pam, a very funny character who enlivened the strip with his shenanigans. Although old enough to draw a pension, Kit Carson never let his age interfere with his adventures, filled with chases, fights, duels, and challenges. His was an idealized figure, that of the old pioneer in a fast-disappearing frontier. Albertarelli drew his inspiration from a book by Truslow Adams, and his *Kit Carson* appeared in the pages of *Topolino* from July 15, 1937, until October 1938.

The sequel to the adventures of Kit Carson, written by Federico Pedrocchi and drawn by Walter Molino, was quite different. The Old West had vanished and Kit Carson moved his operations to Mexico, where he fought assorted outlaws and adventurers such as the despicable Carvajan or the power-mad Tuerto. In these later adventures, which appeared in the weekly *Paperino* from July 6, 1939, to August 15, 1940, he was aided by the mysterious "White Amazon," a female Zorro. At the end of the strip, Kit Carson was depicted as a very old man who would tell of his adventures to an audience of his grandchildren. (In the 1950s Gianluigi Bonelli added the character of Kit Carson to the *dramatis personae* of his *Tex Willer*.)

A classic of the Golden Age of Italian Comics, Rino Albertarelli's *Kit Carson* was reprinted in book form by Milano Libri. The episodes drawn by Molino were published in the deluxe anthology *Le Grandi Firme del Fumetto Italiano*.

G.B.

KITCHEN, DENIS (1946-) American underground comics artist, writer, editor, publisher, and entrepreneur born August 27, 1946, in Milwaukee, Wisconsin. A graduate of the University of Wisconsin at Milwaukee's School of Journalism, Kitchen says, "none, thank God," when asked about his art training.

Unlike many of his underground compatriots who sprung up as part of the alternative "comix" movement of the late 1960s, Kitchen never restricted himself strictly to the underground. He was one of the few who accepted commercial assignments, worked for "straight" magazines, and contributed to other usually taboo ventures.

Kitchen made his first appearance in an underground comic of 1969 which he wrote, drew, published, and distributed himself. Mainly a melange of sometimes-funny, sometimes-not vignettes about Milwaukee, *Mom's Homemade Comics* number one sold its complete run of 4,000 copies and was later reprinted by one of the then-existing underground publishers.

However, being a Milwaukee-based cartoonist, Kitchen found it impossible to deal with the flighty, often-incompetent San Francisco/Berkeley-based underground publishers, and he formed Kitchen Sink Enterprises in 1970. In the years since then, Kitchen Sink has published hundreds of titles, including *Bijou Funnies*, *Home Grown*, *Bizarre Sex*, and *Snarf*. Kitchen contributed to many of these with a simple, cartoony style. *The Crow*, another Kitchen comic, was very popular and two movies based on the comic were filmed in the 1990s. Kitchen Sink has also published reprints of classic comics such as *Li'l Abner* and *Alley Oop*. Kitchen's company produced 78 rpm records by underground cartoonist Robert Crumb, ran an underground comic syndicate which serviced the burgeoning underground newspaper market of the late '60s, operated a cartoon art studio, and produced a variety of underground-oriented novelties that were usually comic-related. In 1970, Kitchen helped found the *Milwaukee Bugle-American*, an underground newspaper for which Kitchen drew a strip in his now-familiar bigfoot style. The paper lasted for a couple of years.

When the alternate comix movement began to flounder in 1974, Kitchen made a deal with Cadence Industries—Marvel Comics''s conglomerate parent company—to edit *Comix Book*, which was ostensibly meant to be an underground comic book for audiences and general distribution. Despite Kitchen's best efforts, all three issues published were both financial and artistic disasters. Many of the top underground cartoonists

Denis Kitchen, "Ingrid the Bitch." © Kitchen Sink Enterprises.

refused to cooperate, citing their traditional reluctance to participate in straight ventures. Distribution was spotty and usually inept.

In the last 20 years Kitchen has devoted all his time to his publishing venture under the name Kitchen Sink Press. It has become one of the more important publishers of books in comic form.

J.B.

KLOTJOHAN (Sweden) Klotjohan was the name of one of those beings from northern mythology that never seem to fail to reach an enthusiastic public when they are handled by Scandinavian creators. The prefix "klot" in this particular troll's name means "ball," and it aptly described the little tyke's looks. Klotjohan's body was a round, black, furry ball. His unkempt head was a bit on the oval side, with a roundish nose and saucer eyes holding pupils as black as coal. For good measure this troll was endowed with comparatively large hands and feet and a tail that was almost twice as long as the little fellow stood tall.

This lovable little creature was a creation of Swedish cartoonist Torvald Gahlin, a staff member of the Swedish newspaper *Dagens Nyheter*. By means of his sharp wit Gahlin also became a radio personality. *Klotjohan*, for much of the strip's 36 years, appeared in *Dagens Nyheter*, after having been created for the weekly *Vårt Hem* ("Our Home") in 1935. Two years earlier, Gahlin had created another comic strip, *Fredrik*, well known and cherished for the "f" alliterations of the funny feature's star. *Fredrik* was started and remained loyal to *Göteborgs Handels-och Sjöfartstidning*. During the last three years of *Klotjohan's* existence, from 1968 to 1970 when Gahlin decided to end the feature, that strip appeared in a farmer's trade journal.

"Klotjohan," Torvald Gahlin. © Torvald Gahlin.

Torvald Gahlin, one of the pioneers of the Swedish comic strip, displayed an original cartoon style from the very start—unmistakable roundish noses and very thin arms and legs—in a conscious effort to have his work differ from the American comic imports then appearing in the weekly press of Sweden. While trying to be different, *Klotjohan* also was a parody on all kinds of children's strips, Klotjohan being a Chaplinesque troll constantly colliding with modern society. Gahlin was awarded the Adamson (the Swedish comics' Oscar) for both *Fredrik* and *Klotjohan* in 1970.

W.F.

KNERR, HAROLD H. (1882-1949) American cartoonist born September 4, 1882, in Bryn Mawr, Pennsylvania, into a family of German descent. During his Pennsylvania schooldays Harold H. Knerr enjoyed something of a "Katzenjammer Kid" boyhood, sliding down roofs, doctoring automobile engines, and playing pranks on his elders, before realizing his dream of becoming an amateur balloonist. "Then I spent my two years raising hell in a Philadelphia art school," confided Knerr in 1942. "My first newspaper work was drawing pictures of gravestones atop the oldest graves in a local cemetery for the *Philadelphia Record*."

Still in Philadelphia, Knerr went to work for the *Ledger*, where he drew an animal strip of uncertain merit, *Zoo-Illogical Snapshots*; in 1902 he joined the staff of the *Inquirer*, where he created no fewer than four kid strips. Two of these are noteworthy: *Scary William*, about a young daredevil not unlike the one he himself had been, and *The Flenheimer Kids*. *The Flenheimer Kids* (which starred two hellraising twins and a peglegged sea captain) was, in terms of quality of style and wit, several notches above the other *Katzenjammer Kids* imitations which were appearing at the same time, and when Hearst had to look for a new artist to continue the adventures of the Katzies he immediately selected Knerr.

From 1914 on Knerr's fame merged with that of the *Kids*. Knerr did create another strip in 1926, the tender and funny *Dinglehoofer und His Dog*, and in the early 1920s he illustrated a series of humorous articles, "This Dumb World," written by comics editor Bruno Lessing. Through all this the Katzies remained the object of his constant care. An innovator in his own right, Knerr brought to the strip a better organization but faithfully preserved its hectic pace and diabolical inventiveness. As critic Jim Walsh observed, "Certainly no one ever accomplished a more brilliant feat of continuing another man's original conception than did Knerr during the 36 years that he drew the *Katzenjammer Kids*."

Knerr also maintained the characters' inimitable speech, sprinkling it with tongue-in-cheek quotes from Shakespeare ("Lay on, MacStuff!"), the Bible ("Der Flesh iss veak!"), and fairy tales ("Vot do you see from der turret, sister Ann?").

Knerr, who was a shy, bald, bespectacled man, never married. His only passion—aside from cartooning—was flying private airplanes, which he continued to do despite the heart ailment which darkened the last years of his life and to which he finally succumbed. On July 8, 1949, Harold Knerr was found dead on the floor of his apartment in the Blackstone Hotel in New York City, leaving behind him the legacy of a comic genius on a par with that of Dirks, Opper, and McManus.

M.H.

KNIGHT, CLAYTON (1891-1969) American cartoonist, illustrator, and writer born 1891 in Rochester, New York. After graduating from the Chicago Art Institute, Clayton Knight enlisted in the Lafayette Escadrille, saw much action over France during World War I, and was once shot down and gravely wounded. After the war he resumed his career as an illustrator and writer, authoring many books and articles on aviation and air warfare, often in collaboration with his illustrator-wife, Katherine Sturges Knight. Clayton Knight's illustrations for *Collier's* drew the attention of the editors at King Features, who asked Knight to draw the illustrations for *Ace Drummond*, an aviation strip just created for them by World War I air ace Eddie Rickenbacker (1934).

Featuring the predictable team of youthful pilot-adventurer Ace Drummond and his grizzled, cynical mechanic Jerry, the strip was not too distinguished as it involved the two heroes in a series of disjointed adventures from China to South America. In spite of Knight's soaring depiction of flight scenes and limitless skies, which were his forte (he never bothered much with characterization or continuity), the strip never caught on and was dropped in the late 1930s (in 1936 a movie serial of *Ace Drummond* was produced by the team of Ford Beebe and Clifton Smith).

Somewhat longer-lasting was *Ace's* companion feature on Sundays, *The Hall of Fame of the Air*, which extolled the lives and times of aviators from all parts of the world (although after the start of World War II it restricted itself chiefly to the exploits of Allied pilots).

Soon after the outbreak of hostilities in Europe, Clayton Knight started the Clayton Knight Committee to help American pilots enlist in the Royal Canadian Air Force (for this work he received the Order of the British Empire). In 1942 he was one of the founding members of the Wings Club, and later was named official historian of the 8th, 11th, and 20th Air Forces. In this capacity he was present at the Japanese surrender ceremonies aboard the U.S.S. *Missouri* in 1945.

Clayton Knight is more famous as an illustrator and painter than as a cartoonist. His contributions to the literature of aviation are also considerable: *Hitch Your Wagon* (with Robert C. Durham, 1950), *The Story of Flight* (1951), *Lifeline in the Sky* (1957), and *Plane Crash* (1958).

During his lifetime Clayton Knight received more distinctions, civilian as well as military, than can be mentioned here. He died of a heart ailment in Danbury, Connecticut, on July 17, 1969.

M.H.

KOBAYASHI, KIYOCHIKA (1847-1915) A Japanese print and woodcut artist born August 1, 1847, in Tokyo, Kiyochika Kobayashi studied photography with Renjo Shimooka, and traditional Japanese printmaking with Gyōsai Kawanabe and Zeshin Shibata. Kobayashi's love for cartooning developed under the influence of Charles Wirgman, a correspondent for the *London Illustrated News* and the founder of the illustrated monthly *Japan Punch* in 1862, who taught him Western-style painting. Mixing photography, Japanese print techniques, and Western painting, Kobayashi developed his own distinctive style in a series of prints which he did from 1876 to 1881 called *Kōsenga*. These depicted scenes of Tokyo in the early days of the Meiji era.

From 1882 to 1893 Kobayashi created a great many historical prints. From 1894 to 1905 he devoted himself to war prints of the Sino-Japanese and the Russo-Japanese conflicts. He also worked as a cartoonist (again influenced by Charles Wirgman), creating many cartoon series for the satirical weekly *Maru Maruchinbun*: *Kiyochika Punch* (1881), *Shinban Sanju ni Mensō* (1882), *Hyakumensō* (1883), *Hyakusen Hyakushō* (1894-85), and *Kyoiku Iroha Tango* (1897), among others.

Kobayashi became a staff artist for the *Niirokushinpo* and contributed many cartoons. He also drew many illustrations for newspapers and magazines and founded his own art school, Kyochika Gajuku, in 1894. He influenced a number of cartoonists such as Yasuji Inoue and Beisaku Taguchi.

Kiyochika Kobayashi spent his later years in obscurity until his death on November 28, 1915.

H.K.

KOHLSAAT, ROLAND (1913-1978) German artist and writer born May 24, 1913, in Hamburg. The son of a merchant, Roland Kohlsaat attended public school and secondary school in Hamburg. At Kunstgewerbeschule Hamburg (the Hamburg College of Arts and Crafts) he studied under Professor Wohlers. After graduation he worked as a painter of portraits, horses, and landscapes. It was not until after World War II that he started working for the press, doing illustrations, cartoons, and comic strips.

His first comic strip was an adaptation of Erich Kästner's famous novel *Emil und die Detektive* ("Emil and the Detectives"). It appeared in *Funkwacht*, a weekly radio guide that, in time, transformed into *TV*, a weekly television guide. In the early 1960s he returned to *TV* for some time with two strips, *Plisch und Wisch* and *Tele Wischen* (pronounced television). *Tele Wischen* was very well received by the public but not by the new editor-in-chief of *TV*, which had merged with another television weekly. The discontinuation of the comic strip drew lots of reader protest, but it was then Roland Kohlsaat who refused to revive the feature after the new editor-in-chief begged him to do so. Kohlsaat did continue to write and draw *Plisch und Wisch* for *TV* for several years.

It was in 1953, however, that Kohlsaat created his most famous comic strip, *Jimmy das Gummipferd* ("Jimmy the Rubber Horse"). This strip began one night in 1953 when the editors of *stern* contacted him to develop a comic feature for their children's supplement *sternchen* by the next morning. About half an hour later, he had conceived the basis of a comic strip that would run for nearly 24 years. The feature was retitled *Julios abenteuerliche Reisen* ("Julio's Adventurous Voyages") in the late 1960s, and was discontinued in 1976 when Kohlsaat became incapacitated and could no longer continue working. The editors of *stern* felt the feature was so much Kohlsaat's brainchild that they discontinued the strip even though some basic ideas and outlines for a continuation may have existed.

While the feature lasted, Kohlsaat maintained a high-spirited story line, writing and drawing fantastic stories full of artistic verve. Kohlsaat also did a regular full page of gag cartoons for the weekly *Das Neue Blatt*. These cartoons usually featured some very curvaceous ladies. Kohlsaat's artwork was also known to help increase the sales of a number of books that he worked for as illustrator. Roland Kohlsaat died February 1, 1978.

W.F.

KOJIMA, GOSEKI (1928-   ) Japanese comic book artist born November 11, 1928, in Yokkaichi, Mie. After graduation from high school, Goseki Kojima (no relation to Koo Kojima) worked as a billboard painter. In 1950 he went to Tokyo in the hope of becoming an illustrator, but he worked instead as a *kamishibai* artist, creating short illustrated stories which he narrated himself to an audience of children.

In 1957 Kojima started to draw comic stories for a company specializing in producing comic books for rental libraries (these books were not sold on newsstands); his output was enormous. A few of his best or more popular works are: *Onmitsu Yūreijō* ("an illustrated story," 1957); *Yagyū Ningun* (1959); *Chōhen Dai Roman* (a series of adaptations from great novels and kabuki stories done from 1961 to 1967); and many ghost stories which were later published in magazines. In 1964 Kojima was voted the most popular artist in his field by the readers.

Starting in 1967 with *Doninki*, Kojima then worked for comic magazines, creating successively *Oboro Jūninchō* (1967), *Akai Kagebōshi* (a comic strip adaptation of Renzaburō Shibata's famous ninja novel, 1968), *Kozure Okami* ("A Wolf and His Cub," Kojima's most famous creation, 1970), *Guremono* ("Delinquent Youth," 1974), and many others.

With *Kozure Okami* (scripted by Kazuo Koike), Kojima became one of the most highly praised artists in Japan; he is regarded as the top *Jidaimono* artist (Jidaimono is a popular Japanese genre set in ancient times) along with Sanpei Shirato. After ending *Kozure Okami* in 1976, he went on to draw *Kawaite Soro, Tatamidori Kasajin, Hanzo Nomon,* and *Bonachi Bushido.* All of these were bloody tales of samurai warfare.

Goseki Kojima's graphic style is realistic and he can render his characters' most subtle emotions. His line, at first very delicate, became firmer with time. Kojima uses both pen and brush in his drawings, making for a warm and personal touch. He has influenced many comic book artists in Japan (Ryōchi Ikegami, Takami Nagayasu, Tsuyako Nishimura, Haruo Koyama, to name but a few). Regarded as the ideal comic strip artist for adult stories, Kojima has also done many illustrations for books and magazines. His sense of composition and his detailed draftsmanship have placed him in the forefront of Japanese artists.

H.K.

KOJIMA, KOO (1928-   ) Japanese cartoonist and illustrator born March 3, 1928, in Tokyo. Koo Kojima decided to become a cartoonist at age 15. He studied at the Kawabata School of Fine Arts and later at the Taiheiyo School of Fine Arts. Along with his fellow students Giichi Sekine, Kouji Nakajima, and Tatsuo Baba, Kojima organized the Dokuritsu Mangaha ("the unknown cartoonists' group") in 1947. At the start of his career Kojima produced many magazine cartoons, panels, and etchings, but his name became famous as a creator of adult comic strips such as *Sennin Buraku* (1956), *Miss Doron Ototo* (1957), and *Kuroneko Don* ("Don the Black Cat," 1958).

More adult comic strips followed, with an emphasis on melodrama, after his first venture into the humor strip in 1959 with *Chūsingura.* A simple listing will suffice to show Kojima's extraordinary creativity: *Oretacha Rival Da!* ("We are Rivals!," 1960); *Ahiruga Oka 77* (which inspired a series of Japanese television cartoons) in 1961; *Uchi no Yomehan* ("My Wife") and *Nih on no*

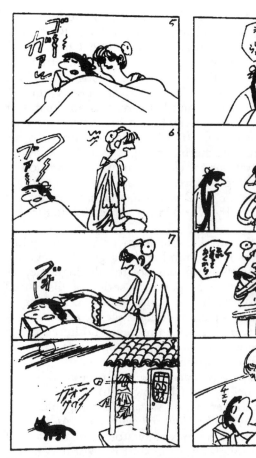

Koo Kojima, "Sennin Buraku." © Kojima.

Kaāchan ("Japanese Wives") in 1966; *My Name Is Natsuko* (1968); *Tama no Kashi Monagotari* (1969); *Oumaga Tsuji* (1971); *Ano Eka Kūn* (1975); and others.

Kojima has also drawn a great many cartoons, magazine and book illustrations, and covers. In this aspect of his work he is most noted for the more than 100 covers that he did for the weekly *Manga Sunday.* His stories since the late 1970s have been published mostly in *Big Comic Original,* a comics magazine that, according to Fred Schodt, "serializes many long-running, popular works by older and famous artists."

Kojima is famous for the beautiful and glamorous women whom he lovingly draws into all his work. His girls have large, dewy eyes, generous lips, thin and long noses, and sensuous bodies. If one word was to define Koo Kojima's art, it would be eroticism. His stories are as erotic as his girls are, and his line is very elegant and sinuous. As a matter of fact, when Kojima took over Kon Shimizu's *Kappa* after the latter's death in 1974, he turned this fantasy series into an erotic strip.

H.K.

KÖNIG, RALF (1960-   ) Ralf König was born in 1960 in Soest, Westphalia, where he grew up, attended school, and completed an apprenticeship as a carpenter. But working with wood was not exactly what he had in mind for a career. König may not have thought he would become an internationally known comic strip artist when his first comics were published when he was 19. These first comics were a creative way he could come to terms with being gay, and showed the humorous side of problems he was experiencing. Friends who read his work found it true to life and

Ralf Konig, "Muttersorgen" ("A Mother's Worries"). © Ralf Konig.

encouraged him to carry on—which he has, with success among both homosexual and heterosexual readers.

Ever since he first began writing and drawing comics, König's material was published either by gay magazines or by book publishers in either paperback editions or comic albums. While developing his simplistic style and realistic dialogue, König studied at the State Academy of Art in Düsseldorf from 1981 to 1986. In 1988 he received the first award for his comics work, the Joop Klepzeiker Prize, in Amsterdam. He was awarded a Best German Comic Artist at a comics salon in Grenoble in 1990 and won best German Comic Artist and Best International Comic Artist in Erlangen and in Barcelona, respectively, in 1992. In 1996 he was nominated for best international comic strip at the salon in Angoulême.

König is best known for his comic albums *Lysistrata*, *Der bewegte Mann* ("Man on the Move"), *Pretty Baby*, *Kondom des Grauens* ("Killer Condom"), *Beach Boys*, and *Bullenklöten* ("Cop's Balls"). In 1993 he started a series of albums titled *Konrad und Paul*, centered around the exploits of two young homosexuals, Conrad and Paul. Here, like in other books before, Konig no longer deals exclusively with gayness but with general themes, while the protagonists of his stories are obviously gay and live in a gay world. *Konrad und Paul* has a cast of supporting characters that had appeared off and on in earlier works.

König, because of the frankness of his language and of his caricatures, has also been fairly successful in raising the hackles of conservative critics. In fact, there have been efforts to ban some of his comics, like *Bullenklöten*, for reasons of obscenity and morality. However, these efforts have been unsuccessful so far. This in part may be due to the fact that König's readership does not only consist of gays. His stories contain some hilarious humor for both homosexuals and heterosexuals.

König is respected as an artist in addition to becoming a commercial success, with some of his works transformed into motion pictures. *Der bewegte Mann* hit the screen in 1994 and was so successful that, in 1995, it received the Golden Screen Award with an Asterisk, a German Motion Picture Industry prize for films that are box-office hits. With 6.5 million tickets sold, *Der bewegte Mann* was the most successful film of the year. The film version of *Kondom des Grauens*, however, did not live up to expectations. Arguably the film would have been better as a filmed version of the puppet play based on the original comic. The latest project is a 26-episode animated series of *Konrad und Paul* for television and for movie theaters.

Comics of Ralf König so far have been translated into 11 languages and have appeared in 17 countries. Total print run for his book editions is in excess of 5 million copies.

W.F.

KONING HOLLEWIJN (Netherlands) *Koning Hollewijn* ("King Hollewijn") is one of the many comic strips created by the very prolific and successful Marten Toonder, whose studio's comic strips and animated cartoons netted him the public's admiration and praise, and led to his title: the Dutch Walt Disney.

Koning Hollewijn was created in 1954 and was published as a daily strip in the newspaper *De Telegraaf/ Nieuws van de Dag*. With over 5,000 episodes under its

"Koning Hollewijn," Marten Toonder. © Marten Toonder.

belt, the strip started strongly commenting on Dutch politics in 1971. A number of the exploits of *Koning Hollewijn* were reprinted in book form. The strip ended in July 1972.

Koning Hollewijn's story concept was fairly unusual for a comic strip; the hero was a bald, white-bearded, bespectacled old King who was an introvert. Constantly busy at self-analysis, the good King lost all touch with reality while his court remained busy trying to get him to face "real life." His shapely secretary, Wiebeline Wip, a lively extrovert, usually succeeded in interesting him in the situation at hand and in making sure that her employer did not fall for any tricks. The pathetic hero and the sparkling heroine were the backbone of this Toonder strip that used humans (although in caricature) instead of the anthropomorphic animals of so many Toonder successes.

Given the large number of strips produced by the Toonder studios, it would be asking the impossible to expect all of them be done by Toonder. In fact, probably 80 percent of all of the Dutch comic artists got their start in or were associated with the Toonder studios at one time. Thus, *Koning Hollewijn* for some time was drawn by Ton Beek (a Dutch comic artist born August 18, 1926), who was with the studios from 1946 to 1959 before he moved to his own comic series, most notably *Birre Beer*, published in *Handelsblad* and first reprinted in album format in 1964. Beek has since been doing *Yogi Bear* and *Huckleberry Hound* comics that in Holland are leased by Geillustreerde Pers. Like so many others, Beek is proof that Toonder did not merely employ artists he felt could work in his style. After a period of learning, they could very well make it on their own if they so desired.

W.F.

KOTZKY, ALEX (1923-1996) American artist born September 11, 1923, in New York City. After a public school education, Kotzky attended the Art Students League on a scholarship in 1941. His intention was to become an illustrator and he studied under George Bridgman, the greatest of contemporary anatomy artists.

While an art student, Kotzky penciled for DC Comics (started August 1940) and drew backgrounds for Will Eisner's *Spirit* comics (starting November 1941).

After wartime service from September 1943 to February 1946, he returned to the comic book field, working on the *Plastic Man*, *Doll Man*, and *Black Hawk* titles for Quality from 1946 to 1951. In 1951, Kotzky joined the Johnstone and Cushing Agency, the foremost comic strip advertisers; he handled the Ford, Dodge, and other auto accounts. By 1954, Kotzky was freelancing and doing illustrations for medical magazines; he was also periodically ghosting *Steve Canyon*, *Juliet Jones*, and *Big Ben Bolt*, as well as drawing the Sunday advertising comic strip *Duke Handy* for Phillip Morris cigarettes.

In the late 1950s Harold Anderson, head of Publishers Syndicate, contacted Kotzky about a new strip idea submitted by Nick Dallis, author of *Rex Morgan* and *Judge Parker*. The strip that developed was *Apartment 3-G*, which debuted on May 8, 1961, and has remained a solid fixture of Publishers-Hall's battery of story strips.

Kotzky's art retained its basic slick realism with a strong infusion of lightness and humor. The artist claimed that the newsprint crunch of the 1970s actually worked to his advantage; because of space and format strictures, he was forced to concentrate on faces—bringing an emphasis to characterization. Kotzky's style was confident and comfortable but not outstanding, a perfect marriage with Dallis's respectable story line. After Dallis died in 1991, Kotzky took over the writing of the strip until his own death on September 26, 1996, in New York City.

R.M.

KOZURE OKAMI (Japan) *Kozure Okami* ("A Wolf and His Cub") was created by Kazuo Koike (script) and Gōseki Kojima (art) for the comic weekly *Manga Action*. It first appeared in August 1970.

Kozure Okami is a period strip set in the Edo era and features the adventures of Ittō Ogami, former high executioner of the realm, and his son, Daigorō. Ittō was the target of assassins hired by the powerful Yagyū family; he escaped assassination but his wife, Azami, was killed, and he vowed vengeance on the Yagyū clan. Giving up his life as a samurai, he and his son became paid assassins. Soon people were calling father and son the "wolf and his cub."

In the long saga that then unfolded Ittō and Daigorō, escaping ambushes and traps set by their enemies, succeeded in slaying Retsudō Yagyū's four sons and his daughter; Retsudō himself lost an eye in one of their encounters. In 1974 a new enemy came into the story: the ambitious and murderous Kaii Abe, who opposes both Yagyū and the Okamis.

Kozure Okami was a revenge story filled with violence and passion, but it also depicted with rough tenderness the relationship between father and son, stressing the family loyalties and ties which have become loosened in modern Japan. When reprinted in book form the strip became an instant best-seller (over five million copies sold) and inspired several motion pictures, a television series, and a number of records. It ended its long run in 1976 after more than 8,400 thrill-packed pages.

H.K.

KRAAIENHOVE (Netherlands) *Kraaienhove* ("Raven Manor"), a fascinating and intelligent combination of horror and adventure genres with wit and parody, was a creation of the very gifted Dutch comic artist Willy Lohmann. Lohmann, born May 7, 1936, in Zutphen,

"Kozure Okami," Gōseki Kojima. © Manga Action.

Netherlands, was only 24 when, in 1960 after a thorough education, he started the comic strip *Bazurka en Jampie Hoed* in the newspaper *Algemeen Dagblad*. Two years later he moved on to even greater things, creating *Kraaienhove*, which started in the newspaper *Het Parool* on December 21, 1962.

The stage was set in the first episode, entitled "Het eerste verhaal" ("The First Tale"). In it a vegetable dealer approaches an old manor that might have come straight from a horror movie set. The house gives him the shivers, as do its owners, Lucius and Grizelda. The exquisitely counterbalanced blacks and whites of the artwork create a moody atmosphere that befits a Gothic tale and seems to explain the vegetable dealer's (and all the neighbors') fears. At the same time the reader's mind is eased by a cartoony touch and by the presentation of Lucius and Grizelda as harmlessly eccentric, if surrounded by an air of mystery.

Lucius is perfectly impractical but superintelligent; his wife, Grizelda, is a parapsychological marvel. Lucius is the embodiment of the mad scientist, forever experimenting to find the explanation for everything. To him, knowledge is power, yet he would never dream of using this power for his gain. (Besides, the way some of his experiments turn out, there is not much to be gained by them anyway.) His counterpoint is magical, mystical Grizelda who more than once proves that ambition and intuition may be more powerful than science.

Kraaienhove has developed by leaps and bounds over the years, always staying true to its special flavor but going off more into the direction of detective mystery at one time or becoming more of a parody at another. The result, because of the strip's extraordinary graphics, is always pleasing. This has also led to the strip's

"Kraaienhove," Willy Lohmann. © Willy Lohmann.

"Krazy Kat," George Herriman. © King Features Syndicate.

"Krazy Kat," George Herriman. © King Features Syndicate.

being added to the lineup of features published in the Dutch comic weekly *Pep*, with stories done especially for that magazine and coloring perfectly blended in with the strip's mood.

W.F.

KRAZY KAT (U.S.) Universally acclaimed as the greatest comic strip, George Herriman's *Krazy Kat* began inauspiciously as a minor part of Herriman's first strip for the Hearst papers, the quasi-daily *Dingbat Family* which opened in the *New York Journal* on June 20, 1910.

As a kind of comic tailpiece to the human action in *The Family Upstairs* (which had become the *Dingbats'* new title as of August 1, 1910) Herriman involved the family animals (a cat and a bulldog) in a nether side-show at their feet: in effect, a separate little gag going on within the main strip. Later a mouse was introduced into the floor level drama and was shown sneaking in to sock the cat with a stone. The little animal byplay delighted the public and by August 17, 1910, the miniscule action had been encased in its own Lilliputian set of panels (at that date, the disgusted mouse first uses the disparaging term "Krazy Kat!"). Minus a title, this separate section of *The Family Upstairs* strip ran with the *Dingbat* saga until July 1, 1911, when the first wholly individual and titled cat-and-mouse strip appeared in the temporary absence of *The Family Upstairs*. Titled *Krazy Kat and Ignatz*, the new feature was reincorporated into *The Family Upstairs* on July 18, 1911, where it resumed its previous untitled run.

For two more years, the wonderful little cat and mouse vaudeville team remained locked into the *Dingbat* opus, until a general page widening in the Hearst evening papers permitted the addition of a vertical, page-high, six-panel strip beside the five horizontal strips already running. On October 28, 1913, the first episode of what was at last to be a continuing *Krazy Kat* strip appeared in this space in the *New York Journal*.

The separate *Krazy Kat*, even in its odd vertical format, was a considerable hit at the time, and Hearst was sufficiently impressed to start Herriman on a Sunday *Krazy Kat* page, the first of which appeared on April 23, 1916. It was in these early Sunday pages that Herriman's graphic and poetic fancy first flowered to their fullest, dazzling the handful of readers (including Hearst) who were able to grasp the wonderful things Herriman was doing in the visual and narrative arts: pulling apart backgrounds in every panel, fluidly shifting scenes to fit mood and dialogue, utilizing the stark, angular shapes of the great American deserts to offset the colorful grotesqueness of his animal characters and their Byzantine interplay. What had been simplistic vaudeville in the plain, bare daily strips of the 1910s turned to operatic grandeur of concept and execution in the Sunday pages.

Before long, Krazy, Ignatz, and their brick-plagued romance had reached and gripped the attention of intellectuals and artists, from John Alden Carpenter, who wrote a full-length ballet based on *Krazy Kat* in 1922, to Gilbert Seldes, otherwise an indifferent and crotchety critic of the popular arts, who was moved to virtually deify *Krazy Kat* in print in his watershed work of 1924, *The Seven Lively Arts*.

Delighted with the response of intelligent readers, Herriman and Hearst enlarged upon the sparse content of the daily strip in the early 1920s, and transformed it into the daily version of the Sunday extravaganza that it remained for the next two decades. It was then that the great Herriman cast of characters, already partly developed in the seminal Sunday pages, were fully rounded into their complex roles in the ceaseless flow of the *Krazy Kat* drama. Offisa Bull Pupp, at first a very infrequent figure in the daily *Kat* of the early 1910s (who might turn up as a mailman or a baker as well as a kop), hit his characteristic club-wielding stride in the initial Sunday pages, then his full imaginative integration into the *Kat* theme after 1921. Developing beside him were such perennials as Mrs. Kwakk-Wak, Joe Stork, Kolin Kelly (the brick baker), Don Kiyote, the Krazy Katbird and the Krazy Katfish, Ignatz's wife and kiddies ("Mizzuz Mice" and Milton, Marshall, and Irving), Sancho Pansy, Mock Duck, Bum Bill Bee, Walter Cephus Austridge, Dr. Y. Zowl, Mimi, Kiskidee Kuku, Mr. Meeyowl and his son Gatita, and many, many, more.

It is part of the record, however, that the strip made no money for the syndicate after the 1920s, and that its continued appearance was due to Herriman's lifetime contract and Hearst's personal affection for *Krazy Kat*. It was folded on Herriman's death in 1944 quite simply because there was no profit left in it.

It is understandable in this context why only one minor publisher risked a book based on *Krazy Kat* during Herriman's lifetime (Saalfield, *Krazy Kat and Ignatz*, 1934), and why only two book collections of the strip (Henry Holt's *Krazy Kat* of 1946, and Nostalgia Press/Grosset & Dunlap's *Krazy Kat* of 1969) appeared after his death; together with a Herriman-illustrated pamphlet edition of the Carpenter ballet score, they constitute the only referential record of this major strip. (There were a number of animated cartoons based on the *Krazy Kat* strip; the first and best were the Herriman-supervised Hearst-Vitaphone releases of 1916-17; those which followed from other studios are only related to the Herriman work by the borrowed title.)

B.B.

KRESSE, HANS G. (1921-1992) Hans G. Kresse was a Dutch comic artist and writer, born December 3, 1921, in Amsterdam. Self-educated in art, Kresse's first comic strip was published in *De Verkenner*, the monthly magazine of the Dutch scouts, when he was 17. The strip was *Tarzan van de apen* ("Tarzan of the Apes") with obvious Hal Foster influences. Like Foster's first *Tarzan*, Kresse put the text below his comic strips in many cases. Also for *De Verkenner*, Kresse did *De Avonturen van Tom Texan* ("Adventures of Tom Texan") from 1940 to 1941. At the age of 23, he was one of the first artists to join the Marten Toonder studios. While there, he did strips like *Per Atoomraket naar Mars* ("To Mars by Atomic Rocket") and, for the newspaper *Trouw*, the daily strip *Robby Robijn* (1945-46). The Toonder influence on Kresse's work started showing strongly in *Robby Robijn*.

In 1946 the first episode of *Eric de Noorman* ("Eric the Norseman") was published in the Netherlands. In both plot and art it showed strong Toonder influences, the first adventure being a compromise between a Toonder suggestion of Atlantean science fiction combined with Kresse's concept of a historic hero. The series reached its climax around 1952 in the "Sword of Tyrfing" cycle, and continued in more routine fashion until 1964 in a number of newspapers and book reprints. In 1951, the

Hans G. Kresse, "Eric de Noorman." © Kresse.

Flemish newspaper *Het Laatste Nieuws* included the strip in its pages and started the weekly magazine *Pum Pum* (named after a character of the *Eric* strip). The first page of the magazine featured a serialized novel with large-sized illustrations of Eric's youth.

In addition to *Eric*, Kresse also created *Matho Tonga*, a Western for *De Kjeine Zondagsvriend* that was later continued in *Pep*, the Dutch weekly comics magazine founded in 1962. After withdrawing from comics for some time, Kresse returned to the medium with *Zorro* (1964), *Vidocq* (1965), and *Erwin* ("Son of Eric," 1966), all published in *Pep*. In 1972 Kresse started a historic series about North American Indians in the time of the Spanish invaders.

Despite his own inclinations as a writer, Kresse had to introduce speech balloons into his artwork in the 1960s. The addition of color to his artwork lent a new dimension to his already superb handling of black and white effects.

Kresse died March 12, 1992. As his health had been failing for some time and he wanted some control over who continued his prestigious series on the Native Americans, he had a clause added to his contract with the publisher that, if the series was to be continued after his death, the artwork should be handled by Dick Matena.

W.F.

KRIGSTEIN, BERNARD (1919-1990) American comic book artist born March 22, 1919, in Brooklyn, New York. Primarily a painter and illustrator, Bernie Krigstein entered the comic book field to earn extra money for his family before serving in the army during World War II. Most of his prewar work was uninspired superhero material for MLJ. After he returned from the war, however, Krigstein's interest in the field as an art form increased and he had short stints with Novelty (1947, on the *Bull's Eye Bill* Western strip), Fawcett (1948, on the Western *Golden Arrow* and jungle *Nyoka* features), and several other groups (Pines, National,

Hillman) before landing with Atlas in 1950. He was used there mainly on crime, horror, and science fiction stories. They were all second- and third-rate stories, but editor Stan Lee gave Krigstein considerable artistic freedom and he used these tales to experiment with the makeup and panel breakdown of the comic book page. And although some of the material was interesting, little of it matched the material he began producing for E.C. in 1953.

Krigstein joined E.C. in the last years of its vaunted "New Trend" and was one of the final arrivals in a stable that already included talents like Kurtzman, Davis, Crandall, Ingels, and others. But Krigstein was undoubtedly the most artistically talented—and the hardest to handle from the conformity standpoint. He was interested in expanding the formats of the comic page, and he used the three dozen or so stories he produced for E.C. to accomplish that goal, much to the chagrin of editors Bill Gaines and Al Feldstein. Whereas Feldstein wrote stories to fit E.C.'s relatively standard seven-panel page, Krigstein constantly altered the page layouts to suit his purposes. The captions that Feldstein wrote to explain what he visualized as one large panel were more often than not chopped up and spread across several of Krigstein's smaller ones. Krigstein was redesigning the comic book page along his own lines, and in the process produced some of the most powerful, innovative, and sophisticated storytelling techniques ever seen in comic books. His best known story is undoubtedly *Master Race*, and its 1955 appearance in *Impact* made it perhaps the most advanced graphic

Bernard Krigstein, "The Flying Machine." © William M. Gaines, Agent, Inc.

story of its time. The story was eventually reprinted in Nostalgia Press's 1971 *E.C. Horror Library*.

E.C.'s color books folded in early 1956, and after contributing material to the short-lived Picto-Fiction series and more stories for Atlas, Krigstein turned to commercial illustration. He eventually devoted his career to painting, concentrating primarily in oils, watercolors, and pastels, and became an accomplished painter with several awards and many one-man and group shows to his credit. He died on January 8, 1990, at his upstate New York home.

J.B.

"Kriminal," Luciano Secchi and Roberto Raviola. © Editoriale Corno.

KRIMINAL (Italy) The first comic book to feature an antihero as protagonist in the wake of *Diabolik*'s success, *Kriminal* appeared for the first time in August 1964.

Kriminal, who was dubbed the King of Crime, was a character of unusual cruelty and wickedness. The very first issue introduced very strong elements of sex and sadism, and this raised an immediate outcry from a number of civil groups, which denounced *Kriminal* as an "immoral publication." There began a long series of lawsuits and seizures that by then involved many other titles from different publishers attracted by the lucrative market for sex-cum-violence comic books. Finally the publisher of *Kriminal*, Andrea Corno of Editoriale Corno, became tired of the controversy and threw in the towel, radically altering the personality of the antihero. To put it succinctly, *Kriminal* became in short order the ex-King of Crime and switched from his antisocial status into the position of occasional defender of the law. The period of his fights with his nemesis, Commissioner Milton, of his surrealistic car flights, of his pitiless and senseless killings, was definitively over.

Married now, *Kriminal* became a suave gentleman-burglar in the tradition of Arsène Lupin, and his adventures, in the company of his trusted Oriental assistant Shan-Ton, had toned down considerably. One of the most famous creations of the *fumetto nero* ("black comic strip"), *Kriminal* was first published as a monthly, then as a fortnightly, and finally as a weekly (the only one of its kind). *Kriminal* was the product of a smooth-working team signing "Magnus and Bunker" (in actuality Luciano Secchi and Roberto Raviola) who gave *Kriminal* an unsurpassed excellence of themes, mingling social and political satire with the killings, and an undeniable graphic quality. Unfortunately, the feature passed into the inept hands of mindless scriptwriters and mediocre draftsmen and the comic book finally folded after nearly 400 issues in 1973.

G.B.

KRÜGER, HANS MARTIN (192?-198?) Hans Martin Krüger (*nom de plume* Hans Martin) was born in the Sachsen-Anhalt region in the 1920s (the exact date of his birth is not known, at the artist's insistence). He grew up in the Harz mountain region in the 1930s and developed a love for drawing cartoons in school. Nevertheless, he decided to study natural science but in the 1940s he was handed a rifle and sent to war. Several shell splinter wounds and years as a prisoner of war changed his outlook on life. He had to work in the dismantling program, then worked on farms and as a gardener, and finally as a dramatic adviser.

He started a self-education program in order to develop his earlier penchant towards drawing, aiming towards the styles of Uderzo and Mordillo. In 1956 he started getting regular work from the cartoon pages of *TV-Fernsehwod* and *Neue Post*. In 1960 he drew his first comic strips for *Bild und Funk*, a radio and TV weekly. This strip starred Mufti, a toy donkey, and his friends in fairy tale adventures written by Karl-Heinz Barth. The series ended in 1968 despite the fact that 80 percent of children and 50 percent of adults regularly read the stories. Also with Karl-Heinz Barth as writer, Krüger drew comics for *Wochenend* for several years. These were adaptations of fairy tales like "Ali Baba."

In 1969, Krüger began drawing comic strips for *Hör Zu*, another radio and TV weekly. The first of these was *Jak-ki und Paff*, the fantastic story of a little boy and his rotund friend, the flying dragon Paff. The story was written by Jörg Ritter. This was followed up by the more substantial adventures of *Die Unbesiegbaren* ("The Invincibles"). This comic strip dealt with the adventures and misadventures of medieval knights in a completely humorous vein. The first two stories were reprinted in book form, and three records based on the comic strip were released. In 1975 the strip was revived, after a change in editorial policy had almost crowded comics out of *Hör Zu*. However, trouble developed over who actually owned the series, so it was axed again and not revived. Krüger died in the 1980s, with the date of his death as uncertain as he had wanted the date of his birth to be.

W.F.

KUBERT, JOE (1926-   ) American comic book and comic strip writer, artist, and editor born in Brooklyn, New York, during 1926. Kubert broke into the comic book business while still a student at New York's High School of Music and Art; in 1939, according to the artist, Harry "A" Chesler took him into his comic book shop at five dollars a week. Kubert says Chesler told him, "I can't use your work, but you show some talent. How about coming up here after school every day for a couple of hours. Just sit up here and draw. I'll have the other guys come and kind of critique your stuff."

After that unorthodox initiation, Kubert eventually began to publish work with the Holyoke group in

1942, drawing adventure strips like *Volton*, *Flag-Man* and several others. Also during the 1940s, Kubert drew for many other groups: at MLJ (1942-43), he drew *Boy Buddies* and *Black Witch*; at Quality (1942-43), he drew *Phantom Lady* and *Espionage*; at National (1943-49), he worked on many strips, including *Johnny Quick*, *Zatara*, *Newsboy Legion*, *Hawkman*, *Dr. Fate*, and *Flash*; and he also worked sporadically for Timely, Avon, Harvey, Fiction House, and others.

Artistically, Kubert's early work was crude but promising. Influenced mainly by Hal Foster and Alex Raymond, and later by comic book artist Mort Meskin, Kubert began to develop into a highly stylized craftsman, his work always utilizing stark blacks, heavy shading, and dynamic design and composition. His figures were not always anatomically correct, but they were fine studies of figures in action.

Perhaps Kubert's finest work came during the 1950-55 period when he was an editor at the St. Johns group on a short-lived prehistoric strip called *Tor*. The group's enterprising publisher, Archer St. John, allowed artists to package the complete book, so Kubert was given the opportunity to own, write, edit, draw, letter, ink, and color the *Tor* feature. Over its short-lived run, *Tor* carried much of Kubert's most brilliant drawings and most inventive stories. The strip became a comic book legend, so much so that National eventually allowed Kubert to revive the feature in 1975.

After the productive St. John period, Kubert continued to freelance, but most of his work was for National. He began to concentrate on war strips, and he and writer Bob Kanigher collaborated on two fine war features, *Sgt. Rock* and *Enemy Ace*. In particular, *Enemy Ace* was outstanding; a strip which took the

Joe Kubert, "Tarzan." © Edgar Rice Burroughs, Inc.

enemy point of view—in the form of World War I flying ace Baron Von Richthofen—the feature became a showcase for fine aerial artwork, sensitive and humanistic characterizations, and Kubert's consistently interesting layouts and page compositions. But throughout the 1950s and 1960s, Kubert also worked on other strips, most notably the excellent *Viking Prince* sword-and-sorcery strip, the revived *Hawkman*, and several others.

During 1966 and 1967, Kubert left comic books and drew the *Green Berets* syndicated newspaper strip for the Chicago Tribune-New York News Syndicate. Although it was an interestingly drawn feature, it was done during a time of increasing hostility towards war features, and Kubert returned to National as an editor in late 1967. He handled many features but the most notable was the National renditions of *Tarzan*. His work on the strip during the 1970s has garnered considerable acclaim for its "classic interpretation."

Since 1976 Kubert has devoted most of his time to the School of Cartoon and Graphic Art that he founded in Dover, New Jersey. The school has turned out such talent as Rick Veitch, Steve Bissette, Tom Yeates, and Timothy Truman. He has kept his hands at comics and illustration at the same time, briefly drawing the *Winnie Winkle* newspaper strip in the 1980s and contributing illustrations and covers to many comic books. In 1996 he published *Fax from Sarajevo*, a harrowing account of the civil war in Bosnia.

J.B.

KUDZU (U.S.) Doug Marlette used his southern roots and his years as a prizewinning editorial cartoonist for the *Atlanta Constitution*, the largest newspaper in Georgia, to shape the world of *Kudzu*, about a skinny young man with aspirations of being a writer and a desperate need to leave his tiny rural hometown of Bypass, North Carolina.

Kudzu began syndication on June 15, 1981. Some 16 years later, he's still stuck in Bypass working for a beer-bellied, redneck good ol' boy, Uncle Dub, at the family garage. It's Kudzu's desire to move to New York City and write for the *New Yorker*. (Marlette himself moved to New York to become editorial cartoonist for *Newsday*, Long Island's largest newspaper.)

In addition to good writing and art, Marlette's terrific cast of characters keeps *Kudzu* consistently funny. Over the years, the fundamentalist evangelist Rev. Will B. Dunn has come to rival Kudzu as the leading character of the strip. Rev. Dunn is the wildest preacher in comics since *Li'l Abner*'s Marryin' Sam. Dressed all in black, a homage of sorts to country singer Johnny Cash's man-in-black image, he's as interested in becoming a powerful televangelist as he is in saving souls. The good reverend has a passion for watching soap operas (no doubt to see sin in action so he can recognize it) and winning the church league basketball trophy. One is left with the impression Rev. Dunn has often bet the collection plate offering on the game. He is one of the funniest rogues in all comics.

Rev. Will B. Dunn, more than the other characters, allows Marlette to use his editorial cartoonist skills in *Kudzu*, which varies from gag-a-day to short continuity format. In one daily he's shown interviewing spiritualist Bhagwan Hasheesh (a name Al Capp of *Li'l Abner* fame would have been proud of) about his message. After learning the message is just "have a nice day," Rev. Dunn proclaims it dumb. Bhagwan Hasheesh asks him if he owns a fleet of Rolls Royces, and Dunn ends the strip saying, "Have a nice day!"

Still, Kudzu himself is the heart of the strip. He's surrounded by traditional Southern "steel magnolia" women. His manipulative mother blackmails him emotionally to keep him in Bypass. The love of his life, blonde cheerleader-goddess Veranda, knows he exists but rarely admits it in public. For Veranda, watching the Miss America beauty pageant on television takes on religious significance. She and her talking mirror both know she has the potential to cause even the President of the United States a "major bimbo eruption." Kudzu's intellectual soulmates are Doris, his mute pet parrot whose thought balloons tell volumes, and Maurice, an African-American man his age who shares many of his interests but is much more realistic about life.

The strip can swing from Kudzu being introspective in a quietly humorous way to Rev. Will B. Dunn having a manic hellfire-and-brimstone conflagration of out-of-control riotous humor.

B.C.

KUHN, PIETER JOSEPH (1910-1966) Pieter Joseph Kuhn, a Dutch writer, comic artist, and graphic artist born May 22, 1910, joins Marten Toonder and Hans G. Kresse as one of the three biggest names in Dutch comics. Kuhn received art schooling at the Kunstnijverheidschool "Quellinus," which was followed by a course in lithography with the Senefelder printing office. He received his lithographer's diploma in 1929 and applied his artistic talent to advertising drawing. During World War II he created *Kapitein Rob* ("Captain Rob"), a daily adventure strip with running narrative below the pictures that first appeared in the newspaper *Het Parool* on December 11, 1945. *Kapitein Rob* lived through 72 adventures in *Het Parool* before the series suddenly ended when Kuhn died on January 20, 1966. The story "Rendezvous in Jamaica" was never completed in *Het Parool*. The Dutch fanzine *stripschrift* reprinted the last episode up to its untimely end, some 60 episodes beyond the last one appearing in *Het Parool*. Quite apparently, Kuhn had worked two months ahead of publication.

The first story, "De Avonturen van het zeilschip de Vrijheid" ("The Adventures of the Sailing Vessel *Freedom*"), was written and drawn by Kuhn as "a tale for boys, based on reality, in order to enlarge their maritime, geographic, and general knowledge." However, the first adventure's texts fell short of Kuhn's own expectations. Therefore, he started a cooperation with Dutch journalist Evert Werkman, who wrote most of the exploits of Captain Robert van Stoerum.

Kuhn, a sailing enthusiast, identified with his character, who sailed around the world in search of adventure. Whenever possible, Kuhn visited the places his hero was to visit. If traveling was out of the question, Kuhn pursued extensive research so his facts would be correct. Thus the strip had an overall realism that was responsible for the success of *Kapitein Rob*. With the addition of Professor Lupardi, the inevitable mad scientist, the comic strip took a turn toward science fiction.

Practically all of the captain's adventures were reprinted in book form. Foreign editions were published in England, Finland, Denmark, Germany, France, Italy, Spain, Poland, Brazil, and other countries. Some of these editions used speech balloons instead of the narrative below the strip.

W.F.

KULAFU (Philippines) One of the very first Filipino artists to illustrate *Tarzan* was Johnny Perez. His work appeared in *Bannawag*, a periodical written in Ilokano, in 1934. Appearing in the same publication was another jungle hero called *Kulafu*, the Filipino Tarzan, and it was drawn by Francisco Reyes (the elder).

The works of Rudyard Kipling and Edgar Rice Burroughs, as well as the myths and legends of feral children, have influenced many variations of the jungle hero theme. In 1934, Francisco V. Coching drew *Marabini*, the jungle girl, for *Liwayway*. During the late 1940s and the early 1950s he wrote and illustrated the *Tarzan*-inspired jungle strip, *Hagibis*, which also appeared in *Liwayway*. For *Pilipino Komiks* he created *Dumagit* in 1953.

Nestor Redondo, whose *Tarzan* illustrations have been published by various American publications, drew *Diwani* in the 1950s. It is considered by many to be the most beautifully rendered jungle novel to appear in comic books, rivaled only by *Rima*, which was also done by Redondo for DC Comics (U.S.). In 1963 he teamed up with Mars Ravelo to do *Devlin* for *Redondo Komix*. He also did *Tani*, which was later drawn by Vic Catan.

Larry Alcala did a hilarious strip containing *Tarzan*, and Alfredo Alcala did a satire on *Tarzan* for his humorous feature *00 Ongoy*, about a simian private eye. One of the most popular of the *Tarzan*-type strip heroes was *Og*. The strip was drawn by Jess Ramos and was eventually made into a movie starring Jesus Ramos.

On October 21, 1971, the weekly comic book *Nora Aunor Superstar* serialized *Tarzan and the Brown Prince*. It was illustrated by Franc Reyes (the younger). It ran consecutively for 16 chapters until February 14, 1972. This feature was made into a movie starring Steve Hawkes as Tarzan and Robin Aristorenas as the Brown Prince. Later on, Franc Reyes illustrated *Tarzan of the Apes* for National (U.S.).

The first artist in the Philippines to work on the syndicated Sunday *Tarzan* feature was Alex Niño. He also drew *Korak, The Son of Tarzan* for DC (U.S.). But before working on any American jungle strips, he illustrated, in the various *Tagalog Komiks*, many jungle series such as *Sargon*, *Tsannga Rannga*, *Gruaga*, and *Mga Ma tang Naglilivab* ("The Eyes That Glow"). Niño stopped doing *Korak* when he left the Philippines to visit the United States, and the strip was turned over to the capable Rudy Florese.

Virgilio Redondo contributed to the long list of tree-swingers by writing and illustrating the exciting jungle adventure *Buntala*. This was drawn in a format reminiscent of Hal Foster's *Tarzan*. Elpidio Torres visualized the stirring experiences and the romantic escapades of *Robina*, the jungle maiden.

Other artists who have drawn *Tarzan* for various publications are Jesse Santos, Frank Magsino, Edna Jundis, Pit Capili, Seg Belale, and Danny Bulanadi. The following individuals have illustrated *Tarzan*-type characters for foreign publications—Steve Gan, Sonny Trinidad, Tony Zuñiga, and Noly Zamora.

O.J.

KUMA (Germany) *Kuma* was Germany's very own jungle boy strip in the time-honored Kipling vein. It might very well be argued that *Kuma* was a Spanish strip as the artwork was done by Spanish artist Rafael Mendez. However, as the comic series was produced originally for a German readership, just as many American comic books are now produced in Spain or in the Philippines, Kuma definitely was a German comic strip.

When, in April 1971, the comic book *prima* (soon retitled *primo*) was started, it contained funnies and reprints of the *Prince Valiant* strip. Issue number 22 of 1972 introduced Arturo del Castillo's excellent Western *Randall*, and the first issue of 1973 featured material from the now defunct *Trinca*. The trend toward adventure comics had been set. Issue 18 of that same year contained the first original entry to the Kauka line of adventure comics: *Kuma*.

Kuma was a sandy-haired boy who grew up among the animals of the African jungle. His best friend was Sharim the wolf. Kuma spoke all of the animal languages; this came in very handy in the first story, when Kuma was captured by a native tribe and put into a hut where a cobra was supposed to finish him off. With a glowing description of what the freedom of the jungle outside meant, Kuma convinced the deadly snake not to waste its poison on him and to help in the escape effort.

In order to justify the introduction of this adventure strip, much care was given to add a decidedly educational touch by depicting in true-to-life (almost academic) delineation as many animals as could be fitted into the stories without detracting from the dramatic structure of the story. This was slightly overdone, however, as it turned the animals into actors with quite a bit of dialogue. This may have accounted for the fact that *Kuma* did not turn into the success that had been hoped for. The formula was much more readily accepted in foreign countries, but in Germany the feature was discontinued after several continued stories in *primo*, in the *Action Comic* albums and in the digest-sized *Super Action*.

This series will be remembered for its hints of Wayne Boring in the depiction of humans.

W.F.

KURTZMAN, HARVEY (1924-1993) American comic book and comic strip artist, writer, and editor born October 3, 1924, in New York City. After studies at the High School of Music and Art and at Cooper Union, Kurtzman's first comic book work appeared in 1943 on Ace's *Magno* and *Unknown Soldier* adventure features. In 1945, he produced an aviatrix strip, *Black Venus*, and then drew *The Black Bull* for *Prize*. Also during this time, Kurtzman created *Silver Linings*, an acclaimed but rare strip, for the Sunday supplement of the *Herald-Tribune*. He moved to Timely and several other groups in 1945 and produced humor features and gags, most notably *Hey Look*, a one-page gag strip.

In 1950, Kurtzman moved to E. C. and produced several fine science fiction stories for the burgeoning "New Trend" line. Within six months, he was editing a war/adventure book called *Two-Fisted Tales*. *Frontline Combat* followed immediately, and Kurtzman wrote and drew pencil layouts for almost all of the two books' tales. Perhaps the best description of his totally unique and refreshing material came from artist Gil Kane. Kurtzman "had a feeling for humane things, a

Harvey Kurtzman, "Air Burst." © William M. Gaines, Agent, Inc.

feeling for profundity. There was a reek of death, a sense of futility about war that just never occurred in anything else I've read in comics," Kane said.

Kurtzman also began E.C.'s *Mad* in November, 1952, and the book immediately became an American phenomenon. It is impossible to adequately describe all of Kurtzman's innovations here, but among them were his introduction of popular humorists to comic books; parodies of every facet of American life, including comics, movies, television, magazines, and advertising; development of the humor talents of Wood, Elder, and Davis; and his supervision of *Mad*'s transition from color comic book to black-and-white magazine.

Kurtzman left *Mad* in 1955, but *Playboy*'s Hugh Hefner hired him in 1957 to staff his new humor magazine, *Trump*. Thanks to a lavish budget and great talent, the book was an artistic success. But it was a financial disaster, and folded after two issues. Kurtzman then headed an artists' syndicate that published *Humbug*, a 15-cent black-and-white comic that lasted only 11 issues. Despite its short stay, however, Kurtzman—who was limiting himself to writing and editing—produced some of his sharpest, timeliest, and most impressive satire here. He and publisher Jim Warren then became partners in a low-budget humor magazine called *Help!* Kurtzman's "Public Gallery" introduced some of the earliest work by underground cartoonists Jay Lynch, Robert Crumb, and Gilbert Shelton.

Shortly before *Help!* folded, Kurtzman and Elder launched *Little Annie Fanny*, a sexual pollyanna and parody of *Little Orphan Annie*, in the October 1962 issue of *Playboy*. It was the most lavish comic strip ever produced in America. And keying off the exploits of *Annie*, Kurtzman wrote some of the 1960s and '70s most mature and biting satire. In the 1970s, he also drew underground material for *Bijou* and produced four paperbacks of original material, most notably *The Jungle Book*, which contained four stories written and drawn by Kurtzman.

From 1980 to 1985 Kurtzman turned out a comic strip titled *Betsy's Buddies*, in collaboration with his former student Sarah Downs. He also briefly published *Nuts!*, a humor magazine in paperback format. In his later years he wrote two books of memoirs, *My Life as*

a *Cartoonist* (1988) and *Harvey Kurtzman's Strange Adventures* (1991). He died in Mount Vernon, New York, on February 21, 1993.

J.B.

KUWATA, JIRŌ (1935-) Japanese comic book artist born April 17, 1935, in Osaka. At the age of 13, while he was still a first-year student in junior high school, Jirō Kuwata had his first comic strip published. The strip was *Kaiki Seidan*, a science-fiction story that Kuwata created under the influence of Osamu Tezuka's *Tarzan no Himitsukichi* ("Tarzan's Secret Base"). At 15, Kuwata created a new strip, *Daihikyō* ("The Big Unexplored Lands"), which was published serially in *Tanteiō*. From then on, Kuwata devoted himself entirely to comics, drawing *Rocket Tarō* for the monthly *Omoshiro Book*, *Maboroshi Kozō* for *Shōnen Gahō*, and *Tantei Gorō* ("Goro the Detective") for the monthly *Bokura* (1955-56).

In 1957 Kuwata's first popularly acclaimed strip, *Maborashi Tantei*, a detective feature, appeared in *Shōnen Gahō*. The next year he created his greatest comic strip, *Gekkō Kamen* ("The Man with the Moonlight Mask," also a detective strip). *Gekkō Kamen* met with great success and was followed by a number of other comic features: *8-Man* (about an android detective) and *Android Pini* (a science-fiction story), both in

Jirō Kuwata.

Konstantin Kuznjecov, "Three Lives". © Konstantin Kuznjecov.

1960; *Mao Dangā* and *Chōken Leap* ("Leap the Super Robot Dog"), both in 1965; *The Time Tunnel* in 1967, and many others.

Kuwata's line and art style are icy-cold and metallic, well-suited for science fiction and similar stories. The influence of the American comic strip masters can be found in Kuwata's love for contrasted compositions, but he has evolved a style of his own. In turn he has influenced a number of young Japanese artist such as Takahuru Kusunoki, Haruo Koyama, and Yū Matsuhisa. In the 1980s Kuwata had an epiphany and converted to Buddhism; since that time he has been doing religious comic books devoted to the life of Buddha and to Buddhism's doctrine and precepts.

H.K.

KUZNJECOV, KONSTANTIN (1895-19??) Serbian comic artist between two world wars. Of his education and private life, little is known. Konstantin Kuznjecov was Russian, born in Saint Petersburg on May 3, 1895. After the Bolshevik Revolution, he moved to Serbia, living first in Pančevo then in Belgrade, where he began to work in applied art.

Kuznjecov had a permanent job painting advertisements in the large department store Mitić, and he also illustrated books, magazines, and daily newspapers, and drew caricatures. Before World War II, he published about 30 comics. His first comic was *Majka* ("Mother"). It started in installments on January 4, 1937, in the 61st issue of the comics magazine *Mika Miš*. *Majka* featured "romanticized historical events from Serbian past," and with his second comic endeavor, *Kraljević Marko* ("Prince Marko"), and some of his subsequent comics, such as *Knjaz Miloš* ("Duke Miloš"), constituted one thematic circle of Kuznjecov's work. In fact it was a genre; knowledge of Serbian his-

tory, literature, folklore, and epic tradition were necessary to understand these comics.

Kuznjecov adapted several world-famous novels, primarily Russian, into comics, including: *Hadži Murat* (1937-38) by Leo N. Tolstoy, *Stenyka Razyn* (1940) and *Christmas Eve* by Nikolay V. Gogol, *Don Quxote* (1940-41) by Cervantes, and three works of Aleksandar S. Pushkin: *The Queen of Spades* (1940), *Fairytale about Tzar Saltan* (1940), and *Fable about Little Golden Rooster* (1940). Around this time, he also created comics based on the Arabian Nights and other fairytales: *Sinbad the Sailor* (*Mika Mis*, 1938), *Aladin and His Magic Lamp* (1938), *Ali Baba and 40 Thieves* (1938), and *The Magic Flute* (1940-41).

Between 1937 and 1938, three related comics appeared in *Mika Miš*: *In the Kingdom of Apes*, *In the Wild West*, and *The Shipwrecked*. All three featured two anthropomorphic chimpanzees, Sony and Tony, who were, by stylization and ambiance, neighbors of Mickey Mouse and Donald Duck. The fifth circle are classic adventure stories: *Mysteries of Chicago* (1937-38), *Orient Express* (1938), and two episodes about Ben Kerigan, an Intelligence Service agent ("Descendant of Ghengis Khan" and "Green Dragon," 1937-38).

Kuznjecov's most effective comics were his stories of mysticism, most successfully *Grofica Margo* ("Duchess Margot"), *Baron vampir*, and *Tri života* ("Three Lives"). These comics, first published in *Mika Miš* between 1938 and 1940, unrolled in elegiac and picturesque landscapes, dark forests, stilled swamps, abandoned greenfields, quiet graveyards, and lonely castles. In the stories, Kuznjecov attempted to create an atmosphere mixing Gothic novels and the horror movies that were popular between the two world wars.

The erudition of this author is best shown by the fact that he wrote all but five of the scripts for his approximately 40 comics. The quality of his work showed in its success abroad, mostly in France.

Evidently, until World War II he worked for only two magazines, *Mika Miš* and *PZ*. When Belgrade was bombarded and occupied by Germans in April 1941, Serbian publishers stopped publishing their magazines. Suddenly word got around, from sources unknown, that Kuznjecov was working for S Department, in charge of propaganda for the occupational German military command of Serbia. This rumor was true. He designed and illustrated posters, booklets, leaflets, and other propagandic materials for the Nazis and was also the caricaturist of the satirical-humorous magazine *Bodljikavo prase* ("Porcupine"), published also by S Department. The crescendo of this activity was the starting of *Mali Zabavnik* ("Little Entertainer") magazine on December 1, 1943. Of the staff, only the editor was named on the masthead; authors, artists, and writers all remained anonymous, fearing the retaliation of their neighbors and the Resistance movement. Five comics appeared in the first issue; at least two can be ascribed to Kuznjecov (the style is obvious): *Between Love and Fatherland* and *Frog Prince*.

After World War II, Kuznjecov managed to escape into the West; to Austria, according to some hints. It seems that he continued with drawing and illustration there. The year of his death is not known.

S.I.

KYOJIN NO HOSHI (Japan) *Kyojin no Hoshi* ("The Star of the Giants"), created by Ikki Kajiwara (script) and Noboru Kawasaki (artwork), made its debut in the May 1966 issue of *Shōnen* magazine.

The story related the growth of Hyūma Hoshi (Hyūma is derived from the word "humanism"), the son of Ittetsu Hoshi, once a famous ballplayer on the Kyojin team whose career had been cut short by the war. Ittetsu wanted his son to be a player with the Kyojin (the most famous baseball team in Japan) and trained him from childhood for this purpose. After a promising start as a pitcher for his high school team, Hyūma was scouted by 11 different professional teams (but not the Kyojin!) and he turned down all offers. Training intensively, he finally passed the test of the Kyojin and was accepted into the club.

The rest of the strip followed Hyūma as he experienced the vicissitudes of the competitive life, winning some, losing some. A father-son rivalry developed when Ittetsu was hired as coach for the rival Chūnichi Dragons. Ittetsu coached the powerful black batter Armstrong Ozma to defeat his son. Hyuma won the first challenge but lost to Ozma on the second. He then developed a new pitching method with which he

"Kyojin no Hoshi," Noboru Kawasaki. © Shōnen.

defeated Ozma decisively, but the effort had been strenuous and Hyūma tore his arm muscles. On this mixed note of victory and sorrow the strip ended, as Hyūma left the Kyojin and baseball to the plaudits of his fans (March 1971). *Kyojin no Hoshi* was more than a simple baseball strip; its central theme was a young man's coming of age and the ambiguous relation between son and father. The strip was published in book form (19 books selling over 5 million copies) and inspired a series of animated cartoons as well as a stage play and several novels. It also extended the vogue of the comic strip from children to young adults.

H.K.

LABORNE, DANIEL (1902-1990) French cartoonist Daniel Laborne was born in Verneuil sur Avre, in Normandy, on October 6, 1902. Upon graduation from vocational high school, he started his career as an industrial draftsman; when the Great Depression hit France in 1930 and he was laid off, he turned his drawing abilities to illustration and cartooning. His humorous drawings and caricatures soon appeared in a number of French magazines, including the venerable *Chat Noir*, to which he was one of the last contributors. Later he extended his freelance activities to the daily press, and his sports illustrations were published as early as 1938 in the Paris evening paper *Ce Soir*.

It was in the pages of another Paris daily, *Le Petit Parisien*, that he created in 1939 his first comic strip, the famous *Lariflette*, which was to last for almost half a century. The title character, Désiré Lariflette, was a typically French "little man," bent on his comfort, his leisure, and his meals. Perpetually wearing a collapsed cylinder hat and a puzzled expression, he tried to cope with the multifarious vagaries of life, the nagging of his formidable wife Bichette, and the pranks of his young son Tatave.

After a two-year hiatus during World War II, *Lariflette* resurfaced in 1945 in the children's weekly *Coq Hardi*, and a little later in syndication to French and foreign newspapers. The character grew to even greater popularity in the immediate postwar period and gave rise to two spin-offs, *Polop le Caïd* ("Polop the Toughie"), featuring the exploits of his wiseguy pal, and *Tatave*, which starred his unruly son. Laborne drew the daily adventures of Lariflette until ill-health finally forced him to abandon the character in 1988; he died two years later at his home in Argenteuil, near Paris.

Laborne received a number of distinctions during his lifetime, but he was proudest of having been deputy-mayor of Montmartre. He was a conscientious and unassuming craftsman whose talents were recognized by French historians only after his death.

M.H.

LANCE (U.S.) Warren Tufts' self-syndicated *Lance* (distributed by Warren Tufts Enterprises to start on Sunday, June 5, 1955) was one of the last full-page Sunday strips, intended to be reproduced in the *Prince Valiant* manner. It was certainly the best of the page-high adventure strips undertaken after the 1930s, although inferior to Tufts' own preceding half-page daily, *Casey Ruggles*. Like *Ruggles* (which Tufts abandoned to United Features in order to have complete control over his own work), *Lance* was a historically oriented strip, taking place around the Kansas and Missouri area in the 1840s rather than in California during the gold rush days.

The hero, Lance St. Lorne, is a second lieutenant in the U.S. 1st Dragoons, serving at Fort Leavenworth, Kansas. The Dragoons are fighting the Sioux, and the strip narrative develops from this situation, introducing later on—as with *Casey Ruggles*—a number of actual historical figures, including Kit Carson. Again as in *Ruggles*, Tufts is a forceful, realistic storyteller for adults: blood flows copiously where necessary, and the extramarital sexual relationships among the characters are related frankly. Tufts' raw, hard-bitten style and content strikes a sharp contrast with Harold Foster's bland art and cheerful narrative of the period in his *Prince Valiant*.

The strip audience of the time was no more ready for *Lance* than they had been for *Casey Ruggles*, however, and newspaper editors began to feel that the relatively tepid public response did not justify a full page for Tufts' strip. Tufts was forced to supply a half-page, then a third-page version. Some papers dropped the strip before it had run a year, and its original distribution was not extensive. Others carried it into its third year and then cut it. Because Tufts never had much interest in discussing the details of his work, it is impossible to pinpoint the date of the last Lance strip distributed, but the last episode printed in the several subscribing newspapers available for review was on

QUAND FAUT Y ALLER...

— Allons, Lariflette, réveillez-vous !

— Je sais que vous êtes bien ici !

— Mais la loi le veut : votre tour est venu...

... de connaître les joies des vacances !

Daniel Laborne, "Lariflette." © D. Laborne.

May 12, 1957. Like *Ruggles*, *Lance* deserves the time and effort of a full reprinting.

B.B.

THIS IS THE WORST PART OF THE HOLIDAY... WAITING FOR THE AIRPORT BUS!

"The Larks," Jack Dunkley. © Daily Mirror Newspapers Ltd.

LARKS, THE (G.B.) *The Larks* is a gag-a-day family situation strip introduced in the *Daily Mirror* on August 5, 1957. First scripted by the radio comedy writing team of Bill Kelly and Arthur Lay, then by Robert St. John Cooper, it was written by television scriptwriter Brian Cooke since 1963. Cooke, himself no mean cartoonist in his prewriting days, brought the characters of the Lark family out of the working class and into the middle class. A typical balloon of 1961 has the wife and mother, Sal Lark, addressing her little lad Stevie thus: "You keep your thievin' cake-'ooks off these, young Stevie, or there'll be dead trouble!" In the strip's later years, apart from the occasional "flippin'," Sal's speech became more refined. Sam Lark, the breadwinner, worked in a white coat at the local supermarket, run by tightfisted Mr. McCreep. The other Lark child was Susie, and for a few years the children were allowed to grow up naturally within the strip. Once Stevie had started work and Susie started school, however, their ages were frozen, as were those of the Newley family next door, with their young twins, Nicholas and Louise. A running gag was Sam Lark's attempts to teach Mike Newley to drive. Other regulars included Milkie the Milkman and the Larks' cat, So-so. The latter is believed to be the only cartoon cat who thinks in rhyme!

The Larks was drawn by Jack Dunkley in his familiarly flexible line. It is no longer being published.

D.G.

LARSEN, KNUD V. (1930-   ) Knud V. Larsen, Danish comic artist born in Copenhagen on May 3, 1930, now lives in Småland, Sweden. He has been drawing ever since he can remember; he started practicing magic tricks at age 8 and got interested in hypnotism at age 16. All of these interests came in handy years later, when he decided to create a comic strip of his own, *Dr. Merling*. The main character of the strip,

Albert Merling—an illusionist by profession—is the alter ego of Knud V. Larsen, who derived the name from King Arthur's wizard Merlin and used it when performing his own magic tricks. Larsen tried to sell the comic strip as far back as 1963, but at the time most Scandinavian newspapers were buying comics from foreign markets. So the strip did not start until 1970. It is now carried by, among other papers, *Berlingske Tidende* of Copenhagen and *Helsingin Sanomt* of Helsinki. Reprints have also appeared in the Swedish comic book *Serie-Pressen*.

Before turning his alter ego into a comic strip based in the 1870s, Larsen took time to study graphic art from scratch. In 1951 he finished his studies in painting and decorating, and up until 1954 he taught art at the technical school of Frederiksberg, Denmark, while at the same time perfecting the magic tricks he performed.

He worked up to the position of art director in an advertising agency and, under four pseudonyms, did book illustrations and newspaper cartoons. He always dreamed of doing a comic strip, and his perseverance finally paid off. His knowledge of human psychology, which he acquired through performing magic tricks, may have been of additional help.

Larsen's imagination never fails to produce interesting reading, thanks to plots bordering on the fantastic and occult. He is recognizably fascinated by the age of Jules Verne, and his bold and very personal style employs a special technique to include details from illustrations of the 1870s; his style also evokes the necessary mood for making this type of strip a success.

W.F.

LARSON, GARY (1950-   ) The creator of the unique panel *The Far Side* was born on August 14, 1950, in Tacoma, Washington. He particularly liked *Mad* magazine and Gahan Wilson's *Playboy* cartoons during his adolescence, even though he displayed no particular inclination then toward the cartooning profession. After graduating from Washington State University with a communications degree in 1973, he moved to Seattle. Employed as a music store clerk, he created six animal cartoons and submitted them to the nature magazine *Pacific Search* in 1976. All were accepted, and after Larson got a job with the Humane Society, his panel, now titled *Nature's Way*, was promoted to the *Seattle Times*. When his feature was canceled by that paper two years later, the cartoonist impressed the *San Francisco Chronicle*'s reticent editor with his twistedly funny panel, which resulted in a five-year syndication contract with Chronicle Features. Given its permanent title, *The Far Side*, by the syndicate, the panel officially debuted on January 1, 1980. Universal Press Syndicate began distributing it four years later, allowing Larson a 14-month sabbatical starting in late 1988. Upon his return, new releases were reduced to five days a week, allowing more opportunity for the development of increased merchandising, color features in his best-selling books, and animated projects handled by his company, FarWorks.

Since abruptly retiring *The Far Side* on the first day of 1995, the private artist has kept busy developing new projects, in addition to studying jazz guitar and writing a children's book.

B.J.

"Voila! . . . Your new dream home! If you like it,
I can get a crew mixing wood fibers and saliva
as early as tomorrow."

Gary Larson, "The Far Side." © Universal Press Syndicate.

LASSWELL, FRED (1916-   ) As an eight-year-old tyke leaving Gainesville, Florida, for Tampa, Fred Lasswell may well have been whistling and singing "Barney Google, with his goo-goo-googly eyes" (the hit song of 1923), without the remotest inkling that he'd be drawing the adventures of Billy De Beck's shrimp-sized hero under De Beck's supervision in another 10 years. But that, of course, is exactly what happened.

Born in 1916 in Kennett, Missouri, (not far from the Kentucky homeland of the Snuffy Smith ménage, which he was later to guide to continuing fame after their creator's death), Lasswell and his parents moved to Gainesville when he was six. In Tampa two years later, he attended Hillsborough High School, from which he graduated into a job as sports cartoonist for the *Tampa Daily Times* circa 1928. A devotee of the pen and ink work of Charles Dana Gibson, Lasswell developed his comic techniques on the *Times* until a poster he had done for a golf tournament at the nearby Palma Ceia Club in 1933 attracted the eye of the golfing rover Billy De Beck. De Beck, who had reached the age where he wanted to groom a younger man to help him with the *Barney Google* strip, saw in Lasswell's skillful lines just the potential talent he wanted.

He called Lasswell at the *Times* and asked if he wanted to go to work on *Barney*. Lasswell accepted, and for the next nine years until De Beck's death in 1942 he worked and traveled with De Beck constantly, until his style was virtually identical to that of his mentor. Lasswell's continuation of *Barney* was—in its early years, at least—one of the most successful prolongations of a major comic in strip history. (Lasswell's work on the Sunday *Bunky* was even more effective, though the strip was dropped in the early 1950s.) Later, when Lasswell was forced, by a King Features' edict prohibiting continuity in the syndicate's humorously drawn strips, to drop narrative for day-to-day gags, the fine edge of the strip was dulled. Lasswell's artistry, however, has not flagged, and the daily and Sunday *Barney Google and Snuffy Smith* remains a visual pleasure on any comic page it graces.

Lasswell himself is a remarkable man of many accomplishments: a flight radio operator in World War II; creator of a major wartime strip, *Hashmark*, for *Leatherneck Magazine;* inventor of a successful citrus fruit harvester; member of the American Society of Agricultural Engineers; developer of a technique to enable the blind to read comic strips on their own; and winner of many strip awards, including the Reuben in 1964. Snuffy would remark that Lasswell was "tetched in the haid"—with genius of a very memorable sort.

B.B.

Lasswell, affectionately known to all as "Uncle Fred," has kept remarkably active at an age when most people dream of retiring. In addition to turning out *Barney Google and Snuffy Smith* daily and Sundays, he has produced a number of *Draw and Color with Uncle Fred* videos and developed his own web page on the Internet. He received the National Cartoonists Society's Elzie Segar Award for outstanding contribution to the art of cartooning twice, in 1984 and 1994. The only surviving charter member of NCS, he celebrated 50 years with the society in 1996.

M.H.

LAT *see* Khalid, Mohamed Nor.

LAVADO, JOAQUIN (1932-   ) An Argentine cartoonist born in Mendoza on July 17, 1932, to Spanish immigrants, Joaquin Lavado (better known under his pseudonym "Quino") displayed drawing abilities at an early age. One of his maternal uncles, Joaquin Téjon, was a commercial artist, and he often would draw to amuse his nephew (who was to recall years later: "To me it was a thing of magic; that is when I decided to become a cartoonist"). Quino studied at the Buenos Aires Art Institute, contributing hundreds of cartoons and humor pages to Argentine publications all the while. In this phase of his career Quino distinguished himself as a graphic historian and critic of his time and his people, with his keen political perceptions and his depictions of television and its myths. In 1963 an anthology of his best cartoons, *Mondo Quino*, was published with great success in Buenos Aires.

In 1964 Quino created his great comic strip *Mafalda*, at first as a Sunday page, and, starting in 1973, as a daily strip. This humorous saga of a precocious and argumentative little girl was greeted with universal acclaim. Quino is regarded as the foremost Argentine cartoonist, and his work is being published throughout the world. Since discontinuing *Mafalda* in 1973, he has devoted his talents to illustration and humor cartooning.

L.G.

LAVINIA 2.016 (Spain) Enric Sío's first work as an independent and original cartoonist was *Lavinia 2.016 o la guerra dels poetas* ("Lavinia 2016, or the War of the Poets"), which first appeared in issue 68 (January 1968) of the Catalan-language monthly *Oriflama* and continued until issue 76 (October 1968).

The script, by Emili Teixido, described life in a city of the future, easily recognized as Barcelona, under a

matriarchal regime where words are prohibited and the image triumphs (a theme similar to that of Ray Bradbury's *Fahrenheit 451*). The poets revolt and decide to use words once again, for which they are jailed and prosecuted. Starting from this premise, Sío opened on a parodic style not too well defined at first, but his graphic evolution was so swift that before long he had achieved the very personal style that he was later to utilize on *Sorang* and *Nus*, the other two works corresponding to the first stage of his artistic development.

A political work in code, where the symbols are very elementary, *Lavinia* presented, in humorous and caricatural guise, well-known personalities of the Catalan cultural left: singers, writers, playwrights, and poets, who mingled freely and interacted with comic strip characters like Snoopy, mythic figures like Bonnie (of Bonnie and Clyde), reminiscences of childhood readings, images from advertising, and toys and montages of news pictures.

L.G.

LAZARUS, MEL (1927-   ) American cartoonist, born in Brooklyn, New York, on May 3, 1927. Mel Lazarus was educated in public schools and hated the whole process ("I even flunked art in high school," he revealed proudly in 1964). After high school he freelanced for magazines, then became assistant on Al Capp's *Li'l Abner* (he was later to recount these experiences in a novel entitled *The Boss Is Crazy, Too*). In the early 1950s he created two weekly panels, *Wee Women* and *Li'l One*, both about precocious children.

In February 1957, Mel Lazarus (under the pseudonym "Mell") launched his first full-fledged comic strip, *Miss Peach*, about a classroom full of rebellious kids. It met with instant success. In 1966, in collaboration with artist Jack Rickard and under the pseudonym "Fulton," he produced the short-lived *Pauline McPeril*, a tongue-in-cheek adventure strip taking off on Pearl White's cliff-hanging serial *The Perils of Pauline*. Mel (or Mell, as he prefers to spell his first name) Lazarus was to be more successful with *Momma*, a rollicking strip that he created in November 1970, based on the "Jewish mother" stereotype.

An avowed admirer of Walt Kelly and Charles Schulz, Lazarus is a member of that small group of cartoonists who helped revive the humor strip in the 1950s and 1960s. His creations, while not on a par with *Peanuts* or *Pogo*, occupy nonetheless an honorable place in what has come to be called "the sophisticated school" of comics.

In 1973 and again in 1979 Lazarus was named Best Humor Strip Cartoonist by the National Cartoonists Society; and in 1982 he won the coveted Reuben Award. Very active in his profession, he served as a board member of NCS in the 1980s and was its president from 1989 to 1993.

M.H.

LEAV, MORT (1916-   ) American comic book artist, born in New York City on July 9, 1916. Leav's only art training came in WPA-sponsored adult education courses during the Great Depression. By 1936, however, he was handling daily and Sunday strips, along with sports and editorial cartoons for Editors Press Service, a South American syndicate based in New York. He broke into comic books in 1941 when he joined the S. M. Iger shop and began drawing a minor feature called *ZX-5, Spies in Action* for Fiction House.

"Lavinia 2.016," Enric Sío. © Enric Sío.

He later drew *Doll Man* and *Uncle Sam* for Quality and *The Hangman* for MLJ while still with Iger.

In 1942, the shop began packaging books for Hillman, and it was then that Leav designed his most famous character. Writer Harry Stein had invented a supporting character called The Heap, and while most other artists laughed Stein's idea off, Leav visualized a hulking, brutish, eight-foot-tall green and brown swamp monster covered with hair. His eerie, illustrative approach to The Heap's first appearance (which came in the *Skywolf* strip in *Air Fighters Comics*) helped create one of the slickest and most original stories produced at the time.

Leav also began working for Busy Arnold's Quality group in 1942 and became a staff artist on features like *Blackhawk* and *Kid Eternity*. Always underrated throughout his career, Leav's work was never artistically overshadowed, even though Quality boasted recognized talents like Lou Fine, Jack Cole, and Reed Crandall. Forced to leave Quality when he was drafted in 1943, Leav turned his attention to illustrating army magazines. His work is probably best noted for his devastating caricatures of Adolf Hitler as a hairy, unkempt petty tyrant.

After the war, Leav did several *Captain America* tales for Timely and several love stories for Ziff-Davis before becoming art director and chief artist at Orbit Publications in 1946. For eight years, he drew almost all the covers and lead stories for books such as *Wild Bill Pecos*, *Wanted*, and *Patches*. Leav left Orbit in 1954, and after two years as a freelance commercial artist, he joined the prestigious Benton and Bowles Advertising Agency. There he drew some of the first television storyboards and became the agency's "TV art director." He is now retired.

J.B.

LECTRON, E.   *see* Fine, Louis.

LEE, JIM (1964-   )   American comic-book artist Jim Lee was born in Seoul, South Korea, on August 11, 1964. He came to the United States as a youth and received most of his education at American schools. Lee graduated from Princeton University with a degree in psychology; he is largely self-taught in art. His love of art and of comics triumphed over his formal studies, and he got his first job in the field in 1987 at Marvel, where he worked as one of the artists on *Alpha Flight*. It was his work on the *Punisher War Journal* the next year that brought him to the attention of fans. After that he went from strength to strength, capping his career at Marvel with the second series of *X-Men*, which he pencilled; its first issue was published in five

Jim Lee, "X-Men." © Marvel Comics.

different editions with a total print run of 8 million copies.

That same year, 1991, saw Lee and other Marvel artists form their own company, Image Comics. At Image he created *WildC.A.T.S. Covert Action Teams* in 1992 and *Stormwatch* in 1993. These both came under his own Wildstorm Productions imprint, which also publishes *WetWorks* and *Team 7,* along with the highly successful *Gen 13,* released initially as a miniseries in 1994, and the next year as a regular monthly series. In 1996 he was contracted by Marvel to produce new stories for *Iron Man* and *The Fantastic Four.*

He is known for his attention to detail and for the sense of motion and excitement he imparts to his compositions. He is the most talented and creative of the Image Group, and not coincidentally the most self-effacing (his release of the first issue of *Gen 13* with 13 variant covers can be chalked up to youthful exuberance). If the comic-book universe undergoes an irreversible implosion, as many predict, Jim Lee is the most likely to succeed in some other artistic field.

M.H.

LEE, STAN (1922-   ) American comic book and comic strip writer, editor, and publisher, born Stanley Lieber in 1922 in New York City. As a youth, Lee won the *New York Herald Tribune* essay contest for three consecutive weeks; at 17, he entered the comic book industry as an assistant editor and copywriter for the Timely comics group owned by Martin and Arthur Goodman. At the time, Joe Simon and Jack Kirby were the group's editors, but when the pair moved to National in 1942, Lee was promoted to editor. He held that post as the company changed names from Timely to Atlas and finally to Marvel, and only relinquished his editorship in 1972 when he was promoted to publisher and editorial director.

During the 1940s, most of Lee's writing was done for the Timely superhero groups. His best work probably came on the *Captain America* and *Young Allies* strips, but he also wrote stories for superhero strips like *The Witness, The Destroyer, Jack Frost, Whizzer,* and *Black Marvel.* As editor, he was also responsible for producing material for the Timely group's war, crime, funny animal, and humor books. When William Gaines' E.C. group turned comic book publishers' attention to horror, war, and science-fiction titles during the 1950s, Lee led the Atlas group through several tough years. Although the group offered some fine artwork—including material by Basil Wolverton, Jack Kirby, Joe Maneely, Al Williamson, Joe Orlando, and many others—Lee's scripts were always rushed and usually below par. In fact, the Atlas years were prolific but artistically vapid for Stan Lee the writer.

It was not until 1961 that he began producing outstanding comic book stories and formats. Together with artist and compatriot Jack Kirby, he formulated the Marvel group of superheroes, starting with *The Fantastic Four* and *Spider-Man* and later expanding to *Dr. Strange, Thor, The Hulk, Sub-Mariner, Daredevil, Iron Man,* and many others. But all the features were founded on one basic premise: that even though the character was a hero with some sort of superhuman ability, he had human failings, emotions, and foibles the teenaged reader could identify with. Spider-Man, for example, had girl problems, a doting grandmother, and not much of a personality. Johnny Storm, the Human Torch, was erratic and unreliable, and all of

Lee's other creations had similar character defects. Strangely enough, however, with the exception of Ditko's early *Spider-Man* renditions, Lee had all the characters portrayed as noble in bearing and majestic, often belying their essential, albeit sometimes adolescent, humanity.

Lee's material catapulted the Marvel line to pop-culture status throughout the 1960s, and sales responded in a like manner. Lee was celebrated as the savior of the comic book, the great innovator, and his personal reputation kept pace with his characters' popularity. He went on lecture tours to college campuses, made broadcast media appearances, and even held an "Evening with Stan Lee" at Carnegie Hall in 1972. Comic book fans bestowed on him six consecutive "Alley" awards between 1963 and 1968. He was instrumental in the formation of the Academy of Comic Book Arts (ACBA), and Simon & Schuster published his *Origins of Marvel Comics* in 1974.

Over the years, Lee has also worked on several syndicated comic strips, including *My Friend Irma* (1952), *Mrs. Lyons' Cubs* (1957-1958), and *Willie Lumpkin* (1960).

J.B.

In 1972 Stan Lee became Marvel's publisher, and in 1978 he moved to California to supervise the operation of its film and television arm, where his performance has been less than stellar. Aside from his writing of the *Amazing Spider-Man* newspaper strip (started in 1977) and an occasional comic-book story, he has now almost totally abandoned creative activities. Furthermore, his record as a publisher has also come under fire of late: his egomaniacal insistence on taking credit for every story Marvel ever published ("Stan Lee Presents . . .") and his shabby treatment of Jack Kirby, Steve Ditko, and others of his most talented collaborators have drawn special criticism from fans and historians alike.

M.H.

LEHNER, RENÉ (1955-   ) A Swiss comic artist born April 3, 1955, René Lehner grew up with comic books and began drawing while he was still quite young. Although he never pursued formal art training, he continued to doodle and draw, and in 1974 he cofounded *Comixene,* the first German comics fanzine. Around the same time, he sold some of his cartoons and gag strips to various publishers. After leaving *Comixene,* he also began publishing his cartoons on his own. In 1981 he moved to Spain with his family; later he lived in Hamburg before returning to his native Switzerland.

Finally an idea took form that Lehner pursued with a vengeance. He created Bill Body, a sports enthusiast with an egg-shaped head and a penchant for getting into all kinds of predicaments. In addition to developing the *Bill Body* comic strip, Lehner began producing animated cartoon shorts of his character in the "comic factory" he cofounded with Rinaldo Schweizer. At first these cartoons were just short sight gags and blackouts used as fillers between advertising segments on privately owned German commercial television, which was then in its infancy. Eventually production was stepped up so that Bill Body could appear in 15- and 30-minute programs on German commercial TV and state-owned Austrian public TV.

While originally influenced by the Franquin school of drawing, Lehner, who signs his work simply

*René Lehner, self-portrait
... and his best-known character,* Bill Body

"René," has developed a style and concept of his own for the lovable and highly marketable *Bill Body*.

W.F.

LEHNER, SEBASTIJAN (1921-1945) Born in 1921 in Osijek (now in Croatia), Sebastijan Lehner traveled to Belgrade in the autumn of 1938 to pursue a career in comics. Incredibly, when the Belgrade comics magazine *Paja Patak* ("Donald Duck") launched its inaugural issue on October 3, 1938, the 17-year-old Lehner was represented with three realistic serials. The magazine, owned and edited by Djuradj M. Jelicic, featured Serbian translations of popular American comics like *Radio Patrol*, *Felix the Cat*, and *Little Orphan Annie*, along with original Serbian comics by such artists as Zika Mitrovic, S. Petkovic, Marijan Ebner (pseudonym of Dragan Kalmarevic), and J. Uhlik. In such company,

young Lehner's comics, although clearly the work of a beginner, showed great promise, which was confirmed in later issues. Despite their weaknesses, his *Mysterious Island in the Pacific*, *Inhabitants of Planet Monip*, and especially *Dzarto, Prehistoric Hero* gained a loyal readership. Titles defined genre affiliation unerringly. Lehner's main characteristics were clearly visible even then: strictly visual stylization; inclination toward monumentality and long, epic adventure serials; and a determination to write all his texts himself.

After *Paja Patak* folded following its 24th issue, Lehner was hired by Milutin S. Ignjacevic to work on his new magazine *Mikijevo carstvo* ("Mickey's Domain"). For the first issue, published on February 23, 1939, Lehner drew *Gospodar sveta* ("Master of the World"), which was based on Jules Verne's *Maitre du monde*. He also did the serial *Dzarto, sin Sunca* ("Jarto, Son of Sun"), a tale subtitled "Hero of Prehistoric Era." In August 1939 Lehner's other well-known serial, *Sigfrid*, inspired by the medieval German saga of the Nibelungen, started. It belonged to a genre (adventure-fantasy) and subgenre (epic sword-and-sorcery) that Lehner liked best. His third serial, *Princ Bialco*, started ambitiously in 1941 but was never finished. In April the Nazis rolled into Serbia, and Serbian publishers ceased producing newspapers and magazines.

On December 1, 1943, during the third winter of the German occupation, there appeared a new Belgrade magazine, *Mali zabavnik* ("Little Entertainer"), which contained five comics. Contributors were anonymous so that the resistance forces couldn't retaliate against them for collaborating with the Nazis. People quickly recognized Kuznjecov's style, but only in 1995 was it discovered that a certain Vsevolod Guljevic, about whom virtually nothing is known, also worked on the magazine. Lehner's comics appeared too, now titled *Nibelunzi* and subtitled *Zigfrid*, clearly a continuation of the prewar *Sigfrid* serial. Set in pencil probably by Lehner, it was inked probably by Guljevic or Kuznjecov. It certainly seems to have been a collective effort.

The circumstances of his death have never been officially confirmed, but very soon after the Germans' defeat in Serbia, Lehner was killed. Most likely he was executed by partisans for collaborating with the Nazi occupation forces.

S.I.

LEHTI, JOHN (1912-   ) American artist, born in Brooklyn, New York, on July 20, 1912. Lehti grew up in Brooklyn and studied at some of the finest art schools in the nation: the Art Students League (under George Bridgman, Frank Dumond, and Nicholaides), the National Academy, the Beaux Arts Institute, and Grand Central Art School under Harvey Dunn, probably the greatest influence on his art and approach to work.

In 1935 Lehti's first published work appeared in pulps; his dry-brush drawings ran in Street and Smith and Double Action group magazines. Within three years the pulp market had narrowed and the rarer illustration assignments were going to the top artists only.

Fortunately for Lehti and other pulp illustrators, comic books were emerging as a new market—for artists as well as readers. He joined the staff of Detective Comics and worked on four titles: *The Crimson Avenger*; *Sgt. O'Malley of the Redcoat Patrol*; *Steve Conrad, Adventurer*; and *Cotton Carver*. During this time, just before split assignments, Lehti and others wrote, drew, inked, and lettered their own titles.

During the war Lehti served in Europe, collecting a Bronze Star, a Purple Heart, and four bronze Battle Stars. Returning to the United States, he was offered the position of art editor with Leigh Danenberg's Picture News, a comic-book-format hodgepodge with everything from news angles developed by the legendary Emil Guvreaux (Bernard McFadden's editor on the *New York Graphic*, who, among other achievements, launched Walter Winchell) to Milt Gross cartoons, among the last drawn by the comic genius, from his hospital bed.

Picture News lasted approximately six issues, evidently neither beast nor fowl to readers; in the spring of 1946 Lehti sold a comic strip to King Features—*Tommy of the Big Top*—which ran until 1950. With the strip's demise he returned to Detective Comics for one year to do pencils for *Big Town* (crossing paths, coincidentally, with Dan Barry, whose place he took; Barry had left to work for King Features). For a while, in 1949, he also worked on *Tarzan*.

This time it was the comic book industry that was hit by relatively hard times—in the early 1950s—and Lehti switched to Western, where he worked on several titles until 1954, including *Lassie, Space Cadet,* and *Flash Gordon*.

In 1954 Lehti sold *Tales from the Great Book* to Publishers Syndicate. It was a Sunday feature, dramatizing the most exciting and heroic parts of the Bible. Stories were continued, and what was lacking in historical precision was compensated for by a great sense of drama—a legacy, no doubt, of Harvey Dunn's classroom lectures. *Tales* was a natural Sunday feature for many newspapers and had a healthy run, to 1972. Lehti later returned to Detective Comics and worked on *Sgt. Rock* and *The Loser*.

Lehti's art is that of a very competent craftsman—never outstanding in the sense of setting trends or breaking ground, but ahead of many contemporaries in technical accuracy and capturing moods. From 1967 to 1970 he headed a production team of animators working on 13 animated Tales from the Great Book; earlier experience in animation included storyboard work on the television cartoon *The Mighty Hercules* in the early 1960s. After self-syndicating a weekly panel again based on biblical stories, he retired in the 1980s.

R.M.

LEISK, DAVID JOHNSON (1906-1975) An American artist born in New York City on October 20, 1906, he was better known as "Crockett Johnson." Johnson grew up on Long Island and returned to New York for art courses at Cooper Union. His first job had him doing advertising work in the art department of Macy's Department Store. He also did freelance magazine art, mostly of the design variety.

In the early 1940s, Johnson drew a little weekly comic strip for *Collier's Magazine. The Little Man with the Eyes* became the unofficial title of this nameless feature; as the major action consisted of the face's moving eyes, the captions carried the concept.

This feature overlapped with a newspaper comic strip he created in 1942 for New York's experimental newspaper *PM. Barnaby*—a whimsical strip about a boy's fairy godfather, the latter's weird assortment of ghostly friends, and the boy's unbelieving parents. The strip was destined to become one of the classics of comics history.

In addition to creating one of the few "intellectual" strips in the *Little Nemo–Krazy Kat–Pogo* fraternity, Johnson introduced an innovation to the form of the comic strip: machine-lettered balloons. Interestingly, however, there has been virtually no follow-up by other artists to this innovation.

The typeset dialogue, Johnson maintained, was to ensure the maximum amount of space for the continuity—a fact that illustrates his primary concern with story over art in *Barnaby*. Eventually other interests became more important than *Barnaby* itself and he turned the strip over to Jack Morley and Ted Ferro.

Reportedly he kept close tabs on the strip (indeed, he returned to write the farewell episode when the strip folded in 1952), but Johnson was interested in other things. He wrote several children's books alone and with his wife, Ruth Kraus (*Harold and the Purple Crayon* was their most memorable collaboration), and then turned to oil and acrylic painting; he characterized his painting style as "non-objective, mathematic and geometric."

This man who remembered no great fondness for comic strips as a child and to whom *Barnaby* was only a passing episode in his life nevertheless remains one of the giants of comic history. His strip was an inspired creation, striking in originality of conception and presentation. He died in Norwalk, Connecticut, on July 11, 1975.

R.M.

LEONARD, FRANK (1896-1970) Born in Port Chester, New York, on January 2, 1896, Frank E. Leonard (later to be known as "Lank" Leonard, creator of *Mickey Finn*) went from high school to the Eastman Gaines Business College in 1914. In the army in 1917 and 1918, Leonard became a traveling salesman in the early 1920s, then did animation with Bray Productions in 1926. He finally landed a syndicate sinecure between 1927 and 1936 with a sports-personality and news feature distributed by the George Matthew Adams Service, doing magazine sports art on the side. Leonard's real fame and fortune began in 1936, when he created his new strip concept, *Mickey Finn*, and it was accepted by McNaught Syndicate for major promotion and sale.

Mickey Finn was the first and almost the only strip to deal sympathetically with the police foot patrolman in a large city. (The comparative glamour of the earlier *Radio Patrol* is evident.) Leonard opted for humor and character over crime and violence, however (although there was plenty of the latter at points in the narrative), and the public seemed to like the theme and creative combination. This led to a wide circulation of *Finn* in its first few years, especially when the real focus of the strip turned from Mickey's exploits to those of his knockabout Irish uncle Phil Finn. (The emphasis in the Sunday page was on Uncle Phil almost from the outset.)

A professional basketball player after high school, Leonard became an ardent golfer in later years. Hiring the very capable Morris Weiss to continue *Finn* while he went into semi-retirement a year and a half before his death, Leonard took a novel step for a strip cartoonist in asking his readers to vote on whether or not Phil Finn should marry a much younger sweetheart named Minerva Mutton. The readers voted 30 to 1 that he should, and Leonard saw them married on the newspaper pages a few days before his death at Miami Shores on August 1, 1970.

B.B.

LEWIS, BOB *see* Lubbers, Robert.

LIAO BINGXIONG (1915-   ) After a difficult childhood, Chinese cartoonist Liao Bingxiong graduated from Guangzhou Normal School at age 17, in the midst of World War II. That year his anti-Japanese comic strips began to appear in newspapers. The strips, which would eventually total 27, gave Liao's view of why the Chinese would eventually defeat the Japanese invaders.

During the war years, Liao also began drawing *Spring and Autumn in Cat Kingdom*, the general title for 100 color cartoons with animal characters that would make his reputation as one of China's greatest cartoonists. The cartoons, which were exhibited successfully in 1946 in Chongqing, openly attacked the political and economic abuses of China's Nationalist government, which was then battling the Communists. Wanted by the government for the criticism he expressed in his cartoons, Liao changed his name and fled.

After the Communist victory and the establishment of the People's Republic of China, Liao returned from Hong Kong and became vice president of the Chinese Artists Association, Guangdong Branch; he also worked as director of the Guangzhou Literature Federation Publishing Department. But he continued to criticize government wrongdoing in his cartoons, and in 1957 he was denounced as a "rightist" and removed from his positions. For 20 years he was forbidden to draw cartoons and forced to work in various positions, including as a physical laborer. When the Cultural Revolution finally ended in 1976, he resumed cartooning.

Liao's artistry has been recognized both in his homeland and internationally. Many exhibitions of his work have been organized around the globe. Two of his cartoons, one from the earlier *Cat Kingdom* series and the other, "Self-portrait," an acknowledged masterpiece from his later years, are in the permanent collection of the International Cartoon Art Museum in Florida.

H.Y.L.L.

LIBERATORE, GAETANO (1953-   ) An Italian cartoonist and illustrator born on April 12, 1953, in Quadri, Liberatore is better known as Tanino, which is short for Gaetano. After graduating from an art school, he moved to Rome, where from 1974 to 1978 he worked for advertising agencies and drew record covers. In 1978 he started contributing to the newly

Gaetano Liberatore, "Ranxerox." © Gaetano Liberatore.

Liao Bingxiong, "Spring and Autumn in Cat Kingdom." © Liao Bingxiong.

launched lampoon magazine *Cannibale*, which printed his black-and-white short stories *Tiamotti, Saturno contro la Terra*, and *Folly Bololy*. Also appearing in the pages of that magazine were the first adventures of *Rank Xerox*, written by Stefano Tamburini and drawn by Pazienza and Liberatore. For the biting satire magazine *Il Male* (1978-82) he created short stories, illustrations, and several covers.

In 1980 Liberatore contributed to the opening issue of the magazine *Frigidaire* with the new and muscular version of *Ranxerox* (renamed under pressure from the famous producer of photocopiers), based on an idea and a script by Tamburini. Ranxerox is an android built by a student during a campus protest. The android, whose circuits are crossed, escapes the police after they kill his master and mates with an amoral teenager, Lubna, who becomes his mistress. Together they live some shocking adventures amid the urban decay and moral degeneration of an indeterminate metropolis that combines features of Rome and New York. More than the plot, it is the violence and hyperrealism of many scenes—depicted with powerful and colorful graphic style—that bear witness to contemporary moral and social squalor.

The sudden success of *Ranxerox* made Liberatore internationally popular. His hero's adventures were printed in France, Spain, Greece, Canada, the United States, and Japan. Many young artists drew inspiration from his style. In 1982 Liberatore moved to Paris, where he worked mainly on painting and illustration for posters and magazine and disk covers (for example, for Frank Zappa's *The Man from Utopia*). For some time he was also active as a fashion stylist for the Italian TV program *Mister Fantasy*.

Ranxerox adventures have been reprinted in three books released between 1981 and 1997. Illustrations and drawings by Liberatore have also been collected in *Plasmando* (1992). Liberatore and Tamburini are the protagonists of the comics adventure *La leggenda di Italianino Liberatore* ("The Legend of Little Italian Liberatore," 1995), written and drawn by Pazienza.

G.C.C.

LIBERTY KID (Italy) On November 13, 1951, in the pages of the new, pocket-sized comic magazine *L'Intrepido*, published by the brothers Del Duca, *Liberty Kid* started its checkered career. The feature was drawn first by the painters Toldo and Albanese, then taken over by Lina Buffolente, who carried it until its demise early in 1960.

As his name implied, Liberty Kid was a lover of freedom. He was a Southerner who could not countenance the practice of slavery, and for this reason he left his father's home to join the Union army. The tall, fair-haired hero fought bravely on all fronts and helped the Union achieve victory. The Civil War over, he became President Ulysses Grant's favorite secret agent; sent to all parts of the Western Hemisphere, Liberty Kid saw to it that justice and democracy prevailed.

Liberty Kid was more of a soap opera than an adventure strip (the same applies to most of the Del Duca productions). The hero's exploits were often a gimmick meant to introduce old people or harmless black children molested by unscrupulous louts. The story line complacently depicted white-haired mothers looking for their dead sons amid the rubble of the battlefield, or bereaved wives waiting in vain for the return of their lost husbands. Yet, in the midst of all the pathos, a

good story would occasionally be told, with flashes of inspiration and some good, zestful artwork.

G.B.

LIEFELD, ROB (1967-   ) The wunderkind of American comics, Rob Liefeld was born October 3, 1967, in Orange City, California. His only training consisted of some art courses during his high school years. He started contributing to fanzines while still in his early teens, and he had his artwork professionally published for the first time in the mid-1980s in the short-lived *Megaton* comic book.

His work soon attracted the attention of the two major publishers in the field. In 1988 he freelanced for DC, working most notably on *Warlord*; and the following year he went to Marvel, where he created the character Cable for *The New Mutants*. In 1991 the first issue of *X-Force*, which boasted Liefeld's cover and interior art, sold an astonishing 3 million copies. Later that same year Liefeld, dissatisfied with working conditions at Marvel, left to cofound Image Comics with five other Marvel defectors, Jim Lee and Todd McFarlane among them. *Youngblood*, his first creation at Image, sold 700,000 copies of its first issue (April 1992), a number never before realized by any independent comic-book publisher. Amid much acrimony and a flurry of lawsuits, however, he broke with his partners at Image in 1996. While continuing to publish *Youngblood* under his own Maximum Press imprint, Liefeld that same year contracted with Marvel to produce a number of issues of *The Avengers* and *Captain America*.

There has been much bashing of Liefeld in the fan press and on the Internet, where he has been accused of (among other sins) bad writing and slapdash draftsmanship. The critics miss the point, however: Liefeld's appeal has little to do with art or creativity; rather, it resides in his ability to titillate the adolescent minds of his fans with depictions of brawny heroes wielding gigantic weapons and big-busted women sporting skimpy outfits. With this caveat in mind, he could more aptly be compared with Madonna than with Jack Kirby.

M.H.

LIEUTENANT BLUEBERRY (France) In 1963 writer Jean-Michel Charlier and artist Jean Giraud (signing simply "Gir") created the adventures of Lieutenant Blueberry for the French magazine *Pilote* in a story called "Fort Navajo." (When the story branched out into a highly successful series, it became known as *Lieutenant Blueberry*.)

Lieutenant Blueberry was the most vigorous, exciting, and authentic Western to come along since the early *Red Ryder*. Lieutenant Mike S. Blueberry, a somewhat disillusioned soldier bearing a strong resemblance to French actor Jean-Paul Belmondo, was drawn with a sure hand by Gir. An officer with the mythical Seventeenth Regiment of the U.S. Cavalry, he is headquartered at Fort Navajo, an army encampment in the New Mexico territory. More often than not, however, Blueberry seems to be pursuing his own private wars, whether against gunrunners or marauding Apaches, quite independently from any official authority. In his adventures he finds help and succor from his inseparable companion Jimmy McClure, whose fondness for whiskey is only equaled by Blueberry's partiality to fighting and gambling.

"Lieutenant Blueberry," Gir (Jean Giraud). © Editions Dargaud.

All the characters in the series, from the hero down to the lowest walk-on, are highly individualized—their faces look lived-in. Gir's depiction of action is masterful, his delineation of background sharp and assertive, and his use of color nothing short of inspired. From its inception in 1954 *Lieutenant Blueberry* was been a revelation and a treat to those who appreciated the comics primarily for their graphic and plastic qualities.

Excellent as it was, however, the strip could have been made even better had Gir been allowed to write his own scenarios. Unfortunately he was saddled with Charlier, who, for all his other virtues, did not have a genuine feel for the Western mythos. Furthermore, Charlier was so eager to show off his textbook knowledge of the American West that he could never pass up an opportunity to cram every irrelevancy or cliché into his text. Yet *Lieutenant Blueberry*, thanks to Gir's brilliant artwork, remained one of the masterpieces of the European comics. *Lieutenant Blueberry* has had numerous book reprints, all of them published by Dargaud.

In the 1970s Gir devoted more and more of his time (as Moebius) to other, more cutting-edge projects, and Blueberry's appearances became increasingly sporadic. In 1985 Colin Wilson took over *La jeunesse de Blueberry* ("Blueberry's Youth"), a spin-off title retracing the hero's adventures prior to his enlistment in the army; and in 1991 William Vance started drawing the main series on scripts supplied by the creator. A number of *Blueberry* episodes drawn by Gir have been reprinted in the U.S. by Marvel and other publishers.

M.H.

LIFE IN HELL (U.S.) As a child, Matt Groening dreamed of becoming a writer; he showed little artistic ability. The incisive portrayals of contemporary angst in his *Life in Hell* grew out of a series of crudely drawn doodles Groening began producing in 1977. The reflections and experiences of a rabbit named Binky (an image chosen because it both represented the helplessness of the character and was the only recognizable

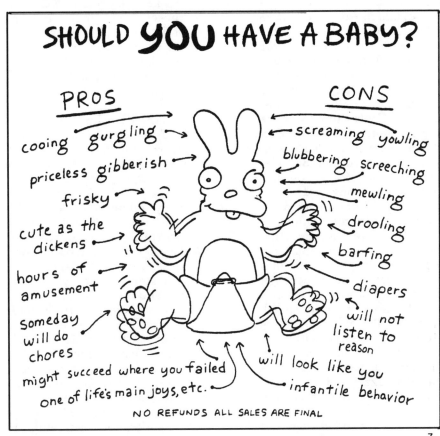

"Life in Hell," Matt Groening. © Matt Groening.

"Li'l Abner," Al Capp. © United Feature Syndicate.

animal Groening could draw), they dramatized human alienation with savage humor.

In 1978 the new-age graphics publication *Wet* published several of Groening's cartoons. The next year, the leading alternative weekly in the area, the *Los Angeles Reader*, picked the strip up, and in April 1980 *Life in Hell* became a regular feature. An employee of the *Reader*, Groening self-syndicated his work, and by 1983 it was appearing in about 20 college and alternative newspapers. In 1984, *Reader* coworker Deborah Caplan independently published a collection entitled *Love Is Hell*, which sold out its edition of 20,000 almost immediately, and the next year Caplan took over the syndication of the series, forming the *Life in Hell* Cartoon Company and the Acme Features Syndicate with Groening. The two, who were married in 1986, now distribute the strip and license use of its images on such products as posters, T-shirts, and greeting cards.

In his first year, Binky changed from a confrontational character to a victim, and his popularity increased exponentially. "The more tragedies that befell this poor little rodent," Groening reports, "the more positive response I got." Although the strip has remained minimally drawn, reflecting the influence of such Groening favorites as James Thurber and Charles Schulz, its range of topics and characters has increased. It now includes Binky's girlfriend Sheba; his even more beleaguered illegitmate son Bongo, graced with only one ear to distinguish him from Binky; and two plump little humans, Akbar and Jeff, who wear identical Charlie Brown sweaters and tasseled fezzes and who operate a series of sleazy businesses such as the Liposuction Hut.

In addition to *Love Is Hell*, which was reissued as a trade book in 1985 by Pantheon, *Life in Hell* has given rise to several successful collections, including *Work Is Hell* (1986), *School Is Hell* (1987), *Childhood Is Hell* (1988), and *The Big Book of Hell* (1990). But Groening's animated television series *The Simpsons*, begun in 1989, "makes the *Life in Hell* Company look like a drop in the bucket," the author admits. Nevertheless, the audience of the shrewdly iconoclastic newspaper feature continues to grow as the strip continues to address the universal themes of "the hellishness of most people's jobs and love lives and fear of death."

D.W.

LI'L ABNER (U.S.) *Li'l Abner*, drawn from the outset by Al Capp (Alfred Gerald Caplin), began as a daily strip on August 20, 1934, with the Sunday page following on February 24, 1935. Released initially by United Features, the strip has been distributed since June 1964 by the New York News Syndicate. Aside from the relatively unimportant World War II bond-selling Sunday half-page, *Small Change* (initially *Small Fry*), and a Sunday third-page companion strip with which the Sunday *Abner* began publication (and which lasted 16 weeks) named *Washable Jones*, *Li'l Abner* has been the only strip bylined by Capp. He did the unsigned story line and art on *Joe Palooka* (nominally by Ham Fisher) in 1933 before starting *Abner*; and while his *Fearless Fosdick* (a takeoff on *Dick Tracy*) has been a strip-within-a-strip of great popularity, it has always been signed Lester Gooch, to kid the Tracy creator, Chester Gould. Capp's signature in the early daily *Abner* episodes was "Al G. Cap," the second "p" being added only with the 25th episode. A similar early confusion can be noted in the Sunday page bylines.

Readers took a careful, interested look at the new daily strip from the moment the 19-year-old, six-foot-three Li'l Abner Yokum was depicted chest-deep in a Kentucky mountain pool of 1934 thinking about dinner back in his parents' log cabin. The artistry was eye-catching, the concept amusing, and the setting novel. (Only Capp himself had used contemporary hillbilly characters and settings in comic strips before, when he was ghosting *Joe Palooka*.) And the public chuckled gleefully when Abner upset New York society scions while visiting his sophisticated and wealthy Aunt Bessie Bopshire in the big city during the first daily story, a situation in which Abner played the cherished American folk-hero image of the noble and naive backwoodsman to the hilt. Readers were delighted, too, with the antics of Abner's "mammy," Pansy Yokum, and her spavined, browbeaten husband, Lucifer Ornamental Yokum. They howled as the strip's other comic characters entered the scene, such as the red-nosed and pompous-bellied Marryin' Sam, sweating on a 1935 Sunday page in an elaborate histrionic attempt to swindle Mammy Yokum out of " 'fo' dollahs." But they were driven to bite their nails during a weekend wait when a swindler named Payne Morland closed a 1935 Saturday episode by firing an automatic pistol bullet into Abner's stomach at point-blank range.

And so the strip went during its initial decades: surprise upon chuckle upon suspense, reflecting such highlights as the first appearance of Sir Cecil Cesspool, with a cigarette holder as long as a Fu Manchu fingernail dripping ashes on the majestic bosom of Lady Cesspool as he schemed to snare the Bopshire billions; the strange and final exit of one of the strip's early major characters, Abijah Gooch, galloping in tandem muleback over a hill with the shotgun of a murderous mountaineer at his head; the flesh-and-blood Garden of Paradise called the Schmoo, in his proliferating millions; the nefarious, deep-cavern skullduggeries and discoveries of Hairless Joe and Lonesome Polecat, not the least of which was the powerful, steaming Kickapoo Joy Juice; etc., etc.

The prompt, far-flung fame of *Li'l Abner*, which put it on the front pages of innumerable Sunday comic sections from Philadelphia to Los Angeles by the late 1930s, led to a filming of the strip by RKO Studios in 1940, with an unimportant but skillfully made-up cast. Later, it was produced as a major Broadway musical comedy in 1957 (hit song: *Jubilation T. Cornpone*) featuring such stars as Julie Newmar, Stubby Kaye, and Jerry Lewis, some of whom also starred in the 1959 Paramount color film version. A series of animated cartoon shorts featuring the inhabitants of Abner's hometown, Dogpatch, and produced in color by Dave Fleischer for Columbia were released in the mid-1940s, while Dogpatch itself serves as the name of a contemporary Disneyland-style amusement park in Kentucky based on Capp characters. (A short-lived soft drink called Kickapoo Joy Juice was marketed for a time in the 1950s, but it failed because of poor marketing techniques.) A number of paperbacks, comic books, and one hardback (prefaced by John Steinbeck) have featured reprints of the Abner strip since the 1930s, and its characters have served as the basis for many artifacts and toys.

Li'l Abner abandoned some of its focus on Abner and his family in later years, to cover the adventures of other associated characters for weeks at a time; Fearless Fosdick was long delayed in reappearing: the taut, gut-twisting narrative suspense of the first years of the strip vanished almost completely, but *Abner* remained

a graphically delectable strip, with still-surprising and bizarre characters and events—one of the daily and Sunday treats of any newspaper. *Li'l Abner* ended on November 13, 1977.

B.B.

"Lilla Fridolf," Torsten Bjarre. © Torsten Bjarre.

LILLA FRIDOLF (Sweden) *Lilla Fridolf* ("Little Fridolf"), written by Rune Moberg and drawn by Torsten Bjarre, had its origins in Swedish radio. The funny adventures of the little, plump man had been a popular radio series that made the transition into comic strips in 1957. The series having long since ended, Lilla Fridolf continues to entertain readers in comic annuals that were started in 1958 and in a comic book that was started in 1960.

Lilla Fridolf, however, seems an unlikely choice for a comic strip character. Who would believe that a stout, small, henpecked husband could work out in a series of his own? Readers in Sweden know the answer, for they are well entertained by the exploits of Fridolf and his domineering wife Selma. Both Fridolf and Selma are over 50 years of age, they already have grandchildren, and Fridolf is working in an office while Selma takes care of their house in the suburbs. For the most part, *Lilla Fridolf* is sheer situation comedy spiced with marital bickering. Drawn in a clear cartoon style similar to that of American comics, it nevertheless differs from American comics in the way family life is depicted. With all the bickering going on and the many odd situations Fridolf gets into, *Lilla Fridolf* is a very entertaining and enjoyable comic feature.

It is therefore not too much of a surprise that Torsten Bjarre won the 1971 Adamson, the Swedish comics award given annually by the Swedish Comics Academy, for his work on *Lilla Fridolf* along with his work on *Oskar* and *Flygsoldat 113 Bom* ("Air Force Private No. 113 No-hit"), all of which have established him as a comic artist emulated by younger colleagues.

W.F.

LILLE RICKARD OCH HANS KATT (Sweden) *Lille Rickard och hans katt* ("Little Richard and his Cat"), created, written, and drawn by Swedish artist Rune Andreasson throughout its 22-year run, was one of a rare breed: the Swedish daily comic strip.

Andreasson, a self-educated comic artist who graduated from high school and Göteborg's theater school, has dedicated most of his work to the entertainment of young readers, finding an ideal tool for this task in the comic strip and comic book media. He got the idea for *Lille Rickard och hans katt* about 1940 while a student studying English. Andreasson's class was reading a story titled "Dick Wittington and His Cat," and the youth was inspired to draw 80 pictures illustrating the tale. Some 10 years later, the memory of Dick Wittington sparked life into Andreasson's boy-hero, Lille Rickard, who is never without his cat while roaming the world in search of adventure.

Lille Rickard och hans katt started in Stockholm's evening newspaper, *Aftonbladet*, on December 23, 1951; it proved one of the nicest Christmas gifts imaginable. In the first strips Rickard leaves his hometown together with his tiny pet cat, forever to stumble into new adventures until the final curtain call in 1973. Swedish daily comic strips, which started in 1929 with Ruben Lundqvist's *Herr Knatt* ("Mister Little") and were continued in 1933 with Torvald Gahlin's *Fredrik*, have always been few and far between. Most daily strips in Swedish newspapers have been foreign imports. The weekly magazines became the seedbed of Swedish comic art much more easily, although they too started out with foreign comic imports. It is therefore quite an achievement to have produced for 22 years an indigenous comic strip that held its own against British and American strips.

At the time he started *Lille Rickard och hans katt*, Andreasson had already had comic strip experience, having done *Brum* for the weekly *Allers* since 1944. While working on *Lille Rickard*, Andreasson also created *Bamse* (about a bear) and *Pellefant* (about a very much alive toy elephant). Through syndication *Lille Rickard* has become Andreasson's best-known work, inside and outside Sweden. *Pellefant* has also been exported; it won him the Adamson, the Swedish Comic Academy's top honor, in 1969.

W.F.

LINDOR COVAS (Argentina) Walter Ciocca created *Lindor Covas el Cimarron* ("Lindor Covas the Untamed") as a daily strip for the Buenos Aires paper *La Razón* in 1956.

"Lindor Covas," Walter Ciocca. © La Razón.

Lindor Covas is part and parcel of the tradition of *gaucho* literature, alongside the famous epic *Martín Fierro*. Its hero is a gaucho, a South American horseman who lives on the pampas, along with his tough companions or with the women who drift in and out of his at times brutal sex life, like Sisina the prostitute or Rita the half-breed. Full of the fatalism characteristic of gaucho tales, Lindor's wanderings are a succession of misfortunes and mishaps, and the hero suffers tribulations parallel to those of Martín Fierro, although he lives in a later period and sometimes experiences happy moments, such as the creation of the tango. The language of *Lindor Covas* is that of the people, and it's so thick with gaucho expressions that on occasion the author feels compelled to include a translation into modern-day Spanish.

Before *Lindor Covas*, Ciocca had written and illustrated a number of stories for *La Razón*, including *Juan Cuello* (1949); *Santos Vega* (1951); *Hilarion Leiva* (1953); and foremost, his two previous successes, *Hormiga Negra* ("Black Ant," 1953) and *Fuerte Argentino* ("Fort Argentina," 1954). Ciocca's style imitates the quality of the wood engravings that illustrated the first editions

"Lille Rickard och hans katt," Rune Andreasson. © Bulls Pressedienst.

of *Martín Fierro*, with a technique that frequently uses chiaroscuro to add power to the images.

In 1962 Carlos Cores directed and interpreted a motion picture based on three episodes of *Lindor Covas*.

L.G.

LINK, STANLEY J. (1894-1957) Stanley Link was one of the few strip artists who stayed put. Born in 1894 in Chicago to a lower-middle-class laboring family, Link (whose *Tiny Tim* was a household name for 20 years) never left the Chicago area until he moved to his final home in nearby Long Beach, Indiana. As a teen, he attended night school and took a correspondence course in cartooning while working full-time at a number of jobs. Finding his first cartooning job with a Chicago-based animated-cartoon company at the age of 16, Link soon developed his natural facility through the repetitive work of endlessly drawing animation frames. Joining the navy in 1917, Link used his cartooning ability in presenting chalk talks on military subjects to groups of sailors while the young Benny Kubelsky (later Jack Benny) played the fiddle for background effect. After freelancing for a time in the early 1920s, Link was hired by Sidney Smith as an assistant on *The Gumps*, and he created the character Ching Chew for the Sunday adventure continuity featuring Chester Gump; he also drew the bulk of that continuity from 1923 until Smith's death in 1935.

In the meantime, Link introduced the popular, philosophical panel *Ching Chow* as a daily feature for Smith's syndicate, the News-Tribune group, and began his own strip, a Sunday feature about a boy shrunk to minuscule size, *Tiny Tim*, in 1933. This latter half-page feature became a great favorite, especially with children, which is not surprising, as it was one of the few newspaper comics deliberately aimed at youngsters. But Link got into serious trouble with his syndicate when he refused to continue *The Gumps* after Sidney Smith's sudden death in 1935, believing that an artist's creation should die with him and not be picked up by other hands. The strip was then at the height of its nationwide popularity, and as a master of the Smith style and story line, Link was the syndicate's obvious choice to carry on. Link refused to budge, however.

In the end, the syndicate held a contest for a *Gumps* artist (after desperately courting such artists as Rube Goldberg for the job), which the late Gus Edson won. Link, in bad grace with the syndicate, found much of his *Tiny Tim* continuity now rejected, his rewriting criticized, and his long-range plans for developing the strip arbitrarily changed in directions he was known to dislike. Link was never able to establish deliberate sabotage of his work, but he sensed it strongly, and this demoralized him and adversely affected much of his later *Tiny Tim* continuity. Eventually the strip was folded in the postwar period, and Link undertook a semi-autobiographical family strip called *The Baileys* for the News-Tribune Syndicate, which he continued until shortly before his death in Long Beach, Indiana, on December 24, 1957, at the age of 63. An extremely amusing and inventive cartoonist and continuity writer at his best, as he was while working on *The Gumps* and the early *Tiny Tim*, Link seems to have precipitated his own creative demise in mid-career by his very questionable decision not to continue *The Gumps*, which he could almost undoubtedly have rendered nearly as well as Smith himself. The sincerity of his conviction, however, cannot be questioned, and his later difficulties can only be regarded as tragic and unjustifiable.

B.B.

LITTLE ANNIE FANNY (U.S.) *Playboy* publisher Hugh Hefner and *Mad* creator Harvey Kurtzman produced two issues of a slick satire magazine called *Trump*, but *Playboy*'s financial empire being weak at the time, the magazine folded. But the pair reunited and Kurtzman and Will Elder premiered *Little Annie Fanny* in the October 1962 issue of *Playboy*.

The feature is an American comic-art landmark simply because it exists. As Hefner puts it, the strip had "an expensive birth. Instead of flat, fake color . . . we decided *Little Annie Fanny* should be rendered in full color, just as the commercial artist does for a magazine illustration, and then reproduced in the same elaborate, expensive four-color separation and process printing as we use for . . . the rest of the magazine." In short, *Little Annie Fanny* was the ultimate comic strip, production-wise. Every panel was a full-color painting.

The story line was simple: Little Annie, beautiful and zaftig, is a sexual Pollyanna. And from there, Kurtzman took off, lampooning everything. He satirized liberals, conservatives, woman's libbers, unions, Ku Klux Klanners, the FBI, and anything else pompous or overblown. And if his stories weren't as spontaneously hilarious as his early *Mad* work, they showed an unprecedented satiric maturity and development. By comparison, his *Mad* work was sophomoric.

Artistically, Will Elder handled the feature with anatomically exaggerated completeness. And while the art too lacked the *Mad* zaniness, it also showed an increased awareness of what is visually funny. Over the years, many other fine illustrators worked on *Little Annie Fanny*. Jack Davis' and Al Jaffee's wild backgrounds added the most to the feature, while Russ Heath's and Frank Frazetta's drawings blended well with the prevailing Kurtzman-Elder style.

The strip also featured several outstanding supporting characters, including Sugardaddy Bigbucks, the Daddy Warbucks imitation and obvious big-business scion; Wanda Homefree, Annie's idealistic girlfriend; and Solly Brass, the slick press agent with the pie-in-the-sky schemes.

A collection of *Annie Fanny* adventures, *Playboy's Little Annie Fanny*, was published in book form.

J.B.

The heroine pursued her free-spirited career through the 1970s and well into the 1980s. She got to meet a number of personages in the news at the time, from the Ayatollah Khomeini to Marcello Mastroianni, in a series of zany encounters. Among the artists who worked on the feature, additional mention should be made of Arnold Roth, Terry Austin, and underground cartoonists Gilbert Shelton and Robert Crumb. The last *Little Annie Fanny* episode appeared in the September 1988 issue of *Playboy*.

M.H.

LITTLE ANNIE ROONEY (U.S.) King Features' *Little Annie Rooney*, an adventure strip about a 12-year-old girl, drawn by five artists and scripted from the start by Brandon Walsh, first appeared in 1927. The Hearst syndicate's competitive reply to *Little Orphan Annie*, Walsh's *Rooney* strip was first drawn by Ed Verdier in a sharp, simple style similar to that of Ernie Bushmiller. He signed himself, cryptically, Verd. The same name

"Little Annie Rooney," Darrell McClure and Brandon Walsh. © King Features Syndicate.

was supplied by King Features for the printed byline. On May 11, 1929, a second, unknown cartoonist, working in a cruder style, took over the strip. Verd's signature vanished, but his byline was retained. The third Rooney artist began work on the strip on July 22, 1929. This was Ben Batsford, who took over the famed *Doings of the Duffs* strip in the mid-1920s and went on to author and draw *The Doodle Family* (later *Frankie Doodle*) through the 1930s. Batsford was the first to draw Walsh's principal *Rooney* character (after the heroine herself), the orphan-asylum head, Mrs. Meany. Batsford's temporary stint was completed on October 6, 1930, when King Features finally located an artist they felt was ideal for the strip: Darrell McClure, who began his long-lived association with *Annie Rooney* on that day.

The 27-year-old McClure, earlier the creator of King Features' *Vanilla and the Villains*, also began to draw the Sunday half-page, which first appeared on November 30, 1930. McClure's style quickly became much more realistic and detailed than those of his three predecessors on the strip, but he made no essential change in the appearance of Annie Rooney herself: the short black bangs, patched dress, black sandals, and white socks remained the same. McClure did change Annie's dog, Zero; early in 1931, he shortened the dog's muzzle considerably, gave him a black button nose, and reduced his size. Mrs. Meany was also altered markedly from Batsford's concept, but chiefly in the direction of collective small details of face and dress.

The McClure strip had genuine eye-appeal and exciting graphic movement. For the first time, Walsh's rather sophisticated script and story line had art that complemented it. But the work on both the daily strip and Sunday half-page (especially when the latter was

enlarged to a full weekly page) was more than the meticulous McClure could handle, and a fine adventure-continuity artist, Nicholas Afonski, was commissioned to draw the Sunday strip after 1932. With Afonski, Walsh developed a new boy-hero for the Sunday page, Joey Robins (whose parents had adopted Annie), and a new feature character, an Oriental adventurer named Ming Foo. Annie was absent for long periods from the new Sunday page in the 1933-35 period, while Joey and Ming Foo went adventuring around the world; then the two were given their own Sunday space in a strip called *Ming Foo* beginning March 17, 1935, which shared *Annie Rooney*'s page thereafter. Annie, of course, continued her escapades in the McClure and Walsh daily strip, and resumed them in the Afonski and Walsh Sunday strip after March 1935.

Curiously, for someone who had gone on the record (in King Features' *Famous Artists and Writers* for 1949) as having accepted the authorship of *Little Annie Rooney* to "write a strip under my own name," Brandon Walsh waited long enough to do it: his first printed byline on *Rooney* appeared on Sunday, August 25, 1935 (although he had been given a handwritten byline on an early Sunday Rooney page-topper called *Fablettes*, a weekly gag sequence with nonrecurrent characters replaced by *Ming Foo*). Earlier, only the drawing artists' signatures had appeared on the daily or Sunday strip, and the daily strip was still being bylined Darrell McClure late into the 1930s. King Features' records, and Walsh himself, however, attest that Walsh wrote *Annie Rooney* from the start.

After Walsh's death in 1954, *Little Annie Rooney* continued in its role as King Features' leading second-string strip for another decade. With McClure at the helm until the end, the Sunday page folded on May 30, 1965, and the daily strip on April 16, 1966. Only two obscure reprints of the strip appeared, in the 1930s.

B.B.

LITTLE BEARS AND TYKES (U.S.)   The first publication of James Swinnerton's *Little Bears and Tykes* in anything that could be called a comic strip format appeared in the *San Francisco Examiner* on June 2, 1895. This was a small square filled with black-and-white bear cubs saying and doing various amusing things with a common theme. Previously, Swinnerton had drawn his cubs (called, in occasional *Examiner* captions, the Little Bears) in humanized postures for special spot art, including daily weather announcements in a small box on the editorial page, from 1893 on. Now, as features multiplied in the *Sunday Examiner*, the Swinnerton bears panel was added to the new children's page. When Swinnerton added a few kids to the bears' antics on Sunday, the paper's caption writer referred to the "Little Bears and Tykes," a term that somehow became distorted over the decades and emerged half a century later in some texts on comic strips as "Little Bears and Tigers," a work that never existed.

The Swinnerton bear cubs lacked individuality and had no separate names in his panel series for the *Examiner*. There was no continuity of action within the panel, either: each cub was engaged in a small spot gag with a caption. (Although some of this was in dialogue form, none of the cubs' remarks were rendered in balloons.) In essence, the cub panel differed little from such earlier character panel sequences as the early English *Ally Sloper*: The drawing was the crucial element, while the dialogue was incidental and largely disposable. There was, accordingly, little in the Swinnerton panel series to anticipate the comic strip art form that was soon to emerge in New York.

However—and this is a vital point—the *Little Bears and Tykes* panel was the first regularly repeated original character cartoon series in a newspaper. It made a portion of the reading public aware that a newspaper could bring them a familiar set of figures on a given day (Sunday) with fair regularity, and that augmented newspaper sales.

Swinnerton carried on the *Little Bears* (dropping the Tykes) in the added 1897 color comic section of the *Examiner*, then took them to New York with him when he joined Hearst's strip artists in that city. They appeared there sporadically until 1901, when the last one or two *Little Bears* appeared as comic section half-pages. It seems apparent that Swinnerton thought of the *Little Bears* as a strip of essentially regional appeal (the bears being derived from the California state flag and seal emblem), and best replaced with his newer, New York work, such as *Mount Ararat* and *Little Jimmy*.

B.B.

LITTLE IODINE (U.S.)   Little Iodine started her obnoxious career as a recurring character in Jimmy Hatlo's humor panel *They'll Do It Every Time*; the readers grew so fond of this juvenile monster that, in 1943, a Sunday color half-page titled *Little Iodine* was added to the *They'll Do It* panel.

Iodine is a contary-minded, stubborn, and grudge-bearing little pest whose pranks, deceptions, and connivings are the bane of her suburban neighborhood. Her favorite target is her own father, the meek and petty Henry Tremblechin, whose dreams of getting a

"Little Iodine," Jimmy Hatlo. © King Features Syndicate.

raise or a promotion from his boss, the foul-tempered Mr. Bigdome, are always thwarted by his progeny's diabolical inventions and her implacable (if contrived) candor. Iodine's mother, Effie Tremblechin, gets scarcely better treatment from her flesh and blood, whose greatest pleasure is aping her mother's one-upmanship and social pretenses. When she grows tired of bedeviling her parents, Iodine, often aided and abetted by her boyfriend Sharkey, exercises her nefarious talents against the world at large, in the form of broken windows, false police alarms, and a superb contempt for the rules of accepted behavior—all of which contribute to making Little Iodine a female counterpart to the Katzenjammer Kids.

Jimmy Hatlo drew his strip in a skillful, if somewhat cluttered, way, and his characters were always depicted in a very funny vein. After Hatlo's death in 1963, *Little Iodine* was taken over by former assistant Bob Dunn (in 1967 Dunn turned over the drawing of *Little Iodine* to Hy Eisman, while continuing to write the stories). Their collaboration proved harmonious and fruitful, lasting for almost 20 years, until the strip's discontinuation in 1986.

Little Iodine has appeared in comic books and was also reprinted in paperback form. In 1946 it was made into a movie, without apparent success.

M.H.

LITTLE JIMMY (U.S.)   James Swinnerton's *Little Jimmy* (first titled just *Jimmy*) opened in the Hearst Sunday comic sections on February 14, 1904, in an episode titled "Jimmy—He Goes for the Milk." Jimmy, an eight- or nine-year-old boy with a round head and button nose, was sent out to buy milk for the family dinner, but he managed to get so entangled in street events on the way that he was hopelessly late, showing up with a broken milk pot as well. This became the theme of most of the early *Jimmy* episodes, as the strip moved from its initial inside half-page position to full, front-page spread. Appearing sporadically at first, *Jimmy* had become a regular weekly page by the 1910s, running by then in the second-string Hearst Saturday comic sections.

"Little Jimmy," James Swinnerton. © King Features Syndicate.

Jimmy Thompson, to give the boy's full name (his first name, of course, was Swinnerton's own nickname), expanded his range of activities in the second decade of *Jimmy*, and added a child friend, the baseball-cap-wearing Pinkie. (Pinkie owned a bulldog named Buck, which was the prototype of Beans, the dog Jimmy himself would later own.) The Sunday *Jimmy* page was dropped for a time at the close of the 1910s, then revived in early 1920 as *Little Jimmy*, with a strong emphasis on the Nevada and Arizona desert regions, which Swinnerton had come to love over the past 15 years. (The Thompson family went there on vacation.) In 1922, Jimmy acquired the first of his several pets, the bulldog Beans. This was followed by a small bear cub in the summer of 1924 (who bore little resemblance to the Swinnerton cubs of the 1890s), which Jimmy called "Lil Ole Bear," and by a Mexican fighting rooster named Poncho in early 1928. (By this time, Jimmy had been shipwrecked on a fantastic island with a drooping-moustached Mr. Batch, an earlier strip creation of Swinnerton's; traveled to Mexico; been to Hollywood; and generally gotten around.) A return to the American Southwest in the late 1920s was permanent, however, and it was here that Jimmy met the last of his regular kid companions, a Navaho canyon kid, borrowed from the popular Swinnerton *Good Housekeeping* color page of the 1920s and 1930s, *Canyon Kiddies*. A knowledgeable older Indian brave named Somolo also entered the strip at this time; Somolo was able to talk to animals, and he involved Jimmy and his pals and pets in numerous funny or weird desert experiences.

Little Jimmy began as a daily strip on July 24, 1920, with Jimmy's daily experiences paralleling those in the Sunday pages for the most part. The daily was dropped in the late 1930s (last date in most Hearst papers was October 25, 1937), while the Sunday page was replaced for a few years in the 1940s by Swinnerton's *Rocky Mason*. Revived in 1945, the Sunday page continued until April 27, 1958, when Swinnerton retired from comic strip work to devote himself to painting his famed desert-scapes. Often charming, enormously informative in its later years about Navaho Indian life and desert wildlife in general, and a particular delight for younger children, *Little Jimmy* deserves selective reprinting. (It should be mentioned that considerable stretches of the daily and Sunday strips were ghosted by Doc Winner in the 1920s and 1930s; these were always left unsigned by Swinnerton.) *Little Jimmy* was reprinted many times in collections and paperbacks from the 1900s to the 1940s.

B.B.

LITTLE JOE (U.S.) One of seven new Sunday half-page strips added to the *New York News* and *Chicago Tribune* family of comics on October 1, 1933, Ed Leffingwell's *Little Joe* was the first major syndicate strip to be set wholly in the contemporary cattle ranch West. Joe, a chapped and booted kid of about 13, lives with his widowed mother on a ranch managed by an old cowhand (and probably gunfighter) named Utah. Utah and Joe quickly come to dominate the narrative, which is an admixture of single-episode gag-finish pages and continuing series or semi-humorous stories of varying lengths. At the outset, the strip seems to have been entirely drawn by Leffingwell, Harold Gray's cousin, letterer, and background aide of the time. The story and dialogue seem to be largely Gray's, however, and by 1936, most of the human figures are clearly his, to remain so through the mid-1940s. Effectively, *Little Joe* must be regarded as an additional Gray strip from its inception in 1933 to at least 1946, when the strip returned primarily to weekly gags and the artistry of Leffingwell and (after his death) that of his brother, Robert, also a later Gray aide.

The combination of Leffingwell's background style (his handling of the western landscape, especially the rocky gorges and mountainsides of the cattle states, is stunning) and Gray's lively figure work made *Little Joe* one of the most visually attractive strips of the 1930s and 1940s. Its wide popularity in syndication seems to have reflected this appeal, as much as it did the amusement and suspense afforded by Gray's mature, cynical, and hard-bitten narrative.

Until American's involvement in World War II, the *dramatis personae* of *Little Joe* consists of wise and just Indian tribes (Gray felt strongly that the American Indian had gotten a very dirty deal from the white man), brutal gunmen, conniving rival ranchers, rustlers, an occasional eastern tenderfoot, gigantic bears, and—in the late 1930s—the comic figure of a Mexican general whose rank and stature at any given time depend on the political complexion of his native country. When out of power, Ze Gen'ral, as he calls himself (and is called in a small companion strip to *Little Joe* that ran in the 1940s), hangs out on Joe's mother's ranch and goes adventuring with Joe and Utah for a long period of time. After 1941, wartime comes to the West of *Little Joe*, and even a submarine-landed invading party of Japanese saboteurs (whom Utah captures and quietly puts to work on his shorthanded ranch as convenient slave labor for the duration) is introduced. Ze Gen'ral takes command of a Mexican division in the war, the ranch characters suffer through rationing, gun down saboteurs, torment draft dodgers, and undergo the general narrative dislocation of most strip characters during the war. Afterwards, Gray seems to have felt he had exhausted the potential of *Little Joe*, and he returned full-time to *Annie*. The Leffingwell brothers continued the strip as a Sunday gag filler until the late 1950s, after which its distribution by the News-Tribune syndicate is obscure, since it was dropped by both parent papers.

Between its gag periods, *Little Joe* could be an intelligently written, well-drawn, and gripping strip. It is definitely a minor classic and merits reprinting in permanent form.

B.B.

LITTLE KING, THE (U.S.) Making its premiere appearance in Sunday comic sections on September 9,

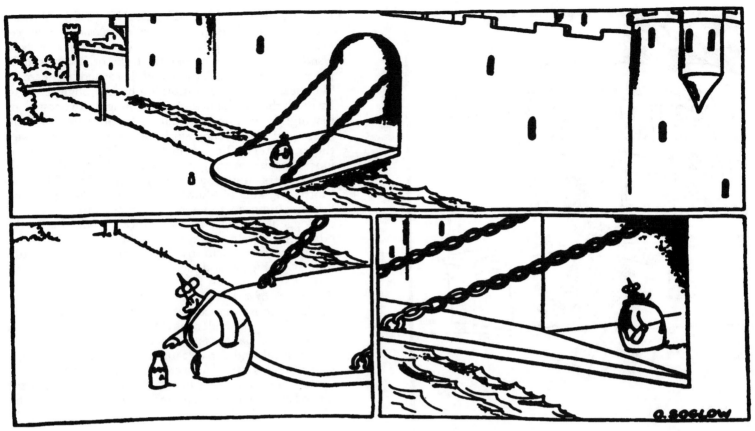

"The Little King," Otto Soglow. © King Features Syndicate.

1934, *The Little King* succeeded the artist's similar page, *The Ambassador*, and the earlier magazine version in the pages of the *New Yorker*. *The Ambassador* was a stop-gap feature that ran between Hearst's signing of the talented Soglow and the expiration of the contract with the *New Yorker* for *The Little King*.

Soglow was a magazine panel cartoonist whose drift to strip ideas was manifested in the *King* pages, one of those rare, spontaneously popular features that burst onto the scene full-blown.

Curiously, although the character was a favorite in comic pages and in Max Fleisher-Paramount animated cartoons for 35 years, the king had no name. Likewise, his kingdom was never named, and the queen and their comely daughter (who appeared with less frequency through the years) were also nameless. But these facts meant little to the understanding of the strip.

Soglow's kingdom was zany and unpredictable—sometimes almost surrealistic—and presided over by a consistently unconventional king. The Little King outraged stuffy ambassadors, surprised dignified ladies, interrupted official functions for childlike games, and, all in all, was the king of the common, uninhibited, playful, irreverent folk. As such he is one of the classic comic creations, strikingly original in broad conception and endearing in individual shenanigans.

King Features' chief Joe Connelly's suggestion to populate the strip with more characters resulted in such figures as Ookle the Dictator (six months in 1940), but few new faces lasted long; they were superfluous.

In the days of top strips, *Sentinel Louie*, a half-pint palace guard with a generous torso, carried on his antics in evidently different neighborhoods of the same kingdom. And *Travelin' Gus* was a short-lived Sunday feature about an inveterate bus rider's trips to strange neighborhoods, presaging some of Mr. Mum's travels and echoing Soglow's *New Yorker* days.

After more than 40 years with King Features, *The Little King* had become one of the most familiar of comic creations: the shrimpy stature, the pointed beard, and the ever-present crown (in bed and swimming pools!). He never spoke, and indeed Soglow's world was almost always silent. The occasional dialogue appeared without benefit of balloons in keeping with Soglow's stark, simple artwork. There was no shading, backgrounds were scarce, and the figures were really glorified stick figures.

Continuing quietly in the 1970s, *The Little King* lost some of its pizzazz and much of its earlier surrealistic flavor. The feature ended on July 20, 1975, a few months after its creator's death.

R.M.

LITTLE LULU (U.S.) *Little Lulu* first appeared in June 1935 as a single-panel gag cartoon by "Marge" (Marjorie Henderson Buell) in the *Saturday Evening Post* magazine. In 1945, Western Publishing Company obtained the rights to the feature for its *Dell Four Color* and *Color* series of specials, commencing with number 74 in June 1945. Nine more "one-shot" issues of *Little Lulu* followed, and in January 1948 the first regular issue was published, beginning a long and successful series.

Marge was not responsible for any of the stories or artwork in the comic book or the subsequent newspaper strip. For some 14 years, the comic book was written by John Stanley, whose storyboarded scripts were then adapted into the artwork. Stanley did finished art on the covers. The newspaper strip, produced for the Chicago Tribune-New York News syndicate by the staff of Western Publishing, ran from 1955 to 1967. It was a daily strip done first by Woody Kimbrell, and, for its last six years, by writer Del Connell and several

"Little Lulu," Marge Henderson. © Marge.

LITTLE NEMO IN SLUMBERLAND (U.S.) Winsor McCay founded his masterpiece *Little Nemo in Slumberland,* which first appeared in the pages of the *New York Herald* on Sunday, October 15, 1905, on a very simple premise: each night Little Nemo is carried in dream to Slumberland, and each morning he is brought back to earth by the rude shock of awakening. In the course of his nightly wanderings, Little Nemo enters a little deeper into his dream-world, meeting along the way the characters who become his guides and companions: Flip, the green, grimacing dwarf; Impy the cannibal; Slivers the dog; the quackish Dr. Pill; and Morpheus, king of Slumberland, and his daughter the Princess (whose name we will never learn).

Doggedly, Winsor McCay proceeds with his methodological exploration of the dream. Lovingly he details its transpositions, its visions, its transformations. Graphically and pictorially, he re-creates its sensations, the sense of free fall, of flight, the feeling of dizziness, of estrangement. Like Freud, and with a similar purpose, he explores the depths of the unconscious. From the evidence of McCay's letters there can be no doubt that these explorations were in part autobiographical, and in part cautionary. McCay gave shape to his dreams in order to exorcise his demons.

Yet there has never been so luminous a treatment for so Faustian a theme. Slumberland is a country of no

artists, including Roger Armstrong. Both Stanley and Kimbrell developed and/or created a number of supporting characters who peopled Little Lulu's neighborhood.

From the start, *Little Lulu* was a strip about childhood and childhood fantasies, dwelling on the title character, a little girl in a typical urban neighborhood. Along with the other neighborhood kids, especially her "boyfriend," Tubby Tompkins, Lulu Moppet would get into endless dilemmas, often the products of overactive youthful imaginations. Superb characterization made even the most minute crisis funny, and for that reason the *Little Lulu* comics by Stanley are nostalgic favorites among collectors, many of whom consider it the best "kid strip" of all time.

Based mainly on the popularity of the comic books, *Little Lulu* was in demand for merchandising, including dozens of story and activity books produced by Western's book division and a series of animated cartoons produced by Famous Studios.

During the 1950s, Western's comic book division produced a great many giant specials with names like *Little Lulu and Tubby Halloween Fun* and *Little Lulu and Tubby at Summer Camp.* Many of these spotlighted a charming series by Stanley in which Lulu, as babysitter to little Alvin, would ad-lib fairy tales about the evil Witch Hazel and a small apprentice witch, Little Itch. In addition, Tubby had his own comic book for 49 issues from 1952 to 1962.

In 1972, Western Publishing assumed full ownership of the feature and Marge's byline was dropped. *Little Lulu* continued to appear in its own magazine and in various issues of *Golden Comics Digest* and *March of Comics.* The title came to an end in April 1984.

M.E.

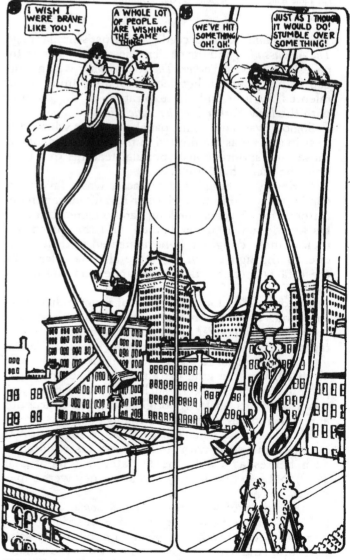

"Little Nemo in Slumberland," Winsor McCay.

"Little Orphan Annie," Harold Gray. © *Chicago Tribune-New York News Syndicate.*

shadows, and its light is the vibrant light of the early Renaissance painters. The grace of baroque composition and the freedom of Art Nouveau design touch its storybook palaces, its fairy-tale landscapes, the dress and poise of its characters. In this brightly lit universe, if the protagonists look shadowy (although there is a definite psychological progression as the action advances) it is because the hero is subordinate to the vision.

The last *Nemo* page appeared in the *Herald* of April 23, 1911. In the meantime McCay had gone over to Hearst (as so many other cartoonists had done before him), where he blissfully continued Little Nemo's adventures (under the title *In the Land of Wonderful Dreams*) from April 3, 1911, to July 26, 1914. Then, after a 10-year absence, *Little Nemo* was revived by the *Herald* from 1924 to 1927, after which it disappeared, this time for good.

Little Nemo's success had been immediate. In 1908 it was made into a musical (with a score by Victor Herbert); in 1909 McCay himself animated it (it was his first film cartoon). Greeting cards in the likenesses of Nemo, the Princess, and Flip were printed in England. Then there was a 20-year silence from 1927 to 1947. In 1947 Robert McCay (Winsor's son and his model for Little Nemo) tried to syndicate the old *Little Nemo* pages, but he was unsuccessful. Only in the late 1960s and early 1970s was interest in *Little Nemo* rekindled. In 1969 Garzanti published in Italy a hardbound collection of *Little Nemo* pages, and an American version appeared in 1972, issued by Nostalgia Press.

M.H.

LITTLE ORPHAN ANNIE (U.S.) According to legend, Captain Joseph Patterson of the *New York News* received a submission from *Gumps* assistant Harold Gray in 1924, performed a sex change on the strip, and thus gave *Little Orphan Annie* to the world. Whatever the circumstances of her birth, the little red-haired

orphan girl soon developed into one of the truly classic figures of comic strip—and indeed, of American pop-culture—history. The strip debuted on August 5, 1924.

The first few years saw Annie in vaguely humorous, often sentimental, continuities—similar to *The Gumps*, another story strip long before the commonly acknowledged birth of story strips. In the early years the *Annie* Sunday page was an entity unto itself and complete within each day's page.

The feisty, curly-haired heroine—who, like all her fellow characters, was drawn with blank eyes—fended for herself in the early days against bratty playmates and bossy protectors. Her only true friends were her dog Sandy and her doll Emily Marie. About the time that the doll left the strip as a prop, "Daddy" Warbucks entered.

With the evolution of Warbucks from a henpecked member of the idle rich (his wife disappeared from the strip in short order) to an adventurous soldier of fortune, international businessman, and the richest man in the world, the strip took on its special meaning.

But more than novels in strip form (thus epitomizing the unique art form that is the comic strip), Gray's tales were morality plays. They were parables, folktales, told with Bunyan-like simplicity, allegory, and characterization.

Thus Gray wrote tales that gripped, that were at once fanciful and glaringly real. Characters were easily identified by their names: Warbucks was originally a munitions manufacturer; Mrs. Bleating-Hart a hypocritical do-gooder; Fred Free a wandering, kindly soul; J. Preston Slime a cynical, two-faced reformer. In time Warbucks (and more so his Oriental associates Asp and Punjab) assumed supernatural powers. These men were always present in the nick of time, dispensing justice arbitrarily, ruthlessly, and quietly.

Gray's art is not to be overlooked and is as important a factor as his writing; his drawings are simply as dramatic—and as suspenseful and pregnant—as the text. In his reserved, heavy lines, Gray created a world that was his own. Seldom have plot and art been so perfectly fused as in the integrated, very personal statement that was *Little Orphan Annie*.

Criticism has been harsh through the years against Gray for his (conservative) political views and his alleged propagandizing, but in the end, Gray needs no posthumous defense. *Annie* was one of the five top strips for decades; at its height it was the basis for two movies, a long-running radio serial, and countless merchandising items.

When Gray died in 1968, his syndicate did the unforgivable: farming out *Annie* to a succession of artists and writers who understood nothing of Gray's fragile creation save the most superficial—and erroneous—stereotypes. In early 1974 a youngster was given the strip with the intention of transforming art and story: Annie was to become a with-it kid. A barrage of complaints and cancellations brought back the Annie of her prime, via reprints starting with the classic Jack Boot murder story of 1936.

R.M.

Following the success of the Broadway musical (and later movie) *Annie* based on Harold Gray's characters, the syndicate decided to do a relaunch of the strip, with original stories this time. In December 1979 *Annie* (as the feature was now renamed to capitalize on the Broadway and upcoming Hollywood versions) made its appearance, drawn and written by Leonard Starr, who had been doing *On Stage* up to that time. Starr remained remarkably faithful to the original: he did bring a more contemporary look and feel to the feature, but otherwise his interpretation has been uncannily respectful to Gray's creation, without being slavish. Now approaching the third decade of its existence, *Annie* has proved the only successful revival of a classic comic strip to date. (*Little Nemo*, *Pogo*, and *Buck Rogers* all failed on their second go-round; the jury is still out on *Terry and the Pirates*.)

M.H.

LITTLE PEOPLE, THE (U.S.) When Walt Scott relinquished the Sunday *Captain Easy* in February 1952, he began his own *Huckleberry Hollow*, a Sunday comic featuring the doings of talking animals. It debuted on February 24, 1952.

The NEA comic, possibly created in answer to the success of *Pogo*, soon took second billing to *The Little People*. This new Sunday strip first appeared on June 1, 1952, based on characters that Walt Scott had drawn for a special NEA Christmas series of strips the previous year. Solely a Sunday page, *The Little People*, with *Huckleberry Hollow* as a top strip, continued until Scott's death; the last page appeared on September 6, 1970.

Scott, a former Disney artist and versatile cartoonist, packed a lot of charm into *The Little People*. The little folks are forest dwellers, the friends of friendly animals and fearful of bigger people and fiercer animals. They have enormous heads with floppy ears and impish expressions, and enormous feet.

In the beginning the little ones lived in a big log and made toys for Santa, but the Christmas theme soon vanished and the happenings in the Valley of the Small People became simple humorous situations on a cuter, smaller scale. Among the regular cast of little people were Cork, Chub, Wembly, Woosh, Weesh, Loop, Jink, and Old One.

R.M.

LOBAČEV, JURIJ (DJORDJE) (1909-   ) One of the most important Serbian comics authors, Jurij Lobačev was born on March 4, 1909, in the city of Skadar (then under Turkish control, now in Albania). His father, Pavie Lobačev, was a Russian diplomat. A month after Jurij's birth, he was transferred to Centinje, the second-largest city in Montenegro. From 1912 to 1914 the family lived in a succession of places: first Serbia, then Macedonia, Italy, and Crete. In 1916 Pavie Lobačev was promoted to consul general in Thessaloniki (Greece). But after the Russian Revolution toppled the czarist regime, the Lobačevs decided not to return to their native country. Instead, they settled after World War I in the newly created nation of Yugoslavia, which consisted of the former kingdoms of Serbia and Montenegro along with territories that used to be part of the Austro-Hungarian or Turkish empires.

Jurij Lobačev took the first name Djordje at this time; it was a name he would keep until being exiled from Yugoslavia in 1949. In 1922 he moved to Belgrade, where seven years later he finished secondary school and became a student of the Philosophical Fac-

Djordje Lobačev, "Hajduk Velijko." © Djordje Lobacev.

ulty. He eventually graduated from the Department of the History of Arts.

In 1934, after losing his job as a clerk in a building firm, Lobačev devoted himself completely to the new medium of comics. He published his first comic, *Krvavo nasledstvo* ("A Blood-smeared Inheritance"), under the pseudonym George Strip in installments in the Belgrade weekly magazine *Panorama*, beginning March 23, 1935. His scriptwriter for this initial and rather naive work was a close friend, Vadim Kurganski. Their second collaboration, *Zrak smrti* ("Death Ray")—based on the Alexei Tolstoy novel *Hiperboloid of Engineer Garin* and published in the magazine *Strip* beginning April 10, 1935—was only slightly better. Up until Yugoslavia became involved in World War II, Lobačev published some 30 long comics. For all but five of them he wrote the script himself. The most successful of them was *Princeza Ru*, which was published in France, Italy, and elsewhere.

During the war Lobačev worked as a technical editor for the illustrated magazine *Kolo*, which was published in Nazi-occupied Belgrade. He published only one comic during the war, *Biberce* ("Pepper-sized Boy"), in the magazine *Kolo*. The comic, based on a Serbian folktale about a small boy who defeats an evil giant, was banned by the Germans after the 10th installment. Nevertheless, a small Serbian publisher quietly printed the entire story as a comic book. In 1942 Lobačev became active in the resistance movement, and when Belgrade was liberated by Soviet and partisan forces in October 1944, he joined the advancing Allies, fighting all the way to Vienna, where he was wounded. After recovering, he returned to Belgrade in 1945.

In 1949, after a rift had developed between the Soviet Union and Yugoslavia, Lobačev, like many other Yugoslav citizens of Russian origin, was deported to the U.S.S.R. There he created *Hurricane to the Rescue*, which was probably the first Russian comic ever; in 1967 it began to be published in installments in the magazine *Kostyor*, which was based in Leningrad. However, after just a few installments, the regional committee of the Soviet Communist Party ordered publication of the strip to cease, declaring that comics were harmful to youth. However, Lobačev managed to publish his work in Serbia. For *Pegaz* magazine he completed an adaptation of *The Wizard of Oz*. He also drew comics inspired by Serbian folk traditions, drew a new version of *Baron Munchausen*, and created, in 1991, *Bajke A. S. Pushkina* ("Fairy Tales of A. S. Pushkin").

As of 1997 he was still doing new artwork for Belgrade comics publishers and visiting the city once a year.

S.I.

LOCHER, RICHARD (1929-　　) A Pulitzer Prize-winning editorial cartoonist for the *Chicago Tribune* in 1982 and the cartoonist for the *Dick Tracy* comic strip since that year, Dick Locher was born in Dubuque, Iowa, on June 4, 1929. He studied art at the University of Iowa, the Chicago Academy of Fine Art, and the Art Center of Los Angeles. He also served as a pilot in the U.S. Air Force. Working in a freelance art studio in Chicago, Locher met *Dick Tracy*'s creator, Chester Gould, in 1957. Gould asked him to be his assistant and Locher agreed, working for Gould for four years before starting his own advertising firm. Among other jobs, he was part of the team that developed the design of

Ronald McDonald and other characters representing the fast-food chain. Locher credits Gould for informing him of an opening for an editorial cartoonist at the *Chicago Tribune*. That was in the 1970s, and before then Locher had never done any editorial cartooning; now it's his passion.

With his experience as a former assistant to Gould on *Dick Tracy*, Locher was the logical choice to take over the artwork when Rick Fletcher, the artist who had succeeded Gould on the strip, died. Locher was teamed with scriptwriter Max Allan Collins, who had written *Dick Tracy* since Gould's retirement in December 1977. Then in 1992, Collins was abruptly fired by Tribune Media Services, the syndicate that owns *Dick Tracy*. He was replaced by Mike Kilian.

Locher readily admits that while he enjoys his comic-strip work, editorial cartooning is his preference. His editorial cartoons can be brilliant. While adequate, his artwork for *Dick Tracy* lacks the verve of both Gould's and Fletcher's work on the strip. It continues to maintain the stark black-and-white look with ample use of the classic Tracy profile and other stylistic elements created by Gould. Although the strip scored an increase in readership in 1990 when the Warren Beatty *Dick Tracy* movie was released, Locher has been fighting an uphill battle against comics editors' preference for humor over story strips. He has also suffered from scripts that for a time during the end of Collins's tenure depended too much on nostalgia and on bringing back old villains. The Kilian era of scriptwriting has not brought glory to America's most famous detective either.

Still, *Dick Tracy* may survive another decade of syndication. Locher has the talent, as his tight yet ornate editorial-cartooning style, replete with biting, dead-on caricatures, proves. However, he needs stories that excite him to take Tracy from the flatfoot cop he is today to the premier detective of yore.

B.C.

LOIS LANE (U.S.) Lois Lane is, amazingly enough, as old as Superman himself. She made her first appearance in National's *Action* number one for June 1938, the issue that introduced the *Superman* strip. She has been Superman's major love interest ever since.

Lois Lane, because she was part and parcel of the first comic book superhero feature, became the model for all future comic book love interests. And because creators Siegel and Schuster included a woman in *Superman*, most superhero imitators included one, too.

As originally conceived by the creators, Lois Lane was nothing more than a bitch—a conniving, self-serving, egotistical reporter with few ethics and fewer morals. She was not your typical girl-next-door, apple-pie woman. Perhaps the greatest example of her viciousness was her hatred of Superman's alter ego, Clark Kent. She rarely missed an opportunity to degrade or humiliate him.

This led to the classic comic book love triangle—Superman–Clark Kent–Lois Lane. It too became a prototype for almost all comic book superhero love affairs. It has also been scrutinized by psychiatrists and psychologists, and school-aged child throughout America recognize Lois Lane as Superman's girlfriend.

As the years went on, however, her character changed subtly and she finally made the transition from repulsive bitch to curious scatterbrain. Although not as aesthetically pleasing, this characterization made Lois Lane all the more saleable.

After appearing virtually everywhere Superman appeared, Lois Lane, National finally decided, was ready for a solo feature. After two appearances in *Showcase* in 1957, she was finally awarded her own title in March 1958. In that book, Lois Lane handled just about every possible situation: at one time or another she married virtually everyone in the "Superman family," from Superman himself to Clark Kent to Batman and Lex Luther; she fought and won a bitter rivalry for Superman's affection with Lana Lang, Superboy's sweetheart; and she became any number of superheroines and developed and subsequently lost any number of super powers. All this while she remained a reporter for the *Daily Planet*.

Kurt Schaffenberger, who worked on *Captain Marvel* and other adventure strips, is most often cited as the definitive artist. Lois also had a sister, Lucy, a former airline stewardess who sometimes doubled as Jimmy Olsen's love interest.

Noel Neill is most often remembered as the television incarnation of Lois Lane (from the *Superman* television series starring George Reeves), and Neill even conducted a college lecture tour concentrating on her Lois Lane career.

J.B.

Superman's Girlfriend Lois Lane (as the comic book was officially titled) came to an end in October 1974. It was briefly revived (as simply *Lois Lane*) in 1986. As for Lois herself, she came back with a vengeance in *Lois & Clark* (based on the television series) in 1994.

M.H.

LONE RANGER, THE (U.S.) In 1938 the editors at King Features decided to adapt Fran Striker's hit radio program, *The Lone Ranger*, into a comic strip; written by Striker himself, the new feature debuted on September 10, 1938, and was at first drawn by Ed Kressy, who was replaced by Charles Flanders early in 1939.

The Lone Ranger (whose identity is kept secret) is the sole survivor of a band of Texas Rangers cowardly gunned down in an ambush by a gang of outlaws circa 1890. Vowing to avenge his fallen comrades, he dons a mask and starts a career of fighting alone against crime. Mounted on his faithful white horse Silver, and accompanied by his loyal Indian companion Tonto (who had earlier rescued him from the clutches of the Cavendish gang), he is the scourge of the numerous evildoers plying the West. The Lone Ranger overcomes them all, leaving on the scene the existential trace of

his passage in the form of a silver bullet, before uttering his famous victory cry "Hi-Yo, Silver!" and riding into the sunset.

The Lone Ranger was one of the longest-running Western strips, disappearing finally in December 1971. Its popularity was greatest in the 1940s, when it gave rise to its own comic book (drawn by Tom Gill most notably, and written first by Striker, and later by Paul Newman). There were also Lone Ranger novels, and in 1938 William Witney and John English produced a stirring screen version of the strip, which was followed by three more movies and by a long-running television series (with Clayton Moore as the Lone Ranger and Jay Silverheels as Tonto).

A jazzed-up movie version, *The Legend of the Lone Ranger*, starring Klinton Spilsbury, briefly came (and went) in 1981; it prompted the New York Times Syndicate to attempt a revival of the newspaper strip that same year. Despite eye-pleasing graphics by Russ Heath and atmospheric writing by Cary Bates, the feature lasted only from September 1981 to April 1984.

M.H.

LONG SAM (U.S.) The brainchild of Al Capp, who created it and wrote its earliest sequences, *Long Sam* debuted on May 31, 1954, for United Feature Syndicate. The artist was Bob Lubbers, journeyman cartoonist who had been doing *Tarzan* and was later to draw *Secret Agent X-9* (under the name Bob Lewis) and *Robin Malone* and assist on *Li'l Abner*.

Long Sam was a hillbilly strip, built on the clever device of a sexy young girl who had never seen, or been allowed to see, a man. Sam was incredibly leggy and naive, her good looks and innocence getting her into many scrapes. Her constant companion and "protector" was Mammy.

Unfortunately but inevitably the device did not last forever; Sam just had to run into a man eventually. It was a one-gag or, rather, a one-theme strip; and it turned into a routine hillbilly feature. In many ways it was a copy of *Li'l Abner* instead of the reversal of it. It last appeared on December 29, 1962.

But during its run *Long Sam* showed much quality. Capp's original continuities were interesting, as were the tales after the original theme was discarded; Capp's brilliant brother, Elliot Caplin, supplied the scripts. Lubbers's art was always exciting—supple, full of motion, with a command of composition and anatomy. His style had much verve and deserved a better fate than a succession of near-great features throughout the years.

R.M.

LÖÖF, JAN (1940-) From his earliest years, Jan Lööf, a Swedish illustrator and comic book artist born in 1940 in Trollhättan, showed a fascination with drawing. Thus, it comes as no surprise that he started studying art in Stockholm in 1959. His main interest centered on drawing three-dimensionally, to create an illusion of space in his pictures. In 1965 he undertook the first steps that led to comic strips; he worked on picture books for children. The first of these, *En trollkarl i Stockholm* ("A Wizard in Stockholm"), was followed the next year by *Morfar är sörövare* ("Grandpa Is a Pirate") and *Den flygande hunden* ("The Flying Dog"). His publisher felt that his style would also be suited to a comic strip. Lööf jumped at the chance and came up

"The Lone Ranger," Charles Flanders. © King Features Syndicate.

McClelland then moved to a rival newspaper, the *Daily Sketch*, where he produced his best-drawn strips: *Scott Lanyard* (1955) and *Jimmy Gimmicks* (1957). Unfortunately neither caught on. He then emigrated to Canada, and found work on the *Toronto Telegraph*. He reportedly died in the 1980s.

D.G.

McCLURE, DARRELL (1903-1987) American cartoonist and illustrator born February 25, 1903, in Ukiah, California. When Darrell McClure was nine, his parents moved to San Francisco. McClure, who later asserted that, "from the age of six, I never once swerved from the ambition to be a newspaper strip artist," was encouraged in his artistic endeavors by his mother. In 1917 and 1918 he studied at night in the California School of Fine Arts, and later attended a cartooning school, working variously as lumberjack, cowhand, and sailor. In 1920 he got his first professional job as a tracer in a small Los Angeles animation studio; when the studio folded, he went back to San Francisco and worked as a commercial animator. When this also failed McClure went to New York on a freighter, via the Panama Canal, and tried unsuccessfully to land a job at one of the newspaper syndicates. Discouraged, he went back to sea, plying the North Atlantic as a seafarer.

In 1923, a chance reunion with fellow Californian Jimmy Swinnerton led to McClure taking a job at King Features Syndicate as an apprentice artist. After five years of ghosting for a number of King Features cartoonists, McClure was finally given the go-ahead to create his own strip, *Vanilla and the Villains*, which debuted on September 10, 1928. After little over a year, the strip folded and, after an attempt to do *Hard Hearted Hicky*, McClure in 1930 went on to take over Brandon Walsh's faltering *Little Annie Rooney* daily strip (October 6), and to draw the newly minted *Annie Rooney* Sunday half-page (November 30).

In 1933 McClure relinquished the Sunday *Annie Rooney* to Nicholas Afonski (or Afonsky) in order to create a Sunday page of his own, *Donnie*, about the sea adventures of an enterprising teenage boy (not unlike Walsh's and Afonski's contemporary *Ming Foo*). Debuting in 1934, *Donnie* met with scant success despite its evocative qualities and McClure's loving knowledge of the sea, and the artist went back to the *Annie Rooney* Sunday page (1937). McClure drew the daily and Sunday adventures of the spunky little waif and her dog Zero until the strip's demise in 1966. During World War II McClure produced his last comic strip creation, *Ahoy McCoy*, for *All Hands*, the U. S. Coast Guard magazine. He retired in the late 1960s to his California hometown, where he died on February 27, 1987.

Darrell McClure will be chiefly remembered as the definitive artist on *Little Annie Rooney*, a strip he served well despite the lunacies of the plot, and as the creator of two charming, if underrated features: *Vanilla and the Villains* and *Donnie*.

M.H.

McDOUGALL, WALTER HUGH (1858-1938) American artist born in Newark, New Jersey, on February 10, 1858. The young McDougall entered and quit a military academy in 1874—learning more about life on the streets of Newark and about his early love, art, from his father, a painter.

Shortly thereafter McDougall broke into the growing field of illustrated journalism when he was hired by the *New York Graphic*, the first illustrated daily paper in America. Here, and on *Harper's Weekly*, where he sold sketches and cartoon ideas, he met many of the great early illustrators and cartoonists: A. B. Frost, C. J. Taylor, Gray-Parker, Theodore Wust, W. A. Rogers, and of course, Thomas Nast.

In the early 1880s he sold some drawings and ideas to *Puck* magazine; one favorite for years afterward was a comment on the watering of milk—a dairy farmer being startled by a cow, not knowing what it was.

And on October 30, 1884, he made history with his front-page cartoon in the *New York World*, "The Royal Feast of Belshazzar Blaine and the Money Kings," an exposé that is credited with losing New York—and the presidential election—for James G. Blaine to the benefit of Grover Cleveland.

McDougall scored a first on May 21, 1893, when his cartoon "The Possibilities of the Broadway Cable Car" became the first printed in color in an American newspaper. And on Feb. 4, 1894, in the same *New York World* pages, his collaboration with magazine cartoonist Mark Fenderson, "The Unfortunate Fate of a Well-Intentioned Dog," became the first color comic strip in an American newspaper.

During this period McDougall was also drawing full-page editorial cartoons in color for the *World*, and illustrating Bill Nye's weekly column for the American Press Association of Col. Orlando Jay Smith, making McDougall the first syndicated cartoonist.

In 1898 he drew probably the largest single-panel cartoon in color in an American newspaper—a double-page affair for the *New York American*—and once had front-page drawings in color in New York's *Herald*, *World*, and *American*, all on the same Sunday!

Among his Sunday features for the *Philadelphia North American* were *Fatty Felix*, *Peck's Bad Boy*, *The Wizard of Oz* (with continuity by Baum), and *Handsome Hautrey*. For the Western Newspaper Syndicate, and later T. C. McClure, he drew the long-running *Hank the Hermit and His Animal Friends*. His daily comic strips into the 1920s included *Absent Minded Abner*, *Teddy in Africa*, *Gink and Boob*, and *The Radio Buggs*.

Other projects in his long career included a play, *The Summer Boarder*, written with Henry Guy Carleton; the short-lived *McDougall's Magazine;* and an animated campaign cartoon for the Democratic National Committee in 1912.

McDougall was indeed in the forefront of several movements in the comics, and the graveyard of yesterday's titles is crowded with dozens of his minor strips. His friendship with the famous in art, journalism, and politics would seem to imply as strongly as study of his work that much of McDougall's success must have been due to personal contacts and camaraderie. His drawings were stiff and awkward, though full of a certain earthy and crude humor. He never matured to a facile style, and there was a direct correlation between the anatomical accuracy of his figures and obvious laboring at the drawing board. Ralph Pulitzer refused to rehire McDougall to do strips at the *New York World* because he "didn't like his style."

Nevertheless McDougall was a pioneer; if not as polished as Frost, facile as Opper, funny as Dirks, or inspired as the early Herriman, he was prolific and influential and was there when it all started.

McDougall committed suicide in 1938.

R.M.

McEVOY, JOSEPH PATRICK (1895-1955) Creator of *Dixie Dugan* and a noted novelist and humorist, Joseph Patrick McEvoy was born June 27, 1895, in New Burnside, Illinois, where he went to school. He attended the Christian Brothers' College in St. Louis, Missouri, and the University of Notre Dame. While attending the latter, he obtained his first newspaper job as office boy on the *South Bend* (Indiana) *News*. Later a reporter for the same paper, he parlayed his writing talent into a position as humor writer for the *Chicago Tribune*, where he wrote a series of comic poems called *Slams of Life* (these were collected into a book of the same name, with illustrations by Frank King, in 1919). In the early 1920s he did a weekly account of the doings of a typical Midwestern American family called *The Potters*, with illustrations by John H. Striebel, also for the *Chicago Tribune*. With a hit Broadway play based on this series (printed in book form with a dust jacket by Striebel in 1923), *The Potters* carried McEvoy into New York theatrical writing, where he authored such hits as *The Comic Supplement* (a revue based on the comic strips of the 1920s), *Americana*, and the *Ziegfeld Follies* of 1924 and 1926 (aside from the W. C. Fields skits).

Transferring *The Potters* to the Hearst papers in 1924, McEvoy saw the play adapted as a feature film with W. C. Fields in 1926. His first novel, *Show Girl*, which featured Dixie Dugan, was serialized in *Liberty* in 1928, then published in several printings by Simon & Schuster the same year. Dixie reappeared in two later novels as well: *Hollywood Girl* (1929) and *Society* (1931). A remaining major novel of the period, *Mister Noodle* (1931), was subtitled "A Novel of the Comic Strips" and dealt hilariously with the newspaper strip syndicate world of the time. It was drawn in large part from McEvoy's own experiences scripting *Show Girl*, the comic strip based on his Dixie Dugan novels.

With art by Striebel, *Show Girl* was begun in various subscribing papers on October 21, 1929, and emphasized the "fast," sensational Hollywood and Broadway show business life of the time (Flo Ziegfeld himself was caricatured—as Flo Zigfold—in the first week of the new strip). But with the Depression souring American life, the frivolous theme of *Show Girl* was felt to be hampering the new strip's potential circulation. The strip title was changed to *Dixie Dugan* in the mid-1930s, and Dixie was eased out of show business and into a mainstream working-girl existence: her strip became one of the most widely read in America.

In the mid-1940s, McEvoy left the scripting of *Dixie Dugan*, turning that task over to his son, Renny, who continued the strip with Striebel until the late 1960s. Famed for film script work in the 1930s, columns for the Hearst newspapers, and a long series of engaging articles for *Reader's Digest*, McEvoy died in 1955.

B.B.

McFARLANE, TODD (1961-) American comic book artist born April 16, 1961, in Calgary, Canada. After attending Eastern Washington University, where he earned a bachelor's degree in graphic design, Todd McFarlane went to work for Marvel in 1985 as a penciler on the *Coyote* title for their Epic Comics imprint. That same year he crossed over to DC Comics, drawing for the Infinity Inc. line of comic books.

It was with *The Incredible Hulk* and *The Amazing Spider-Man*, however—two of Marvel's flagship titles that a burned-out Stan Lee and a succession of second-

stringers had allowed to go stale—that McFarlane rose to fame. Starting in 1987, his dramatic rendering of these two superheroes, coupled with a kinetic sense of visual storytelling, rescued the venerable features from the doldrums, and in 1990 he was allowed to write his own stories. The McFarlane-scripted *Spider-Man* number one broke all previous sales records for a single comic-book issue.

McFarlane was among the Marvel defectors who founded Image Comics late in 1991. "When I quit Marvel, I was the top-paid guy and I couldn't spend all the money they were paying me," he later declared in an interview. In May 1992, under his own Todd McFarlane Productions imprint, the first issue of *Spawn*, written and drawn entirely by the author, came out and sold over one million copies, a record for an independent comic book title. While visually dynamic and fast-moving, the early issues of *Spawn* had laughable dialogue and desultory plots—weaknesses McFarlane remedied by bringing in talented wordsmiths such as Alan Moore and Neil Gaiman to write the scripts. The title has been a constant top-seller since its inception and has given rise to a number of spinoffs as well as to several action figures marketed by Todd McFarlane Toys. In May 1997 the animated *Todd McFarlane's Spawn* debuted on HBO, and a live-action *Spawn* movie was released in August 1997.

M.H.

McLOUGHLIN, DENIS (1918-) British cartoonist and illustrator born April 15, 1918, at Bolton, Lancashire, and educated at Dearden's Private School and Sunninghill School prior to winning a scholarship to Bolton School of Art in 1932. His first professional work was done for Ward and Copley Studio in Manchester, drawing realistic illustrations for John Noble's Sixit Club Catalogue (1934). His first cartoons were for Atlas Stores and he entered the comics field by drawing three covers for Sunday supplements imported from the United States for market sales (1938). He was called into the Royal Artillery (1940) and during his service he painted 50 humorous and pinup murals for Woolich Depot. Freelancing in his spare time, he drew the book jacket for *Navy Colt* by Frank Gruber, the first of 700 of this type. In 1944-45 he drew three complete cartoon books: *Laughter for Home and Front*, *New Laughs for All*, and *Laughter Parade*—the publisher, Kangaroo, changed his name to David McLoughlin. The same publisher issued his first complete comic book, *Lightning Comics* (1946), which included a Western and a science-fiction strip, two fields in which he would excel.

In 1947 he was exclusively contracted by T. V. Boardman, a prolific publisher of novels and comics, and created their house style. His many book jackets and paperback covers belong to this period, as does creation of the famous trademark, the Boardman Bloodhound, that he also sculpted for a trade exhibition. For the Boardman comics, 12-page booklets printed in excellent two-tone gravure, he created the detective *Roy Carson*, the spaceman *Swift Morgan*, and the covers for such U.S. reprints as *Blackhawk*. He also took over the *Buffalo Bill* series, formerly a reprint of the Swiss strip by Lennart, improving it considerably with his expertise in the Old West, while drawing and compiling 13 *Buffalo Bill Annuals* (1949-1961).

After Boardman's retirement from publishing, McLoughlin wrote and drew the book *Derek the Tor-*

George McManus, "The Whole Blooming Family." © King Features Syndicate.

toise (Dean), and compiled the *Encyclopedia of the Wild West* (Doubleday, 1973). In between he drew the serial strips *Saber* and *Big Hit Swift* for *Tiger* (1967), *Fury's Family* for *Thunder* (1970), and *Power the Danger Ranger* and *Terror in the Tall Tower* for *Wizard* (1974). He continues to be a forceful contributor to British comics, working in the American style, which he much admires. Although he slowed down in the 1990s, he still draws an occasional war comic book.

D.G.

McMANUS, GEORGE (1884-1954) American cartoonist born in St. Louis on January 23, 1884. At 16, George McManus became cartoonist (and later fashion editor) for the *St. Louis Republic*, where he published his first comic strip. Of that effort, *Alma and Oliver*, McManus later said, "It was a terrible mess and wouldn't get by high school editors today."

In 1904 McManus went to New York and started a long association with Joseph Pulitzer's *World*. Over the years he contributed a variety of comic features in the hope that one (or more) would click. They were: *Snoozer*; *The Merry Marcelene*; *Panhandle Pete*, one of the first in a long line of comic strip bums; *Nibsy the Newsboy in Funny Fairyland*, an unabashed but beautiful imitation of *Little Nemo in Slumberland*; *Cheerful Charley*, about a stone-faced Indian; and *Let George Do It* (a phrase that was to become famous). But the most popular and best of McManus's strips for the *World* was *The Newlyweds* (1904), the first of his family strips.

In 1912 McManus moved to William Randolph Hearst's *New York American*, transferring *The Newlyweds* with him, under several alternate titles (*Their Only Child*, *Baby Snookums*, etc.). But McManus was still not satisfied artistically and he started experimenting again with several ideas in the period from 1913 to 1918,

George McManus, "Their Only Child." © King Features Syndicate.

simultaneously creating *Rosie's Beau*, a humorous girl strip; *The Whole Blooming Family*, about a much put-upon husband and father; and *Spareribs and Gravy*, a take-off on scientific explorers; as well as the feature for which he was to receive world acclaim, *Bringing Up Father*.

McManus also worked on animated cartoons (producing notably the *Snookums* series with Emile Cohl) and contributed occasional illustrations to magazines, but he remained first and foremost an artist of the comics. His elegance of line and elaborate mise-en-scène have been widely imitated but never equalled; every cartoonist has, at one time or another, borrowed some of McManus's pungent aphorisms, but none has ever matched his impeccable timing and delivery.

McManus's popularity was as great as his artistry. Countless awards from art groups and civic organizations were heaped upon him. On the occasion of *Bringing Up Father*'s 25th anniversary a Congressional dinner was held for him in Washington, and he continued to receive innumerable fan letters from simple citizens and government leaders alike until his death in Santa Monica, California, on October 22, 1954.

M.H.

McNEILL, HUGH (1910-1979) British cartoonist and illustrator, born in Manchester of Scottish parents on December 13, 1910, Hugh McNeill received a secondary school education and attended Manchester School of Art evening classes from 1925 to 1927. He became a four-year apprentice at Kayebon Press, a Manchester advertising studio. His first published drawing was a gag cartoon in *Topical Times* (1927).

McNeill tried comic strips in response to an advertisement in a local newspaper by D. C. Thomson, which was seeking artists for its new comic publications, *Dandy* and *Beano*. His first original character, *Ping the Elastic Man* (July 30, 1938), in *Beano*, was an indication of the special kind of wild whimsy that would make his comic work stand out. Then came *Simple Simon* (1938) for *Dandy*, and McNeill's most enduring character, *Pansy Potter*, for *Beano* (1938). Comic strip work suited his sense of humor and proved more rewarding to his employers than advertising work. They extended him to the main comic publisher, Amalgamated Press, and he created *Simon the Simple Sleuth* (March 4, 1939) for the new comic *Knockout*, and *Professor P. Nutts* and *Binky & Granpop* (both March 18, 1939) for the revamped *Jolly Comic*. His style so suited *Knockout* that he rapidly took over, creating *Deed-a-Day Danny* for the colored front page and making the already-established *Our Ernie* conform to his own wacky wit.

Unhappily, war curtailed his burgeoning career and he was conscripted into the Royal Army Service Corps. He continued to draw his *Knockout* characters, and, when posted overseas in 1943, he drew his *Danny* pages on air letter forms that were the same size as reproduction.

Hugh McNeill, "Deed-a-Day Danny." © *Knockout.*

After demobilization McNeill returned to *Knockout* with *One Eyed Joe* and *Two Toof Tom* (1946) and others, then showed a new side to his art by taking on an adventure strip, *Tough Tod & Happy Annie* (1947). He expanded this style further with *Deadshot Sue* (1949), *Highway Days/Dick Turpin* (1951), adaptations from films (such as *King Solomon's Mines*) in *Sun*, and the superhero *Thunderbolt Jaxon* (1949) in *Comet*.

A third change of direction occurred on February 27, 1954, when A.P. launched the gravure weekly *Jack and Jill* for younger children. McNeill not only drew these front page children, he also revived Harry Hargreave's *Harold Hare* from *Knockout*, but with his own new nursery style, plus a touch of his old fantasy. The character was virtually reborn. Harold grew so popular that he was given a weekly comic of his own, *Harold Hare's Own Paper* (November 14, 1959), and a newspaper strip in the *Sunday Pictorial* (1960).

In 1961 McNeill took on the adventures of the son of Andy Capp, Buster, in the comic of the same name, and from February 25, 1967, he drew *The Trolls*, a two-page strip adapted from the familiar little dolls, for *Tina*, a girl's comic. Meantime, he created and drew many characters and strips, all with the great humor and charm that has marked his work from the start.

"Hughie," as his friends called him, died on November 22, 1979, in Sussex, on the eve of being presented with the Ally Sloper Award for a lifetime devoted to comics. He never knew he was going to receive the award.

D.G.

McWILLIAMS, ALDEN (1916-1993) American artist born 1916 in Greenwich, Connecticut. A graduate of the New York School of Fine and Applied Arts, Al McWilliams started his career in pulp magazines before becoming one of the pioneering comic book artists in 1935.

For Western (his most constant comic book employer from 1935 to 1942) McWilliams contributed both writing and artwork (with a strong leaning to science fiction) to such diverse features as *Captain Frank Hawks*, *Gangbusters*, *Space Cadets*, *Stratosphere Jim*, and *Flash Gordon*. During the same period he also worked for Centaur (*Skid Davis*, 1939) and Quality, where his forte from 1940 to 1942 was war stories (*Spitfire*, *Atlantic Patrol*, *Captain Flag*, *Destroyer 171*).

After three years in the army during World War II, McWilliams was discharged in 1945 and promptly resumed his comic book career, developing *Steve Wood* for Quality and *Young King Cole* and *Sergeant Spook* for Novelty, as well as a number of crime stories for Gleason. Al McWilliams is best noted, however, for his newspaper strip work which began in 1953 with the science-fiction daily *Twin Earths*, written by Oskar Lebeck and distributed by United Feature Syndicate. When *Twin Earths* folded in 1963, McWilliams went on to draw *Davy Jones* (a sea adventure strip that he had originated with writer Sam Leff in 1961). Later came *Dateline: Danger!* (1968-1974, for Publishers-Hall Syndicate), an excellent spy adventure strip with scenarios by Allen Saunders. In his later years he drew the *Star Trek* and *Buck Rogers* strips, and assisted John Prentice on *Rip Kirby*.

Al McWilliams also did a great deal of advertising work and never stopped working for comic books. (*Man From UNCLE* and *I Spy* were two of the titles he contributed to in the 1960s.) A talented and unassuming craftsman, Al McWilliams always managed to make a distinguished contribution to every feature on which he worked. He died in March 1993.

M.H.

MADAM AND EVE (South Africa) A comic strip about a "wannabe liberal" white housewife and her street-wise black maid, *Madam and Eve* satirizes the new South Africa through one of society's oldest and closest—yet most distant—interracial relationships. Gwen Anderson and her assertive maid Eve Sisulu verbally tangle about household matters, while also commenting in rather critical terms about changes in postapartheid South Africa.

Madam and Eve's tremendous success can be attributed to its understated irony and to the fact that its two lead characters are given almost equal chances to come out on top. Madam does so through her dominant position and use of blunt force, while Eve employs a more conniving and subtle style. Playing off current events, the strip also pokes fun at the high-and-mighty and society at large, paying no attention to rank, color, or class. It aims to make South Africans laugh at themselves, while also making them squirm a bit.

Madam and Eve was started in 1992 by Harry Dugmore, Stephen Francis, and Rico Schacheri, three non-South African-born transplants from Botswana, New York, and Austria. They have worked together since 1988, first on the satirical magazine *Laughing Stock*, and then in another branch of the parent publishing company. The first newspaper to pick up the strip in its original 12-panel format was the *Weekly Mail and Guardian*. The four-panel version was first introduced in the *Johannesburg Star*; seven dailies and three magazines now carry *Madam and Eve*, and efforts are being made to syndicate it abroad.

American influences, such as the one-two gag punch of Johnny Hart, the political humor of *Doonesbury*, and the philosophical style of Bill Watterson, are acknowledged by Dugmore. According to him, *Madam and Eve* uses "cynical humor which people love. Sometimes we are hard-hitting, but we also bring a certain warmth to the strip." Dugmore, who has a Ph.D. in history, is very much aware of the wide berth *Madam and Eve* has been given by the authorities, as it has held up for ridicule, without incident, the few scandals that have blemished the Mandela administration. Government largesse and inefficiency were targeted in the daily strips for weeks on end, as well as in *All Aboard the Gravy Train* and *Somewhere over the Rainbow Nation*, two of the four bestselling *Madam and Eve* collections that have been published.

J.A.L.

MAFALDA (Argentina) Created first as a weekly page for the Buenos Aires magazine *Primera Plana* on September 29, 1964, *Mafalda* soon became a daily strip as well, published for the first time in this format in March 1965 by the newspaper *El Mundo*.

With a highly individual and simple graphic style, its creator Quino (pseudonym of Joaquin Lavado) humorously related the adventures of Mafalda, an argumentative little girl who refused to be integrated into the adult world. Her extraordinary insight and precociousness allowed Mafalda to understand, better than her elders, the situations of the world at the time. From the mid-1960s to the mid-1970s (when Quino decided to abandon his strip) the author seemed to share his character's astonishment in the contemplation of a world bent on its own destruction. This work mirrored the contradictions of the thinking man, when confronted with mindless individuals merely intent on existing, through the mediation of a little girl.

"Madam and Eve," Harry Dugmore, Stephen Francis, and Rico Schacheri. © Rapid Phrase Entertainment.

"Mafalda," Quino (Joaquin Lavado). © Quino.

Mafalda and her little friends—Felipe the idealistic dreamer; Susanita the already adult little girl, obsessed, like her mother, with boys and money; Manolito the future businessman, and others—with their deep psychological insights, judged the world in which they live. For this reason, the strip transcended the concrete Argentine situation which gave rise to it, and reflected the universal anxieties, obsessions, and preoccupations of the time.

Mafalda was published in book form (1968), translated into six different languages, and distributed widely throughout Europe and Latin America. Its success, like that of *Peanuts*, led to its rapid commercialization, with hundreds of toys, dolls, and gadgets of every description, and a series of animated cartoons for television.

L.G.

MAGER, CHARLES AUGUSTUS (1878-1956) Creator of the famed *Monks* strip series of 1904-1913, and the later *Hawkshaw the Detective*, Charles Augustus "Gus" Mager was born 1878 in Newark, New Jersey. Growing up in Newark, the son of middle-class German immigrants, Mager went through the old-world comic humor magazines sent to his parents by relatives in Germany as he attended grammar and high school in his hometown, basing much of his emerging cartoon style on the work of Wilhelm Busch and others. Getting his first newspaper job with the Hearst papers in New York at 20, Mager had already sold a number of spot gag cartoons to the American cartoon magazines of the time, and provided the same sort of material for Hearst's *New York American* and *New York Journal*, from which they were sent to other Hearst papers for reprinting. Mager's early talents leaned toward humorously drawn animals, and his gag cartoons emphasized this element, particularly African jungle fauna such as tigers and monkeys. Before long, Mager's gags had a running title for their occasional daily appearance: *In Jungle Land* (sometimes also *In Jungle Society*).

From this springboard, the young, just-married Mager launched his first gag sequence about a separately named animal, *Knocko the Monk*, which first appeared in the *Journal* on April 25, 1904. The public loved *Knocko*, and Mager gave them a continual series of *Knocko* episodes for the rest of the year. He made a brief stab at another kind of strip (with humans), *Everyday Dreams*, then turned back permanently to his monkey characters, introducing a *Rhymo the Monk*, then reintroducing *Knocko*, and adding fresh figures every few months: *Henpecko the Monk, Groucho the Monk*, etc. Finally, in 1910, he created *Sherlocko the Monk*; this became his most popular figure and eclipsed public interest in the earlier *Monk* strips. Most of his subsequent work focused on Sherlocko and his involvements with the other *Monk* characters, and it was the Sherlocko character (a close parody of Doyle's Sherlock Holmes) that he took with him when he left Hearst and joined the staff of the *New York World* to create *Hawkshaw the Detective*, a humanized version of the old *Sherlocko* strip, on February 23, 1913. Mager continued with *Hawkshaw* (aside from a brief attempt in 1922 at a small-town family-type strip, largely ghosted for him by another artist, called *Main Street*, and to circulate a renovated *Sherlocko* strip on his own in 1924) for the rest of his life, adding it to Rudolph Dirks's *Captain and the Kids* page in 1931, and continuing with it there until his retirement in the late 1940s.

Living continually in Newark, Mager had built a sizable home there and now took up his lifetime hobby of serious painting in earnest, selling paintings to the permanent collections of the Newark Museum and the Whitney Museum in New York, among others. A devoted naturalist, as his early strip work suggested, Mager also drew a feature page titled *Games and Gimmicks* for *Outdoor Life Magazine*. He published only two small books (aside from comic book reprints in *Tip Top Comics* and elsewhere) in his lifetime, and died on July 17, 1956, at the home of his son, Robert, in Murrysville, Pennsylvania, where he had been ill.

B.B.

MAGER'S MONKS (U.S.) Charles A. Mager's series of interrelated and simultaneously running daily *Monk* strips (*Knocko the Monk, Rhymo the Monk, Sherlocko the Monk*, etc.) that ran in the first two decades of this century and were the direct source of the Marx Brothers' acting names, first appeared in Hearst's *New York Journal* on April 25, 1904, in the form of a *Knocko the Monk* ("He Always Says What He Thinks") episode. Earlier, Mager had done spot animal gags for the morning and evening Hearst papers, incorporating these after a time into an editorial page feature called *In Jungle Land*, or, alternatively, *In Jungle Society*, which ran through 1903 and 1904. Like its predecessor gag feature, *Knocko the Monk* appeared every second or third day on the *Journal* editorial page, alternating with other quasi-daily strips of the period, such as *Johnny Bostonbeans* and *Mr. E. Z. Mark*. Mager dropped *Knocko* at the end of 1904 and turned to human characters in a short-lived strip called *Everyday Dreams*. The public didn't care for this, demanded more Mager Monks, and by mid-1905 Mager had satisfied them by introducing *Rhymo the Monk*, which ran in the *Journal* through the rest of the year.

Mager's early simian characters were small apes, with a multiplicity of facial hair and baggy human clothing. Gradually, as his strips continued, his monks became more humanized and their settings became contemporary houses and cities. Each of his title characters had a quirk or obsession reflected in his name,

"Mager's Monks," Gus Mager.

and as these strips increased in variety of titles after 1905, running intermixed in the *Journal* as the already mentioned *Knocko* and *Rhymo, Tightwaddo the Monk, Groucho the Monk, Nervo the Monk, Hamfatto the Monk,* etc., their layout became standardized as an upright, oblong set of six panels per episode.

The popularity of the *Monk* strips was enormous, and various vaudeville comics of the 1910s adapted Mager's titular idea for themselves, so that Hickos, Sharpos, Plumpos, *et al,* flourished for a while. This fad died down with the closing of most of Mager's *Monk* strips in the early 1910s, but it was recalled by a vaudeville monologuist named Art Fisher who improvised the names of Groucho, Chico, Harpo, and Gummo for four of the five Marx brothers during a 1918 poker game.

Mager's future was settled, however, when he introduced *Sherlocko the Monk* in the *Journal* for December 9, 1910. The first *Sherlocko* was a lovely take-off on A. Conan Doyle's *Sherlock Holmes* detective stories, complete with an admiring aide named Dr. Watso, and a neat six-panel mystery-and-solution involving Tightwaddo the Monk. Before long Mager was drawing just the one title for Hearst, and felt he deserved a Sunday page. Hearst had no place for Mager in his already jampacked four-page Sunday section, and Mager began to shop around. He found a sympathetic ear at the *New York World,* and left Hearst's *Journal* (where the last *Sherlocko* ran on February 23, 1913, followed by one or two old *Monk* strips the *Journal* still had on hand) to undertake a Sunday *Sherlocko* for the *World.*

In the meantime, Doyle's representatives in the United States had gone to court to suppress Mager's *Sherlocko* title as an infringement of copyright. (Worried, the *World* asked Mager to find new names for his two principals, which he did, but this is another story that can be found in the entry for *Hawkshaw the Detective.*)

B.B.

MAGGIE AND JIGGS *see* Bringing Up Father.

MAGSINO, FRANK (1937-) Frank Magsino was born on December 3, 1937, in San Jose, Occidental, Mindoro, an island in the Philippines famous for its wild buffalo, the tamaraw. Frank Magsino attended the University of Santo Tomas and majored in art, but left school when he was offered a job working for Araneta University doing a variety of art chores. From there he went on to work for Hontiveros Associates Incorporated, doing layouts, illustrations, and advertisements for Pepsi Cola. He also did a stint with Adver Incorporated in commercial art.

From 1961 to 1968, Magsino worked as a freelance artist doing covers and interior art for several magazines such as *Women's World* and the comic-oriented publications *Liwayway* and *Bulaklak.* He illustrated many short stories and novels that appeared in these Tagalog comic magazines.

He continued his education in the United States, receiving a Bachelor of Arts degree from the San Francisco Academy of Art. Galleries in Europe, the Philippines, and the United States have sold many of his works in oil, acrylic, tempera, and watercolor. Though much of his art was done in the classical manner, dealing with traditional subjects, his later endeavors were varied and eclectic in approach. Ventures into the fields of surrealism and fantasy brought further acclaim to his works.

Despite his heavy commitment to painting, Magsino experimented with a variety of strips and did some cartoon features, as well as some artwork for Marvel's *Conan* comic book (U.S.) in the early 1970s. He is no longer much involved with comics.

Being ambidextrous, Magsino drew and painted with his right hand and did his lettering with his left. He was one of the very few individuals who used a brush to do his lettering.

O.J.

MAIN STREET (U.S.) Decidedly the flattest and least interesting Gus Mager strip, and a very minor strip in its own right, *Main Street* was created by Mager as a

Sunday page for the *New York World* shortly before his popular *Hawkshaw* page folded in mid-1922. It appeared first in nationwide syndication by the *World*'s Press Publishing Company on April 22, 1923.

A bad mistake as a strip, *Main Street* attempted to present too many ill-defined characters at once (the residents along a middle-sized town's Main Street). Its style, an odd mixture of Mager faces and ghosted torsos done in a pseudo-McManus manner, was not captivating. Although some of the individual weekly gags and situations were good, the lack of strongly defined central figures ultimately sank the strip and ended Mager's career with the *World*.

By the extent of his more frequent appearances, Henry Meek, a henpecked husband, might be said to have been the strip's main character, but other families and individuals such as the Millers, the Ticks, and the Smithers shared the confused scene. Within a few months, *Main Street* had been dropped by most of the subscribing papers initially attracted by the Mager name and the reputation of *Hawkshaw*, and it disappeared from the *World* itself late in 1924.

B.B.

MAISON IKKOKU (Japan) In *Maison Ikkoku*, artist Rumiko Takahashi pursues the male fantasy of the hopeless slob who gets the perfect woman. What separates *Maison Ikkoku* from other such stories, however, is the fact that Takahashi is herself a woman. Serialized in the weekly magazine *Big Comic Spirits* from November 1980 to April 1987, *Maison Ikkoku* was the first title by a woman to become a popular hit in a Japanese men's comics magazine. (Another well-known work of hers, *Urusei yatsura*, was the first title by a woman to be a popular hit in a Japanese boys' comics magazine, and ran more or less concurrently with *Maison Ikkoku*.)

The hero of this charming romantic comedy is young Yusaku Godai, a resident of the dilapidated Maison Ikkoku apartments who failed to pass the college entrance exams on his first try and, as the story opens, is preparing to take the exams again a year later. Yusaku is indeed a slob, and, like most men his age, has his share of impure thoughts, but he falls genuinely in love with the Maison Ikkoku's new superintendent, the young and beautiful widow Kyoko Otonashi.

An awkward love-quadrangle quickly forms, as Yusaku must deal with Kozue Nanao, who has declared herself to be his girlfriend, and vie for Kyoko's attention with Shun Mitaka, another young man who is not only older, better-looking, wealthier, and better mannered, but is also a nice guy. Shun seems to have everything going for him, and Yusaku seems to have nothing going for him but his sincerity. Fortunately for Yusaku, Kyoko turns out to be more than a pretty face: she is strong-willed, stubborn, sometimes short-tempered, surprisingly witty, often silly, and eccentric enough to be more attracted to Yusaku than to Shun. Double entendres, slapstick humor, and Takahashi's trademark puns abounded, as did hilarious and poignant plot twists.

When Viz Comics translated *Maison Ikkoku* into English, it skipped several of the early episodes and changed the plot somewhat, feeling that English-language readers might be confused by the motif of the college entrance exams.

Takahashi's other works include *Ranma 1/2*, *The Mermaid Saga*, *One Pound Gospel*, *Rumic World*, and *Inu Yasha*.

M.A.T.

MAL *See* Judge, Malcolm.

MALAYA (Philippines) The word *malaya* means "freedom" in the Tagalog dialect; it is also the name of the most intriguing Filipino underground cartoonist. No one knows for sure whether this pen name applied to an individual or to a group of artists. However, there are many who speculated that Malaya was actually a group of individuals illustrating under one name to protect themselves from political pressures that could be brought upon their families, relatives, friends, or themselves. This theory is plausible because of the variety of styles and approaches that the work bore.

Malaya submitted comic strips, editorial cartoons, political illustrations, and humorous features to conservative and radical publications alike. Adding to the mystery, many of the envelopes that contained these works were mailed in various segments from different localities.

According to some individuals the earliest known appearance of Malaya's work was sometime in the 1950s, but definite documentation of these strips is difficult to obtain because of the rarity and obscure nature of the publications.

From January 3 to April 1, 1963, a daily strip titled *Dili Ako Mahadlok* ("I Am Not Afraid") appeared in the now-defunct newspaper *Leyte Express*. It was written in Cebuano, one of the many dialects of the Visayan region, and dealt with the atrocities perpetrated by rich landlords and their spoiled offspring against the hapless tenants of the vicinity. Many of the sequences in the strip were actual incidents, thus bringing forth the wrath of the landlords. All copies of the paper were confiscated and destroyed, but the elusive Malaya seemed to disappear into thin air. Many of the inhabitants later denied the existence of the publication for fear of the consequences.

In 1967, after a heavy typhoon, an airplane appeared out of the blue skies in the area of Bago Bantay in Quezon City. The plane dropped leaflets containing several comic strips concerned with the excessive power of the Church over the populace. On the last page of the pamphlets the name Malaya was scribbled. This led to a rumor that Malaya was an eccentric millionaire who crusaded against wrongdoers; after all, only someone extremely rich could afford to use a plane and print thousands of leaflets.

In 1971, a new publication, *Kalayaan International*, appeared on the scene. No one knew who published it. Copies were available in various Filipino stores throughout the San Francisco Bay Area in California, as well as in the lobby of the International Hotel located on Kearney Street, a block away from the tourist-infested Chinatown area. In the February/March issue of the newspaper (volume 1, number 6) there appeared several editorial and political cartoons signed by Malaya. The *Kalayaan* quickly disappeared, and Malaya has not been heard of since.

O.J.

MALE CALL (U.S.) Milton Caniff created *Male Call* (one of his more lighthearted contributions to the war effort) for the Camp Newspaper Service in 1943. The

"Male Call," Milton Caniff. © Milton Caniff.

year before, Caniff had been drawing another strip for the GIs with Burma (one of the sexy leading ladies of *Terry and the Pirates*) as its heroine, but the Chicago Tribune-New York News Syndicate had objected to the use of the character, which led Caniff to produce an altogether original strip. Named *Male Call* by the staff of the Camp Service, it had as its heroine the fondly remembered Miss Lace.

Miss Lace was a pretty, scantily clad, not overly shy brunette whose relations (usually innocent, as it turned out) with soldiers on every arm (whom she invariably called "general" or "admiral") constituted the gist of the strip's weekly gags. Miss Lace enjoyed a quite deserved popularity with the GIs and ranked as one of the major pinups of the war years, alongside Rita Hayworth and Betty Grable.

Caniff lavished as much care on the done-for-free *Male Call* as he did on *Terry* (for which he was highly paid), and some of his best work of the period can be found in the strip. He certainly enjoyed throwing in risque lines and situations which he could not have done with the relatively more inhibited *Terry*. The last weekly *Male Call* strip appeared on March 3, 1946, signaling the end of the war era.

A collection of *Male Call* strips appeared in 1945, and in 1959 Grosset & Dunlap reissued the entire feature as it had originally appeared during its three-year run.

M.H.

MALLARD FILLMORE (U.S.) In 1994 the people of the United States proved conservatism still had appeal by voting in a Republican Party majority to both houses of Congress for the first time in 40 years. That same year, King Features recognized the lack of a true politically conservative syndicated comic strip and successfully launched Bruce Tinsley's *Mallard Fillmore*. Mallard's namesake is Millard Fillmore, who served as the 13th President of the United States from 1850-53. (As a member of the Whig party, Millard Fillmore would have considered today's Republicans the lunatic liberal fringe.)

Cartoonist Bruce Tinsley has done conservative-inspired editorial cartoons for a number of years. He claims that *Mallard* is drawn for the average person—the forgotten American taxpayer who is sick and tired of a liberal media and cultural establishment that acts like he or she doesn't exist.

The premise is that Mallard Fillmore, recently fired from his job on a newspaper, is forced to find work at a television station, WFDR. He's hired not because he is a good journalist, but because he is "an amphibious American." Mallard is continuously at odds with his ultraliberal news director. Physically, Mallard is a duck whose squat body is squeezed into a tweed jacket. He also favors a fedora with press passes stuck in the band and regimental-stripe neckties. If Mallard resembles any prior cartoon ducks physically, it's neither Donald Duck nor Uncle Scrooge, but Marvel Comics's now-defunct Howard the Duck.

For Tinsley, the ethically challenged administration of President Bill Clinton has been fodder for endless gags. Both gag-a-day and brief continuity concepts have been used. In the spring of 1996, the strip portrayed President Clinton and Sen. Edward Kennedy of Massachusetts taking a road trip to attend college spring-break parties in Florida. For more than a week, Bill and Teddy drove south in a convertible, bantering back and forth about booze, babes, and partying. In another episode, Mallard, unable to sleep, decided to do something "really mind-numbing . . . like counting Veep: one Al Gore, two Al Gores, three Al Gorezzz . . ." And President Clinton has been shown on his knees seeking spiritual guidance from the divine Elvis. The King of Rock and Roll tells the President, "You even look a little like me in my, uh, mature years. Watch out for the Big Macs, Bill."

Mallard Fillmore is a brilliant example of niche marketing by King Features. The newspaper business is competitive, and papers are anxious to keep readers. *Mallard Fillmore* allows King Features to offer a counterpoint to *Doonesbury*. A good number of papers publish *Mallard Fillmore* and *Doonesbury* together on the editorial or op-ed page seven days a week. Because knowledge of American politics is critical to enjoyment of the strip, *Mallard Fillmore*'s popularity is an American phenomenon.

B.C.

MANARA, MAURILIO (1945-   ) Italian cartoonist and illustrator born September 12, 1945, in Luson (Bolzano) and better known as Milo, short for Maurilio. As a student in architecture and at the academy of arts in Venice, he painted and sculpted, and then to earn his living decided to exploit his vocational drawing ability.

He started in 1962 drawing pocket-size criminal and erotic comics that became very popular in Italy at the time: the series *Genius, Jolanda de Almaviva,* and a few episodes of the series *Terror* and *Cosmine.* He also drew 15 issues of the monthly *Telerompo* (1973-75), lampooning Italy's state-controlled television system. In 1974 he started drawing some adventures, and then some episodes of the series *Il fumetto della realta,* for the *Corriere dei Ragazzi;* in 1975 he was asked by the same magazine to draw the artwork for a series written by

Milo Manara, cover illustration for Glamour International. © Edizione Glamour.

Mino Milani, *La parola alla giuria* ("The Verdict of the Jury"). In this series, a famous historical figure (for example, Nero, Oppenheimer, Custer, or Helen of Troy) was brought to trial, letting the readers judge if he was guilty or not guilty. During this experience Manara's graphic style changed completely.

In 1976 Manara drew for *Corrier Boy* three episodes of the new character *Chriss Lean*, written by D'Argenzio, and then started contributing to the monthly *Alter Linus* with the story *Lo scimiotto* ("The monkey," 1976-77), written by Silverio Pisu. It was the adaptation of a famous 15th-century Chinese novel that tells the wanderings and adventures of a monkey that epitomizes man in search of wisdom and freedom from all kind of submission. The author's political interpretation transformed the monkey into a symbol for China's president, Mao Tse-Tung. Manara contributed to some collective works printed by the French publishing house Larousse, illustrating five episodes of *L'histoire de France en B.D.* (1978), and some episodes of *L'histoire de Chine* (1979).

Manara was extremely prolific in 1978. He illustrated some episodes of Enzo Biagi's *Storia d'Italia a fumetti*, drew the adventure *L'uomo delle nevi* ("The Snowman") written by Alfredo Castelli and set in Tibet, and began to write and draw for the French magazine *A Suivre* the black-and-white series *HP e Giuseppe Bergman*. While working on this peculiar graphic novel, the author himself toured the world in search of adventure and eventually met Hugo Pratt (HP), who became in the novel adventure personified.

In 1981 Manara wrote and drew for the Italian magazine *Pilot* a western adventure titled *L'uomo di carta* ("The paperman"), and in 1983 he published his first erotic story, titled *Il gioco* in the Italian magazine *Playmen*, and named *Le Declic* in the French *L'Echo des Savanes*. His superb skill in rendering the glamour of the female figure and the daring sexual situations depicted made Manara famous as an erotic author. Making the most of his talent as an erotic illustrator, over the years Manara drew *Il profumo dell'invisible*

parts one (1985) and two, *Candid Camera* (1988), and *Il gioco* parts two (1991) and three.

His friendship with Pratt gave birth to two graphic novels written by Hugo and drawn by Milo. The first, *Tutto ricomincio con un estate indiana* ("It all Started Again with an Indian Summer") was printed during 1983-85 in the magazine *Corto Maltese*. This graphic novel, set in 17th-century New England, described in critical terms the puritanical attitude of the American colonial period through a dramatic story illustrated in a masterly way. The second, *Il gaucho*, which started in 1991 in the Italian magazine *Il Grifo* and then shifted to the French *A Suivre*, is an adventure set in 19th-century Argentina. Also in 1991 Manara drew the colored book *Cristoforo Colombo* based on Biagi's script. Because of his admiration for Federico Fellini, with whom he was on good terms, Manara was authorized to draw two short stories based on film ideas the movie director could not shoot: *Viaggio a Tulum*, published in the magazine *Il Grifo* (1991). Manara also illustrated the posters of two of Fellini's movies, *Intervista* (1987) and *La voce della luna* (1990).

Manara over the years has produced several portfolios, including *Erotique* (1984), *Le Declic* (1984), *Nubinlove* (1985), and *Un' estate indiana* (1987). He has also illustrated several books by Wilbur Smith, Richard Allen, Pedro AlmoDovar, and other writers, and has created artwork for advertising campaigns.

Most of Manara's works has been reprinted in book form by many publishers. Manara was awarded a Yellow Kid in Lucca (1987) and has received many other prizes abroad. The movie *Declic* (1985), shot by French director Jean-Louis Richard and inspired by Manara's homonymous comics story, was a flop mainly because it lacked the joyful eroticism and the sarcastic remarks against bourgeois moral prejudices of Manara's erotic stories.

G.C.C.

MANDRAKE THE MAGICIAN (U.S.) Author Lee Falk and artist Phil Davis joined forces to create *Man-*

drake the Magician in 1934. Distributed by King Features Syndicate, Mandrake appeared first as a daily strip on June 11, 1934, and then as a Sunday page in February 1935.

In his coat-and-tails suit, opera hat, and black-and-red cape, Mandrake is the quintessence of all the music-hall magicians Lee Falk admired as a child. (It is interesting to note that Mandrake, with his neatly parted hair and trim moustache, was modelled after Falk himself.) In the beginning Mandrake was an actual magician endowed with supernatural powers but later he took on a more human, more believable, persona. As a master of hypnotism and illusion (skills he learned in Tibet) Mandrake uses only his superior faculties of intelligence, resourcefulness, and courage to triumph over his enemies. These have included masters of black magic pitting their power against Mandrake's white magic, mad potentates, and invaders from outer space.

In the course of his exploits, Mandrake is assisted by his faithful companion Lothar, king of a faraway African tribe, whose Herculean strength often wins the day where Mandrake's magic has failed. He also met his match in the person of Princess Narda, who tried to do him in on several occasions before settling into what seems to have become a morganatic union of sorts. In later years Mandrake's twin brother Derek and his younger sister Lenore were also introduced into the strip. Today, Mandrake leads an existence of comfort and ease on his secluded country estate, Xanadu, in the company of the ever-faithful Narda. He occasionally leaves his placid lifestyle, however, to engage in secret missions for the good of world peace on instructions from the UN-related organization Inter-Intel.

Lee Falk's writing was pithy and literate, his scenarios very imaginative, ranging from straight adventure to mystery story to science-fiction, and the story line was ably complemented by Phil Davis's elegance of line (at least before illness forced Davis to rely more and more on his assistant-wife). After Davis's death in 1964, the drawing was taken over by Fred Fredericks, who is still doing it today.

Mandrake met with immediate success from the outset and spawned a host of imitators, especially in the comic books of the 1940s and 1950s. It was made into a movie serial in 1939.

M.H.

MANGUCHO Y MENECA (Argentina) A long-lasting humor strip, Mangucho y Meneca was created in 1945 by Robert Battaglia (initially under the title Don Pascual, then changed to Mangucho con Todo, before assuming its most recognizable name). The series unfolded its gags (usually with continuity from week to week) in the pages of the comic magazine Patoruzito. It ended in 1977 when Patoruzito ceased publication.

Mangucho y Meneca's protagonists were the resourceful Mangucho and his girlfriend Meneca. Mangucho, a chubby boy always wearing an oversized cap, had a large bag of tricks that he used to get out of every conceivable predicament. He worked for a shopkeeper in a Buenos Aires suburb, Don Pascual, a gullible and easily frightened little man. Other popular characters in the strip included the megalomaniacal and slightly crazy inventor Agustín, Mr. Naña, and the dim-witted Taraletti.

L.G.

MANI IN ALTO! (Italy) Tea Bonelli's Edizioni Audace, which had offered so many imitations of Tex Willer, came up in 1952 with an original and welcome interlude: Mani in Alto! ("Hands Up!"). It was very different from their usual, run-of-the-mill productions in both style and content. The story featured not one, but several leading characters. Eventually the snappy

"Mandrake the Magician," Lee Falk and Phil Davis. © King Features Syndicate.

young Sergeant Teddy Starr emerged as the strip's most popular protagonist, but the others were so well portrayed as to vie with him for attention. Foremost among them was the old boozer, Cherry Brandy, whose name was fitting: hot-tempered and clownish, he was the comic sidekick so often depicted in American movies. Cherry Brandy's effervescent personality won him his own comic book some time later. Another star of the series was Cora, a beautiful, long-haired brunette, who often embarked on her own independent adventures. In recognition of his large cast, Rinaldo D'Ami (who wrote and drew the feature under the pen name Roy D'Amy) presented on the cover the faces of his characters, each of them enclosed in a star design: Teddy, Cherry, Cora, Little Svetola, Chinese Yo-Yo, and Corporal Cicoria.

In addition to adventures in which all the characters participated, there were individual escapades that ranged from the dramatic to the humorous, depending on the character. D'Ami, who was trained in the Venetian School of Asso di Picche, combined realistic drawings with caricatural or stylized figures.

Mani in Alto! was often reprinted in various formats, and, in spite of its short-lived career, is most deserving of mention.

G.B.

MANNEN SOM GÖR VAD SOM FALLER HONOM IN (Sweden)

Mannen som gör vad som faller honom in ("The man who does whatever comes to his mind") is a creation of Swedish cartoonist and comic artist Oskar Andersson, best known by his initials O.A., which also served as a pseudonym. O.A. started selling his cartoons to *Söndags-Nisse* (Sunday Troll), a Swedish humor weekly of the time, at the age of 20 in 1897. He was employed as a regular contributor to *Söndags-Nisse*, whose editors realized the fantastic talent they had found. Their faith in O.A. was well founded, as he became one of the best-known Swedish cartoonists.

O.A. read all that he could find of the American comic strips of his day, and in 1902 created his *Mannen som gör vad som faller honom in*, a comic strip of which some 20 episodes graced the pages of for *Söndags-Nisse* until 1906. The man who is following his each and every whim is a sour-faced libertarian living out his free will against morals and mechanization. He is also a deeply pessimistic being, reflecting the inner essence of O.A. An episode in which the man pulls a folded car out of his coat pocket, and then drives away in it seems harmless enough. Even the man's disposal of his opened umbrella after it has stopped raining seems innocent, but cutting off his fingers after shaking hands with a person he dislikes, or watching a dynamiting site at close proximity while others warn the man from a safe distance, strongly hints at O.A.'s pessimism and morbid concern for self-destruction. It is a pessimism of life, a reflection of death foreshadowing O.A.'s suicide in 1906. Thus, more than anything else, *Mannen* was a kind of self-portrait of O.A., as was much of his other work, consisting of comic strips, cartoons, and book illustrations.

The dark side of O.A. was obscured, however, by satire and humor, and by precise pen-and-ink rendering of his subjects. O.A. wanted his headstone to read simply "Here rests O.A." He no doubt was aware of the irony of this inscription, as he has been kept very much alive through reprints of his work, which has long been internationally known.

W.F.

MANNING, RUSSELL (1929-1981) American comic book and comic strip artist born in Van Nuys, California, in 1929. After graduation from high school, Russ Manning enrolled in the Los Angeles Art Institute. After a short stint as a comic book artist, he was drafted in 1950 and sent to Japan, with the prospect of being shipped to Korea. This did not happen, however, and Manning's duties, such as mapmaking and drawing cartoons for the base newspaper, remained peaceful.

Discharged in 1953, Manning met Jesse Marsh, who was then drawing the *Tarzan* comic book for Dell Publications. On Marsh's recommendation Manning joined the Dell art staff, working on their entire line of comics at one time or another. In 1965 Manning succeeded Marsh on *Tarzan* and his work was hailed by comic fans everywhere. This prompted ERB, Inc. and United Feature Syndicate to assign the *Tarzan* daily strip to Manning in 1967, and the Sunday the next year. While Manning's work continued to be critically acclaimed, the feature itself was a commercial failure. In 1972 Manning left the daily *Tarzan* strip (which went into reprints) to concentrate on the Sunday and to draw *Tarzan* comic books especially designed for the European market.

When the Los Angeles Times Syndicate decided to launch a *Star Wars* newspaper strip in 1979, the editors asked Manning to take charge of the artwork. He drew the feature until ill health forced him to relinquish it to Alfredo Alcala in 1981. He died on December 1 of that year in Long Beach, California.

Russ Manning has been hailed in the United States and in Europe as *Tarzan*'s third great comic strip artist (along with Hal Foster and Burne Hogarth). His work

"Mannen som gör vad som faller honom in," Oskar Andersson.

has proven as enduring as that of his illustrious predecessors.

M.H.

MANOS KELLY (Spain) Created in 1970 in the Spanish magazine *Trinca, Manos Kelly* was the work of cartoonist Antonio Hernandez Palacios.

Manos Kelly was a Spanish explorer who served as a guide to General Scott at the time of the Guadalupe treaty of 1848. With his companion in adventure, Siglo, he lived a multitude of experiences in the age of the gold rush, the Californian missions, and the wagon trains. A defender of the oppressed Indians and a man who went his own way without regard to prejudice or material gain, Kelly was one of the most singular heroes in the already crowded mythology of the American West.

To produce his strip, Hernandez Palacios made use of a highly personal technique in which he energetically etched out the figure of his robust hero and played with shadows and light in a style that was never one-dimensional. The quality of chiaroscuro, here rendered in full color, contributed a new dimension to the feature. The light that enhanced the images was bright and fiery, always done in warm tones, with the foregrounds remaining monochromatic. The whites were thus given additional value, directing the reader's attention, and accentuating the fast pace of the narrative.

Palacios, the author of another comic strip with similar qualities, his very personal version of *El Cid*, drew the last *Manos Kelly* story in 1984.

L.G.

MARC, RALPH *See* Marcello, Raffaelo Carlo.

MARCELLO, RAFFAELO CARLO (1929-   ) Italian cartoonist and illustrator born November 16, 1929, in Ventimiglia, near the French border. After art studies in local schools, Marcello sent samples of his work to a number of publishers in Italy and France. After being accepted at SAGE, a French publisher of comic books, he decided to settle in Paris in 1948. His first series (which he signed Ralph Marc) were *Loana*, a jungle strip starring a blonde bombshell lording it over the natives in Africa (an obvious ripoff of *Sheena, Queen of the Jungle*), and *Nick Silver*, detailing the exploits of a justice-fighting private eye.

In 1950 Marcello embarked on a long and extraordinarily prolific career as a newspaper-strip illustrator, while continuing to work as a comic book artist. Working for Opera Mundi, the largest press syndicate in France, he drew hundreds of stories, usually adaptations of popular novels such as *Ben-Hur, Oliver Twist*, or *Jane Eyre*. Since most of these adaptations comported a copious text running under the pictures and no balloons, they were not authentic comic strips, except for their presentation in horizontal rows of panels and their publication in daily newspapers. Switching to the rival Mondial-Presse in 1956, the artist continued turning out innumerable series, including such classics as Stendhal's *The Charterhouse of Parma* and *The Red and the Black*, and Henry Fielding's *Tom Jones*.

In 1971 Mondial-Presse folded, and Marcello began freelancing full-time for comic books and comic weeklies. Again the sheer volume of his output proved astonishing. Contributing to every possible publication in the field, he illustrated Westerns (*Buffalo Bill, Daniel Boone*), science-fiction tales (*John Parade, Space Patrolman*), romance stories (*Mylene, Star Ballerina*), costume epics (*The Unknown Rider*), and of course adaptations from novels (*The Quest for Fire, The Black Tulip*). His most notable creation during this time was *Docteur Justice*, which he drew on original scripts by Jean Ollivier for the weekly magazine *Pif* from 1970 to 1977. Benjamin Justice, a flying doctor working for the World Health Association, practiced expeditive justice against gun runners, drug traffickers, and despoilers of the wilderness more than he practiced medicine.

An artist of great facility, gifted with a supple line, he was always proficient and craftsmanlike; but being without personal style or originality, he made no lasting contribution to the medium. He deserves mention, however, for his massive presence in all facets of comics production. Possibly exhausted by the crushing workload he had imposed on himself for the previous 40 years, in 1989 Marcello returned to his hometown where he now lives in semiretirement, drawing an occasional story for such popular Italian comic books as *Tex Willer* and *Zagor*.

M.H.

"Manos Kelly," Antonio Hernandez Palacios. © Trinca.

Rafael Marcello, "Ben-Hur." © Opera Mundi.

MARI AGUIRRE (Spain) On April 14, 1968, the young cartoonist Juan Carlos Eguillor started *Mari Aguirre* in the magazine *El Correo Español-El Pueblo Vasco*.

Mari Aguirre was a young and pretty girl living in the mythical city of Bilbania (a transparent parody of the Basque city of Bilbao, where her comic strip adventures were published) in a world dominated by money, social stratification, and the love of material comfort. Rebellious and energetic, Mari tried without success to escape from her family and her native city. She continually encountered characters from advertising and comic strip heroes such as the Phantom, as well as real human beings. In the first incarnation of the strip she worked for a spy organization and had a number of adventures in which she fought her most famous enemy, the villainous Valmaseda. On December 28, 1968, Mari was killed and buried with full honors.

On August 29, 1970 *Mari Aguirre* was resurrected in the pages of the magazine *Mundo Joven*, and then taken back by the publication in which she lived her first adventures. Although the stories previously occupied an entire page, the second version of *Mari Aguirre* was published in the space of only one or two strips. The strip has since been discontinued.

Eguillor's style was very individual, a little naïf, elementary and simple, and his drawings were infested with weird cultural onomatopoeias which, instead of phonetically reproducing noises, rang out the names of philosophers or singers.

L.G.

MARIJAC *see* Dumas, Jacques.

MARKOVIĆ, MOMCILO-MOMA (1902-1977) The author of one of the most popular Serbian comics between two World Wars, Momcilo-Moma Marković was born in 1902 in Belgrade. Marković was among several authors who modernized Serbian comic art and illustration and harmonized it with international comics methods.

Marković studied in Paris at Ecole Nationale des Arts Decoratifs. After he had graduated, around 1933, he returned to Belgrade and worked as a book illustrator and painter. From 1932 to 1935 he was the editor and illustrator of the Belgrade magazine *Jugoslovenče*. Between 1935 and 1941 his comics were published in the most popular youth magazine of that time, *Politikin Zabavnik*, as well as in the best Serbian satiric magazine, *Ošišani Jež* (after World War II this magazine was renewed as *Jež*). His two most popular strips were *Rista*

Sportista ("Rista The Sportsman"), which appeared in *Politikin Zabavnik*, and *Stojadin*, which was popular in *Ošišani Jež*. The stories for both series were written by Mica Dimitrijevic and famous Belgrade actress Ljubinka Bobic.

Rista Sportista was about boys from Belgrade who were chasing a soccer ball and often found trouble and adventures. *Stojadin* was a witty comic about a common Serb who lived in Belgrade. The author defined him in these words: "You meet Stojadin everywhere: in the life, in the street, in politics, while shopping, in coffee bars . . . everywhere. He is our typical 'common man,' witty and cheerful, always an optimist and opportunist."

During World War II, after the occupation of Belgrade, the Nazis sent Marković to a concentration camp in Austria. After several unsuccessful attempts to run away from the camp, finally he succeeded and moved to territory liberated by the Allies in Italy. For some time, he worked in the Royal Air Forces Service as an editor of the RAF magazine. Toward the end of the war, he was moved to the British Army Headquarters, which published the soldier magazine *Union Jack*. After the war he did not want to return to communist Yugoslavia and emigrated to Canada in 1951. It was then that a family tragedy occurred: his son Mirko, who had stayed in Belgrade during the war, was killed in an attempt to cross the border illegally and join him. Marković's wife suffered a nervous breakdown and was hospitalized, and this tragedy affected his career. Although he tried to continue his art in Canada, he had little enthusiasm and a poor mental condition. Eventually, having lost the will to create, he accepted employment at the Department of Highways of Ontario County, where he worked until his retirement. He was awarded a medal for his professional contribution to the development of railways.

Moma Marković never integrated into Canadian society. He never published any comic there, and his works were never exhibited during his lifetime. He is not even in the Catalogue of the National Gallery in Ottawa. In 1980, three years after his death, his paintings (not his comics) were exhibited during the Anniversary of the Railways Development in Ontario. After the exhibition had closed the paintings were returned to the Ministry offices.

S.I.

MARK TRAIL (U.S.) In 1946 Ed Dodd, a journeyman cartoonist who had drawn the nostalgic *Back Home*

Again for United Feature, sold *Mark Trail* to the *New York Post*.

It was an unlikely matchup; the *Post* was perhaps the nation's most decidedly urban newspaper and the new comic strip dealt with outdoor, nature themes. But within four months the fledgling New York Post Syndicate had sold *Mark Trail* to 50 newspapers, and by 1950 the new Post-Hall Syndicate under Bob Hall had doubled that client list.

Mark is the archetypal outdoor person—although in modern garb, not an old backwoodsman. He is a handsome, pipe-smoking conservationist and wildlife expert. His girlfriend, Cherry, is one of the comics' most patient female leads. She is a demure, dark-haired beauty without much passion, who is always awaiting Mark's return. Scotty is Mark's young friend, a recent college graduate with degrees in biology and wildlife management. He works for an international wildlife concern. Doc is Cherry's gentle father, whose main function in the strip is to chaperone Mark and Cherry—when they can manage some time together. Rounding out the cast is Mark's trusting, lovable Saint Bernard, Andy.

Mark Trail is notable for the trails it blazed; it predated the ecology movement by decades. When nature lore was still esoteric to the masses, it was common stuff in *Mark Trail*. Through the years the strip has received many awards and recognitions. Dodd's philosophy in the strip was to take his readers outdoors and tell them of the fun and beauty of nature. There is a heavy dose of education but little pedantry.

The characterizations of the strip are strong. Incidents showcase emotions rather than vice versa, and the continuity moves at a brisker pace than many of its fellow story strips. The art is solid, somewhat heavy but not stiff or lacking in action. Naturally, the animal world is depicted with painstaking accuracy. Dodd and his assistants—animal artist Tom Hill and journeyman cartoonist Jack Elrod—produced an informative, well-paced action, adventure, and romance strip. Elrod took official credit for the strip upon Dodd's retirement in 1978.

For years the Sunday *Mark Trail* has been given to nature notes. A daily panel, also distributed now by Field Newspaper Syndicate (the successor to Hall), is *Mark Trail's Outdoor Tips*. The strip is now distributed by King Features.

R.M.

MARMITTONE (Italy) *Marmittone* was created in the pages of the *Corriere dei Piccoli* on January 29, 1928, by Bruno Angoletta, an illustrator of children's stories and a former caricaturist for *L'Asino*.

Marmittone (whose name can be loosely translated as "rooky") is derived from the "marmitta," the huge pot out of which soldiers' rations are ladled; the term is applied to a novice and simple-minded soldier, and the protagonist of the strip was true to his name. Marmittone compulsively saluted any man in a uniform, including movie ushers and hotel bellmen; on his first day of training, he was so eager to fall in that he bumped into the captain and fell on him. Because of his bewildered incompetence he spent most of his days in the stockade.

At first *Marmittone* unfolded its six panels on a half-page of the magazine, but it was later increased to 12 panels covering a full page, a sure sign of the success encountered by the hero (or rather antihero). This success was justified because *Marmittone* was read by thousands of soldiers for whom the army (and later the war) was only a silly game they were forced to play. The years went by and, despite all the bellicose propaganda spewed out by other Italian comic heroes, *Marmittone* continued to violate every military regula-

"Mark Trail," Ed Dodd. © Field Newspaper Syndicate.

"Marmittone," Bruno Angoletta. © Corriere dei Piccoli.

tion in the book. In 1940, however, Italy went to war, and a caricature like Marmittone could no longer be tolerated; he was eliminated in 1942. It is interesting to note that, while Marmittone usually ended up in jail in the last panel of each strip, in the final episode he was thrown in prison in the very first panel.

G.B.

MAROTO, ESTEBAN (1942-   ) Esteban Maroto is a Spanish artist born in Madrid. He served his apprenticeship in comic drawing as an assistant to Manuel López Blanco on the adventure series *Las Aventuras del F.B.I.* in the early 1960s. Together with Carlos Gimeénez, he began an independent artistic career a little later, with such strips as *Buck John* and *El Príncipe de Rodas* ("The Prince of Rhodes"). In 1963 he worked in Garcia Pizarro's studio, which was producing comic features for the English market. He then joined the group of Selecciones Illustradas in Barcelona, where he drew *Alex, Khan y Khamar, Beat Group,* and *Amargo*.

Maroto definitively established his strong personality and mastered his unique graphic style with his long series *Cinco por Infinito* (1967); this was followed by *La Tomba de los Dioses* ("The Tomb of the Gods") and by two exceptional heroic-fantasy stories, *Wolff* (1971), and *Manly*. In the 1970s he devoted his talents to illustrating and developing comic stories for Warren Publications.

Probably the most remarkable draftsman in Spanish comics today, Maroto has received numerous awards from amateur and professional organizations in Spain, Europe, and the United States.

L.G.

It was Warren that contributed most to Maroto's appreciation in the U.S. through its magazines *Eerie, Creepy, Vampirella,* and *1984* (later changed to *1994*), for which the artist drew numerous short stories. Among his works in the 1980s, mention should be made of *Prison Ship* and of *Manhuntress,* a science-fiction series scripted by Bruce Jones. In the latter part of the decade Maroto devoted himself exclusively to illustration; he came back to comics in 1993, drawing *Zatanna* for DC Comics and later working on a number of titles published by Topps.

M.H.

MARRINER, WILLIAM (ca. 1880-1914) Billy Marriner stands as one of the most talented and influential, but most forgotten and tragic stories in the comics.

Details of his early life are obscure—obituaries dealt with the circumstances of his death and omitted biographical data—but his first major work appeared in the pages of *Puck* magazine in the late 1890s. His signature then was an elongated "Marriner" in contrast to the compact signature of his later career. But his drawings also were stretched out, and he is notable in the musty pages of old issues of *Puck* for the unorthodox formats of his panels.

Also his drawing style differed from those of its neighbors: Marriner was definitely of a new wave of comic artists in a day when Gibson imitators still dominated. A. Z. "BB" Baker, Gus Dirks (the brother of Rudy), and Henry "Hy" Mayer were technical cousins of Marriner. Their styles were loose and free. Marriner's, in particular, was delicate and wispy—his rambling drawings would include essential lines that would become decorative tools. Smoke wound around the panel; horizon lines grew into borders; his signa-

ture itself, often in a sea of white space, would serve as a balance in the total effect.

He touched on all subjects, but soon kid cartoons predominated his drawing board. Gags with adults inevitably contained a gratuitous kid or two. He became so popular in this genre that *Puck* began heralding Marriner's kid cartoons.

And inevitably—given the flux in the comic industry at the turn of the century—he joined Opper, Howarth, and other *Puck* cartoonists into the funny pages. As with all funny-paper comic artists in those days who were not under contract to Hearst or Pulitzer, Marriner had many outlets and generally freelanced.

From 1902 to 1905 he worked for the *Philadelphia Enquirer,* the *New York World* (briefly), and T. C. McClure Syndicate. It was with the latter organization that he formed a permanent association.

His first comic was *Foolish Ferdinand,* which, like all the features for McClure and other early syndicates, gave Marriner and his fellows greater circulation in America than Hearst artists. *Mary and Her Little Lamb* was a longer-running feature, and *Sambo and His Funny Noises* ran until Marriner's death. The latter strip concerned the efforts of two white boys to wreak mischief on little black Sambo. But, in a manner that predated *Gerald McBoing-Boing* by generations, Sambo was able to confound his tormenters with strange sounds.

Marriner's most enduring and engaging effort, however, was *Wags, the Dog that Adopted a Man.* It concerned what the title implied: the harried pet-hater made it his life's effort to rid himself of the pup which had decided on him ("My Nice Man") as an owner. *Wags* ran from 1905 to 1908, with reprints years thereafter by boilerplate syndicates.

Wags was the only strip among Marriner's many that regularly featured an adult. His kids—indeed all his characters—had enormous heads, larger-than-normal feet and hands, button eyes, and Opperesque upper lips. The world in which they moved was Marriner's traditionally wispy and slightly distorted universe.

Marriner's personal life is in contrast to the innocent world of children that he drew. Clare Victor Dwiggins, with whom he worked on the *Enquirer,* remembered that Marriner, a little fellow, liked big women. Ernest McGee remembers Jimmy Swinnerton's theory that Marriner was drunk when he died in a house fire.

Swinnerton's suspicion is confirmed by contemporary reports. Marriner in 1914 was working for *Cosmopolitan* magazine and owned a house in Harrington Park, near Closter, New Jersey. He was on one of his frequent benders, during which time his wife inevitably packed herself and their son off to New York City until he dried out. On this occasion, after a visit to nearby Westwood, Marriner swore to a neighbor, "If my wife doesn't come home tonight I'm going to burn down this house and the whole village!"

Early on the morning of October 9, Marriner died in a fire that consumed his home. Early reports suggested a burglary mishap as the real cause; a gunshot report was never explained.

This tragedy nipped in the bud one of the most promising careers in the story of the comics. Billy Marriner was in his early 30s and his work was enjoyed by an entire nation—and many of his fellow cartoonists—when he took himself from their midst.

R.M.

MARSTON, WILLIAM MOULTON (1893-1947)

When comic books first became a medium for original material, there was considerable scrambling for the right formats. National struck first with *Superman*, and literally dozens of companies followed suit. Seriously lacking in the infant industry, however, was a female hero, and it remained for non-comics writer W. M. Marston to create one—Wonder Woman.

Born in Cliftondale, Massachusetts, on May 9, 1893, Marston had discovered the lie detector in 1915. By 1919, he was a member of the Massachusetts state bar, and by 1921 had secured a psychology doctorate from Harvard. During the 1920s and 1930s, he lectured at many universities, served on government study groups, was vice president of an advertising agency, wrote books on several topics, and syndicated psychology articles to newspapers and magazines.

In 1941, he turned to comics and created *Wonder Woman*; the strip made its first appearance in *All-Star* number eight (December 1941). Using the pen name Charles Moulton, Marston used the strip to express his latest theories on the psychology of the male-female relationship. Aided by the stolid, linear artwork of H. G. Peter, the feature was an instant success and was soon appearing regularly in *Sensation* and in its own magazine.

Next to the archetypal *Superman*, Marston's work is the most scrutinized in comics. Today's feminists claim it was years ahead of its time, with Wonder Woman doing everything a man could do and more. They see it as a story of a woman fulfilled. On the other hand, detractors find lesbianism, bondage, and sadomaso-chism. In his 1953 attack on comics, Dr. Fredric Wertham singled out *Wonder Woman*, calling it "one of the most harmful" crime features on the market. But despite the relatively recent, and outré, interpretations placed on the strip, there is little to indicate that Marston's young readers were particularly aware of the feature's psychological implications. In fact, since the strip continued without Marston and his theories for over 25 years, it appears readers never treated *Wonder Woman* as anything more than just another comic book story.

Marston wrote all the *Wonder Woman* stories—and the short-lived 1944 syndicated strip—until his death on May 2, 1947. Regardless of one's opinion of the feature, however, Marston's work is easily the most thought-provoking and unique ever produced for comic books. *Wonder Woman* continues to be published 50 years after its creator's death.

J.B.

MARTIN, EDGAR EVERETT (1898-1960)

American artist born in Monmouth, Illinois, in 1898. Abe Martin's father was a college biology professor, and Martin later said his first drawings were of bugs in his father's laboratory. Hooked on art, the young Martin left college in his junior year to study at the Chicago Academy of Fine Arts. Although there is no record of his having taken the Landon correspondence course, he must have done so, because he joined NEA Service in Cleveland just about the time other graduates were also signing up; Landon himself had just been named art director.

After a few immediate failures with strips, *Boots* was introduced in 1924 as a daily strip and caught on with the service's subscribing newspapers. The Sunday page did not fare as well; it was originally a top strip for the *Our Boarding House* page, running from 1926 to 1931. Martin then began a full Sunday page of his own—*Girls*—on Oct. 11, 1931, but by 1933 (on July 30, to be exact) the popular blonde Boots popped up as a character and on Sept. 9, 1934, the title was changed to *Boots* for the Sunday comic.

Although *Boots and Her Buddies*, as it came to be called, was an obvious takeoff on *Polly and Her Pals* right down to the alliteration, the resemblance soon

William Moulton Marston, "Wonder Woman." © National Periodical Publications.

Edgar Martin, "Boots and her Buddies." © NEA Service.

stopped. Boots was a flapper, who, like Blondie, eventually married and settled down. She was often sexy, but was she plump or thin? Martin's art was often confusing—encompassing clever design devices, but awkward composition. The lettering was annoyingly backhanded and the square balloons so angular that they detracted from the art.

Nevertheless, *Boots* through the years had qualities, such as inclusion of the latest fashions, that attracted a loyal set of fans. Martin gave the top strip to a pudgy couple from the main strip, Babe and Horace, and featured Boots, Babe, and other girls in popular paper cutouts on the Sunday pages. Martin's art, with all its visual distractions heightened, was continued by his assistant, Les Carroll, on a Sunday page after Martin's death on Aug. 31, 1960.

R.M.

Menny Martin, "Ayos!" © Pinoy Komiks.

MARTIN, MENNY EUSOBIO (1930-   ) Menny Martin was born on February 2, 1930, in Manila, Philippine Islands. He started to draw at the age of 13 and realized that he had a natural knack for cartooning. Two of his brothers, Jess Torres and Elpidio Torres, were well known in the field of art, so his artistic ability might well have been inherited.

In 1950 Martin started to work for *Pilipino Komiks*. He did his first comic character, *Kelot*, for *Tagalog Klasiks*. In 1951 he won first prize for his work in *Pilipino Komiks*. Later he attended the University of the East and in 1955 he finished his schooling in the field of commerce. He continued to do cartoon strips and won another major award in 1956 for his work on *Little Hut*. In 1958 he became an editor of *Espesyal Komiks*.

Through the years Martin has created and illustrated numerous cartoon characters for the many comic publications in the Philippines.

Creative, imaginative, and gifted with a great sense of humor, Martin is one of the most popular cartoonists in his country. His work has a uniquely Filipino touch and flavor, and he has the ability to capture and portray the foibles and idiosyncrasies of his fellow countrymen and to use this effectively in his continuous array of jokes, gags, puns, and comedy situations.

Among his favorite subjects are mothers-in-law and sexy women.

O.J.

MARTIN MYSTERE (Italy) Originally titled *Martin Mystere, Detective of the Impossible*, the comic created by Alfredo Castelli made its first appearance in the magazine *Supergulp* in 1978. Since 1982 the series has been published monthly in book form by the publisher Sergio Bonelli, and so far nearly 20,000 comics pages of *Martin Mystere* have been produced.

Martin Mystere is a peculiar detective who does not investigate criminal cases but mysteries concerning the world's great enigmas from the distant past to the present: old civilizations, monsters and mythical creatures, legendary heroes, long lost books, historical figures, secret societies, unexplainable events, imaginary worlds, impossible inventions, powers of the mind and magic, UFOs, and aliens. Born in America but raised in Europe, Martin Mystere is knowledgeable in many fields, from archeology and anthropology to history and computer sciences. He possesses a large personal library and huge archives stored in his personal computer; these are a valuable source of information for his adventurous explorations, for writing books, and for his own TV show *Martin's Mysteries*.

Martin lives in New York City, but he is perennially traveling in search of mysteries and their solutions. This wandering life disturbs his relationship with his fianceé, Diana Lombard, in spite of her calm patience, sense of irony, and deep feminine wisdom. Martin's most loyal and devoted friend, always at his side, is Java, a representative of the Neanderthal race, born in Mongolia and now an American citizen. Java communicates by gestures and grunts, but posesses an acute intelligence, completely different than that of modern man, that allows him to sense by instinct all kinds of dangers and to communicate mentally with animals. The many differences in character between Martin and Java only complement their partnership, based on trust and mutual understanding.

Some of the many villains who try to prevent Martin from unraveling the mysteries of the world are recurrent: the powerful Men in Black, who shape the course of history by targeting and eradicating beliefs, ideas, and opinions that might disrupt the accepted view of world history (for example, evidence that UFOs exist or that highly developed civilizations preceded our own); Martin's archenemy Sergej Orloff, the wealthy leader of a group that shares Martin's interests, but for evil purposes rather than for learning; Mr. Jinx, an expert in computer sciences who grants men's secret and forbidden desires at a Mephisophelean price; and an ineffable trio of scoundrels among whom the deliciously sexy Angie stands out.

Martin's stories are fictional but extremely well-grounded in fact. Informative elements are woven throughout the narrative, allowing the reader to be entertained while at the same time learning about history, current events, geography, science, the arts, language, mythology, and cultures past and present. Spinoff series of *Martin Mystere* have appeared since 1992 in the magazine *ZonaX* and also some stories with Dylan Dog have been published.

So far, Castelli, the main scriptwriter of the series, has been assisted in his task by 21 collaborators, including Vincenzo Beretta, Andrea Pasini, and Carlo Recagno. The artwork, originally produced by Gian-

"Martin Mystère," Alfredo Castelli and Leo Filippucci. Martin Mystère is greeted in New York by all his Italian friends from the comics.

carlo Alessandrini, the graphic creator of the character, has been carried on over the years by 37 artists, including Giampiero Casertano, Franco Devescovi, Lucio Filippucci, Esposito Bros., Paolo Morales, Guiseppe Palumbo, and Rodolfo Torti. *Martin Mystère's* adventures are scheduled for publication in the United States under the name *Martin Y* in 1997 by Dark Horse.

G.C.C.

MARVELMAN (G.B.) Recluse astroscientist Guntag Barghelt, while working in his secret laboratory on an island in the Mississippi, finds the keyword to the Universe: "Kimota!" When uttered, this dynamic word endows the speaker with all the natural power that exists. Seeking a young lad of honesty and integrity to use this power only against evil, Barghelt is saved from young thugs by crew-cut Micky Moran, copyboy on the *Daily Bugle*. After subjection to atomic treatment, Micky is able to save his benefactor from the evil Herman Schwein by shouting "Kimota!" At the magic keyword atomic power crashes down and immediately Micky becomes Marvelman, Mightiest Man in the Universe.

Born more of necessity than ingenuity, the *Marvelman* comic book weekly began at number 25 (February 3, 1954); number 24 was the last British edition of the American comic book *Captain Marvel*. The changeover was devised to continue the sales of its predecessor, which had suddenly ceased upon the filing of the famous lawsuit brought by National Comics against Fawcett Publications in America. *Captain Marvel* became *Marvelman*, Billy Batson became Micky Moran, Station Whiz became *Daily Bugle*, "Shazam" became "Kimota," and Dr. Sivana became Dr. Gargunza.

On the same day *Captain Marvel Jr.* was re-created as *Young Marvelman*, while Freddy Freeman became Dicky Dauntless, not a crippled newsboy but a messenger boy in the Transatlantic Messenger Service. And

"Marvelman," Don Lawrence. © Marvelman Family.

from October 1956 *Marvel Family* comic book became *Marvelman Family*, with *Mary Marvel* replaced by *Kid Marvelman*. Publisher Leonard Miller (of L. Miller & Son) was the impresario behind what became Britain's longest-lived and most popular superhero.

The architect of this venture was cartoonist Mick Anglo, with editors W. A. Knott, Anthony Miller, and later D. W. Boyce. Artwork was originally shared by King-Ganteaume Productions and Anglo's Gower Studios. Cartoonists on the series included R. Parker, Don

Lawrence, Norman Light, James Bleach, Stanley White, Denis Gifford, George Parlett, Leo Rawlings, and Ron Embleton. The last issue, number 370, was published in February 1963. There was also an annual for both characters.

Nearly 20 years later, Dez Skinn, a British comics-buff-turned-publisher, acquired the revival rights to *Marvelman* and reintroduced him to a new young audience in the monthly comic *Warrior*. The artist this time around was Garry Leach. The original run was from 1982 to 1985. Skinn then interested a small American publisher and so introduced *Marvelman* to the States. When mighty Marvel Comics stepped in and claimed infringement on their registered copyright name, the publisher changed *Marvelman's* name to *Miracleman*. What the British publisher Top Sellers thought is not known—for the record, they published a monthly *Miracle Man* back in the 1950s.

D.G.

MARY MARVEL (U.S.) Flushed by the success of *Captain Marvel Jr.*, the first spinoff of the monumental *Captain Marvel*, Fawcett decided the time was right for a lady Marvel. Otto Binder subsequently created *Mary Marvel* in *Captain Marvel Adventures* number 18 (December 1940). The next month it began appearing regularly in *Wow* and then in *Mary Marvel* comics in 1945. Otto's brother, Jack Binder, was the strip's major artist.

Mary Marvel's origin was a strange one. Unlike orphans Billy (Captain Marvel) Batson and Freddy (Captain Marvel Jr.) Freeman, Mary Bromfield was living a comfortable childhood with a well-to-do family. But Billy later learned that she was his long-lost twin sister, and he saved her just before she was kidnapped. Billy scoffed at the thought of Old Shazam giving his

"Mary Marvel," Jack Binder. © Fawcett Publications.

magic powers to a girl, but when Mary yelled the magic word (Shazam) in a crisis, she was immediately transformed into Mary Marvel. Her reaction was to exclaim "My! What a lovely costume!" And except for the short sleeves and a demure miniskirt, hers were the same gold-and-orange togs worn by Captain Marvel himself.

The *Mary Marvel* feature was one of the best produced in the 1940s, but it was the weakest of the Marvel Family troika. Although Binder had the foresight to revise the meaning of the magic word for her—Shazam now stood for Selena's grace, Hippolyta's strength, Ariadne's skill, Zephyrus' fleetness, Aurora's beauty, and Minerva's wisdom—Mary Marvel was never treated like a girl. In fact, she was almost always treated like just another Marvel. Despite all his talents, Otto Binder only rarely managed to imbue Mary with any real female characteristics. And even though girls were buying hordes of romance comics, Mary Marvel never had the slightest hint of a romantic interest!

Artistically however, Jack Binder handled the strip with a verve and style rarely seen in his work. Known more for his organizational talents rather than his artwork, Binder constantly produced clean, pretty, and interesting interpretations. His backgrounding and panel details struck an aesthetic balance between C. C. Beck's cartoonish *Captain Marvel* and Mac Raboy's illustrated *Captain Marvel Jr.*

In *Wow* number 18, the Binder brothers created still another Marvel, the lovably fraudulent Uncle Dudley Marvel. Claiming to be related to Mary Batson Bromfield, he wanted to organize Shazam, Inc. to profit from the Marvel Family powers. A W. C. Fields lookalike, he wore a tattered imitation of the majestic Marvel costume and had absolutely no powers—even though he claimed all the family prowess. He was eventually proven to have a "heart of gold" and was made an honorary Marvel—the family even humored his superpowered delusions! Never more than a supporting character, he added much to *Mary Marvel* and the whole Marvel cadre.

Mary Marvel continued to appear in *Marvel Family* until 1953, but she stopped appearing on a regular basis after *Wow* and *Mary Marvel* were discontinued in 1948. She was revived by National Periodicals in 1973, but only made occasional appearances in *Shazam!* comics from 1973 to 1978.

J.B.

MARY PERKINS *see* On Stage.

MARY WORTH (U.S.) In 1932 Mary Orr (niece of *Chicago Tribune* editorial cartoonist Carey Orr) created *Apple Mary* for Publishers Syndicate. The title character was a middle-aged woman who had been reduced to selling apples on street corners by the market crash. (She was no doubt inspired by a Damon Runyon character of the same ilk named "Apple Annie"—herself the heroine of the successful 1933 Capra movie *Lady For a Day* and its later remake *A Pocketful of Miracles*.) The series met with instant success in the bleak 1930s but, as the United States was slowly getting out of the Depression, the worthy but indigent Mary became more and more irrelevant.

In 1940 Martha Orr left *Apple Mary*, and the strip, rechristened *Mary Worth's Family*, was entrusted to writer Allen Saunders and female cartoonist Dale Conner (their byline was "Dale Allen"). The strip was

"Mary Worth," Ken Ernst and Allen Saunders. © Field Newspaper Syndicate.

considerably revamped and Mary, along with her new surname, acquired a less shabby, more dignified persona. The metamorphosis was hastened by Kent Ernst, a cartoonist of the new school of no negligible talent, who had succeeded Dale Connor in 1942 and who now endeavored to remove from Mary any vestige of her earlier slightly déclassé existence. Further shortened to *Mary Worth*, the strip seems today almost exclusively peopled with artists, actresses, promising executives, and other glamourous types to whom Mary dispenses motherly advice with deadpan impartiality.

The seeming conventionality of the series can be attributed not so much to either Allen Saunders (whose scripts were often excellent) or Ken Ernst (who made imaginative use of framing and composition) as to the inevitable limitations of the soap opera genre.

Saunders retired in 1979 and the scripting of the feature passed into the hands of his son, John Saunders. When Ernst died in 1985 he was succeeded by his longtime assistant, Bill Ziegler, who had to quit in 1990 due to illness. *Mary Worth* is now drawn by Joe Giella and distributed by King Features Syndicate, which in 1996 characteristically wrote of the heroine that "this confidante of the comics dispenses kindness and wisdom to all who enter her life."

A few *Mary Worth* episodes were reprinted in paperback form by Dell in 1964 and by Avon in 1969.

M.H.

MASTER OF KUNG FU (U.S.) In the early 1970s the martial-arts craze (fueled mainly by Bruce Lee's movies) was sweeping the country. It was therefore inevitable that a comic book on the theme would come out sooner or later—which it did right on cue in issue number 15 (December 1973) of *Marvel Special Edition*, an oversized line devoted to movie adaptations.

The hero (or antihero) of the piece was Shang-Chi, reportedly the son of that archfiend of Oriental menace Fu Manchu. Trained in all the martial arts, and particularly in kung fu, the youth was sent by his cunning father to fight Fu's nemesis, Sir Denis Nayland Smith of the British Intelligence Service, and his associate Dr. Petrie. When he realized how evil his father really was, Shang turned against him, but like most do-gooders he only found himself the target of both opposing forces.

On this premise writer Steve Englehart built an intriguing tale of suspense and derring-do; he was ably abetted in his efforts by Jim Starlin, who provided a kinetic visual flow to the fast-paced stories. The series turned out to be so popular that *Marvel Special Edition* changed into *Master of Kung Fu* with issue number 17 (April 1974). Additionally, a black-and-white comics magazine, *Deadly Hands of Kung Fu*, came out on the same date.

The original team soon departed, however, and the title experienced a number of ups and downs, faring well under capable artists and writers (Doug Moench with Paul Gulacy or Gene Day, for instance), going dismally down in the hands of time-serving hacks. At any rate the kung fu craze was played out by the beginning of the 1980s in favor of the kickboxing fad, and *Master of Kung Fu* was discontinued in June 1983 (*Deadly Hands* had only made it to February 1977, but for the record it should be noted that the title was revived for an issue in 1991).

M.H.

MATENA, DICK (1943-) Dutch comic artist born April 24, 1943, in Den Haag (The Hague), where he grew up and went to school. In school he enjoyed a certain notoriety for the charicatures he made of his teachers. After leaving school he became assistant in a photo shop, tried several other jobs, and finally landed a job that afforded him a chance to display his artistic talents painting and drawing window displays for a huge department store. Realizing Matena's talent, his boss suggested that he apply for a position in the Toonder Studios. Marten Toonder, whose studio does everything from cartoons to graphic design, gave young Dick Matena a chance.

Matena stayed with the Toonder Studios from 1961 to 1968, working on a freelance basis for four of these years. He received intensive training for work on the Toonder strips. In 1966 he drew his first comic strip, *Polletje Pluim*, an animal strip, that was published in the women's magazine *Prinses*. This led to *De Argonautjes* ("The Argonauts"), on which he started working with writer Lo Hartog van Banda in 1967. The feature first appears in 1968 in the Dutch weekly comics magazine *Pep*, founded in 1962. It was soon followed by the humorous adventures of the knight *Ridder Roodhart*, starting in *Pep* in 1969. Once again the writer was Lo Hartog van Banda.

Dick Matena turned writer/artist in 1970 for *De Grote Pyr*, a comic strip that quickly caught on. It was an exceptionally funny comic series in the vein of *Asterix*, seasoned somewhat by a grain of Jacovitti. The hero of this series, a Viking chieftain, was very

Dick Matena, "De Zoon van de Zon." © Marten Toonder.

worried about his son, who would rather sing than fight despite his superb build. Nevertheless, it was usually the son who solved all of the Norsemen's troubles.

In ensuing years Matena turned to realistic artwork. The science-fiction epic *Virl*, published in 1977, marked the definitive change. He impressed readers with his literary adaptations and comic biographies of famous people like Mozart and Edgar Allan Poe. One of the highpoints of his current work was titled *Alias Ego*. In 1992 Matena started a series of comic albums about an adventurer, *Flynn*, and also revived *De Grote Pyr*.

Matena knows how to give the comic page just the right amount of animation. His firm line, balance of black and white, care for detail, and storytelling prowess make his stories highly entertaining.

W.F.

MATSUMOTO, REIJI (1938-   ) Japanese comic book artist born January 25, 1938, in Tokyo. Reiji Matsumoto started drawing at an early age and while still in high school he sold his first strip, *Mitsubachi no Bōken* ("The Adventures of Honeybee"), to the monthly *Manga Shōnen* in 1954; the following year it was picked up by the Western edition of the *Mainichi Shogakusei Shin bun Seibuban*, a daily newspaper for schoolchildren.

After graduation Matsumoto created *Kuroi Hanabira* ("Black Petal," a girl strip) for the monthly *Shōjo* (1957). Many more creations were to follow: *Denkō Ozma*, a science-fiction strip, in 1961; *Zero Pilot*, a war strip, in 1962; *Gohikino Yōjimnō*, a Western strip, and *S no Taiyō*, a girl strip, in 1967. In 1968, three new Matsumoto titles were published: *Akage no Hitotsu* (which told of the friendship between Hitotsu, a big red bear, and Yuki, a young girl); *Sexaroid*, and *Kōsoku Esper* (both science fiction). After this, Matsumoto created such titles as *Yojigen Sekai* ("The Four-Dimensional World," 1969); *Mystery Eve* (a science-fiction strip, 1970); *Otoko Oidon* (one of his most famous creations, 1971); *Gun Grontier* (a Western, 1972); *Uchū Senkan Yamato* ("Space Battleship Yamato," 1974), which inspired a series of animated cartoons; and others. In 1977 he produced the very successful *Captain Harlock*; Harlock and his other creations have kept him busy (and rich) up to this day.

Matsumoto is a versatile artist who has created comic strips for boys, girls, and adults with equal ease. He is noted for the wide range of his undertakings, from humor strips to war tales, and he is especially good at depicting alluring young ladies, animals, weapons, machines, and insects (his predilection). In his early strips, Matsumoto was greatly influenced by Osamu Tezuka (like every other young Japanese cartoonist) but he quickly came into his own with a style full of zest and vitality.

Reiji Matsumoto, "Otoko Oidon." © Reiji Matsumoto.

Matsumoto is also known as an avid comic book collector. His wife, Miyako Maki, is a famous illustrator of women's comic books.

H.K.

MATTOTTI, LORENZO (1954-   ) Italian cartoonist, illustrator, and painter born January 24, 1954, in Brescia. While a student in architecture in Venice, Lorenzo Mattotti turned to comics. His first short works were printed during 1975 in the Italian magazines *La Bancarella* and *King Kong*, and in the French publications *Biblipop* and *Circus*. In 1977 he contributed to *Eureka* and drew *Alice brum Brum*, written by Jerry Kramsky (Fabrizio Ostani) and printed in book form by the publisher Ottaviano. In 1978 he drew *Tram Tram Rock-Tram Tram Waltz*, written by A. Tettamanti, for the magazine *Secondamano*, and *Huckleberry Finn*, adapted by Tettamanti from Mark Twain's novel and printed in book form by Ottaviano. In 1979 he drew *Agatha Blue* for the magazine *Canecaldo*, and *Mandrie*

sulla sabia, written by Ostani, for a supplement of the magazine *Eureka*.

In 1980 Mattotti started collaborating to the monthly *Linus* with the story *Ale tran tran*, written by Tettamanti, and contributed to other magazines such as *Nemo in blue, Panorama*, and *Satyricon*. In 1981 he developed other short works for different magazines and drew for the monthly *Alter Alter* the story *Incedenti*, written by Tettamanti and dealing with social ostracism. The following year he drew for *Secondamano* the weekly strip *Jazzamentos*, based on a Kramsky script, and for *Alter Alter* he drew *Il Signor Spartaco* (to which Kramsky added the text after the artwork was done), a tale which does not narrate any action, but the protagonist's interior evolution.

In 1983 Mattotti joined in Bologna Giorgio Carpinteri, Igort, Marcello Jori, and other artists in founding the group Valvoline which gave birth to an insert for the magazine *Alter Alter*. There Mattotti published the story, based on a Kramsky script, *Dottor Nefasto*, about a mad doctor who wants to conquer the world. In the

Lorenzo Mattotti, © Lorenzo Mattotti.

same year Mattotti started drawing the series for children *Barbaverde*, written by Ostani, printed in the *Corriere dei Piccoli* and continued up to 1988.

In 1984 Mattotti began contributing to the fashion magazine *Vanity* with covers and illustrations. In the same year he worked for different magazines but, above all, he wrote and drew the story *Fuochi* published by installments in *Alter Alter*. The plot is quite simple: a battleship has the task of destroying a little island, but one of the sailors, attracted by the colors and creatures of the island, tries to prevent his companions from doing it. What is fascinating in this story is the artwork midway between realism and abstractionism, and the existing narrative tension among words and colors. With *Fuochi* Mattotti's reputation grew considerably on an international scale. In the following years he contributed increasingly with short comics stories and illustrations to many foreign magazines. In the United States Mattotti's contributions appeared in the magazine *La Dolce Vita* in the years 1987-88, and *L'uomo alla finestra* ("The man at the window") a long poetic and melancholy story based on a script of Mattotti's former wife L. Ambrosi, and printed in book form in the same year 1992 in Italy, France, Germany, Holland, and Finland. Many of Mattotti's comics stories have been reprinted in book form in several countries.

Mattotti's graphic activity has also included illustrations of books (worth mentioning is Collodi's *Pinocchio* in 1990), book and CD covers, calendars, portfolios and serigraphies, posters, and advertising campaigns. Mattotti received a special prize in Lucca (1986), a Caran d'Ache in Rome (1995), and other prizes abroad.

G.C.C.

MAURICIO *see* De Souza, Mauricio.

MAUROVIĆ, ANDRIJA (1901-199?) The history of Yugoslav comic strips began in 1935 when Andrija Maurović decided to create the comic strip *Vjerenica mača* ("The Sword's Fiancée") for the first Yugoslavian comic magazine, *Oko*. The father of Yugoslav comic strips was born in Kotor in 1901, and during his career Maurovič drew over 150 comic strip episodes. He lived very modestly for years in his very poor Zagreb home, alone, without any financial help, except for his small pension. Years ago Maurović was the highest-paid art-

Andrija Maurović, "Grucka Vjestica." © Andrija Maurović.

ist in Yugoslavia, earning a lot of money very quickly, but spending it even faster. He reportedly did not possess a single page (printed or original) of any of his comics. He was also unable to remember more than four or five titles of his own comics or his characters. He said that he was turning out comics so quickly that he never found time to look at them after he had finished drawing, or after they were printed.

The fact remains, however, that Maurović was the most important and most productive of all Yugoslav cartoonists. His Western series *Stari Mačak* ("The Old Cat"), published in 1937, was the most popular. Thirty years later Maurović wanted to make a comeback with *Stari Mačak*, and in 1968 *Plavi Vjesnik* published his *Povratak Starog Mačka* ("The Return of the Old Cat"), but the venture proved unsuccessful. It was the last strip drawn by Maurović.

Maurović was a very original, an inimitably realistic artist, and in his drawings no other artist's influences can be found. He has also done some comics directly in color, and these were very much appreciated by readers and art critics. Only one criticism can be made of Maurović. That is that he never used any archives in all his work. Also he never took any long trips, and all the people, animals, costumes, countries, or arms in his comics "were always coming from his head," as he used to say.

Maurović was thrown out of the Yugoslav Republic Society of the Fine Arts when they complained that he had not been paying his membership fees regularly. However, he believed that his colleagues were envious of his art mastery and that the society liked neither comic strips nor cartoonists. He reportedly died in the early 1990s.

E.R.

MAUS (U.S.) The seminal inspiration for *Maus* came in 1972 in a three-page comic book story that Art Spiegelman published in *Funny Aminals* (sic) number 1. In it a little mouse named Mickey was told by his father at bedtime of the holocaust that had been perpetrated against Jewish mice by "Die Katzen," the German cats. It was a simple tale, devoid of rhetoric and highly affecting.

In 1980 when he began to publish his own magazine, *Raw*, Spiegelman decided to amplify and personalize the tale, retaining the cat-and-mouse analogy. The now grown-up mouse Art enticed his father, Vladek, into telling him of his life before and during the Second World War as a Jew living in Poland. There unfolded a horrifying story of persecution and genocide endured by the Jewish mice at the hands (or paws) of the Nazi cats with the tacit complicity of the Poles (portrayed as pigs). Although the use of an animal fable did not in itself trivialize the Holocaust story, naming the Germans the Katzies (with its echo of the pranks played by the comic-strip Katzenjammer Kids) was unfortunate. Furthermore, as many have pointed out, genocide is a policy of extermination whereby killers and victims are members of the same species, which cats and mice definitely are not. At any rate the story ended six years later with Vladek and his wife, Anja, being shipped to Auschwitz (or Mauschwitz, as it is called here).

Later in 1986 all the different chapters were collected into book form by Pantheon with the title *Maus: A Survivor's Tale.* The volume received thunderous critical acclaim and became a bestseller; a few demurs from

"*Maus*," Art Spiegelman. © Art Spiegelman.

some in the Jewish press and elsewhere were quickly drowned by the drumbeat coming from the amen corner. Encouraged by this response and with a grant from the Guggenheim Foundation, Spiegelman set to work on a sequel picking up the story in 1944 and bringing it up to the present. Completed in 1991, it was again published by Pantheon, as *Maus II; From Mauschwitz to the Catskills*, and again there were generally favorable reviews and good sales.

Viewed in its totality *Maus* revealed not only a highly complex structure but also some disturbing flaws in its narrative thrust. While Vladek's story is as grippingly told in the second volume as in the first one (and even more horrifying), many of the exchanges between father and son (and Art's later expostulations upon them) seem contrived to accord with the author's politically correct ideology. In particular Art's attempts to take away the mantle of victimhood from his father's shoulders to wrap it around himself makes Vladek look even more heroic in comparison to his son, who comes out as a mean-spirited, self-pitying weasel (to continue the animal analogy). The interpolated four-page episode "Prisoner on the Hell Planet" wherein Art, accoutered in concentration-camp garb, seems to accuse his mother of having killed herself in order to make him feel guilty, is very revealing in this regard.

Maus remains an important work, although it is neither the literary ("on a par with Kafka") nor the artistic ("comparable to Goya") achievement its more rabid admirers have claimed. In 1996, when minds had had time to sober up and to more lucidly weigh the work on the scales of art and literature, Pantheon issued a special 10th anniversary edition of *The Complete Maus*. It flopped.

M.H.

MAX (Belgium) *Max* is a typical example of the internationalism of today's European comic strips. Conceived by the Belgian cartoonist Guy Herzog (under the pseudonym "Bara") in 1955, it was distributed by the Danish syndicate P.I.B. and appeared for the first time in French (as a daily strip) in the Paris newspaper *France-Soir*. It was later picked up by the Belgian weekly *Spirou* (1963) and, in 1968, by another Belgian weekly, *Tintin*.

Max is an explorer but his methods and attitudes would have made Stanley and Livingstone turn in their graves. He would shoot down maharaja-carrying elephants, make fun of African witch-doctors, bait chest-thumping gorillas, and get into arguments with Mexican taxi-drivers, all to his ultimate chagrin. There is more than a hint of the absurd in Max's character as he imperturbably went on to race Indian fakirs on flying carpets, or rescue mermaids lost on land. The surreal atmosphere was very close to Irving Phillips's

"*Max*," Bara (Guy Herzog). © Bara.

Mr. Mum (a strip that Max predated by some five years).

Max is a pantomime strip and relies chiefly on its drawing style to make its points. Bara's line, deceptively simple in appearance, is actually highly stylized and sometimes almost abstract. With a few strokes of his pen, the author could suggest a whole atmosphere of Oriental bazaars or African jungles, as he could in a few panels (usually three) dissect a whole scene. Max himself was very funny, with his toothbrush mustache, his perpetual grin, and his eyebrows arched high over his pith helmet. There are no other permanent characters in the strip; Max is the entire cast and crew.

For years *Max* was the most widely syndicated European strip (appearing at one time in over 20 newspapers). It was also reprinted in paperback form (by the Editions Dupuis in Belgium). In the late 1960s, however, it started getting repetitive, or perhaps the author was tiring of it, and it was discontinued by *Tintin* in 1972. It continued, however, in the daily press, where in 1994 the strip numbered 10,000 appeared. *Max* has also been reprinted in nine albums to date.

M.H.

MAXON, REX (1892-1973) American artist born in Lincoln, Nebraska, on March 24, 1892. His family moved to St. Louis where Maxon studied at the St. Louis School of Fine Arts and worked on the staff of the *St. Louis Republic*. He moved to New York in 1917 and contributed drawings to a number of New York newspapers, including the *Globe*, the *World*, and the *Evening Mail*. In March 1929, succeeding Harold Foster, Rex Maxon started drawing the daily strip of *Tarzan*, a task that he would carry on (with the exception of a short interruption in 1937-38) for the next 18 years. He was called upon to draw the newly created *Tarzan* Sunday page in March 1931, but this proved too much for his abilities and he turned it over to the returning Foster in September of the same year.

After his departure from *Tarzan* in 1947, Maxon worked mainly in comic books as an illustrator of cowboy stories. In 1954, in collaboration with Matt Murphy, he created for Dell *Turok, Son of Stone*, which he drew until his retirement in 1960. For a while he lived in London before settling in Boston, where he died on November 25, 1973.

Maxon's main claim to fame rests upon his long association with *Tarzan*. His work on the strip, however, was unremarkable and a far cry from the brilliance of Harold Foster and Burne Hogarth, who were drawing the Sunday page during the same period of time.

M.H.

MAX UND MORITZ (Germany) *Max und Moritz* may well be the most famous creation of German artist/writer Wilhelm Busch. It has been an important influence in the development of the comic strip, and in fact, may be counted among the earliest comic strips.

After having produced a large number of full-page funny picture stories for the humor weekly *Fliegenden Blätter* and for the *Münchener Bilderbogen* since 1859, Wilhelm Busch started doing picture-books in 1864 that were published by a Dresden publisher. These books did not turn into an immediate smash success, and so the publisher rejected *Max und Moritz* in 1865 as unsuitable for publication. Busch sent it to Munich explaining that it could be used as a continuous children's story in the *Fliegenden Blätter* and, with slight changes of text, might be reprinted in the *Bilderbogen*. The publisher liked what he got; the rest is history.

Max und Moritz as a story with a story with a cast of continuing characters told in pictures and text that are interdependent, filling most, if not all, of the classic requirements that define a comic strip. Sound effects, for that matter, are not lacking either; "Rickeracke! / Rickeracke! / Geht die Mühle mit Geknacke," (As the farmer turns his back, he / Hears the mill go "creaky! cracky!"). *Max und Moritz* was even met by the same teachers' resentment that confronted comic books in the 1950s.

The most obvious influence of *Max und Moritz* is the pattern it set for *The Katzenjammer Kids*, which is regarded as one of the first genuine comic strips. But *Max und Moritz* and Busch's other work also set a trend that was followed by artists like Carl Spitzweg, Eduard Ille, Adolf Oberländer, Lothar Meggendorfer, Emil Reinicke, and Franz Stuck, who also worked for the *Fliegenden Blätter*. Some of them, like Spitzweg, are better known for their paintings, which proves that "fine art" and "comic art" are not incongruous. It should also be noted that the *Fliegenden Blätter* had a continuing character that was done by different artists: the Bavarian Lion (stepping into the comic pages from the Bavarian coat-of-arms).

The masterful strokes of Busch's art were also copied by the comic supplements of German newspapers in the 1880s and 1890s. His method of telling stories in verse stayed with most German picture stories up to the 1940s. Although designated as literature for children, Busch's work, because of its social satire and biting sarcasm, was also aimed at adults. Nevertheless, comics were simply regarded as kid stuff in Germany up to the late 1960s. This attitude, besides being a gross insult to Busch's wit, consciously denies any such thing as a German comic tradition.

W.F.

MAYER, SHELDON (1917-1991) American comic book writer, artist, and editor born April 1, 1917, in New York City. Shelly Mayer's first comic artwork came when he was an assistant for several New York newspaper cartoonists between 1932 and 1935. In 1935, he became one of the earliest contributors to comic books when he wrote and drew *J. Worthington Blimp* and *The Strange Adventures of Mr. Weed* for the early books of Major Nicholson. Mayer joined the McClure syndicate in 1936, producing editorial odd jobs which including ghosting George Storm's *Bobby Thatcher*. At the same time, he was also editing Dell's fledging comic line.

Mayer resigned both posts in 1939 to assume the editorship of publisher M. C. Gaines' All-American comic book line. That group and the National (DC) line were jointly owned by Gaines and by Jack Leibowitz and Harry Donnenfeld, but the two groups maintained separate staffs and offices until 1945. Under the A-A logo, Mayer was responsible for the direction of *Flash*, *All-Star*, *Green Lantern*, *Wonder Woman*, and several other titles, all among the best selling comic books of the early 1940s.

In addition to his editorial duties, Mayer scripted the *Ultra-Man* superhero strip from 1939 to 1944. *Scribbly*, a feature he wrote and drew, was a delightfully whimsical strip about a boy who wanted to be a cartoonist.

Mayer drew the strip in All-American comics between 1939 and 1944, and then in its own title—Mayer calls it a "novel in comic book form"—between 1948 and 1950.

Mayer resigned as editor in 1948, but continued to write for National. He wrote and drew dozens of children's comics and funny animal books, most notably *Sugar and Spike*, a feature about two children who can walk but can't talk. In 1973, he turned his attention to mystery strips and created *The Black Orchid* for Adventure comics. He had to abandon drawing in 1977 because of eye trouble; he died on December 21, 1991.

J.B.

MECKI (Germany) Mecki was originally the star of the animated puppet films of the Diehl brothers. Eduard Rhein, first editor-in-chief of *Hör zu*, acquired the rights to use *Mecki* as editorial talisman and as a comic strip. For this, the more domestic atmosphere of the original hedgehog in Mecki's films had to be expanded upon. This task was given to Reinhold Escher, who created a number of supporting characters like Charly Pinguin or the Schrat. *Mecki* appeared in *Hör zu* from 1951 to 1972. Up to 1971 a running narrative was included in the picture frames. For the last two years speech balloons were added. The strip was cancelled when Hans Bluhm, the second editor-in-chief of *Hör zu*, was looking for a new attraction, but a revamped version of *Mecki* appeared in October 1975.

During the 21 years of its first run, *Mecki* lived through some 21 continued stories and a large number of single-page gags. Most of these were written and drawn by Reinhold Escher, who was sometimes assisted on the writing by his wife. Some of the stories were drawn by Professor Wilhelm Petersen and Heinz Ludwig. But of these, it is only Escher's art that is slightly reminiscent of Lyonel Feininger's stylistics in *The Kin-der-Kids*.

The star of this strip, of course, was Mecki, a hedgehog with a wife and children. He was both father figure and adventurer, mastering every situation with wit and cunning. His "crew cut" appearance led to a German word for crew cut, *Mecki-Schnitt* ("Mecki cut"). Charly Pinguin, the penguin friend of Mecki, was the wise guy of the group. His high-flying plans were usually wrecked by his own shortcomings, and more often than not by his choleric temperament. The Schrat was a kind of ape-like sloth whose utmost goal seemed to be being lazy. It was only his good nature that motivated him occasionally to act—say, if one of his friends was in a pickle—but even then he was soon overcome by sleep. The stories were sheer escape into an anthropomorphic world of fun and suspense that held reader interest for over two decades because of excellent storytelling, art, and color.

The success of the strip led to books that were published annually and the production of cuddly toys of Mecki and the Schrat. However, the full-page comic strips that appeared until 1978 were not reprinted in book form. After a hiatus of some seven years, *Mecki* was revived in 1985 as a comic strip. It is now a two-tier strip published weekly in *Hör zu*, written and drawn by Volker Reiche, who originally was an underground comic artist before drawing *Donald Duck* for the Dutch Disney magazines. The strip has become a family affair with humorous pranks and gags. Popularity of

the characters is still high; an animated series was developed and produced for television in 1995. The series is loosely based on the original puppet animation films and does not make use of additional characters appearing in the comic strip.

W.F.

MEDIEVAL CASTLE, THE (U.S.) Harold Foster created *The Medieval Castle* as a companion feature to *Prince Valiant*. Conceived as a three-picture strip, usually placed at the bottom of the page, *The Medieval Castle* ran from April 1944 to November 1945.

This slight tale of two young English squires, Arn and Guy, in the time of the First Crusade, is remarkable mostly for its graphic qualities and the minute realism of its details. Into it Foster poured all his knowledge of medieval lore and his love for the period in an abundance of painstakingly detailed vignettes about the lifestyles and mores of the times. In many ways Foster used *The Medieval Castle* as a sketchboard and idea-board for his main feature, *Prince Valiant*. One of the young heroes, Arn, served as the model for Prince Valiant's elder son, also named Arn.

In 1945 a color version of the strip was published by John Martin's House under the title *The Young Knight: A Tale of Medieval Times*, and in 1957 Hastings House again reprinted the strip (in black and white and a slightly altered format) under its original title.

M.H.

MELOUAH, SID ALI (1949-   ) A native of Algiers, Algeria, where he was born on September 23, 1949, Sid Ali Melouah is the foremost cartoonist and comics artist of his country. He exhibited a love of drawing from an early age, and as an outlet for his budding talents he cofounded the first Algerian comics magazine, *M'Quidech*, in 1968. After graduation from the Academy of Commercial Art in Copenhagen, Denmark, he embarked in earnest on a career as a cartoonist, illustrator, and journalist, notably working for the dailies *El Moudjahid* and *Horizons* and for the weekly *Algérie-Actualités*. Equally fluent in the French and Arabic languages, he was instrumental in the creation of the first Algerian magazines of satirical humor, *El Manchar* and *Baroud*.

Melouah has so far divided his comic strip production almost evenly between children's and adult comics. In the former category he has contributed to many international children's magazines, especially in Middle Eastern countries such as Saudi Arabia and Kuwait; he has released a graphic album, *Le grand trésor* ("The Big Treasure") under the auspices of the United Nations. His most significant work, however, has been geared to an adult audience, notably two well-received graphic novels, *La cité interdite* ("The Forbidden City") and *La secte des Assassins* ("The Sect of the Assassins") on themes of Oriental history and legend. His latest effort in this vein was *Pierrot of Bab El Oued*, about a *pied-noir* (literally "black foot," the nickname given to European settlers in Algeria) returning to his native country after 30 years of independence. For the Algerian Department of the Environment he also produced a series of comic strips featuring a bemused (and disgusted) member of the nomadic Touareg tribe confronted with the depredations of modern civilization.

In his dual capacities as an internationally renowned journalist and cartoonist, Melouah has incurred the wrath of the Moslem fundmentalists who are trying to

Sid Ali Melouah, "The Touareg." © *Algerian Department of the Environment.*

overthrow the Algerian government. After several attempts on his life, he had to go underground, and as he wrily stated in a recent letter to the editor of this encyclopedia, "Due to threats on my life, my comics production has become very sporadic of late." He now lives in France.

M.H.

MESKIN, MORTON (1916-1995) American comic book artist born May 30, 1916, in Brooklyn, New York. After studies at Brooklyn's Pratt Institute and New York's Art Students League, Mort Meskin broke into comics in 1938 when he illustrated Fiction House's *Sheena* strip as a member of the S. M. "Jerry" Iger studio. The next year he joined the Chesler shop and produced strips for MLJ like *Bob Phantom, Mr. Satan, Shield,* and *Wizard,* among others. Concentrating on the superhero and adventure strips, Meskin was considerably more polished than recognized geniuses like *Superman*'s Joe Shuster and *Captain America*'s Jack Kirby. Drawing under the pen name "Mort Morton Jr." and several others, his work was illustrative and detailed rather than expressive and gaudy.

In 1941, Meskin joined National and produced probably the best work of his career. Again concentrating on superhero features like *Vigilante, Wildcat,* and *Starman,* Meskin was an early proponent of the cinematic technique. His stylized drawings and flowing panels seem inspired by the motion pictures of the day. His finest work in the 1941-48 National period came on a minor strip, *Johnny Quick.* Initially a variation of National's already successful *Flash* strip, *Johnny Quick* featured cameraman Johnny Chambers as a crime fighter who gained super speed simply by uttering the magic formula "3X2(9YZ)4A." Never an outstanding strip textually, Meskin's cinematic approach to depiction of speed made the strip a landmark. Unlike a sketched series of speed lines utilized by the *Flash* artists of the 1940s or the strobe technique applied later by Carmine Infantino, Meskin drew a series of fully drawn figures per panel. This, of course, gave the impression that *Johnny Quick* was everywhere.

While he was working for National, Meskin also managed to handle work for Marvel (Timely), Gleason, Spark, and several others. Between 1947 and 1949, he and *Batman* artist Jerry Robinson drew some fine material for Nedor's *Black Terror* and *Fighting Yank* strips. Both features were past their prime editorially, but the Meskin-Robinson team's work on the features was the best the strips ever had. In 1949, Meskin moved on to

Prize and drew a whole range of features until 1956. Between 1952 and 1958 he drew weird and horror stories for the Atlas group, and, in 1956, he returned to National. Remaining there until 1965, Meskin drew some fine war, science-fiction, and love tales, but the *Mark Merlin* adventure strip was the finest work he produced in the last part of his comic book career. He was also a member of the Simon and Kirby shop between 1949 and 1955, where he helped create the *Black Magic* book.

Later Meskin became an illustrator and art director for an advertising agency. He retired in 1990 and died in July 1995, but artists like Steve Ditko, Joe Kubert, and Jerry Robinson continue to produce material heavily influenced by his innovative artwork of the 1940s.

J.B.

MESSICK, DALE (1906-   ) American comic strip artist and writer born 1906 in South Bend, Indiana. Dalia Messick's father was a sign painter and her mother a vocational-school teacher. After flunking most of her subjects in high school, Dalia Messick finally graduated at age 20 in 1926. Her only art training came that same year when she enrolled at the Chicago Art Institute for one summer.

In 1927 she was designing greeting cards for a company in Chicago and changed her name to Dale because of the prejudice against women cartoonists among art editors. The Depression found her in New York where she managed to land another job as a greeting card designer at $50 a week. All the while she was haunting comic syndicate rooms trying to find employment as a cartoonist. Some 30 years later she bitterly remembered her experiences: "It was always the same story. They couldn't believe I could draw because I was a woman. They would just put my samples away and say, 'Come on, honey, let's go out and talk things over.'" The final blow came in 1939 when she was turned down by the News-Tribune Syndicate. Mollie Slott, then assistant to Joseph Medill Patterson, liked her work, however. Together, Slott

Dale Messick.

and Messick laid out the premises of a new girl strip whose heroine Dale Messick wanted originally to be a lady bandit. Mollie Slott thought that a newspaper girl was more appropriate; thus, on June 30, 1940, *Brenda Starr, Reporter*, appeared as a Sunday page (in October 1945 a daily strip was added).

With the help of a large and specialized staff, Dale Messick was able to turn *Brenda Starr* into one of the topmost features, with scant regard to verisimilitude ("Authenticity is something I always try to avoid," she once confessed). She retired in 1980, leaving the strip in the hands of Linda Sutter (writing) and Ramona Fradon (drawing).

The success of *Brenda Starr* was a puzzlement to many. Messick's stories were chaotic, to say the least, and her drawing was less than adequate. In a field where women have never been conspicuously successful, however, Dale Messick's prosperous career shines especially bright.

M.H.

MÉZIÈRES, JEAN-CLAUDE (1938-   ) Jean-Claude Mézières is a French cartoonist born September 23, 1938, in Paris. After graduation from high school Mézières, who had shown a marked inclination for drawing, sold his first illustrations to *Editions de Fleurus* at age 17; contributions to *Spirou* magazine followed. In 1957-58 Mézières's first comic strip, a clumsily rendered Western, appeared briefly in the children's magazine *Fripounet*.

Drafted into the army in 1959, Mézières spent 28 months cut off from his professional contacts. Upon his return to civilian life, he became a staff illustrator at the Hachette studio in Paris and later worked for three years in an advertising agency. During his stay with the agency, Mézières was asked to illustrate a short comic strip written by his friend, Pierre Christin, for *Total Journal*, an oil company comic book giveaway. Later he became a member of *Total Journal*'s editorial board. In 1965 Mézières took a pilgrimage to the United States in order to perfect his art and to observe American cartoonists' working methods. The trip lasted a year and a half—well into 1966.

Back in France Mézières resumed his collaboration with *Total Journal* and began to contribute illustrations and cartoons to *Pilote*. For *Pilote* he illustrated *L'Extraordinaire Aventure de Monsieur Faust*, a modern parody of the Faust legend written by Fred (Othon Aristides), in 1967. The strip was not a success, but later that same year, with Pierre Christin (signing "Linus"), he produced the popular science-fiction feature *Valérian*, also for *Pilote*. The strip is still going strong. While still working on *Valérian*, Mézières and Christin have also been producing *Canal Choc* ("Shock Channel") since 1990. In addition to his work as a comics artist, Mézières did the backgrounds and design of Luc Besson's 1997 movie *The Fifth Element*.

Jean-Claude Mézières is among the "new wave" of European cartoonists. While not as revolutionary as some of his colleagues, he nonetheless displays a pleasant—and sometimes striking—graphic style, as well as a keen sense of composition and suspense.

M.H.

MIAO DI (1926-   ) During his childhood, Miao Di became interested in his mother's paper-cuttings for window decorations; this became a lifelong love of and interest in art. While a university student, he was not interested in medicine and education, his majors, and so he switched to study art at North China University and Central Art Academy in the late 1940s. He has worked for the *People's Daily* as art editor since the 1950s. In 1979, *Humor and Satire*, a supplement to the *People's Daily*, was founded, and Miao Di worked there as editor until his retirement in 1990.

His comic strips *Grandpa and Grandson*, created in the early 1960s, and *Xiao Hou's Adventures*, created in the late 1970s, are Miao Di's best-known works and the ones that brought him fame. Each story was told in a four-panel comic strip; the themes were commonly shown with little words and the punchlines were often unexpected.

In his retirement, he has been cartooning actively, especially doing cartoons in brush and ink, traditional Chinese painting techniques, and four-panel comics. He is a member of the China Cartoon Art Commission of the Chinese Artists Association, is advisor to the Chinese News Media Cartoons Research Society, and is a member of the board of directors of the Shenzhou Painting Institute (affiliated with the *People's Daily*). Collected works include *Miao Di Cartoons Collection*, *Cartoon Selection of Miao Di*, *Social Satire Cartoons*, a volume in a series of Chinese cartoons, and *Comic Strip Collection*.

H.Y.L.L

MICHEL (Germany) *Michel* was created by Franz Roscher and published in the Munich newspaper *tz* from September 18, 1968, to December 8, 1969. The rotund Michel is based on the character Deutscher Michel, who, in editorial cartoons, stands for Germany, just as John Bull symbolizes England or Uncle Sam means the United States. Besides the trials and tribulations of Mr. and Mrs. Average, *Michel* also offered comments on local, national, and international politics.

A rather simplistic, yet well-rounded style was one of the faults, and yet one of the charms of this humorous comic strip that sometimes bordered on editorial cartooning. *Michel* had been in *tz* from the day the paper was launched, but a change of editor-in-chief ended this singular German experiment in editorial comic strips while it was still far from its peak of perfection and popularity. The fact that *Michel* was published in only one newspaper did not help to create a sizeable following in cities other than Munich. This says nothing about the success and potential of *Michel* but rather about the state of recognition that German newspapers give to comic strips.

Writer/artist Roscher had an agreement with *tz* to distribute *Michel* nationally, but this effort was never undertaken. When *tz* refused to pay more for the exclusive use of *Michel* and when a new editor-in-chief with a dislike for comics came along, *Michel*'s comic strip life ended. Franz Roscher moved on to other comics but would still revamp the strip for national syndication. *Tz*, after more editorial changes, reintroduced comics to its weekend television supplement, starting out with a Disney Sunday page. The Disney material has since been replaced by *Prince Valiant*.

Miao Di, "Xiao Hou's Adventures." © Miao Di.

"Michel," Franz Roscher. © tz.

"Michel Tanguy," J. M. Charlier and Albert Uderzo. © Editions Dargaud.

Michel was one of a rare breed: the German daily comic strip. It may very well have been the last of its kind for some time to come.

W.F.

MICHEL TANGUY (France) *Michel Tanguy*, France's answer to *Steve Canyon*, was created by writer Jean-Michel Charlier and illustrator Albert Uderzo in the first issue of *Pilote* (October 29, 1959).

Lieutenant (and later Captain) Michel Tanguy of the French Air Force was a hero in the traditional mold; unselfish, courageous, and clean-living, his sole aim in life was to enhance the prestige and power of the French tricolor. At the head of his formation of Mirage fighters, the "Stork Squadron," he was often called upon to impress by his aerial prowess the head of some foreign state in order to gain for France an advantageous political position or simply a large order for French planes (this was during the height of De Gaulle's "politique de grandeur" and Charlier was just doing his bit for "la patrie"). Michel Tanguy often had to fight foreign agents after French secrets, or foil sinister plots designed to show the French Air Force in a bad light (in all fairness it should be noted here that Charlier didn't do anything that Caniff wasn't doing in spades with *Steve Canyon*).

Tanguy, as is usual in adventure strips, had his comic side-kick, Lieutenant Ernest Laverdure, whose bumbling heroics and short temper often landed him in all kinds of trouble from which Tanguy had to rescue him. The adventures of Tanguy and Laverdure, always fast-paced and entertaining, took place all over the planet, from Greenland to Central Africa and from South America to the Pacific.

Charlier, a former pilot himself, gave a good account of the techniques of flight and although his plots sometimes needlessly meandered, he knew how to keep the suspense going. In this he was ably assisted by his artists: first Uderzo, who handled the feature with a deft, light, and even humorous pen until his workload (he was also drawing *Astérix* at the same time) forced him to quit in 1966; then Jijé (Joseph Gillain), who gave the

strip an austere, almost somber look, decried by some, lauded by others, but always interesting to look at.

Michel Tanguy is an adventure strip in the classic tradition, and an aviation strip as worthwhile as any currently done in the United States. All of Tanguy's adventures were reprinted in book form by Editions Dargaud; in the late 1960s it was made into a television series under the title *Les Chevaliers du Ciel* ("Knights of the Sky").

Jijé's death in 1980 interrupted the series in mid-adventure; the story was completed by Patrice Serres, who would illustrate the strip (now called *Tanguy et Laverdure*) until 1988. That same year French television broadcast a new series of *Les Chevaliers due Ciel*, with Christian Vadim and Thierry Redler in the principal roles. Alexandre Coutelis was the last artist to work on the feature (for the length of one episode), as Charlier's death in 1989 also spelled the end of his most notable creation.

M.H.

MICHEL VAILLANT (Belgium) Cartoonist Jean Graton introduced his Michel Vaillant character in a series of short comic strip stories published in *Tintin* magazine during 1957. Their success prompted the editors to establish a regular *Michel Vaillant* feature the next year.

Michel Vaillant is an automobile racer, the standard-bearer of the Vaillante team and the son of the cars' manufacurer. Young, athletic, and clean-cut, he is cast in the mold of the conventional comic strip hero—self-assured, brave, and unimaginative. His first adventure pits him (on the race circuit) against the American champion Steve Warson; in the course of the strip Vaillant and Warson constantly compete against each other (but always in a gentlemanly way), losing and winning in turn before they finally team up on and off the raceway against unscrupulous promoters and dishonest drivers. Most of the action takes place in and around speedways, and Graton is not averse to plugging brands of tires, gasoline, or oil lubricants as a lucrative sideline.

The strip hero's close companionship with his teammates brought on accusations of latent homosexuality,

"Michel Vaillant," Jean Graton. © Editions du Lombard.

been reprinted in many albums). *Michel Vaillant* has also appeared on the television screen and in a number of annuals devoted to more of his adventures.

After jumping from publisher to publisher with his creation in the late 1970s, the author has been releasing *Michel Vaillant* himself, under the imprint Editions Jean Graton, since 1982.

M.H.

MICHELUZZI, ATTILIO (1930-1990) Italian cartoonist and illustrator born August 11, 1930, in Umago (Istria) and died September 20, 1990, in Naples. After graduating with a degree in architecture, Attilio Micheluzzi worked for many years in different African countries; eventually, upset by various coups d'état, he returned to Italy. Because he could not stand the politics connected with licensing public buildings, he devoted himself to comics. In 1972, under the pen name Igor Artz Bajeff, he started drawing short historical stories and biographies for the weekly *Corriere dei Ragazzi*. In 1974, his first comic character, *Johnny Focus*, appeared in *Corriere*, and in 1976 he carried on the drawing of *Capitan Erik*, written by Claudio Nizzi and created by Giovannini, for the same weekly. In 1977 his second creation appeared: *Petra Chérie*, an aristocratic female pilot who lived in Holland and operated as a secret agent against Germany during World War I.

After this he wrote and drew two historical graphic novels: *L'uomo del Tanganyka* ("The Man from Tanganyka," 1978), set in Africa during the First World War, and *L'uomo del Khyber* ("The Man from Khyber, 1980), set in 19th-century India. Between these he adapted Mark Twain's *Prince and the Pauper* to the comics.

In 1980, his third creation appeared in the monthly *AlterAlter*: *Marcel Labrume*, a pleasure-loving and politically indifferent young Frenchman, who in 1940 decides to uphold the honor of his country against the Nazis. In 1982 he illustrated *Molly Manderling*, a long graphic novel written by Milo Milani that examined the political intrigues of a small German court in the 19th century. His next two series were *Rosso Stenton*, about the adventures of an American sailor in China during the 1930s, and *Air Mail*, devoted to the first experiments in air mail service in the United States during the 1920s.

so Graton decided to have Vaillant marry in 1973. The hero continues, however, to shun all semblance of domestic life for the more exciting action in the arena.

Graton possesses one of the most detestable styles in contemporary comics: all his characters look alike, their faces are locked in an expressionless, vacant stare. Only the cars seem alive, and it is they that have assured the phenomenal success of the strip (which has

Attilio Micheluzzi, "Johnny Focus." © Editoriale l'Isola Trovata.

In the second half of the 1980s, features that Micheluzzi wrote and drew included *Bab El Mandeb* (1986), a war adventure set in Africa during the Ethiopian war of the 1930s; *Roy Mann* (1987), the dreamlike adventure of a young American; and a very long adventure in the *Dylan Dog* series (1988). His last work, *Afghanistan*, was published posthumously (and unfinished) in the magazine *Comic Art*.

Micheluzzi's extensive knowledge of history, and his fluency in German, French, and English, allowed him to create competent and accurate stories in different social and historical contexts. With elegant scriptwriting, intelligent characters, and a polished graphic style, Micheluzzi's stories were pleasant to read and epitomize the spirit of comic art.

Micheluzzi received many prizes, including an Alfred (1984) in Angoulême and a Yellow Kid (1990) in Lucca.

G.C.C.

MICKEY FINN (U.S.) Lank Leonard's sympathetic, lightly humorous strip about a big city beat cop, *Mickey Finn*, was released by McNaught Syndicate as a daily on April 6, 1936, and as a Sunday page on May 17, 1936. At the opening of the strip, Mickey (named Michael Aloysius Finn in full) was the working son of a widowed woman who lived with her brother, Mickey's Uncle Phil. A young trial employee at the Schultz Soap Company, Mickey lost his job through a comic catastrophe, but rescued a runaway steer in the street with his bare hands on his way home. Offered a chance to take a police physical as a result, Mickey did, and made the grade. From that point (May 26, 1936), Mickey was a beat patrolman, undergoing continuity escapades in the daily strip and comic escapades in the Sunday page.

At first serio-comic melodrama, the daily narratives gave way in a few years to mildly farcical stories centering on Mickey's Uncle Phil, who was something of a wayward Romeo and con man (though more often conned himself). Early teamed with another patrolman named Tom Collins, and frequently involved with the antic activities of a reporter named Gabby, Mickey found an on again-off again romance with a girl named Kitty Kelly. Other regulars were Clancy the bartender; Sergeant Halligan, Mickey's immediate superior; Mr. Houlihan, Uncle Phil's nemesis; Flossie Finn, Mickey's niece; and Red Fedder, a baseball player.

Sports were central to Lank Leonard's life; he did the sports-page cartoon for over a decade on the *New York Sun* before launching *Mickey Finn*, and he occasionally introduced actual sports personalities into the strip, particularly the Sunday page. Lou Gehrig, Joe Louis, Jack Dempsey, and others appeared over the years. This was a notable aspect of Ham Fisher's *Joe Palooka* strip as well (although the noted figures there tended to be politicians and show people), and for that reason, as well as the teamed appearance of the two strips in many papers (in the *New York Sunday Mirror* they were the front and back page strips for some time), many readers linked the strips in their minds. The personalities of their two heroes assisted in this linkage, of course: both were sweet simpletons with enormous strength and comic companions—Uncle Phil and Knobby Walsh.

Mickey Finn was very much a one-man strip, and it effectively died with the passing of its creator in 1970. The strip was continued, however, by Morris Weiss;

"Mickey Finn," Lank Leonard. © McNaught Syndicate.

the Sunday page was dropped in late 1975, with the dailies coming to an end on July 31, 1976.

An amusing record of certain aspects of Irish social city life in the 1930s, *Mickey Finn* deserves a more permanent record than the handful of comic book reprints it incurred in the 1940s, and should be collected into at least one well-selected volume.

B.B.

MICKEY MOUSE (U.S.) With a sensational new animated film star named Mickey Mouse dancing across the theater screens of America in 1929, it struck a King Features executive as important that the mouse star appear in a comic strip as well. Walt Disney Studios, which had launched the smash box office hit in a short called "Steamboat Willie" a short time earlier, agreed with the executive, and put its artists to work on a daily strip featuring Mickey, the first episode of which appeared in a dubious handful of newspapers on the grim depression date of January 13, 1930.

Scripted haphazardly in odd moments by Walt Disney himself, and drawn by two different artists in its first few months (one of whom was Ub Iwerks; the other a man named Win Smith), the strip was doing a fair job of reproducing the quality of the animated cartoons of the period, but little more. Then by what was little more than a lucky accident, when Smith asked to leave the strip Disney appointed a new studio animator he recalled once having mentioned an interest in strip work, Floyd Gottfredson, to the Mickey comic. The work suited Gottfredson perfectly, and he took to the strip like Donald Duck to a fight. Within a few months the strip began to take on a character and quality of its own, edging away from the broad surrealism of the film cartoons toward a realism consistent with the more straightforward narrative line Gottfredson had introduced, and it was apparent that the strip had

"Micky Mouse," Walt Disney. © Walt Disney Productions.

the creative basis to maintain reader interest and stick around awhile.

More papers took note of the daily strip and added it to their rosters as Gottfredson's story line gathered momentum and suspense from Mickey's cross-country battle with the archvillains Pegleg Pete and Sylvester Shyster, Minnie Mouse in desperate tow. By late 1931, King Features felt that a Sunday page was called for, and after a draft layout was done for the first episode by an artist named Earl Duvall, the new feature was also given to the devoted Gottfredson, the first episode by Gottfredson appearing a week after Duvall's on January 17, 1932. Gottfredson's adept handling of his cast of characters, largely derived and developed from their sketchier film counterparts such as the already-mentioned Pete and Shyster team and Minnie Mouse, but also including the redoubtable Horace Horsecollar, Clarabelle Cow, Pluto, and Minnie's uncle, Mortimer Mouse (bearing the name originally intended for Mickey himself), made the essentially anecdotal Sunday page as enjoyable as the daily narrative. (Later, Gottfredson was able to introduce superb adventure continuity to the Sunday page from time to time as well, and these comparatively rare sequences stand up with the best of the daily stories.) Finding the Sunday page ultimately burdensome, however, Gottfredson dropped it in mid-1938 for good.

Studio developments were in no way reflected in the Gottfredson strip. Here, in a splendid world of his own, an adventuring Mickey continued to fight pirates, fly fighter planes against armed dirigible cities in the air, rescue friends from the hypnotic rays of mad scientists, pursue desert bandits in bat costumes on horseback, match a fighting kangaroo against a gorilla, and other-

wise involve himself hazardously with such friends as Captains Dobermann and Churchmouse, Dippy Dawg (later Goofy), Donald, Gloomy, detectives Bark and Howell, and others, and such devoted enemies as Captain Vulture, the Phantom Blot, the Bat Bandit, Eli Squinch, and the aforementioned Pete and Shyster duo. There was no effective letup until well into the 1940s, when a slowing-down of realism went hand-in-hand with a sophisticated fantasy which, while engaging in itself, was a silk-gloved betrayal of the hard-core action-adventure elements that had made the earlier strip so consistently gripping and delightful.

Then the stories ceased altogether. By the early 1950s, the strip had bowed to a King Features edict which eliminated action-adventure in humorous strips. Against Gottfredson's own recorded preference, the daily strip turned to spot gags, an area in which it did not particularly shine. A certain rare talent, such as a Mort Walker or a Johnny Hart possesses, can transform the dreary joke-book gag format into a paragon of characterization and wit—but Gottfredson's talent simply did not lie in that direction. The popularity of the strip with its old and dedicated readers nosedived immediately and permanently—a situation in which it is hard to perceive King Features's gains from the change of content. (It should be noted that, starting in late 1939, Gottfredson's contribution had become less and less, as he was edged out by such as Al Levin, Bill Walsh, and Roy Williams.)

In any event, the greatness of Gottfredson's *Mickey Mouse* strip during its 20-year heyday cannot be denied, and it is hoped that the good fortune of many Europeans in having countless reprints of all of Gottfredson's early narratives available in bookstores everywhere, as a permanent testament to his genius, will one day be duplicated for Americans.

B.B.

Mickey has had a checkered career in comic strips in the last 20 years. Roman Arambula became the titular artist on the dailies after Gottfredson's retirement in 1975. In 1983 he also took over the Sundays, which Manuel Gonzales had been drawing from 1938 to 1981 (the interim period had been filled in by Tony Strobl, Daan Jippes, and Bill Wright). From 1989 to 1993 the artwork was assured by Rick Hoover. The *Mickey Mouse* newspaper strip now only appears in reprints of old episodes.

M.H.

MIGHTY MOUSE (U.S.) In 1945, a strip based on the *Mighty Mouse* animated cartoons debuted in *Terry-Toons Comics* number 38, published by Timely (later known as Marvel). The magazine showcased charac-

"Mighty Mouse," Art Bartsch. © Paul Terry.

ters from the cartoons produced at the Paul Terry cartoon studio where the first *Mighty Mouse* film, "The Mouse of Tomorrow," was made in 1942. The character, conceived as a parody of *Superman* and originally called *Supermouse* for three films, was the idea of a story man and animator, Isidore Klein, although Paul Terry himself often claimed credit for the idea, as he did with most of his characters. *Mighty Mouse* quickly became the most popular of Terry's cartoon properties and a successful series of films were made, culminating in 1955 when Terry sold his operation to the Columbia Broadcasting System which began the *Mighty Mouse* television program.

The history of *Mighty Mouse* in comic books is a checkered one. The strip's debut in *Terry-Toons Comics* boosted periodical sales such that the first full issue of *Mighty Mouse* was issued in the fall of 1946. Two years later, Timely (then called Atlas) lost its license to the Paul Terry characters and the St. John company took over publication of *Mighty Mouse* and of *Terry-Toons Comics*, which was later changed to *Paul Terry Comics* and finally, for its last issue (number 127), to *The Adventures of Mighty Mouse*. St. John also issued a wide range of specials and giants, including two 3-D editions of *Mighty Mouse*.

The St. John comics were produced in close cooperation with the Paul Terry studios, often employing moonlighting Terry staffers. Many of the covers were drawn by Tom Morrison, a longtime Paul Terry story man and the voice of *Mighty Mouse* in the animated films. Most *Mighty Mouse* adventures were set in Terrytown, a city inhabited solely by mice who were forever at the mercy of invading herds of cats. It was always up to the town hero, the ultramuscled, flying Mighty Mouse, to fend off the invaders.

The same format was followed when the Terry characters shifted to the Pines Company which published *Mighty Mouse* beginning with number 69. In 1958, Dell/Western (later Gold Key) took over *Mighty Mouse* and Pines replaced it with *Supermouse*, based on an imitation previously published by Standard Comics. Charlton also published an imitation called *Atomic Mouse*. From time to time, other superpowered "funny animals" have appeared, but none could match the popularity of *Mighty Mouse*, which finally folded in 1968 under the Gold Key banner. It was unsuccessfully revived twice: by Spotlight Comics in 1987 and by Marvel in 1990-91.

M.E.

MIKE AND IKE (U.S.) These famed derby-hatted twin brothers of Rube Goldberg's initiated his comic-page career when they first appeared nationwide in the four-page Sunday color comic section distributed to many papers by the World Color Printing Co. of St. Louis on September 29, 1907. They weren't called Mike and Ike then; Goldberg—who apparently freelanced the strips to the St. Louis syndicate from San Francisco and/or New York (accounts differ on where he may have been in the fall of 1907)—named the duo Tom and Jerry, and called his strip, *The Look-A-Like Boys*. The World Color Printing feature, which ran until March 22, 1908 (although not every week), was a half-page, six- to eight-panel strip, which appeared in two colors. Tom and Jerry were ne'er-do-well tramps, who panhandled themselves into trouble with everyone from washerwomen to magicians.

Goldberg abandoned the strip when he began his sports-page work for a regular salary in New York, and later seemed to have almost forgotten his first comic strip altogether, never mentioning it (except vaguely) in interviews, autobiographical sketches, or the like. The two derbied twins turned up sporadically in Goldberg's daily miscellany strip for Hearst in the late 1910s, however—and this time as Mike and Ike. The bewhiskered pair of shrimps did minor vaudeville turns in the Army, the Navy, Europe, or wherever Goldberg put them for the sake of a short gag sequence included with other panels and short narratives from day to day, and they made a considerable public hit.

Goldberg did little more with them, though, until he introduced them as regular characters in his long-running continuity Sunday strip, *Boob McNutt*, on August 14, 1927, as the long-lost sons of a farmer couple, for which Boob had been desperately and hamhandedly searching for several months (they are found by Boob performing as acrobats at a circus). From that point on, Mike and Ike remained in the *Boob McNutt* strip until it folded on September 1934. Their joint refrain, identifying themselves to anyone in sight, and sometimes to no one at all except each other, was "I'm Mike," "I'm Ike," which caught on nationally on the schoolyard level for a number of years.

Mike and Ike appeared in no other Goldberg strip, and never appeared solely in a strip of their own (although some papers did run the episodes included in the Goldberg miscellany strips of the 1910s and 1920s as if they were independent material, perhaps under the title *Mike and Ike*). No *Mike and Ike* book exists, nor has there been a cinematic adaptation, either as separate characters or as part of the *Boob McNutt* gang.

B.B.

MIKE MACKE (Germany) *Mike Macke*, created, written, and drawn by Volker Ernsting, was one of the comic strips that replaced the humorous adventures of the hedgehog, *Mecki*, in Germany's largest television weekly, *Hör zu*, when the editors were looking for new attractions.

The first *Mike Macke* story appeared in *Hör zu* on December 23, 1972, and ended after 15 full-page episodes on March 31, 1973. It was a follow-up to an earlier Ernsting comic strip appearing in *Hör zu* in 1972, *Hein Daddel*, about a dune detective and his zany friends working on the seashores of Northern Germany. Still included in *Mike Macke*, Hein Daddel and friends were dropped for *Mike Macke und der Piratensender* ("Mike Macke and the Pirate Station," November 17, 1973, to February 2, 1974) and *Mike Macke: Das Erbe von Monte Mumpitz* ("The Estate of Monte Humbug," October 19, 1974, to May 10, 1975). They were replaced by Airwin, Mike's pet dog, who ran around in Batman costume performing incredible feats.

Hein Daddel was already geared for the readership of a television weekly, but despite zany madcap adventures, it lacked an attractive hero. Thinking back to his television satire, *Sherlock Holmes und das Geheimnis der blauen Erbse* ("Sherlock Holmes and the Secret of the Blue Pea"), which featured more than 100 television celebrities, Ernsting found a blueprint for a hero in Mike (Mannix) Connors. Of course, Mike Macke (which loosely translates into Mike Daft) is a very dis-

"Mike Macke," Volker Ernsting. © *Hör zu.*

tant relative of Mannix, stepping from one improbable situation into the next while being furiously funny, quoting and misquoting, or simply making fun of clichés or getting involved in slapstick routines. Never, however, does he forget that there also is a story that needs telling. In addition to a little help from his dog, this sleuth also has his special gun which shoots rubber tipped arrows with a line tied to them, obviously to facilitate the tracking down of elusive crooks.

Ernsting's satirical comic strip may be unorthodox at times, but it never failed to get its readers laughing. It evoked such strong and favorable response that it alternated with other *Hör zu* features. It was even reprinted in book form. When editorial policies were changed once again, and full page comics like *Mike Macke* were axed in favor of a full page of comics (*Mecki, Mafalda,* and *Siegfried,* the latter depicting the adventures of a Stone Age dragon), Ernsting continued doing gag cartoons for the magazine for some time.

W.F.

MILLER, FRANK (1898-1949) American cartoonist born in Sheldon, Iowa, on October 2, 1898. Frank Miller attended school erratically in South Dakota, Colorado, and California, while showing artistic ability at an early age. Yet his career first took a very unartistic turn. After graduating from Harvard Military School in Los Angeles, he took a position as bookkeeper in a bank. From there he went successively to cattle ranching, accounting, sheep ranching, and mapmaking, among other pursuits; at the same time that he was restlessly shifting from job to job he never lost his taste for drawing. In 1919 he sold his first cartoon and slowly built up his professional reputation. By the mid-1920s Miller decided to make cartooning his full-time profession, working first for the *Denver Post* and the *Rocky Mountain News,* and later joining the art staff of the Scripps-Howard chain of newspapers.

In 1936 Frank Miller went over to King Features Syndicate, creating *Barney Baxter,* an aviation strip, in December of that year. In 1942 he left the strip to Bob

Naylor and joined the U.S. Coast Guard. When the war ended, Miller, instead of going back to his comic strip work, settled on his ranch near the town of Craig in Colorado and turned to painting. His watercolors depicting the life of cowhands and Indians of the Rockies, were critically recognized, and Miller had a number of his works exhibited in galleries and museums.

In 1948, with *Barney Baxter* faltering, KFS called on Miller to take his feature back, which he did. Frank Miller alternated his work between *Barney* and his paintings, just as he alternated his residence between his ranch in Colorado and his home in Daytona Beach, where he suddenly died of a heart attack on December 3, 1949 (*Barney Baxter* was discontinued after his death).

M.H.

MILLER, FRANK (1957-   ) American comic book artist not to be confused with the creator of *Barney Baxter,* to whom he bears no relation. This Frank Miller was born in Olney, Maryland, on January 27, 1957, almost eight years after the other Miller's death. He grew up in New England, where he received his education; coming to New York in the late 1970s, he got his first job in comic books in 1978, working for Gold Key. His big break came the next year when he succeeded Gene Colan on Marvel's *Daredevil*; working first as a penciler, he later also wrote the scripts and made the title into a fan favorite.

Transfering to DC Comics in 1983, Miller created *Ronin,* a manga-style comic-book mini-series set in medieval Japan. In 1986 he conceived *Batman—The Dark Knight,* which depicted an aging and weary Caped Crusader in a Gotham City of the near-future. For the next six years he devoted most of his time to scripting, notably writing *Daredevil: Love and War* and *Elektra Assassin* on illustrations by Bill Sienkiewicz for Marvel and *Batman: Year One* with art by David Mazucchelli for DC. In the early 1990s, he wrote two series for Dark Horse Comics: *Give Me Liberty,* which was graced by Dave Gibbons's outstanding artwork, and *Hard Boiled,* excellently illustrated by another British artist, Geoff Darrow. Only in 1992 did he come back to drawing with *Sin City,* a dark tale of the outer fringes and the lower depths, which he also wrote.

While Miller has proven himself a writer of great ability, his status as an artist is more difficult to nail down. He was strongly influenced by Neal Adams in his work on *Daredevil* and *Batman,* his *Ronin* was clearly inspired by Goseki Kojima's Lone Wolf and Cub, while *Sin City* is a take on José Munoz's dramatic black-and-white rendition of *Alack Sinner* (even the two titles sound similar). So will the real Frank Miller please stand up?

M.H.

MILLER, SYDNEY LEON (1901-198?) Cartoonist born 1901 at Strathfield, N.S.W., Australia, the son of a news agent. After completing his education at Fort Street High School in 1916, he worked briefly at a pharmaceutical importer before becoming a trial apprentice in the Process Engraving Department of the *Bulletin.* Being surrounded by the best black-and-white technique artists of the day inspired Miller to further his interest in art by attending night classes at the Royal Art Society for a short period. In 1917, he joined Harry Julius, who had returned from the U.S. to start *Filmads,* and they produced the first animated cartoons made in Australia. He also did freelance work, selling cartoons to the *Bulletin*, *Aussie*, and, in 1920, *Smith's Weekly*. Later that same year, he was given a contract with *Smith's* and drew political, sports, and general cartoons, in addition to writing and illustrating film and stage critiques. He resigned in 1931 to freelance with Sun Newspapers and the J. Walter Thompson agency.

During the 1930s he ran a weekly strip feature, *Curiosities*, in the *Melbourne Herald*, and *Nature Notes* in the *Daily Telegraph*. In 1938, he created a half-page adventure strip, *Red Gregory*—one of Australia's earliest adventure strips and certainly the best-drawn strip of that genre of that time. The same year, he created *Chesty Bond* in conjunction with Ted Moloney of J. Walter Thompson. Possibly the first five-day-a-week advertising strip, Miller handled it until 1945 when it was relinquished to a series of artists (Mahony, Reilly, Linaker, and Santry) who carried the strip through until 1958. The inclusion of Bob Hope in a wartime sequence of *Chesty Bond* brought the threat of a $200,000 lawsuit, but it was averted.

From 1942 to 1946, Miller published many comic books containing his own characters (*Red Gregory*, *Molo the Mighty*, *Red Grainger*, and others) as well as the work of aspiring comic artists such as Len Lawson, Albert De Vine, and John Egan. In July 1945 he created a daily strip, *Sandra*, for the *Melbourne Herald* that was syndicated in England and ran until November 1946. This strip was immediately followed by *Rod Craig*, which appeared daily until November 1955—the longest run of any daily adventure strip up to that time. *Rod Craig* was syndicated in Jamaica, Paris, and Buenos Aires, and became the first Australian thriller strip to be adapted to radio. Starting in 1948, his single column comic spot, *Animalaughs*, was also appearing in England, Scotland, and South Africa. It was unprecedented for an Australian artist to have two strips being syndicated overseas at the same time.

In December 1955 Miller started a new daily, *Us Girls*, which ran until he resigned in 1957 to enter a partnership in the production of television animation and sound-slide films. He remained in this field until retiring to his painting and copperwork. He died in the 1980s.

Syd Miller was possibly the most prolific and versatile of Australian comic artists. Miller's style was influenced by Norman Lindsay and David Low at the *Bulletin* as well as by the animals of Harry Towntree (England), the dry brush drawings of Bert Thomas (England), and the split-brush technique of Dan Smith (U.S.). Apart from his undoubted skills as an illustrator, Syd Miller helped enrich the field of comic art by his encouragement of Australian artists and writers.

J.R.

MILTON, FREDDY (1948-   ) Freddy Milton is one of the most important representatives of the modern Danish comic artists. Starting in 1975 he acquired a reputation as one of the best funny animal artists of Europe when he drew *Donald Duck* stories for the Disney comic book published by Oberon in the Netherlands. Like Daan Jippes, Milton is one of the modern interpreters of the adventures of the indomitable duck, and his artistic style is based on that of Carl Barks. Milton's Disney work was inspirational for other European artists who wanted to enter the Disney field. Germans Volker Reiche, Jan Gulbransson, and Gabriel

"Tschap" Nemeth are among those his work inspired to knock, successfully, on Disney's doors.

Milton has not concentrated solely on Disney material, however. He also offered his version of *Woody Woodpecker* in two comic albums published in 1978 and 1979; these were very successful. In 1983 Freddy Milton created a funny animal series of his own, *Gnuffen* ("The Gnuffs"), the whimsically funny adventures of a dragon family. The stories, however, do have a penchant toward social criticism. In the United States, *The Gnuffs* were published in *Critters* magazine.

Milton's social criticism has become stronger over the years, and was particularly visible in his semifunny albums for adult readers, like *Villiams Verden*. He has drawn entertaining comics for Danish toy producer Lego, and has also done social satire in comic form which is highly critical of efforts to achieve a European Union. Another of Milton's ambitious projects is an interpretation of the Ten Commandments—in comic form, of course.

W.F.

MING FOO (U.S.) One of the most oddly appealing of adventure strips, *Ming Foo*, by Brandon Walsh and Nicholas Afonski (signing Afonsky), started on March 17, 1935, as a Sunday top piece to Walsh's already-established *Little Annie Rooney*. (Actually the titular hero of the strip and his boy companion, Joey Robins, had first appeared on the *Rooney* Sunday page as early as 1933, and their popularity on the strip prompted King Features to give them their own berth.)

Ming Foo was an Oriental adventurer with inexhaustible patience and unlimited resourcefulness. He was also given to phrase-mongering such as: "It has been truly said: He who could see two days ahead would rule the world!" and "It is written: Even the gods will not help a man who loses opportunity." Joey, on the other hand, was a typical American kid of the "gee-golly" variety. Together with an old sea-captain whom they had met in the course of their wanderings, Ming and Joey went adventuring aboard the captain's yacht, the *Sea Swallow* (the captain did not seem to ever need a name: he was always referred to as "Captain"). Our friends (as Walsh was fond of calling them) met with no paucity of action: pirates along the China coast, cannibals in Borneo, revolutionaries in South America, and other toughs always managed to make life interesting for them.

Afonski's faintly grotesque style was ideally suited for the strip: a little redolent of old book illustration, it gave *Ming Foo* the right humorous touch to match the levity of the storyline. (During the middle 1930s Afonski illustrated another Sunday half-page, *Heroes of American History*, a straight and earnest series of weekly history lessons fortunately—if unintentionally—made impossible to take seriously by Afonski's peculiar line and rendering.) As for Walsh's storytelling, it was positively brilliant, suspenseful, and involved without being overplotted. As Bill Blackbeard noted (referring to Walsh's scripting of *Little Annie Rooney*): "The *Ming Foo* spinoff of the 1930s, however, was first-rate: one of the great adventure strips of all time, suggesting that Walsh's real talent, lay elsewhere than with fleeing and helpless orphans."

Everyone may not agree with Blackbeard's glowing assessment of the strip, but *Ming Foo* was certainly entertaining and was missed by the few readers who

"Ming Foo," Nicholas Afonsky and Brandon Walsh. © King Features Syndicate.

saw it (it had a pitifully low circulation) when it disappeared early in the 1940s.

M.H.

MINNITT, FRANK (1894-1958) Although the name of *Billy Bunter* is still well known and loved in the United Kingdom some 90 years after his creation in 1908, the name of the cartoonist whose comic strip interpretation of the "world's fattest schoolboy" delighted millions of children for a long period remains unknown. This is the continuing tragedy of British comics, where publishers refuse their artists the right to sign their work.

Frank John Minnitt was born in New Southgate, London, on September 3, 1894. A completely self-taught cartoonist, he attended the Hugh Middleton School, where his twin interests, art and boxing, were first developed. In 1914 he enlisted in the Coldstream Guards and soon found himself at war. During action in Flanders he was gassed and buried alive by a shell explosion for three days. The effects of the mustard gas would remain with him for the rest of his life. After his release from the army, he married and found work welding the headlights onto taxicabs. The family moved to Leigh-on-Sea, where the clean air helped the respiratory problems caused by the gas. In Leigh, he began to freelance joke drawings to newspapers, magazines, and comics. By 1927 he had successfully taken over several other artists' strips in the penny comics and was given the chance to draw characters of his own creation. These included *Pat O'Cake* in *Butterfly*, *Breezy Ben* in *Comic Life*, *Darkie and Dick* in *Golden Penny*, and *Jack O'Spades* in *Chips*. Usually short strips of four, or occasionally six panels, they continued with *Nanny the Nursemaid* in *Monster* (1928), *O'Doo and O'Dont* in *Joker* (1929), and from 1930 a string of characters in *Butterfly*.

In 1930, Minnitt tried his luck with the Dundee-based company D.C. Thompson, drawing *Peter Pranky*, *Smiler Smutt*, and *Jimmy and Jumbo* for the boys' weekly *Adventure*. These would all be reprinted (without renumeration for the artist, another typical gambit of British publishers) in the *Sunday Post Fun Section* (1939) under the new titles *Billy Banks*, *Nickum the Nigger*, and *Wee Eck and his Elephant*.

Unlike a contemporary, Allan Morley, Minnitt decided to stick with the Amalgamated Press Comics, which paid slightly better than Thompson. His luckiest editorial encounter was with the A.P. boys' weekly *Pilot*, to which he contributed two "real life" strips about popular stars: *Stainless Stephen*, about a radio comedian, and *Will Hay*, the top British comedy movie star (1937). Minnitt later contributed four unusual strips: *Kiddo the Boy King*; *Ali Barber, the Whisker Wizard of Old Bagdad*; *Bob's Your Uncle*; and *Merry Margie the Invisible Mender*. More interesting than his earlier characters, these strips became so popular that Minnitt soon took over the two-page *Billy Bunter* strip, the top feature in *Knockout*. This strip made Minnitt's reputation.

When the paper shortage of World War II cut down the size of *Knockout* from 28 to 16 pages, *Bunter* became a single page, so Minnitt promptly increased his picture quotient from six to 12 per page, then to 15. After the war, an editorial change resulted in a major crisis. The new editors in charge of the magazine didn't care for what they called Minnitt's "old-fashioned" style, and he found himself out of work.

He was able to find work in the many one-shot and minor comics published in the postwar 1940s, and single-page adventures of all manner of characters flowed from his nib. Beginning with a page in Swan's *Comicolour* (1946), he contributed to nine new titles in 1947, 36 new titles in 1948, and 34 new titles in 1949. He was frequently asked to draw the front covers, as many publishers were proud to have a former top A.P. cartoonist decorating their small eight-page books. He also drew much of the top-class *Frolicomic*, published in full-color photogravure by Martin & Reid. Although Amalgamated Press occasionally provided him some work, it was often embarrassing. He was not asked to draw the special long strips of *Billy Bunter* for the annual *Knockout Fun Book*; instead, he would draw the figure of Bunter while other, more "modern," artists drew the rest of each picture.

His later years were unhappy; he and his second wife spent their days addressing envelopes for a pittance, and he wrote pathetic letters to all the editors he knew pleading for work. Very little came. He died on May 12, 1958.

D.G.

MINUTE MOVIES (U.S.) Ed Wheelan's 1921 creation *Minute Movies* is widely credited as being the first suc-

"Minute Movies," Ed Wheelan. © George Mathew Adams Service.

cessful continuity strip. It is not, but it is an important early factor in the development of the story strip.

Based on Wheelan's earlier prototype, *Midget Movies*, *Minute Movies* was frankly designed for continuity, but its heavy dose of satire makes it confusing, in retrospect, to determine whether its main intent was to parody movie serials or to bring the daily continuity to the comic strip idiom. No matter: in short order *Minute Movies* had a large following; Wheelan had a personal product filled with inside comments and chatter to the readers; and the characters themselves had large fan clubs. The feature wonderfully combined the best magic of the movies—vignettes, titles, synopses—with the freedom and pliability of the comic strip.

The stars were stereotypical: Dick Dare was the dashing hero, Ralph McSneer was the villain, Blanche Rouge the femme fatale, and Hazel Deare the Mary Pickford heroine-type; the rest of the regular cast of characters were also unabashedly lifted from the movies. And so were the plots, which ran in a two-row strip format every day. After a few mysteries, melodramas, and romances, Wheelan followed with shorts, travelogues, and even trailers for upcoming episodes. Much of the charm left the strip—although acclaim from educators was forthcoming—when Wheelan abandoned his own imaginative scripts to pictorialize the classics in the early 1930s. Outlandish satire was replaced with conventional lightness in *Ivanhoe* and *Hamlet*; the strip was also assertedly aimed at children, to the dismay of adults who had thrived on the farce and inside jokes of the earlier *Minute Movies*. The art changed, too, and it is easy to recognize the hand of ghost Nicholas Afonsky, whose work was neater and funnier.

In Wheelan's own private melodrama, he became convinced that William Randolph Hearst exercised a personal vendetta against him when Afonsky was lured away to do the Sunday *Little Annie Rooney*.

Minute Movies left the comic pages in the mid-1930s and resurfaced in *Flash Comics* in the late 1930s and early 1940s.

R.M.

MISS FURY (U.S.) One of the few female cartoonists successful in the action genre, Tarpe Mills started *Black Fury* (soon to be changed to *Miss Fury*) on April 6, 1941, as a Sunday feature for the Bell Syndicate.

Tarpe Mills served her apprenticeship in comic books, working on such titles as *Mann of India*, *Daredevil Barry Finn*, and *The Purple Zombie*. From her comic book work she acquired a very direct, forceful style. Violence, action, and thrills were the hallmarks of the *Miss Fury* Sunday page, along with a sadistic streak that only grew larger after America's entry into World War II. The implied or actual use of the whip was a recurrent theme, as were branding irons, spiked-heel shoes, vicious women fights, clawing, and eye-gouging. In this respect the heroine gave as much as she received at the hands of ruthless gangsters or evil-looking Nazi spies.

The plot was also derived from comic books. *Miss Fury* was, in actuality, wealthy socialite Marla Drake, who donned a black leopard-skin costume to fight crime and subversion in her own way. Tarpe Mills liked to show her heroine's luscious body in various states of undress, but otherwise sex was only implied. *Miss Fury* made her exit from the comic pages at the end of the 1940s, and her passing was much deplored by aficionados of the bizarre.

M.H.

MISS PEACH (U.S.) Mell Lazarus created *Miss Peach* for the *New York Herald-Tribune* on February 4, 1957. The background of the strip is occupied by a mythical establishment of learning called the Kelly School where the children are always one up (or better) on their teachers. The adults of the strip—from the young and pretty Miss Peach, the teacher and titular star of the feature, to her colleague, the homely and pedantic spinster, Miss Crystal, and the harried and frustrated Mr. Grimmis, the principal—are upstaged at every turn, and out of turn, by their clamoring and unruly charges.

In a 1963 interview Mell Lazarus declared, "As a kid I hated school. This strip is my way of getting even."

"Miss Peach," Mell Lazarus. © Field Newspaper Syndicate.

"Mr. and Mrs.," Kin Platt. © New York Tribune.

And indeed the inmates of the Kelly School—the overbearing Marcia, the craven Ira, the uncouth Arthur, and the rest of this ill-mannered and loudmouthed horde—hit back at the school system with a vengeance: they interrupt classes with incongruous questions and irrelevent asides, cheat on exams, misplace books and papers, and generally make a shambles of the whole education process.

One of the funniest of contemporary strips, *Miss Peach* has been reprinted several times in paperback form. It was adapted into several TV specials in the 1980s and it helped Lazarus win the Reuben Award in 1982.

M.H.

MR. ABERNATHY (U.S.) The collaboration of two magazine panel cartoonists, Ralston "Bud" Jones and Frank Ridgeway, *Mr. Abernathy* was launched by King Features Syndicate in October 1957.

A conversation on submission day at the *Saturday Evening Post*'s offices led to the effort by writer Ridgeway and artist Jones. The former's original title was *Mr. Moneybags*, but comic editor Sylvan Byck suggested the change. The Sunday page started about a year after the dailies, which was a King practice in those days.

Abernathy is the typical half-pint multimillionaire, a debonair ladies' man with yacht and servants—the kind of fellow that, by design, virtually no readers would identify with. He is head of Abernathy Enterprises, a nebulous industry engaging in something or other. Always playful and never autocratic, Abernathy lives in studied opulence just as a kid would live in a tree house. His friend is Admiral Asterbloom, who joins him in upper-class pastimes—including girl-chasing, as there are the inevitably pretty girls at every elbow. On the staff are Dudley, the butler; Hilda, the maid; Flossie, Abernathy's secretary; and Monty, his playful dog.

The collaboration worked well; Ridgeway, living in California, wrote the gentle and chuckle-provoking gags, and Jones's art never slipped into the "bigfoot" school as many of his fellows had. He drew *Abernathy* in a modern, stylized, firm pen-line manner, utilizing broad spaces—whites, blacks, Ben Day—effectively, making it a pleasant gag strip.

Jones resigned from the strip in the late 1970s, and Ridgeway carried on alone until his death in 1994. It is now being done by syndicate staffers.

R.M.

MR. A. MUTT *see* Mutt and Jeff.

MR. AND MRS. (U.S.) Clare Briggs's Sunday page strip *Mr. and Mrs.*, dealing with an eternally bickering middle-class couple, began in the *New York Tribune* on April 14, 1919, shortly after he left the *Chicago Tribune*, where he had drawn such once-famed Sunday pages as *Danny Dreamer, Danny Dreamer, Sr.*, and *Sambo Remo Rastus Brown*. Unlike such similar but heavily populated strips as *The Gumps* and *The Bungle Family*, Briggs's *Mr. and Mrs.* rarely featured any characters other than the title figures, Joe and Vi, and their son, Roscoe, who occasionally asks wistfully, like an idiot Greek chorus, "Mamma love Papa?" There is no doubt that *Mr. and Mrs.* accurately reflected a large segment of domestic life as it was in America: it did so with such adamant realism and unadornment that the strip is unrelentingly dull and obvious from start to finish. There is little real humor and invention, and it is hard to believe that *Mr. and Mrs.* was a product of the same pen that created the witty and sharply observant daily panel features such as *It Happens in the Best Regulated Families, Tedious Pastimes*, and *How To Start the Day Wrong*.

The last *Mr. and Mrs.* page drawn by Briggs appeared on January 26, 1930, but the strip continued with a text by Arthur Folwell and art by Kin Platt for almost two more decades—duller and more obvious, if possible, than the Briggs original. This latter pair added a daily *Mr. and Mrs.* strip in the early 1930s in place of the daily panel gags that Briggs drew, and which were reprinted for a time. This was a daily gag strip with no continuity and it ran about as long as the post-Briggs Sunday page. Bad as it was, however, it cannot be argued that the public did not find a familiar and welcome note in the original Briggs strip. As a social record of the times, it has its undoubted value.

B.B.

MR. BREGER (U.S.) Dave Breger's immensely popular World War II panel series, *Private Breger*, about the training and warfare experiences of a shrimpish, bespectacled GI, was first distributed to newspapers by King Features on October 19, 1942, and had its name changed to *Mr. Breger* on October 22, 1945, to reflect its hero's return to civilian life. A Sunday half-page in strip form was issued on February 3, 1946. Originally created as a new weekly panel character series for the *Saturday Evening Post* on August 30, 1941, *Private Breger* caught the fancy of enlisted men at once. Reflecting on the woes of newly drafted men in the peacetime armed forces, its sharply mocking view of officer pomp and ceremony and wryly sympathetic portrait of the put-upon private soldier struck responsive chords. Asked to do a similar panel and strip feature for the new army magazine *Yank*, Breger eagerly agreed, but because the *Private Breger* name was already in copyright use by the *Post* and was being considered for syndication by King Features, he felt he had to coin a new title for his work. He came up with *GI Joe*, shortly to become the most widely used term of reference for the American enlisted man.

As *Private Breger* in the American press and *GI Joe* in the weekly *Yank* and daily overseas army paper *Stars and Stripes*, Breger's freckle-faced little hero was as universally known as Baker's *Sad Sack* and Mauldin's *Willie and Joe*. Mustered out of the service along with his creator in late 1945, *GI Joe* appeared in a farewell book collection of the same name, while *Private Breger*, already celebrated in a book titled *Private Breger's War* in 1944, continued as a civilian newspaper panel character. Its hero now married (to Dorothy Breger), and the father of a son, Harry, *Mr. Breger* carried much of the same wit and comedy into middle-class American life that had made the wartime strip so enjoyable. Too subtle and satirical for many readers, however, and lacking the kind of identification tags the public relishes (such as Dagwood's sandwiches and Snoopy's doghouse), *Mr. Breger* never enjoyed a wide circulation outside the Hearst press (indeed, many ex-GIs never knew the post-1945 strip existed). Partly because of its poor income and partly because Breger owned the rights to his character, King Features folded the panel and strip with its creator's death, the last episode appearing on March 22, 1970.

B.B.

MISTERIX (Italy) *Misterix*, Italy's second masked hero feature, made its appearance in the comic publication *Albi le Più Belle Avventure* on December 12, 1946, only a few months after *Asso di Picche*.

Paul Campani, the artist, and Max Massimino Garnier, the scriptwriter, chose the United States as the locale for their strip. Their graphic style was close to that of Caniff's *Steve Canyon*, while the mood was more inspired by *Batman*. Campani, however, unlike most of his colleagues who were content to depict an imaginary America, was very attentive to authentic detail; instead of the bland treatment usually associated with this kind of feature, he depicted a cruel metropolis similar to the locales of countless gangster movies of the 1940s.

Misterix was in reality John Smith, a reporter for the *Globe* (a cover similar to that of Superman), and the inventor of a special rubber suit powered by nuclear energy. This suit endowed its wearer with extraordinary strength and exceptional powers; unfortunately, as all machines do, it often went haywire (this usually happened at the most critical moment so as to build up the suspense). Misterix's enemies were many, but the most dreaded of all was the evil Takos, a ruthless gang leader who turned out to be the hero's lost brother.

The struggle with Takos unfolded throughout 15 comic books and these episodes were reprinted many times. The most imaginative and enjoyable of Misterix's adventures, however, were those done by Campani for the Argentine market. So successful was the hero in Argentina that in 1948 Editorial Abril of Bue-

nos Aires launched a weekly comic magazine titled *Misterix*. Along with the hero's adventures, it published a host of other strips, most of them by Hugo Pratt.

G.B.

"*Mr. Jack*," James Swinnerton. © *International Feature Service.*

MR. JACK (U.S.) One of the most fondly remembered of early American comic strips was James Swinnerton's *Mr. Jack*, which first appeared as a separate strip (it developed from a strip series about humanized lynxes that Swinnerton was drawing at the time) on November 2, 1902, in a half-page Sunday episode titled, "No Friend of Hers." Several more episodes featuring Mr. Jack (a girl-ogling young and married cat-about-town who inevitably lost out with the fancy women he pursued) appeared over the next few months, separately captioned and without a specific name for the lead character. Finally, on November 1, 1903, it received the title, *Mr. Jack!*, from which point on the strip ran almost weekly until February 7, 1904, when it was abruptly dropped from the Hearst Sunday comic section for good, being continued some time later as an occasional daily strip called *The Troubles of Mr. Jack* from 1912 to 1919.

Again abandoned by Swinnerton, *Mr. Jack* was revived under that title as the companion page-topper for the Sunday *Little Jimmy* on February 7, 1926, first as a single row of four panels, then in a few weeks as a double-rowed strip of eight to ten panels. It continued as such until June 5, 1935, when the last episode appeared (drawn, incidentally, by Swinnerton's frequent ghost, Doc Winner), the Sunday space being filled the following week by a new Swinnerton feature, *Orvie* (later *Lil Ole Orvie*), about a very young, round-headed, and pop-eyed kid.

Mr. Jack seems to have worried Hearst syndicate executives as a character. Initially a married and humanized cat, his hot pursuit of show girls, sometimes thwarted by his wife, apparently seemed too risqué for the juvenile audience of the Sunday comics, and he was shunted to the editorial pages of the daily Hearst papers. When he returned as a Sunday character in 1926, his amorous proclivities were as much in evidence as before, but he was no longer married. Despite this, the vulgarity of the Mr. Jack character, above a page essentially intended for young readers, seems to have gotten him scuttled again in 1935, when the innocent *Orvie* was introduced. One of the best-

"Mr. Kiasu," Johnny Lau. © the Kuppies.

drawn and most amusing of the humanized animal strips, *Mr. Jack* is a minor but memorable feature of its time. (In all likelihood, the character inspired Robert Crumb's *Fritz the Cat* some 50 years later.)

B.B.

MR. KIASU (Singapore) *Mr. Kiasu* was an unusual phenomenon in 1990s Singapore. First of all, it proved to be popular and lucrative in a country not known for comics; second, it made its mark by exploiting negative characteristics of Singaporeans.

Derived from the disparaging Hokkien term meaning desire to be number one at anyone's expense, "kiasu" was often used to refer to brash, obnoxious, and selfish bargain hunters and freebie seekers. The character that goes by that name was created by architect/cartoonist Johnny Lau, with help from James Suresh, Eric Chang, and Lim Yu Cheng, in time for exhibition at the 1990 Singapore Book Fair. From the beginning, Lau and his coentrepreneurs, calling themselves the Kuppies, approached *Mr. Kiasu* in a businesslike way, marketing a slew of products simultaneous with the character's first appearance and self-publishing and using the alternative distribution means of introducing the book at the fair. The latter assured a greater take of profits and retention of all rights by the Kuppies.

The formula worked, for although only one book appears each year *Mr. Kiasu* is known far and wide, with spinoffs including a radio show, a compact disc, music videos, cartoon shows, and other comics titles, as well as arrangements with fast food, travel agencies, and hotel businesses, and merchandising of about two dozen products such as watches, cereals, and school bags. The books have also been translated into other languages for sale in Hong Kong, Indonesia, and Japan.

Mr. Kiasu is a nerdy, bespectacled young man with an insensitive disposition and vulgar behavior. The humor, according to Lau, is a workable blend of the East and West—satire influenced by *Mad* magazine and slapstick comedy emanating from an old Asian comic, *Old Master Q*. Suresh described *Mr. Kiasu* in this way: "His philosophies in life are: to win all the time; bor-

row but never return; cheap is good; pay only when necessary."

J.A.L.

MR. MUM *see* Strange World of Mr. Mum, The.

MR. NATURAL (U.S.) Of all the characters created by Robert Crumb, undoubtedly the most famous of all the "underground" comix artists, Crumb's *Mr. Natural* is easily the most vexing, hardest to interpret, and most subtle.

Since Crumb himself has those characteristics also, he is often cast as Mr. Natural; this, however, is probably not the case. But because *Mr. Natural* as a strip and as a character does run so far afield, it is easy to see why many look upon Crumb and Mr. Natural and find them similar.

Mr. Natural, a white-bearded guru-type in white gown and sandals, began to appear in print late in 1967 in *Yarrowstalks*, an underground paper published in Philadelphia by Brian Zahn. At about the same time, Zahn commissioned Crumb to produce complete books of Mr. Natural and his *Yarrowstalks* characters—which were also appearing in the *East Village Other* and many of the other underground tabloids beginning to emerge. Crumb responded by completing two issues of *Zap*. Zahn disappeared with some of the art, however, and neither book saw print until Crumb moved to San Francisco and teamed with Don Donahue and printer Charles Plymell. The books subsequently appeared as *Zap* number one and *Zap* number zero.

As for the character of the *Mr. Natural* strip itself, perhaps the simplest description is to say that it is a vehicle through which all of Robert Crumb's ideas have flowed. The historical basis for the existence of any real-life Mr. Natural has been bandied about frequently—he has been pegged as a legendary Afghanistanian, a parody of an infamous San Francisco guru popular during the time of *Mr. Natural's* creation, and even a reincarnation of a Dr. Von Naturlich—but it really has little bearing on Crumb's *Mr. Natural*.

At best, this fluffy-bearded pragmatist can be called a lovable old fraud who dispenses wisecracks and occa-

"Mr. Natural," Robert Crumb. © Robert Crumb.

sional sage advice on life to a horde of not-quite-convinced followers. At worst, Mr. Natural epitomizes all the ripoffs and dangerous mindwarping that stemmed from the "hippie" movement during the late 1960s. Probably, however, the inconsistencies in Mr. Natural's character came from Crumb's own ambivalence about the "movement," which drew Crumb and other followers to HaightAshbury in San Francisco. If anything can be firmly stated about this capitalistic cross between Santa Claus and a confidence man, it is that he was infinitely wiser and more realistic than any of his followers. The best-known of his subjects were Flakey Foont, a neurotic city-dweller constantly obsessed with sex and life's true meaning who was never quite sure why he took all the abuse Mr. Natural heaped upon him, and Shuman the Human, a bald truth-seeker whom Crumb often used to poke fun at the latest religious fad.

Mr. Natural, besides appearances in many undergrounds—including two bearing his name—is a favorite merchandising gimmick for those looking to cash in on Crumb's popularity. He has appeared on just about every type of merchandise trying to appeal to the young. Crumb, however, rarely authorized the bastard editions and was paid royalties on them even less often.

J.B.

MR. SCARLET (U.S.) Early in the 1940s, the National and Fawcett groups locked horns over two alleged imitations of the *Superman* feature, and National eventually sued Fawcett, claiming their *Master Man* and *Captain Marvel* strips were plagiarisms. While critics still argue the merits of both cases—National won settlements—National certainly missed attacking another, more vulnerable, Fawcett property, *Mr. Scarlet*, a close imitation of *Batman*. Created by writer Ed Herron and artists Jack Kirby and Joe Simon, *Mr. Scarlet* first appeared in *Wow* number one (Spring 1941), and borrowed many of *Batman's* major concepts. Although Mr. Scarlet was actually prosecutor Brian Butler and not a playboy, he and Batman were both nonsuperpowered crime stoppers. And just like Batman, Mr. Scarlett was cast as a mysterious figure of darkness, prowling the city streets in the dead of night. (His blood-red and silver-trimmed costume quickly scuttled that aspect, however.) And, again like Batman, he used a gun (two, in fact) in early stories, and shortly added a kid sidekick (Pinky Butler).

Unlike Batman, however, Mr. Scarlet sported a moustache, and his entry into crime fighting was based on his desire to bring to justice "those who escape the law through its loopholes." A noble desire, indeed, and writers Herron and Otto Binder kept the strip teeming with cops-and-robbers clichés. Simon's and Kirby's artwork on the strip was pleasant, complete with strange angles and interesting composition, but they were restricted by the standard nine-panel page. The Binder shop handled the artwork in 1942, and Mac Raboy (1941-1942), Harry Anderson (1942-1944), and John Jordan (1944-1948) drew the strip afterward.

Mr. Scarlet appeared in *Wow* for 69 consecutive issues (until Fall 1948), and also appeared in *America's Greatest* from issue one (1941) to issue seven (May 1943).

J.B.

MR. TERRIFIC (U.S.) Along with the premier episode of *Wonder Woman* in *Sensation* number one (January 1942), National introduced a costumed hero backup feature entitled *Mr. Terrific*. Created by writer Charles Reizenstein and artist Hal Sharp, the strip was pedestrian and uninspired, but Mr. Terrific was blessed with a garishly colorful outfit: scarlet tights and face mask, green tunic, yellow gloves, black boots, and a brown waist girdle. Escaping the use of the normal superheroic chest emblem, Mr. Terrific chose to sport a yellow chest patch that righteously promoted "Fair Play."

In reality he was child prodigy Terry Sloane, who was so successful in sports, academics, and business that he was bored by life, and so Mr. Terrific became a crime fighter simply to shake off his boredom. In his first effort, he delayed his planned suicide long enough to don his costume and turn a group of youthful thugs into fine, upstanding young Americans. He also changed their name from the "Purple Dagger Gang" to—as one might expect—the "Fair Play Club." Naturally, he then found a purpose in life and applied his genius to thwarting crime. Most of the scripts by Reizenstein and replacement Ted Udall were similarly simplistic.

Sharp's artwork was flat and linear, but Mr. Terrific's loud costume helped him stand out against the sparse background. Sharp turned the artistic chores over to Stan Asch in 1944, and the versatile Asch handled the feature until its 1947 demise.

Mr. Terrific appeared in *Sensation* until March 1947's 63rd issue, and the character made a cameo appearance with the Justice Society in 1945. He was revived by National, along with their other 1940s heroes, in the mid-1960s for several appearances.

J.B.

MIZUKI, SHIGERU (1924-   ) Japanese comic book artist born March 28, 1924, in Sakaiminato (Tottori prefecture). Shigeru Mizuki attended Musashino Art University but dropped out in 1949 and became associated with Koji Kata. He then started a career as a *kamishibai mangaka* (an artist who specialized in drawing stories in pictures for exhibitions), but the genre's popularity was then at a low ebb and Mizuki went to Tokyo in order to work on comic books.

His first comic book creation, *Rocket Man*, a strip combining elements of horror with a science-fiction theme, was published in 1957. For the next eight years Mizuki became a *kashibonya yō mangaka*, an artist working for comic books circulated in special rental libraries (a peculiarly Japanese institution). Among his works during this period, mention should be made of the following: *Yūrei Ikka* ("The Ghost Family," 1959); *Kappa no Sanpei* (a monster story, 1963); *Akumakun* (about a magician who can conjure Mephistopheles with the help of King Solomon's flute, 1964); *Hakaba no Kitarō* ("Kitarō from the Graveyard") and Mammoth Flower (both 1965); and *Renkin Jutsu* (a tale of alchemy and black magic, 1967).

Shigeru Mizuki is the most talented artist working in the horror/terror genre in Japanese comics today. His ghoulish creations are always tempered, however, with a generous touch of civilized irony. The most striking feature of his unique art is the blending in the same panel of realism and distortion. This imbalance allows him to strike for even greater effects of horror and dread.

Mizuki has also written a number of hardbound horror novels with illustrations by himself. His works have inspired a number of animated cartoons (*Hakabano Kitarō*) and have been adapted to the television screen (*Akumakun, Kappa no Sanpei*).

In an altogether different vein, Mizuki completed his monumental series *Komikku Showa-shi* ("A Comics History of the Showa Era"), about the controversial reign of Emperor Hirohito, in 1994. He was awarded the Japanese Medal with Ribbons in 1992.

H.K.

MIZUNO, HIDEKO (1939-   ) Hideko Mizuno knew from the time she was in third grade that she wanted to be a comics artist. In middle school, she began sending samples of her work to Osamu Tezuka, the undisputed leader of Japanese comics artists, and Tezuka recommended her to the editor of Kodansha Publishing's girls' magazine, *Shojo Club*. She soon began doing small illustrations and four-panel strips for the magazine, and in 1956, at the age of 15, she was asked to create a short story. This debut story, *Akakke ponii* ("Red Pony"), was a Western that featured a free-spirited tomboy who bore no resemblance to helpless-but-pretty little heroines of the melodramas that were the standard fare for Japanese girls' comics—all created by men—at the time. That same year, Mizumo was given her first serial, *Gin no hanabira* ("Silver Flower Petals), a medieval adventure tale of a horse-riding, sword-wielding princess. It was an enormous hit that shattered stereotypes of what Japanese girls wanted to read.

Mizuno made her debut at more or less the same time as two other women, Masako Watanabe and Miyako Maki, and the three became the first women to create narrative comics (as opposed to humor strips) in Japan. All three were tremendously popular, but whereas the other two more or less continued the tradition of domestic melodramas featuring little girls, Mizuno, who was more influenced by the dynamic work of Tezuka than by earlier girls' comics, always pushed the envelope, and her stories, like her lines, were bold. One of her best-known works, *Hoshi no tategoto* ("Star Harp," 1960), was a mythic epic in the style of Wagner that was the first girls' comic to feature romantic love between a woman and a man.

Mizuno again broke new ground in 1969 with *Fire!* ("Freedom!"), a passionate story of a juvenile delinquent's rise to rock stardom, and his encounters with sex, drugs, and rock 'n' roll along the way. Although the theme of *Fire!* may seen corny today, it captured the feelings of the youth of the day, and Mizuno's exquisite technique still shines. *Fire!*, which was published in the teen-oriented weekly magazine *Seventeen*, earned Mizuno the 1970 Shogakukan Comic Award.

Mizuno proved to be a major influence on the subsequent generation of women artists, particularly the innovative artists known collectively as the *Hana no nijuyonen gumi* ("Magnificent 24-Year Group") because many were born in the year Showa 24, or 1949.

Most of Mizuno's better-known work is now available in soft-cover collector's editions, and in 1981 her adventure comedy *Hanii Haniino sutekina boken* ("Honey-Honey's Wonderful Adventures") was made into an animated television series.

M.A.T.

MIZUSHIMA, SHINJI (1939-   ) Japanese comic book artist born April 10, 1939 in Niigata. Mizushima, who dreamed of becoming a cartoonist since his grammar school days, started work as a fishmonger as soon as he finished junior high school. In 1959 he made his debut as a cartoonist, working for the famous Kashibon Manga Kage, a comic company specializing in the publication of comic books for rental libraries.

Working on all of Kage's releases from number 17 to 120, Mizushima created many features, including *Ore wa Yaru* ("I'll Kill You," 1959), *Thrill o Ajiwan Otoko* ("The Man Who Craved Thrills," 1960), *Muteki Dump Guy* (a story about a stock car driver, 1961), *Idaten Santa* (a humor strip, 1962), *Heno Heno Moheji* (a story about a boy who loved a scarecrow, 1963), and *Botchan*, a 1964 comic book adaptation of a famous work of Japanese literature.

In 1965 Mizushima produced his first magazine strip, *Takaou*, which was followed by *Ushitsuki* (an animal strip, 1966) and *Left wa Shinazu* (a boxing strip, 1969). After this, Mizushima specialized in baseball strips, with four consecutive creations in this field: *Ace no Jōken* (1969); *Otoko Doahou Koushien* (1970); *Yakyūkyō no Uta* (1972); and *Abu-san* (1973). These and later sports comics made their author very rich, and since 1978 he has regularly made the list of the highest income-earners in Japan.

Mizushima is now a famous and popular comic book artist. Greatly influenced by the work of playwright Kobako Hanato, his stories are full of warmth and drama. He created so many baseball strips because he is a baseball fan himself.

H.K.

MODESTY BLAISE (G.B.) The official biography of Modesty Blaise reads as follows: Origins: Date of birth unknown. Place of birth unknown. Age, approximately 26. Education: Self-acquired. Excellent. Occupation: Retired. Previous Occupation: Suspected head of "The Network," international crime syndicate based in Algeria. Financial category: Very rich. Present address: London W. 1. Close friends: Only one—William Garvin soldier of fortune (retired). Hobbies: Sculpting precious stones. Future Plans:¿¿¿¿¿

The strip biography tells of a small female child, a war refugee, her memory erased through shock, who escaped from a prison camp in Greece to a displaced persons camp in Persia. She saved an old professor from a thief, and in return he educated her and named her Modesty. Her surname she took from Merlin's tutor. She buried the old man and entered civilization, spinning a roulette wheel in Tangier.

In two years she had taken over her late employer's gang; in two more she was boss of the international crime syndicate "The Network." It was in Saigon that she first saw Willie Garvin, Thai-style fighter, gutter-bred. She bought him out of jail without strings, and from then on he called her "Princess." Partners in crime, they retired to England where Sir Gerald Tarrant, head of British Intelligence, appealed to them for their help in a mission requiring an intimate knowledge of the underworld. Bored with the luxury life, they became unpaid agents for Britain.

The third biography is the correct one: *Modesty Blaise* is a daily newspaper strip created by writer Peter O'Donnell and artist Jim Holdaway. Intended for the *Daily Express*, it was rejected at the last moment, on the grounds that the life of a "fallen woman" was unsuitable to a family newspaper. The *Evening Standard*, another Beaverbrook newspaper, took it on immediately, starting on Easter 1963, and soon the strip was syndicated to 76 newspapers and magazines in 35 different countries.

A major movie was made from the strip in 1966, starring Monica Vitti as Modesty, Terence Stamp as Willie, and Harry Andrews as Sir Gerald. It was directed by Joseph Losey. O'Donnell's first novel, *Modesty Blaise*, was published in 1965. When Holdaway died in 1970, the strip was taken over by the Spanish cartoonist Romero. Thirty-four years after its inception, the strip is still doing well internationally with Peter O'Donnell and Enrique Romero firmly at the helm.

D.G.

MOEBIUS *see* Giraud, Jean.

MOLINO, WALTER (1915-   ) An Italian cartoonist and illustrator born November 5, 1915, in Reggio Emilia, Walter Molino moved with his family to Milan in 1920. There the young Molino went to high school and, upon graduation, entered the University of Milan. Molino, whose father was an art teacher, exhibited an early talent for drawing but decided to follow in the footsteps of his older brother, Antonio, a noted short-story writer (later killed in the Mathausen concentration camp). In 1934 Molino's first drawing was published in the student newspaper *Libro e Moschetto*, on the occasion of Arnaldo Mussolini's death. This was followed by a series of short-lived comic strips for the brothers Del Duca's publications, *L'Intrepido* and *Il Monello*, and a brief stint as an advertising artist.

In 1935, at the formal request of Mussolini and in collaboration with Mario Sironi, Molino originated a series of political and satirical cartoons, published first in *Libro e Moschetto*, and later in *Il Popolo d'Italia*. He also contributed fashion drawings to such publications as *Per Voi, Signori*, and *Arbiter*. In 1936 the humor magazine *Il Bertoldo* was founded, and Molino became one of its most talented contributors. But Molino's talent shone brightest in the series of comic strips starting in 1937 that editor and scriptwriter Federico Pedrochhi asked him to illustrate. "Aside from my work at *Il Bertoldo*," Molino later reminisced, "all I did was draw comic strip after comic strip." During this golden period he drew *Virus, il Mago della Foresta Morta* ("Virus, the Magician of the Dead Forest"), a masterly science-fiction thriller (1938); *Capitan l'Audace* (1939), a tale of intrigue and violence set in 16th-century Italy; the moody Western, *Kit Carson*, which Molino took over from Rino Albertarelli in 1939; the parodic *Don Antonio della Mancia*, about a modern-day Don Quixote; and many others.

In 1941 Molino started his 25-year collaboration with the *Domenico del Corriere*, contributing cartoons, illustrations, and double-page spreads. In 1946, using a clever combination of wash and photographic techniques, he created the spectacularly successful *Grand Hotel*, the soap opera to end all soap operas, an outrageous display of all the clichés the genre has to offer (many of Molino's former fans have yet to forgive him to this day).

In the 1960s Molino retired from comic strip work, concentrating on illustration and cartooning. His work has been amply reprinted and anthologized, as indeed it deserves to be. In 1984 a large retrospective of his works was organized by the Academia d'Arte and later traveled through Italy.

M.H.

MOMMA (U.S.) Thirteen years after launching the acclaimed *Miss Peach*, Mell Lazarus created another very amusing comic strip, which he affectionately named after the meddlesome heroine. *Momma* thus appeared on October 26, 1970, and was immediately recognized as the archetype of so many put-upon, self-sacrificing (though not silent), and unappreciated mothers.

Mrs. Sonya Hobbs is a widowed lady whose three children seldom meet her expectations—or maybe they meet them all too well. Thomas, her 42-year-old son, a successful professional, married and father of one, is still not treated as an adult by Momma. Neither, for that matter, is his wife Tina, "the person my Darling Son saw fit to pick as a wife," whom Mother Hobbs bombards with constructive criticism and unwanted advice, usually regarding raising little Chuckie or performing household duties to more demanding standards.

At age 22, Francis is a failure in her eyes—perhaps justifiably so, particularly when compared to other people's sons. Forever unemployed, always about to get married to some new girl, and always shamelessly sponging off his white-haired mother, he endures her nagging with equanimity while she suffers his ungrateful behavior with dismay. Daughter Marylou, 18, has a different boyfriend every other day, much to her mother's consternation—and pride.

Mrs. Hobbs never read Dr. Benjamin Spock. Her method of bringing up children, regardless of their age,

"Momma," Mell Lazarus. © Creators Syndicate.

rests instead on large quantities of food (since food *is* maternal love, and vice versa) and especially on larger quantities of guilt. Therefore, she tests their love constantly ("minimum daily requirement"), checks to see that her phone is indeed working, and reminds them how sorry they will be when she dies of worry, sorrow, abandonment, or heartbreak. Yet, despite all her aggravations, Momma will admit in some unguarded moment that she does have "fine children, a nice home, warm memories, friends, security, [and] health."

Momma is drawn in the same caricatural style as Lazarus's *Miss Peach*: foreshortened characters with distinguishing features, such as Francis's big jaw and flowing black hair, Marylou's skinny figure and stringy hair, or Mrs. Hobbs's protruding eyes. Its popularity, however, comes from its on-target observations and sophisticated wit. The National Cartoonists Society awarded joint honors to the two series in 1973, 1979, and 1982.

First distributed by Field Newspaper Syndicate and since 1988 by Creators Syndicate, the strip has been reprinted in a number of paperback editions, including *The Momma Treasury* (1978), which also has a funny introduction by the author's mother.

P.L.H.

MONK, JACK (1904-197?) British cartoonist John Asthian Monk was born in Bolton, Lancashire, in 1904. He was educated at a council school, leaving in 1918 with an art scholarship to join Tillotson's Process Engraving as an office boy. He supported himself by doing retouching for catalogues and other publications, while attending evening classes at Bolton School of Art. His first published cartoons were sports drawings freelanced to the *Bolton Evening News Buff*, a Saturday sports edition. He was then invited to join the art staff of Allied Newspapers in Manchester, where he drew fillers, caricatures, and maps for the *Evening Chronicle*. He moved to the northern edition of the *Daily Express* and created a fact strip, *Can You Beat It?*, and *The Funny Side of Northern Towns* (both in 1934).

In July 1936 Monk moved south to Richmond, Surrey, to freelance for the *Daily Mirror*. His first daily strip was an adaptation of the Edgar Wallace novel *Terror Keep*, scripted by Don Freeman. Unfortunately, although rights had been cleared with Wallace's estate, the American syndicate producing the daily *Inspector Wade* claimed prior rights and the strip had to be ended. But Guy Bartholomew, the *Mirror* editor and champion of strips, liked Monk's style and asked him

to create an original detective. The result was *Buck Ryan*, which began on March 22, 1937, and ran for 25 years.

On the side he drew advertising strips for Phillips Stickasoles, and served part time as an auxiliary fireman during the war. At the end of his *Mirror* run Monk turned to comic work, beginning with *Commander Cockle* (1962) in *Lion*, then a number of series for D. C. Thomson's comics, including *Wee Tusky* (1965) in *Sparky*, *Inspector Jellicoe* (1963) in *Hornet*, and *Million Pound Mutt* (1973) in *Debbie*. None of these, however, had an impact similar to that created by his famous detective hero. He died in the late 1970s.

D.G.

MONKHOUSE, BOB (1929-) British cartoonist, editor, comedian, actor, and writer, Bob Monkhouse was born in Beckenham, Kent on, June 1, 1929, and educated at Dulwich College, where he drew the amateur magazine, *Modern Mag* (1943), and freelanced his first strips, *Bobby Brain* and *Professor Poosum*, to *All Fun* (1944). He contributed many different characters to this and the other Soloway Publications, which he followed by two comic painting books for R. & L. Locker, *Bimbo Goes to the Moon* and *Chubby & the Christmas Star* (1946), and the weekly newspaper strip *Just Judy* in the *South London Advertiser* (also 1946).

He passed the aptitude test for trainee animators at Gaumont British Animation and worked on the *Animaland* and *Musical Paintbox* series at the Cookham Studio until his conscription into the Royal Air Force in 1947. In the same year he edited and produced his first complete comic book, *Smasher Comics*, for Tongard Trading. He also wrote and pencilled strips for editor/artist John R. Turner to ink for *Okay*, *Ripping*, and *Winner* comics (1948). He became freelance editor for Martin & Reid comics in 1948, taking over existing titles (*Merry Go Round*, *Merry Maker*, *Funny Tuppeny*, *Jolly Chuckles*, etc.) and creating new titles: *Crash Comics* (1948), in the American superhero style, and *Super Star* (1949).

While his humorous work was much influenced by the animated cartoon style of the American funnies, he also admired the superhero style and created *Oh Boy Comics* (1948) for Paget Publications, drawing the super-adventures of *Tornado*. After four issues the comic was taken over by Mick Anglo, and continued with different artists for some while.

His last strips were for *Amazing and Modern Comics* (1949), published by Modern Fiction and edited by his schoolmate, Denis Gifford. Gifford brought Monkhouse back to cartooning in 1974, after many years as a star comedian and scriptwriter, to chair the first television panel game for cartoonists, *Quick on the Draw*. He also illustrated the book, *The A to Z of Television* (1971), which he coauthored with Willis Hall.

Bob Monkhouse is still very active in the field of comics.

D.G.

"Monsieur Poche," Alain Saint-Ogan. © Alain Saint-Ogan.

MONSIEUR POCHE (France) Alain Saint-Ogan, then at the height of his fame, created *Monsieur Poche* (literally "Mister Pocket") for the weekly *Dimanche Illustré* on October 14, 1934, where it ran as a full page.

Monsieur Poche is a solid citizen, of advanced middle age and ample proportions. Free of money worries (we certainly never see him trying to earn a living) he also feels free to stick his big red nose into everybody's business, ever generous with unsolicited advice, or ready to loudly assert his rights. During a conversation he never lets anybody else speak; in social gatherings he tries to upstage everyone (with usually disastrous results). He is also smug, vainglorious, cowardly, stingy, and loud-mouthed; the portrait, scarcely caricatural, of the typical small-town bore.

Monsieur Poche, a bachelor, was served (not always too well) by his elderly housekeeper, who didn't seem to take her boss's whims or orders too seriously. He was often accompanied by a young boy named Ratafia who is not adverse to taking advantage of Poche's credulity on occasion. Poche's constant companion, a kangaroo named Salsifi, made his appearance one full year after the inception of the strip (on October 28, 1935). A gift from Poche's Australian uncle, Salsifi was an unusual animal whose unpredictable behavior very often lands his master into the most screwy incidents. In 1937 *Monsieur Poche* ended its run in *Dimanche Illustré*. In December of that year it was revived in the pages of *Cadet-Revue* (where it had been preceded by *Zig et Puce*), which often simply reproduced the old *Dimanche Illustré* episodes. In 1940 the feature disappeared for good (in the interim Librairie Hachette had reprinted four volumes of *Monsieur Poche*'s adventures).

While not as famous as *Zig et Puce*, *Monsieur Poche* is a good example of Saint-Ogan's humor, made of subtle little touches and an unfailing eye (and ear) for the ridiculous. The characters of Poche and Salsifi are certainly among the author's most felicitous creations.

M.H.

MONTANA, BOB (1920-1975) American comic book and comic strip artist and writer born in Stockton, California, on October 23, 1920. After studies at the Phoenix Art Institute, the Art Students League, and the Boston Museum School of Fine Arts, Bob Montana broke into comic art as Bob Wood's assistant on Novelty's *Target Comics* in 1940. In 1941, he moved to MLJ and drew a slew of superhero features, including *Black Hood*, *Fox*, and *Steel Sterling*, and, between 1942 and 1945, drew material for Lev Gleason's superhero and crime books.

Without a doubt, however, Montana's greatest comic art contribution came in the 22nd issue of MLJ's *Pep* (December 1941). Almost unnoticed behind the superhero features, he created *Archie*, a teenage humor strip based on the then-popular Henry Aldrich radio show. With Montana at the helm, the strip soon became the most saleable humor strip feature on the market, was the basis for dozens of comic titles, a comic strip, all sorts of merchandising, a radio show, and several television programs.

The *Archie* concept has been roundly criticized because it has never accurately depicted teenage life, but Montana's creation has survived and profited mightily. The artist added a curious collection of stereotyped supporting characters: Archie Andrews's brunette girlfriend, the rich and spoiled Veronica Lodge,

Bob Montana, "Archie." © Archie Comics.

"Moomin," Tove Jansson. © Bulls Pressedienst.

was modeled after motion picture star Veronica Lake; the blond, middle-class Betty was based on one of Montana's old girlfriends; and Mr. Wetherbee, Riverdale High's harried principal, and Miss Beasley, the spinster schoolteacher, were developed from people Montana met during his Manchester, New Hampshire school days. Strangely enough, he created the lovable-but-inept Jughead on the drawing board. "I never knew him," Montana once said.

In 1947, an *Archie* comic strip was started under Montana's byline, and he soon abandoned the comic book line to concentrate on the dailies and Sundays.

Throughout his 35-year stint on *Archie*, Montana never varied his art style. It was always straightforward, uncluttered and unembellished, usually relying on the situation gag and one-liners rather than sight jokes. Montana died of a heart attack near his Meredith, New Hampshire, home on January 4, 1975.

J.B.

MOOMIN (Finland, G.B.) Moomintroll, to give him his full name, has a full figure: a sort of cuddly hippo who walks on two legs and loves something similar called Snorkmaiden. The full Finn Family Moomintroll, to use the title of one of their many books, is headed by Moominpappa, who may be recognized by his top hat and cane; or is more likely headed by Moominmamma, who may be recognized by her apron and handbag. Otherwise, Moomins are much the same, but very lovable in it. They all live in Moomin Valley in Moominland, a Nordic paradise spoiled only by doom-laden Fillyjonks and horrifying Hattifatteners.

Their creator, the artist and author of many children's books, is Tove Jansson, who turned the Moomins into a daily strip at the request of her English publishers and the *London Evening News*. The series began on September 20, 1954, to the instant joy of millions, children and adults alike. The decorative linework, slender yet curvaceous, was something new in strips, and so was the whimsical humor. From 1957 her brother, Lars, wrote the stories for her. At the end of her contract, she gave up completely and let Lars draw the strip, too. He continued until the *News* dropped it on June 29, 1968. Tove Janssen, beset by requests to commercialize her creations, refused, and reacted by writing them into a final, despairing novel, *Moominland*

Midwinter. An excellent hardback volume of *Moomin* from the first strip was published under that title in 1957.

D.G.

MOON MULLINS (U.S.) Moon Mullins (and his earliest strip crony, Mushmouth) arrived on the comics scene by box, being dumped off a delivery van in Jack Dempsey's training quarters at Shelby, Montana, in the first daily episode of Frank Willard's new *Chicago Tribune* strip of June 19, 1923 (the first Sunday page appeared September 9, 1923). In training for his July 4, 1923, fight with Tom Gibbons, Dempsey (shown in this first *Moon Mullins* episode in a dressing gown lavishly decorated with pre-Hitler swastikas) was prominently featured in the sports news of the time, and his presence must have attracted many eyes to the new strip. Moon's idea, once inside the compound, was to rent his own fighter, Mushmouth (whom he calls Wildcat) to Dempsey as a great "punching bag," or spar-

"Moon Mullins," Frank Willard. © Chicago Tribune-New York News Syndicate.

ring partner, but Dempsey has both Moon and Mushmouth thrown out of the camp, minus their box.

This opening episode (badly printed in many papers because of a damaged proof) characterized both the small-time opportunism of the new strip's hero, and the rowdy, slam-bang narrative that was to follow. Essentially, Willard's *Moon Mullins* was *Tribune* publisher Joe Patterson's competitive reply to the success of Hearst artist Billy De Beck's *Barney Google*; and it looked for a few weeks as if Willard was going to develop the boxing world as a strip theme much as De Beck had developed horse racing. Willard veered away from that limited area shortly, however, and never returned: Moon's natural habitat, it turned out, was the circus, the neighborhood pool parlor, and any ritzy mansion he could bluff his way into for a free meal or two.

Moon's full first name was "Moonshine" (given to him by Patterson with an eye on the popular Prohibition term for bootleg liquor), and he had a markedly prognathous, Popeyesque jaw in the early weeks of the strip, which Willard rounded off gradually. Joining a carnival, he met the next regular character in the strip, his love-light, Little Egypt, in the daily episode for July 30, 1923. Losing Egypt for the time being, Moon wanders to a strange town where he moves into a rooming house run by the scrawny, elaborately coiffeured Emmy Schmaltz (March 3, 1924), where the strip took on the general shape it maintained over the next 50 years. Emmy, it turned out some time later, is ardently pursuing the reluctant, plump, and nobly moustached Lord Plushbottom (who resisted her charms until their marriage in 1934). Kayo, Moon's bratty little brother, turns up, as does Mamie, a cook hired by Emmy who turns out to be the estranged wife of Moon's Uncle Willie, the last regular character to enter the strip, in a Sunday episode for May 29, 1927. From that date, the continuing *dramatis comicae* of *Moon Mullins* was complete.

While there was little or no continuing narrative in the anecdotal *Mullins* Sunday page, the daily strip was one of the most intricately-plotted and imaginatively-developed continuing narratives in the comics. Willard and his assistant, Ferd Johnson, mastered the difficult art of maintaining cliff-hanging continuity while mustering a neat daily gag each and every day almost from the outset of the strip. Much of the compelling story pace of the strip and the narrative imagination of the strip's first 15 years ebbed in the early 1940s for some reason, however, and was never effectively regained, although the quality of many of the daily and Sunday gags remained relatively high.

Willard's only *Moon Mullins* companion strip was the four-panel Sunday feature called *Kitty Higgins*, involving the escapades of a young female playmate of Kayo's, which began in early 1930 and was dropped in the 1960s. A number of *Moon Mullins* episodes were reprinted in book form, but no complete daily narratives were published as they originally appeared until a few from the late 1930s were obscurely reprinted in comic books of the period. A comprehensive book is still needed.

Following Willard's death in early 1958, Ferd Johnson took over the *Moon Mullins* strip, which he continued until its demise in June 1991. Johnson's Mullins-Plushbottom menage was much more amiable and clean-scrubbed than the old Willard bunch: the derbies Moon and Kayo both sported disappeared, as did the other antisocial rough edges of the original crew. But there was a marked humor and charm in the latter strip that was very much Johnson's own, and it held the attention of a new generation of readers.

B.B.

MOORE, ALAN (1953-   ) British artist born in November 1953 in Northampton, England. Dropping out of school at age 17, Alan Moore started writing, under the pseudonym "Curt Vile," for the rock magazine *Sounds*. After trying his hand at cartooning with *Maxwell the Magic Cat*, he went back to scripting, working notably for the comic magazines *2000 AD* and *Warriors*. His break came in 1982 with *V for Vendetta*, a tale about a British society of the near-future laid waste by war and ruled by a Fascist government; illustrated with great sensitivity by David Lloyd, *V for Vendetta* was very well received by readers and critics alike.

This success drew the attention of the editors at DC Comics, who brought Moore over to the U.S. in 1983. He made an acclaimed debut writing some of the most suspenseful *Swamp Thing* episodes; then in 1986 came *Watchmen*, illustrated by Dave Gibbons, which definitively established him as one of the modern masters of comic-book storytelling. Two more remarkable stories followed in 1988: a *Superman* tale ("Happy Birthday, Superman!," again with Gibbons) and a *Batman* episode ("The Killing Joke," with art by Brian Bolland).

Back in Britain by the end of the decade, Moore turned out a number of personal projects (some of a political nature), including *Big Numbers* (illustrated by Bill Sienkiewicz), the tale of a small English town disrupted by the opening of a shopping mall; and *From Hell*, one more version of the Jack the Ripper murders, with art by the Australian Eddy Campbell. Since 1996 he has been writing *Supreme* for Rob Liefeld's Extreme Studios, and he is currently at work on the *Judgment Day* miniseries. The recipient of many honors and awards, Alan Moore has also lectured extensively on the subject of comics.

M.H.

MOOSE MILLER (U.S.) A standard King Features-style "bigfoot" humor strip, *Moose Miller* celebrated its 30th year of international syndication in September 1995. Considering the attrition rate of newspaper comic strips, this is a notable accomplishment for *Moose*'s creator, Bob Weber Sr.

Moose Miller was King Features's answer to the instant success of *Andy Capp*, the British import about a drunken but funny lout, that was syndicated in the United States by Publishers Syndicate beginning in September 1963.

Weber's *Moose Miller*, unlike *Andy Capp*, is a devoted family man. With wife Molly, son Bunky, daughter Blip, and a mini-zoo of family pets, from Grits the dog to goats and parrots, it's the type of family you'd wish to be anybody's neighbors but your own. The Miller family's neighbors in the strip, Chester and Clara Crabtree, are often the butt of the Miller's low-rent behavior, such as stealing food from their barbecue.

Fat and extremely lazy, Moose Miller works at not working. He's the kind of guy who gives white trash a bad name. Until the arrival of the cartoon family in Bud Grace's feature *Ernie* in 1988 and Matt Groening's animated family sitcom *The Simpsons* in 1989, the *Moose Miller* clan held the prize as cartooning's most physically unattractive characters.

Alan Moore and Curt Swan, "Superman." © DC Comics.

With sight gags, broad burlesque, slapstick, and old-fashioned bigfoot-style fun, *Moose Miller*, in Bob Weber Sr.'s competent hands, continues the King Features tradition of humor strips. Weber's son, Bob Jr., assisted his father on *Moose Miller*, prior to creating his own feature for King, *Slylock Fox*.

One of a legion of cartoonists who attended the School of Visual Arts in New York City, Bob Weber Sr. credits magazine cartoonist Orlando Busino for getting him to leave technical illustration for cartooning. A raconteur with endless stories about cartooning, Weber has taught cartooning to children all over the northeastern United States for many years.

B.C.

MORDILLO, GUILLERMO (1933-   ) An Argentine cartoonist born in Buenos Aires in 1933, Guillermo Mordillo started his cartooning career in animation and advertising. In 1955 he moved to Lima, going from there to New York, where he got a job as a greeting card designer for the Hallmark Company. In 1966 the peripatetic Mordillo settled in Paris, where he produced books of extraordinary cartoons without captions, such as *Crazy Cowboy*. He also designed posters, greeting cards and merchandising material, all of which bore the stamp of his unmistakable style.

At the same time Mordillo experimented with the comic strip form, laying out his humor pages in rows of panels and creating his series of unforgettable characters, such as the giraffe, the little Tarzan, Superman, and the inflatable woman. These pages were published all over the world in magazines such as *Lui, Oui,* and *Bocaccio*, making Mordillo the most widely published cartoonist of the 1970s. In the last 20 years he has worked almost exclusively in humor and children's illustration.

L.G.

MORONI-CELSI, GUIDO (1885-1962) Italian artist born 1885 in Rome. Guido Moroni-Celsi began his professional career as a portrait artist and humor cartoonist with a series of sketches called *L'Album di Pippo* ("Pippo's Sketchbook") published in *Il Messaggero dei Piccoli*. Under the pen name "F. Sterny," he contributed a number of cartoons to the humor magazines *Il Mulo* of Bologna and *Ma chié* of Naples. In 1926 he started his first comic strip, *Bonifazio*, partly inspired by Swinnerton's *Little Jimmy*, for the juvenile weekly *Il Novellino*, and the same year also contributed to the *Domenica dei Fanciulli*. In 1929 he alternated with Rino Albertarelli in producing the center-spreads of the *Cartoccino dei Piccoli*.

Only in 1930 did Moroni-Celsi do drawings and illustrations in a straight style: these were hunting, battle, and sport scenes for the magazine *Viaggi e Avventure* (Albertarelli, Ballerio, and Rivolo also worked

Guido Moroni-Celsi, "Le Tigri di Mompracem." © Mondadori.

on these pages). In 1934, for the *Corriere dei Piccoli*, he created *Grillo il Balillino* (the "balillas" were Fascist youth), a politically motivated strip featuring the brave deeds of a blackshirted young man.

In 1935, for Mondadori's *I Tre Porcellini*, he produced *Ulceda*, a Western whose title character was the daughter of the Great Hawk of the Prairie. Once again the hero was an Italian—Vittorio Ranghi—who married the beautiful Ulceda at the end of the story. In 1935-36 he published his only science-fiction story, *S.K. 1*, in the weekly *Topolino* (it was reprinted in 1970 by Sansoni); but his best-remembered work remains his illustrated version of Salgari's jungle novels (*I Misteri della Giungla Nera*, *La Conquista di Mompracem*, etc.). Published between 1936 and 1941 (when he was succeeded by Franco Chiletto) in the pages of *Topolino*, they tell in vivid and memorable fashion of the adventures of Yanez, Tremal Naik, and the pirates of Mompracem.

After the war, Moroni-Celsi faded from public favor. He died in Naples in 1962 in utter obscurity, but he was later resurrected as one of "the fathers of the Italian adventure strip."

G.B.

MORRIS *see* Bevère, Maurice de.

MORTADELO Y FILEMON (Spain) The Spanish cartoonist Francisco Ibañez created his comic strip hit in 1958 in the weekly *Pulgarcito* under the initial title *Mortadelo y Filemon, Agencia de Informacion* ("Mortadello and Filemon, Information Agency").

This information agency is made up of a pair of private eyes, Filemon, the boss, and his clever assistant Mortadelo, who is capable of disguising himself as a butterfly or an earthworm. Mortadelo's skill at outlandish transformations and the latent sadomasochism in the duo's relations constitute the main attractions of the strip. The stories are rich in absurd interludes, fist and club fights, madcap situations, and the introduction of the surreal into the mundane world of small-time hoods and scientists as crazy as the two investigators. In a second stage of their adventures, the pair met Doctor Bacterius, an inventor who used them as guinea pigs in his experiments, and they later joined the secret agency TIA (*TIA* in Spanish means "AUNT," a parodic pun on both the fictitious organization UNCLE and the real CIA), which allowed them further scope in their hare-brained exploits around the world.

The adventures of Filemon and Mortadelo were so popular that, in addition to their publication in *Pulgarcito*, they gave rise to two new publications, *Mortadelo*

and *Super Mortadelo*, in which the pair were the star attractions. After Ediciones Bruguera, owners of *Pulgarcito* and *Super Mortadelo*, went out of business in 1986, the pair continued their exploits under the banners of different Spanish publishers.

The success of the strip is so enormous that it can only be compared to that of *Asterix* in France. It soon spawned toys, books, gadgets of all kinds, advertising campaigns, animated films, and publications in numerous foreign countries, garnering the sort of acclaim aimed only at internationally-recognized hits.

L.G.

MORT CINDER (Argentina) *Mort Cinder* was created by Argentine cartoonist Alberto Breccia in 1962; written by Hector Oesterheld, it unfolded over a total of 206 pages in the comic magazine *Misterix*. The protagonist is a criminal with a wide knowledge of neurosurgery; having already lived a series of lives, he is resurrected by the antiquarian, Ezra Winston, who gives him work and studies his history, along with that of Hilaire Belloc.

A masterpiece of the chiaroscuro technique, *Mort Cinder* is bathed in the nightmarish atmosphere of foreboding and terror favored by the author and carried to its limits in *Los Mitos de Cthulu*. Each of the strip's episodes is treated in the author's unique style, always unified by his visual experiences, from the expressionist cinema of Fritz Lang to the films of Ingmar Bergman.

L.G.

MOSLEY, ZACK (1906-1994) American artist born in 1906 in the Indian Territory of Oklahoma. Zack Mosley displayed an early interest in drawing, but

"Mort Cinder," Alberto Breccia. © Editorial Abril.

"Mother Goose and Grimm," Mike Peters. © Grimmy Inc.

spent his youth in nonartistic pursuits such as cotton picker, cowboy, and soda jerk.

His interest in comic strips, manifested by incessant copying of newspaper strips, led him to schooling at the Chicago Academy of Fine Arts, the Chicago Art Institute, and under Carey Orr, the great editorial cartoonist of the *Chicago Tribune*. Mosley claimed that during his student days he assisted in the artwork of *Buck Rogers* and *Skyroads*.

The aviation strip was a natural for Mosley, who loved planes as much as comic art. When he was 11 years old an army Jenny was forced down on the Mosley ranch and Zack instantly fell into a lifelong love affair with aviation. He took up flying, got a pilot's license and earned himself a reserve commission.

In 1933 he sold a strip to the Chicago Tribune-New York News Syndicate, *On the Wing*, one of seven that debuted simultaneously that year. Walter Berndt, creator of *Smitty*, was asked by Captain Patterson of the *News* to make a final decision on the seventh strip between a now-forgotten effort and Mosley's strip. Berndt, with the prearranged vote of editorial cartoonist C. D. Batchelor, picked *On the Wing*.

The strip was short-lived under this name. The main characters were Mack, his pal Bumpy, girlfriend Mary Miller, Steve the flying instructor (who, in the promotional material, was a "thoroughly good scout who will win the heart of every boy"), Pinfeathers, a kid who, like the young Mosley, hung around airports, and Dart, "the villain of the piece. See them moustaches?" A moustache was to reappear immediately on the face of the hero in Mosley's second effort, *Smilin' Jack*. This strip met with greater success and ran as a daily and Sunday page until April 1, 1973.

Mosley retained several assistants, including Ward Albertson, during the duration of *Smilin' Jack*; his research into the latest aviation developments was enormous and Mosley continued to fly a great deal. He owned nine planes and flew to many spots around the world, flew on Civilian Air Patrol antisubmarine flights during World War II, and through the years he designed insignias, posters, and program covers for many aircraft-related events and organizations. Upon the cancellation of *Smilin' Jack* he retired to Stuart, Florida, where he died in January 1994.

Mosley's artwork actually had a handsome naiveté in the early years of *Wing* and *Jack*. His aircraft was, of course, authentic and his girls ranged from pretty to sexy. In later years, many readers saw a mannered crudeness (almost ugliness) in the artwork which, perhaps, as part and parcel of the adventure themes, was appropriate.

R.M.

MOTHER GOOSE AND GRIMM (U.S.) Created by Pulitzer Prize-winning editorial cartoonist Mike Peters, *Mother Goose and Grimm* first appeared on October 1, 1984, as a zany and irreverent takeoff on fairy tales and popular culture—from Snow White and the Magnificent Seven to Mrs. M&M accusing her husband of melting in someone else's hands.

The strip, however, soon focused on the madcap actions and thoughts of Grimm, Mother Goose's dog, and his entourage of animal friends: a pig who adores food, a goldfish named Lassie, and an assortment of various pooches, including the RCA Victor dog. Most of his attention, of course, is directed at Attila the cat, whom he persecutes mercilessly—without ever laying a paw on him. Yet the result is always terrified eyes and raised fur, sometimes even broken bones. Other Grimm favorite targets are the paperboy and the postman, or at least his truck, as Grimm likes to puncture the tires. When the dog catcher's truck and the mail van crash into each other, he jubilantly exclaims, "Is this a great country or what?" For fun, he enjoys chasing cars, raiding garbage cans, playing poker (his wagging tale gives him away), going for rides, watching Carl the Wonder Poodle on TV, and sleeping. In short, he is Everyman's Dog.

For her part, Mother Goose is an old lady with an acerbic viewpoint. While she often indulges her pets and speaks to them (Attila in particular) in baby talk, which makes her seem doddering in Grimm's opinion, she is quite sharp-eyed and sharp-tongued about the world, and herself, as when she sits down to a seven-course dinner—"a pizza and a six-pack"—or confides that the most important thing that she looks for in a man is "a pulse."

Although mostly about these characters, the strip still makes many references to fairy tales (Pinocchio afraid of termites), literary allusions (Frankenstein's monster playing hide-and-seek with the Invisible Man), and current events ("When Euro-Disney fell on bad times, the commissary started serving chicken-dumbo soup"). In addition, Mike Peters loves visual and word plays: 40-year old bald eagles sporting wigs; light bulbs watching a slide of an electric plug approaching the outlet in sex education class; one fly whispering to another, "Your human's open"; a shark ordering a manwich; the wicked witch asking for the children's menu; or Sarge, Dagwood, Nancy, Hägar, Dennis, and Grimm playing "strip poker."

Peters draws in the modern caricatural style that has made him famous as a political cartoonist: thick lines, exaggerated features, and no unnecessary details. Widely distributed by Tribune Media Services, *Mother Goose* was also a television cartoon and has been reprinted in numerous albums and merchandised. It even has its own web site on the Internet (http://www.grimmy.com). For his work, Peters was named Cartoonist of the Year by the National Cartoonist Society in 1992.

P.L.H.

MOTLEY'S CREW (U.S.)   In 1996 Tribune Media Services's *Motley's Crew* celebrated its 20th anniversary of syndication. Sadly, its writer, Tom Forman, also died that year. Since becoming a writer/cartoonist team in 1975, Tom Forman and Ben Templeton had been responsible for a string of syndicated panel and comic strips for TMS. In 1975, Foreman had contacted Templeton with the idea of a strip called *Super Fan* about a blue-collar sports fanatic. TMS liked the idea but wanted to broaden the appeal to humor beyond sports. Forman who earned a degree in government from California State University at Los Angeles found politics and family humor in a factory town dominated by Drudge Industries the perfect stage for his gag writing.

Ben Templeton earned a graphic design degree from the University of California-Los Angeles and had been an advertising art director prior to teaming up with Tom Forman. After *Super Fan* was turned into *Motley's Crew* and successfully launched September 6, 1976, the pair turned their interest in sports into the daily panel plus Sunday *The Sporting Life* which was syndicated in the 1980s.

As with all comic strips, the characters change physically over time. Mike Motley was squat, beer-bellied, and a bit grungy in 1976. Now he's taller, thinner, and the hard blue-collar edge has been elevated to almost middle-class sensibilities. Promotional material from 1976 has Motley saying, "Remember class people bring their own six-pack," or seen in a sleeveless T-shirt turning on the TV, saying, "If there ain't no game on we'll catch the reruns of celebrity bowling."

"Motley's Crew," Tom Forman and Ben Templeton. © Tribune Media Services.

Contemporary themes such as the Olympics, Super Bowl, baseball's World Series, and elections have been a staple for *Motley's Crew*. Since 1977, when President Jimmy Carter visited the Motley family to find out about a real slice of American life, every current American president has been in the strip.

The core characters include Motley's wife Mabel and son Truman who's married to the beautiful Tacoma. Motley's boyhood pal Earl, with Elvis-style sideburns, is a fellow worker at Drudge Industries. Cigar-loving Earl would rather be exercising his elbow at Dolly's Bar than be either at work or home with his wife Abigail. His favorite hiding place in the Drudge factory's warehouse was discovered when he accidentally left behind his copy of *Chicks & Ammo* magazine. Motley explained to a fellow worker it wasn't the photos of women in tiny bikinis but those of guns that turned Earl on. "In high school Earl's locker pin-up was a Model 94 Winchester lever action with an octagonal barrel," he noted. *Motley's Crew* needs an unapologetic politically incorrect working guy to be true to its original premise.

In forays into foreign affairs, Forman and Templeton introduced Yuri Gregorvich Linov, Motley and Earl's guide on their cultural-exchange tour of Russian factories. Later Yuri defected from communist tyranny dressed in drag in a size 48 tutu. Motley got him a job at Drudge Industries but after the fall of communism, Yuri answered the call for expatriates to return to Mother Russia. He now owns a gambling casino in Moscow.

Comic strips are a blend of writing and art. The loss of writer Tom Foreman has put this veteran strip at a crossroads. Only time and reader reaction will in the end determine if a slowly gentrified Motley is as funny as the hard-edged blue-collar guy for whom the good life meant a fresh beer and a good-looking woman to leer at.

B.C.

"Muggs and Skeeter," Wally Bishop. © King Features Syndicate.

MUGGS AND SKEETER (U.S.) Originally billed as one syndicate's answer to Percy Crosby, *Muggs and Skeeter* ironically wound up in the same stable as *Skippy*, outlived it, and went on to become one of the longest-running strips in comic history.

It was introduced in 1927 by Virgil V. McNitt of the McNaught Syndicate, but was released by McNitt's Central Press Association of Cleveland. The following year, Hearst bought the Central Press and Muggs McGinnis (the strip's featured character and original title) was in the same Hearst family as Crosby. Coincidentally, Crosby entered the newspaper world similarly; his drawings first appeared for the Editor's Feature Service of CP. The return of Wally Bishop, *Muggs*'s artist, to Hearst completed another cycle: he had tried (and failed) several strip efforts previously, including *The Golf Bug*.

Originally *Muggs* was an imitation of *Skippy*—the cast included scrappy kids, who were never quite as tough as Crosby's. But eventually the gang grew more domesticated and Bishop's style became his own—rather stiff but quaint and, to the end, old-fashioned. Skeeter, a pal of the young Muggs, was found on a train about eight years after the strip's debut and soon shared the billing.

Other members of the cast included Grandma and Grandpa, with whom the kids lived; Effie Mae, a hillbilly kid in the neighborhood; Beauregard, another friend; and several dogs through the years, including the popular Junior, a dachshund.

Muggs and Skeeter, which never ran as a Sunday page, ran continuities in the adventurous decade of the 1930s, but never to the extent that other strips did; Bishop's thin storylines averaged about a week apiece.

The strip was ended short of a half-century in February 1974. In its prime, it appeared in comic book format and Bishop, who claims to have been the youngest syndicated cartoonist of his day (at 17), eventually wound up subbing for Percy Crosby on occasion.

R.M.

MUÑOZ, JOSÉ (1942-   ) Spanish cartoonist and illustrator of Argentine origin born October 7, 1942, in Buenos Aires. While still in his teens José Muñoz began collaborating on publications put out by the legendary publishing house Frontera, then run by Hector Oesterheld. His first important work was a police serial written by Ray Collins (Eugenio Zappietro) and titled *Precinto 56*, first published in the magazine *Misterix* in 1963. Muñoz pursued his career in relative obscurity until he decided to move to Europe in 1973 and started his fruitful collaboration with the scriptwriter Carlos Sampayo, a fellow Argentinian. In 1975 the duo initiated *Alack Sinner*, which is at the origin of most of their later creations; since that time their collaboration has been continuous and has resulted in an enormous output, in which they have transcended the traditional relationship between artist and writer.

In *Alack Sinner* stories and characters constantly stand at the confluence of past and present, in a world peopled with memories and torn by all the contradictions of society. Influenced by Alberto Breccia and George Grosz, Muñoz dramatically accentuates the private sufferings of his characters, expressionistically voicing their innermost feelings. It is as though Muñoz and Sampayo share a common secret: how to tell, in heartrendingly lyrical accents, stories of love and friendship, of fear and melancholy, of solitude and solidarity, in an atmosphere reeking of cruelty and injustice, chaos and violence, misery and death. The artist's line, pushing to their limits the contrasts between black and white and between light and dark, shapes with righteous anger a world condemned to the torments of social anomie and iniquity. The stories read like a documentary of the lower depths, a travelogue from hell, transfigured in the course of its sordid journey into a demented pictorial fantasy.

Muñoz and Sampayo have also produced a collection of independent stories dealing with South American problems, later published in book form in France as *Sueurs de Métèques* ("Spics' Sweat," 1984). Muñoz has also collaborated on occasion with other scriptwriters, such as Luis Bustos in *Rayos y centellas* ("Rays and Sparks," 1992). Most of Muñoz's stories have been translated in the United States, where they have wielded tremendous influence on a number of American comic book artists.

J.C.

MURPHY, JAMES EDWARD (1891-1965) American cartoonist born November 20, 1891 in Chicago, Illinois. James Edward "Jimmy" Murphy Jr. spent one year at Creighton University in Nebraska. From June to December of 1906 he was a cartoonist for the *Omaha Examiner* and he was about to get a job on the *Omaha Bee* at 16 when a new editor vetoed his prospects.

After the *Bee*-stung bubble, the young Murphy (who was as inclined to move about the country to improve his prospects as did his furniture-dealing parents) went to Spokane, Washington, where he began his career as

José Muñoz and Carlos Sampayo, "Alack Sinner." © Muñoz and Sampayo.

an editorial cartoonist on the *Spokane Inland-Herald* in 1910. A year later he was in Portland, doing editorial drawings for the *Oregon Journal*. By 1915 he had reached San Francisco, where he did editorial cartoons for the *San Francisco Call* (which were also carried in the companion Hearst California evening paper, the *Los Angeles Herald*). His work impressed Hearst, who invited him to come to New York and join the art staff of the *New York Journal* in 1918. It was there that Murphy, intrigued by the processes of drawing comic strips in the offices adjoining his, did his first samples of *Toots and Casper*—and obtained King Features's approval on the strip.

Toots and Casper, daily and Sunday from the outset in a number of the Hearst coast-to-coast papers in 1919, was a bit slow in catching on. Considered a Hearst second-string strip, it ran only as a filler or as a Saturday color comic in Hearst evening papers. But the delightfully zany appearance of Murphy's married team and their baby, Buttercup (who never grew up during the 30 years of the strip), caught many eyes and aroused amusing comments, and before long *Toots and Casper* was a permanent daily and Sunday feature in Hearst's showcase newspaper, the *New York American*. Noting the success of humor-tinged soap opera in *The Gumps* and *The Nebbs*, Murphy altered his content from family gags to involved continuity on a neighborhood problem level—and the public loved it. In a very short time, *Toots and Casper* became one of the most avidly followed strips in the country. A live-action comedy series was filmed in the mid-1920s, but oddly, no book collection was ever published.

In 1926, Murphy added a second Sunday-page strip, *It's Poppa Who Pays*, and in 1934 he introduced the Sunday comic section idea of comic character stamps, which took the public by storm, and spread to strips

Jimmy Murphy, "Toots and Casper." © King Features Syndicate.

from virtually all other syndicates. King Features reportedly gave Murphy a bonus for this wildfire promotional idea, and he moved his family (including his wife, Matilda Katherine, whom he used as a model for Toots) to the West Coast as a result. Here he developed his interests in golf and driving long distances to sightsee, while *Toots and Casper* continued to enjoy great popularity.

Murphy retired from his strip in 1958 as the result of a debilitating illness. He recovered somewhat during the next several years, but did not revive the strip, and died in Beverly Hills, California, on March 9, 1965. His strip, closed down by his earlier decision, died with him.

B.B.

MURPHY, JOHN CULLEN (1919-   ) American illustrator and cartoonist born May 3, 1919, in New York City. As a youth he moved with his family to Chicago and studied at the Chicago Art Institute when he was nine years old. In 1930 the Murphys moved to New Rochelle, New York, where he became friends with Alex and Jack Raymond (later cartoonists themselves) and worshipped the work of neighboring illustrators Norman Rockwell and the Lyendecker brothers.

While in high school he studied at the Grand Central Art School and received a scholarship to the Phoenix Art Institute, where he studied under Franklin Booth. His artistic training then continued at the Art Students League under George Bridgman and Charles Chapman.

Murphy's first professional work was sports cartooning for Madison Square Garden promotions in 1936, followed by covers for *Columbia* and *Liberty* magazines. During World War II he drew on-the-spot war sketches for the *Chicago Tribune* and, while serving on the staff of Gen. Douglas MacArthur, painted portraits of MacArthur and many other military figures.

After the war Murphy worked on Hollywood movie promotions and illustrated for *Esquire, Holiday, Colliers,* and *Look* magazines. In 1949 Elliot Caplin conceived an idea for a boxing strip and contacted Murphy, whose reputation as a sports artist was established through magazine work. *Big Ben Bolt* made its appearance through King Features Syndicate in February 1950.

A supreme compliment to Murphy's talent was the request by Harold Foster in 1971 that Murphy assist on *Prince Valiant*, a task Murphy accepted without sacrificing *Big Ben Bolt*. Since that year he has drawn the Sun-

day feature from script and comprehensive roughs. (He finally had to abandon *Big Ben Bolt*, however, in 1977.)

Murphy's work has been highly regarded by other members of his profession as well. The recipient of the National Cartoonists Society award for story strips in 1971, Murphy has kept the illustrative quality of his strips at a high level, sacrificing neither detail nor visual sophistication.

R.M.

MUSIAL, JOSEPH (1905-1977) American cartoonist born 1905 in Yonkers, New York, Joe Musial attended Yonkers High School and then enrolled at Pratt Institute in Brooklyn. After graduation from Pratt he studied for a year at the Sorbonne.

Back in the United States in 1929, Musial got his first professional job as assistant on Billy De Beck's *Barney Google*. In 1932 he joined the staff of King Features and was assigned a variety of strips to work on. The strips he ghosted at one time or another included: *Thimble Theatre, Bunky, Tillie the Toiler, Pete the Tramp, Elmer, X-9, Little Iodine,* and *Toots and Casper.* In 1956, following "Doc" Winner's death, KFS picked Musial to do *The Katzenjammer Kids* (a very unjudicious choice, to put it mildly).

Being more literate and better educated than most of his colleagues, Musial proved a better choice as King's education director. In that position he was responsible for *Dagwood Splits the Atom*, a comic book explaining nuclear fission; another one on mental health with Blondie as spokeswoman this time; and a flag-waver called *This Is America*. He earned a Congressional citation for each of these publications. Musial also was the author of *The Career Guide for Cartoonists* and lectured extensively as a spokesman for the newspaper strip industry. He died on June 6, 1977, at his home in Manhasset, Long Island.

Impressive as his extraartistic achievements were, Joe Musial will ultimately go down in comic strip history as the man most responsible for the mindless emasculation of *The Katzenjammer Kids*.

M.H.

MUSTER, MIKI (1925-   ) Miki Muster is a Yugoslav cartoonist and cartoon filmmaker born in Murska Sobota, on November 22, 1925. From his earliest childhood Muster liked to draw, and his parents encouraged him in that direction. He wanted to be a cartoonist and to produce cartoon films, admiring the work of Walt Disney very much. After grammar school Muster acquired a diploma as a sculptor at Ljubljana s Academy of Plastic Art.

In June 1952 a new magazine for children, *PPP*, was launched in Ljubljana, featuring a few comics. Since a Walt Disney comic strip that had been ordered did not arrive in time, the editor asked young Muster to draw his own comic strip. It was then that *Zvitorepec*, one of the longest running Yugoslav comics, was born. Since *Zvitorepec* was so very popular among its readers in the Republic of Slovenia (where it started to appear), the publishing house Delo decided to launch a comic weekly titled *Zvitorepec* in 1965. *Zvitorepec*, about a talking rabbit, was influenced by Walt Disney. However, this popular character and his friends, Trdonja and Lakotnik, lived in Slovenian magazines and newspapers for over 20 years, and were reprinted only in *Novi List*, in Trieste, Italy.

Miki Muster, "Zvitorepec." © Miki Muster.

He is no longer involved with comics. Muster's favorite hobby was the cinema, and it eventually became his profession. He produced successful animated commercials for television, as well as for several German firms.

E.R.

MUTT AND JEFF (U.S.) The first continually published, six-day-a-week comic strip, Bud Fisher's *A. Mutt* (later given its more famed title *Mutt and Jeff*) was introduced to an unsuspecting audience on the sports page of the *San Francisco Chronicle* for Friday, November 15, 1907, under the title "Mr. A. Mutt Starts In To Play the Races." (Mutt himself had first appeared in a page-wide racing cartoon by Fisher on the November 10, 1907, sports page, together with Mrs. Mutt.) The idea for the strip was clearly derived from Clare Briggs' horse-touting *A. Piker Clerk*, for the action in Fisher's first episode simply relates how a fanatic bettor (Mutt) gets tips and places bets on three nonfictitious horses running the same day at the local track.

Fisher's born loser, with his scraggly moustache and slept-in clothes, had enormous visual appeal and soon thousands of nonhorseplayers were reading Fisher's witty dialogue and following Mutt's fretful search for the big money. Within a month, the *Chronicle*'s circulation had increased measurably against that of its morning rival, Hearst's *Examiner*. In the meantime, Fisher had informed the readers about Mutt's first name, Augustus, on November 18, 1907, in a panel also portraying Mrs. Mutt, Cicero, and his cat. And, by the end of November, a real plot line had developed within the strip. It was apparent that there was much more to Fisher's strip than the communication of horse tips, and by the beginning of the next month, Fisher (having shrewdly copyrighted his strip title and idea before leaving the *Chronicle*) had been hired by the rival *Examiner* to continue his feature there. (Fisher's last *Chronicle* episode was dated December 10, 1907; his first *Examiner* episode appeared the following day. The *Chronicle* hired Russ Westover to continue *A. Mutt*, starting December 12; Westover's work ran until June 7, 1908, when Westover actually killed Mutt off in the final episode.)

Fisher was not long at the *Examiner* before Hearst had his new talent shipped off to New York—not before, however, he had introduced the character who was to become Mutt's shrimp-sized partner, Jeff, on

"Mutt and Jeff," Bud Fisher. © H. C. Fisher.

March 27, 1908. (Jeff is a lunatic who imagines himself to be James Jeffries, the prizefighter, and is encountered casually by Mutt amid several other asylum denizens in the same episode.)

The first formal *Mutt and Jeff* designation appeared on the pioneer Fisher strip collection, *The Mutt and Jeff Cartoons* (1911), but the title was not used in newspapers until Fisher left Hearst for the Wheeler Syndicate in 1915, the first specific *Mutt and Jeff* logo appearing on September 15, 1916. The first full-page color Sunday *Mutt and Jeff* did not appear, however, until Wheeler distributed it coast to coast on August 11, 1918.

It was not until Fisher had effectual control of his own strip under Wheeler that most of the other characters for which the strip would be famed emerged— Sir Sidney (who met Mutt and Jeff in the trenches during the first World War); Gus Geevum; Jeff's twin brother Julius; and Mutt's brother's Ima—to say nothing of the debauched members of the infamous Lion Tamers' Club. This was also the period when Fisher hired the gifted Billy Liverpool (earlier known only for an obscure strip called *Asthma Simpson, the Village Queen*) who had briefly ghosted Hearst's attempt to continue his own version of *Mutt and Jeff* after Fisher's departure. Fisher's instinct was right: Liverpool's raucously comic drawings made *Mutt and Jeff* probably the most visually funny strip of the 1920s.

By this time, *Mutt and Jeff* had become one of the half dozen best known and most widely read strips in America. *Mutt and Jeff* reprint books proliferated; *Mutt and Jeff* musicals toured the country; animated cartoons starring the duo appeared throughout the 1920s; there was even a ballet and a song (called *The Funny Paper Blues*) which became a hit in 1921.

Some of their popularity declined in the 1930s and 1940s, possibly because of Al Smith's inferior handling of the strip gags and graphics after Liverpool's departure in late 1933. Nevertheless, a major, multiissued series of comic book reprints of the daily and Sunday Smith strip appeared throughout the 1940s, introducing the team anew to millions who had not seen it in their local papers.

Distributed later by the Bell Syndicate, and then by the Bell-McClure Syndicate (until it merged into United Feature Syndicate), *Mutt and Jeff* did not keep abreast of the tone of the times, either in Smith's hands, or in those of the men working on the strip with him. Accordingly, it lost most of its vast outlet of newspapers, and appeared only obscurely here and there, usually in the daily format, for the next 40 years. For most readers, the strip's fund of imaginative vitality faded rapidly in the 1940s, to vanish almost altogether by 1950. Drawn by George Breisacher in the last two years of its existence, it was finally discontinued in November 1983; but as a major strip landmark for all time, *Mutt and Jeff* will never die.

B.B.

MUTTS (U.S.) Every so often a new strip comes along that proves there are still areas of cartooning left to be explored. In American newspaper cartooning *Calvin and Hobbes* set the cartoon world on fire in 1985. Now *Mutts*, launched by King Features on September 5, 1994, is doing the same thing. In fact, with *Calvin and Hobbes* ceasing syndication in 1995 at the wish of its creator, Bill Watterson, *Mutts* became a major beneficiary of the space this opened on many comic pages.

Mutts is the creation of Patrick McDonnell, a 1979 graduate of the School of Visual Arts in New York City. A skilled illustrator, his work has been published in everything from the *New York Times* to *Sports Illustrated* to *Reader's Digest*. McDonnell is also a cartoon historian and coauthor of *Krazy Kat: The Art of George Herriman* (Abrams, 1986). His monthly cartoon *Bad Baby* has been published in *Parent's* magazine for over a decade.

The stars of *Mutts* are Earl, a small white dog with black ears and a patch on his back, and Mooch, a black cat who talks with a lisp. In an *Editor & Publisher* magazine interview, McDonnell said that art is really important. "It's what draws you into a strip. Comics are a visual medium." Thus it is not surprising that *Mutts* is visually exciting. McDonnell is one of the few strip cartoonists to use prescreened Crafting paper to give his crosshatching a different look. Simplicity rules, but it is not the simplicity of a neophyte artist, but that of a trained professional.

Mutts alternates between gag-a-day humor and continuity stories. Sunday pages let McDonnell experiment with layout and color and he takes full advantage, even with the horrific restrictions that space limitations in comics sections dictate today.

Earl, who looks like a dog that has been a feature of McDonnell's illustrations for years, lives in his own comic strip world, not present-day reality. There he and his feline pal Mooch deal with life's basics, such as survival, the weather, their relationship with their owners (who are neighbors), and with other pets, including a large bulldog and Sid the fish, who is tired of life in a fishbowl.

Hip but not cynical, the writing of the strip can be as goofy as the drawings are funny. Earl's owner, Ozzie, and Mooch's owners, Millie and Frank, are integral parts of the humor, as who is more important in the lives of pets than their owners?

Mutts is a comic strip with worldwide appeal that may well earn the pedigree of "classic." McDonnell was awarded Germany's Max and Moritz Prize for best international comic strip artist in 1996. However, the greatest prize may have been when Charles Schultz, of *Peanuts* fame, wrote in the introduction to the first collection of *Mutts* (published by Andrews and McMeel) that Patrick McDonnell keeps coming up with ideas that Schultz wished he'd thought up himself.

B.C.

MYERS, RUSSELL (1938-   ) American cartoonist born October 9, 1938, in Pittsburg, Kansas. After graduating from the University of Tulsa in 1960, Russell Myers joined the Hallmark Company, illustrating and writing contemporary greeting cards. In 1970 he started *Broom Hilda*, a comic strip relating the half-baked exploits of a most unspooky witch, for the News-Tribune Syndicate.

Russell Myers's drawing style—broad, simple, and seemingly easy—and his tongue-in-cheek approach to characterization and situation place him in the tradition of the sophisticated strip. Myers himself is prompt to acknowledge his debts to his famous elders, Charles Schulz, Johnny Hart, and Brant Parker.

Russell Myers, like many cartoonists of his generation, has a genuine love for his medium: he collects original comic art, is knowledgeable in the history of

"Myra North," Charles Coll. © NEA Service.

the form, and he has been a familiar figure in comics conventions throughout the country.

After more than a quarter-century *Broom Hilda* is still going strong; asked in 1996 to comment on his successful career, Myers tersely replied, "Cartooning is fun."

M.H.

MYRA NORTH (U.S.) *Myra North, Special Nurse* (later simply *Myra North*), drawn by Charles Coll and written by Ray Thompson, was created for NEA Service as a daily on February 10, 1936, and as a Sunday on June 12 of the same year.

Myra North was a pretty blonde and, as the title implied, a special nurse whose talents took her far afield from the nursing profession. In one of her first adventures, she traveled to Urbania, "a small African kingdom," to foil the evil designs of a group of conspirators plotting war. In another episode she engaged in a battle of wits with the mad scientist Dr. Zero, who had invented an invisibility process. But her most constant foe was the sinister and ubiquitous Hyster, an egomaniacal and evil mastermind, whose goal was nothing less than total world domination (a popular pursuit among villains of the period). Myra's most famous encounter with Hyster came in a 1937 adventure which took place in "a country ravaged by civil war," obviously Spain transparently disguised under the name of "Morentia."

In some of her other exploits, Myra solved several murders, a kidnapping involving the crown prince of another European power, had a movie role in Hollywood and, in the main, tried her level best to emulate Frank Godwin's *Connie.* In her adventures she was often accompanied by her (innocent) love interest Jack Lane, an insurance investigator.

The adventures of Myra North were inventive and entertaining, and Coll's drawing style barely adequate but pleasing nonetheless. *Myra North* was one of the few girl-adventure strips around, and deserved a longer run than the one it actually enjoyed. For the record, the daily strip ended on March 25, 1939, while the Sunday

page was discontinued not too long afterward, on August 31, 1941.

M.H.

MYSTISKA 2:AN (Sweden) *Mystiska 2:an* (*Mystiska Tvåan*, "The Mystic—or Mysterious—Two"), a Swedish adventure comic, was created and drawn by Estonian Rolf Gohs, who has been living in Sweden since 1946. The series, mostly written in cooperation with Janne Lundström, first appeared in 1970 in its own comic book published by Inter Art, of which Gohs was a founder. When Inter Art folded, Semic Press continued the comic book with two issues per year, arriving at number seven in 1973 before starting the book over with a different concept and a new numbering. In order to step up the frequency of publication, *Det Okända* ("The Unknown," meaning The Twilight Zone) was added to the book. Before this change occurred, there also appeared a continued story of *Mystiska 2:an* in numbers 16 to 26 (1972) of the biweekly *Fantomen* comic book. The series was also remounted in the daily strip format for inclusion in the comics page of the newspaper *Expressen.*

Mystiska 2:an stars two boys, Sacho Taikon and Stefan (whose last name is never told), whose story is told in the classic tradition of boyhood friends as it is represented in the novels of Sivar Ahlrud or Enid Blyton,

"Mystika 2:an," Rolf Gohs. © Rolf Gohs.

for example. Sacho is a gypsy boy whose family lives a Swedish lower-middle-class life. It is quite by intention that Gohs depicts him as any normal boy from any normal Swedish home. Stefan seems to have a well-to-do background; he is intelligent, a logical thinker. Sacho is naive and impulsive. Yet, Sacho is the star of the strip, possibly because he is a "foreigner" like Gohs and shares a number of similar interests (like photography and music) and character traits. With number seven (1973), a girl, Carina, enters the boys' lives.

The adventures of *Mystiska 2:an* take place in and around Stockholm and, as the name suggests, are usually in the mystery and horror vein. The two boys often get involved in intrigue, pitting them against unscrupulous reactionary or fascist groups. They are usually up against the mysterious and the unknown.

In 1987 Rolf Gohs took what must be considered a daring step for a series aimed at readers the age of his youthful heroes: in an episode of soul-searching, Sacho discovers that he is gay and falls in love with an older man. The theme was handled matter-of-factly and without much ado. However, the publishers were not happy with this development. They would have preferred the youthful hero to go on living a straight life of adventure.

The stories, printed in black and white, have the appearance of stark realism and a constant atmosphere of suspense because of the very graphic Gohs style that makes excellent use of black-and-white contrasts. Good writing, excellent art, and social commentary make *Mystiska 2:an* extraordinarily worthwhile reading.

W.F.